"This meticulously curated collection explores the theory and practice of accommodating diversity in multi-level polities. It is essential reading for those who care about how law shapes the balance between convergence and divergence. It teaches us as much about how to study diversity accommodation as about the law itself."

Professor Joanne Scott, *European University Institute*

"The world is multilevel and multicultural, even for those not realizing it. Law is the tool to organize and streamline complexity and this book offers guidance on how diversity can be accommodated between different units in multilevel systems."

Professor Francesco Palermo, *University of Verona and Eurac Research*

Accommodating Diversity in Multilevel Constitutional Orders

This book offers insights into the legal mechanisms that are adopted in multilevel constitutional orders to accommodate the tension between contrasting interests of diversity and unity and the converging or diverging effects they may have on the functioning of a multilevel constitutional order. It does so by targeting mainly the European experience but also drawing insights from other jurisdictions.

The volume draws on a well-rounded theoretical framework that allows a comprehensive discussion of the dialectics in multi-level systems. It focuses on two of the most relevant areas of constitutional law, namely the setup of supranational institutions and the protection of fundamental human rights. Finally, the work presents a fresh legal take on the unity-diversity dichotomy.

This collection is ideal for academics working in the fields of constitutional law, international law, federal theory, institutional design, management and accommodation of diversity, and protection of fundamental rights. Political scientists will also find the discussions very relevant as a foundation for further research in their field. Policymakers involved in constitutional engineering will be interested, as mechanisms of accommodation, convergence, and divergence are increasingly looked at as devices for managing multilevel polities.

Maja Sahadžić, Assistant Professor of Constitutional Law, Institute of Jurisprudence, Constitutional, and Administrative Law and Montaigne Centre for Rule of Law and Administration of Justice, Utrecht University, the Netherlands, and Visiting Professor, the University of Antwerp, Belgium.

Marjan Kos, PhD Candidate and Teaching Assistant, Faculty of Law, University of Ljubljana, Slovenia.

Jaka Kukavica, PhD Researcher, European University Institute, Italy, and Junior Lecturer, Faculty of Law, University of Ljubljana, Slovenia.

Jakob Gašperin Wischhoff, PhD Candidate and DynamInt Research Fellow, Humboldt University of Berlin, Germany.

Julian Scholtes, Lecturer in Public Law, School of Law, University of Glasgow, Scotland, United Kingdom.

Comparative Constitutional Change

Comparative Constitutional Change has developed into a distinct field of constitutional law. It encompasses the study of constitutions through the way they change and covers a wide scope of topics and methodologies. Books in this series include work on developments in the functions of the constitution, the organization of powers and the protection of rights, as well as research that focuses on formal amendment rules and the relation between constituent and constituted power. The series includes comparative approaches along with books that focus on single jurisdictions, and brings together research monographs and edited collections which allow the expression of different schools of thought. While the focus is primarily on law, where relevant the series may also include political science, historical, philosophical and empirical approaches that explore constitutional change.

Series editors:

Xenophon Contiades is Professor of Public Law, Panteion University, Athens, Greece and Managing Director, Centre for European Constitutional Law, Athens, Greece.

Thomas Fleiner is Emeritus Professor of Law at the University of Fribourg, Switzerland.

Alkmene Fotiadou is Research Associate at the Centre for European Constitutional Law, Athens, Greece.

Richard Albert is the William Stamps Farish Professor in Law and Professor of Government at the University of Texas at Austin, USA.

Also in the series:

Challenges to EU Values in Hungary
How the European Union Misunderstood the Government of Viktor Orbán
Beáta Bakó

Accommodating Diversity in Multilevel Constitutional Orders
Legal Mechanisms of Divergence and Convergence
Maja Sahadzic, Marjan Kos, Jan Kukavica, Julian Scholtes and Jakob Gasperin Wischhoff

Constitutional Law and Politics of Secession
Edited by Antoni Abat i Ninet

For more information about this series, please visit: www.routledge.com/Comparative-Constitutional-Change/book-series/COMPCONST

Accommodating Diversity in Multilevel Constitutional Orders

Legal Mechanisms of Divergence and Convergence

Maja Sahadžić, Marjan Kos, Jaka Kukavica, Jakob Gašperin Wischhoff and Julian Scholtes

Routledge
Taylor & Francis Group
LONDON AND NEW YORK

First published 2023
by Routledge
4 Park Square, Milton Park, Abingdon, Oxon OX14 4RN

and by Routledge
605 Third Avenue, New York, NY 10158

Routledge is an imprint of the Taylor & Francis Group, an informa business

British Library Cataloguing-in-Publication Data
A catalogue record for this book is available from the British Library

Library of Congress Cataloging-in-Publication Data
A catalog record has been requested for this book

ISBN: 978-1-032-40980-1 (hbk)
ISBN: 978-1-032-41006-7 (pbk)
ISBN: 978-1-003-35576-2 (ebk)

DOI: 10.4324/9781003355762

Typeset in Galliard
by Taylor & Francis Books

Contents

Illustrations

Figures

Tables

Contributors

Pieter Aertgeerts, PhD Candidate and Teaching Assistant, Institute for European Law, KU Leuven, Belgium.

Pieter Van Cleynenbreugel, Professor of European Union Law, University of Liège, Belgium.

Pedro Coutinho, Assistant Professor, Universidade Lusófona do Porto, Portugal.

Bruno De Witte, Professor of European Union Law, Maastricht University, the Netherlands, and Part-Time Professor, European University Institute, Italy.

Gabriel Encinas, Professor, The Autonomous University of Baja California, Mexico.

Jakob Gašperin Wischhoff, PhD Candidate and DynamInt Research Fellow, Humboldt University of Berlin, Germany.

Marjan Kos, PhD Candidate and Teaching Assistant, Faculty of Law, University of Ljubljana, Slovenia.

Jaka Kukavica, PhD Researcher, European University Institute, Italy, and Junior Lecturer, Faculty of Law, University of Ljubljana, Slovenia.

Alexander Lazović, PhD Researcher, European University Institute, Italy.

Audrey M. Plan, PhD Candidate, Trinity College Dublin, Ireland.

Agata Magdalena Poznańska, PhD Researcher, European University Institute, Italy.

Maja Sahadžić, Assistant Professor of Constitutional Law, Institute of Jurisprudence, Constitutional and Administrative Law and Montaigne Centre for Rule of Law and Administration of Justice, and Visiting Professor, University of Antwerp, Belgium.

Julian Scholtes, Lecturer in Public Law, School of Law, University of Glasgow, Scotland, United Kingdom.

Thomas Verellen, Assistant Professor of European Union and International Law, Utrecht University, the Netherlands.

Foreword

The notions of convergence and divergence are frequently used in comparative law literature. Their original use was to describe the interaction between separate and independent legal orders, that is, essentially, between national legal systems. Due to the separateness of these legal orders, the extent to which their law converged or diverged was a matter of voluntary choice. Convergence was studied much more actively than divergence, and comparative law scholars coined concepts such as transplants, borrowing and migration of legal ideas to describe the mechanisms of this voluntary convergence. Occasionally, states would create institutional mechanisms promoting convergence. A good example of this is the Venice Commission of the Council of Europe, created in the aftermath of the fall of the iron curtain. The opinions delivered by the Venice Commission are not binding on its member states, but help (as the Commission states on its website) 'to ensure the dissemination and consolidation of a common constitutional heritage' and the Commission's role is 'to help states wishing to bring their legal and institutional structures into line with European standards'. In other words, it is designed as a force for constitutional convergence and it understands its role in that way. The scholarly attention to the mechanisms of convergence led many scholars to believe that the process of convergence in public law (and other fields of the law as well) would roll on relentlessly, both within Europe and worldwide. That belief has been shaken in recent years, and divergence between national legal systems seems on the rise once again, as illustrated most dramatically by the erosion of democratic government across the world.

Against the backdrop of this literature on convergence and divergence between separate legal systems, the present volume examines those notions from a particular angle, or rather in a particular context, namely that of multilevel legal systems. In such legal systems, trends towards convergence or divergence are not entirely voluntary. Instead, the system itself may contain mechanisms that order convergence or permit divergence between its constitutive elements. This volume examines a number of those mechanisms. Many studies collected in this volume focus on one particular multilevel legal system, namely the composite system formed by EU law and the law of its member states, whereas other contributions examine federal legal systems or the relation between the European Convention of Human Rights and the law of its contracting states.

Within the multilevel EU system, there is a strong motor of convergence, based on the primacy and direct effect of EU law with their many ramifications, but also strong elements of divergence, most fundamentally the insistence by most national constitutional systems that their constitution is still at the apex of the legal order despite the primacy claim of EU law. Those countervailing claims to precedence are well known and well documented in the literature. The contributions to this volume do not rehearse them but examine, instead, some subtler mechanisms that push towards convergence or divergence, including, for example: the way in which EU legislation increasingly tends to mobilise the national administrative apparatus for the effective enforcement of EU law, thus facilitating the effective convergence between national laws; or the way in which the Court of Justice of the EU, through its internal procedures and ways of operating, socialises new judges coming from very diverse backgrounds into effective contributors to the Court's task to promote convergence. Certain complex legal formulas can serve both to foster convergence or permit divergence, depending on how they are used in concrete cases, as is illustrated by the chapter devoted to the 'interlegal' balancing of rights, and the chapter dealing with how the US Supreme Court and the European Court of Human Rights use the existence of a consensus between the component parts of their multilevel system in order to adjudicate multilevel disputes.

This is just a sample of the interesting contributions that the reader will find here. The volume as a whole is a fine contribution to the comparative law literature on convergence and divergence, as well as to the study of the 'vertical' interaction between legal systems.

Bruno De Witte

1 Introduction

The Dialectics in Multilevel Systems – Mechanisms of Divergence and Convergence

Marjan Kos, Jaka Kukavica and Maja Sahadžić

The Dialectics in Multilevel Legal Systems

The stability and resilience of any legal system depends on its responsiveness to the social reality it aims to regulate.[1] If legal systems are to govern the relations between their subjects, as well as the relations between their subjects and the system itself effectively, they can only do so if they are adaptive to the social and broader factual substratum underpinning it. When legal systems and their norms deviate too far away from the societal norms they relate to, situations inevitably arise where either compliance with the legal framework suffers or pressures to adapt the legal framework to what is acceptable to its subjects will emerge. Either way, the legal system will be torn between ensuring its effectiveness and the attempts to be sufficiently responsive to societal demands to avoid instability or, ultimately, avoid its dismantling. As noted by Krisch, 'law enhances stability only when it is supported by societal circumstances.'[2] Thus, the sustainability of (complex) legal systems strongly depends on the responsiveness of the normative framework to the social reality.

This is true of any unitary legal system but it resonates even more strongly with what this book calls multilevel constitutional systems: legal orders composed of multiple layers of legality (or multiple legalities) that are simultaneously separated and interconnected.[3] These legal systems may form part of a single legal entity,

1 David N Schiff, 'Socio-Legal Theory: Social Structure and Law' (1976) 39 The Modern Law Review 287. For noteworthy applications of such ideas to regulatory theory and the ideas of responsive regulation of markets, see Ian Ayres and John Braithwaite, *Responsive Regulation: Transcending the Deregulation Debate* (Oxford University Press 1995).

2 Nico Krisch, 'Global Legal Pluralism' in Jeffrey L Dunoff and Mark A Pollack (eds), *International Legal Theory: Foundations and Frontiers* (Cambridge University Press 2022) 254.

3 See, for example, 'Online Conference "Multiple Legalities: Conflict and Entanglement in the Global Legal Order"' (*Verfassungsblog*) <https://verfassungsblog.de/category/debates/multiple-legalities-debates/> accessed 21 April 2022. See especially: Hannah Birkenkötter and Nico Kirsch, 'Multiple Legalities: Conflict and Entanglement in the Global Legal Order' [2021] Verfassungsblog: On Matters Constitutional <https://verfassungsblog.de/multiple-legalities-conflict-and-entanglement-in-the-global-lega

DOI: 10.4324/9781003355762-1

such as a (federal) state, or several different legal entities, such as the European Union or the Council of Europe. They may be sub-national, national as well as supra- or international.

One important feature of such systems is their ***complexity***, which is reflected in a large number of mutual relationships between the component units and central authority. On top of all the other challenges to the effectiveness, fairness, equality, accountability, and transparency of a legal system,[4] the challenge of providing clear rules of engagement between the various component units is added to the overall picture. Even on national and subnational levels these issues are linked to the questions of stability[5] but they are even more pressing when it comes to supra-national multilevel systems, where questions of sovereignty and authority may not be fully resolved.[6] On all levels, however, complexity implies a strong need for effective coordination.

Another important feature of multilevel systems is ***diversity***. By their very design, multilevel constitutional systems are tailored to the need of specific interests of their component parts. Often, the design of a multilevel order will (need to) reflect the diversity stemming from the social or legal reality of the system. If there was no such underlying need, the system could simply be constructed as a unitary system. To put it differently, the underlying diversity of social, economic, and political realities is most often the main reason a multilevel legal order is constructed in the first place. In practice, multilevel orders, especially supra- and international ones, express diversity even more sharply. They are often composed of component parts that portray a picture of great social, economic, political, and, consequently, legal diversity.[7] National and sub-national levels display very similar dynamics. Diversity has provoked gradual transformations in the internal structure of states by increasingly leading to the application of federal principles.[8] Primarily due to variations in identity, but also variations in wealth and historical reasons,

l-order/> accessed 21 April 2022. See also Nico Krisch (ed), *Entangled Legalities Beyond the State* (Cambridge University Press 2022).

4 See Nico Krisch, *Beyond Constitutionalism: The Pluralist Structure of Postnational Law* (Oxford University Press 2010), Richard H. Pildes, 'Ethnic identity and democratic institutions: A dynamic perspective' in Sujit Choudhry (ed), *Constitutional Design for Divided Societies: Integration or Accommodation* (Oxford University Press 2008).

5 Maja Sahadžić, *Asymmetry, Multinationalism and Constitutional Law, Managing Legitimacy and Stability in Federalist States* (Routledge 2020).

6 See David Beetham and Christopher Lord, *Legitimacy and the EU* (Routledge 1998).

7 See Pieter Van Cleynenbreugel, 'Asymmetry as a Way to Move Forward with Multi-tiered Integration? A Study of Constitutional Asymmetry in the European Union' in Patricia Popelier and Maja Sahadžić (eds), *Constitutional Asymmetry in Multinational Federalism, Managing Multinationalism in Multi-tiered Systems* (Palgrave Macmillan 2019), Giuseppe Martinico, 'Complexity and Cultural Sources of Law in the EU Context: From the Multilevel Constitutionalism to the Constitutional Synallagma' 8 German Law Journal 205, Richard Bellamy, *A Republican Europe of States: Cosmopolitanism, Intergovernmentalism and Democracy in the EU* (2019).

8 Francesco Palermo, Carolin Zwilling and Karl Kössler, *Asymmetries in Constitutional Law: Recent Developments in Federal and Regional Systems* (Europäische Akademie Bozen/Accademia Europea Bolzano 2009).

even unitary and regionalised states succumbed to pressures founded on the accommodation of diversity.[9] Herein lies the crux of the problem the present book tackles: every multilevel order is torn between the need to justify its purpose, namely effective regulation of social interactions, and the demand to be responsive to the specific needs of the different component parts of the system. To put it more clearly, the tension between unity and diversity is inherent to all multilevel constitutional orders.

The complexity and diversity of multilevel legal systems lead to specific difficulties in their governance. On top of the need to provide an effective and acceptable solution to the issues stemming from the complex relationships between the different levels of legality in the multilevel legal system, while doing this, a balance between *effectiveness (unity)* and *justified compromise*[10] *(respect for diversity)* of the system needs to be struck. The two issues are closely connected, since inadequate solutions regarding either of the two may in turn negatively affect the other.

There have been different theoretical attempts in both legal and political science that aim to offer insights into this problem. They are focused on social, economic, and political factors of diversity,[11] how they reflect on the legal setup of the different supranational, international, regional, national, or sub-national systems,[12] as well as on the practical functioning and the theoretical implications of those solutions.[13] They include studies on the different theories of integration and disintegration of legal systems, federal models, multilevel governance, local self-governance, the

9 Maja Sahadžić. Erika Arban, Giuseppe Martinico and Francesco Palermo (eds), *Federalism and Constitutional Law: The Italian Contribution to Comparative Regionalism* (Routledge 2021).

10 In her work, Sahadžić uses the term 'justified compromise' instead of the frequently used term 'fairness' to emphasize that differences require enabling an equal footing among different categories that do not always have to be just and fair, but rather justified. See Maja Sahadžić, *Asymmetry, Multinationalism and Constitutional Law, Managing Legitimacy and Stability in Federalist States* (Routledge 2020). This thinking is inspired by the Baer's concept of equality in multilevel legal orders which implies that diversity is about treating comparable situations alike, and different situations differently. See in Susanne Baer, 'Equality' in Michael Rosenfeld and Andra⊠ Sajo⊠ (eds), *The Oxford Handbook of Comparative Constitutional Law* (Oxford University Press 2012).

11 Tesfaye B. Mersha and Andrew F. Beck, 'The social, economic, political, and genetic value of race and ethnicity in 2020' 14 Human Genomics, Jose G. Montalvo and Marta Reynal-Querol, 'Ethnic Diversity and Growth: Revisiting the Evidence' 103 Review of Economics and Statistics 521.

12 Liesbet Hooghe and Gary Marks, 'A postfunctionalist theory of multilevel governance' 22 British Journal of Politics & International Relations 820, Andreas Klinke, 'Dynamic multilevel governance for sustainable transformation as postnational configuration' 30 The European Journal of Social Sciences 323, Jitske van Popering-Verkerk and Arwin van Buuren, 'Decision-Making Patterns in Multilevel Governance: The contribution of informal and procedural interactions to significant multilevel decisions' 18 Public Management Review 951.

13 Martino Maggetti and Philipp Trein, 'Multilevel governance and problem-solving: Towards a dynamic theory of multilevel policy-making?' 97 Public Administration 355.

studies of international and regional systems of human rights protection, legal and constitutional pluralism, etc.[14]

Recently, the debates on the construction and the functioning of different multilevel legal orders have become even more interesting for extensive scientific research. The last few decades have made it clear that states as singular actors cannot successfully tackle many global transnational, regional, and local challenges. Addressing global problems such as climate change, migration, pandemics, financial and security crises adds new layers of complexity that require coordination between the different actors on the global and the regional stage.[15] Unconcerted solo efforts to address them would likely make such attempts futile in the long run. By their very nature, climate change and global migration are challenges that are beyond the reach of any single state, both in terms of legal solutions, as well as from the aspect of global solidarity, as the European experience of the last decade has clearly shown. And even regarding some issues that are not inherently global or regional, transnational governance of those areas might be desirable: from the protection of fundamental rights to (international) tax or intellectual property law, states and individuals may benefit importantly from different degrees of integration of those legal areas. Additionally, addressing complex local issues such as autonomy claims, and sub-national positioning toward international and supranational actors also requires a certain degree of coordination between the sub-national entities and the state level.

Efforts to arrive at common responses to these globalised social, political, or economic problems through the creation of the state, sub-state, but especially supra-national and international multilevel legal structures, as apparent from the above, raise many challenges of their own. One of the more prominent problems that have become particularly pertinent in the past decade is the turn towards an identity discourse.[16] Through different manifestations of more intense inter-state cooperation, some states especially turned back to their national and regional

14 For example: Bruno De Witte, Andrea Ott and Ellen Vos (eds), *Between Flexibility and Disintegration: The Trajectory of Differentiation in EU Law* (Edward Elgar Publishing 2017); Peter Hay, *Federalism and Supranational Organizations: Patterns for New Legal Structures* (University of Illinois Press 1966); Patricia Popelier and Maja Sahadžić (eds), *Constitutional Asymmetry in Multinational Federalism: Managing Multinationalism in Multi-Tiered Systems* (Palgrave Macmillan 2019); Lorenza Violini and Antonia Baraggia (eds), *The Fragmented Landscape of Fundamental Rights Protection in Europe: The Role of Judicial and Non-Judicial Actors* (Edward Elgar Publishing 2018); Matej Avbelj and Jan Komárek, *Constitutional Pluralism in the European Union and Beyond* (Hart Publishing 2012).

15 See, for example: Ursula von der Leyen, 'A Union That Strives for More: My Agenda for Europe: Political Guidelines for the next European Commission 2019–2024.' (European Commission Directorate General for Communication Publications Office 2019) <https://data.europa.eu/doi/10.2775/753401> accessed 18 April 2022.

16 Alejandro Arnaiz and Carina Llivina (eds), *National Constitutional Identity and European Integration* (Intersentia 2013); Elke Cloots, *National Identity in EU Law* (Oxford University Press 2015); Christian Calliess and Gerhard Van der Schyff, *Constitutional Identity in a Europe of Multilevel Constitutionalism* (2020).

identities as a shield against multilevel legal arrangements,[17] rather than as a natural constituent part of a common identity.[18] This brought to the surface one of the key issues, which had up until then mostly been discussed within the realm of federal or quasi-federal legal orders:[19] *How do we accommodate the various converging and diverging forces in similar supra- and international multilevel legal systems?*

The age-old question of how the law consolidates the pulls toward unity amongst constituent parts of multilevel systems, on the one hand, and the states' legitimate interests in maintaining their own way of doing things and thus fostering diversity, on the other hand, became an existential question for many such multilevel systems, the European Union and the Council of Europe included. This problem is even more pronounced in legal orders where the question of the final arbitrator ('kompetenz-kompetenz') has not been conclusively answered, in which several legal orders may claim, or do claim the final authority.[20] This has especially been visible in the European Union with the recent examples of the German or the Polish constitutional courts;[21] or in the USA by the recent attempts of some states to design (unconstitutional) statutes that would evade judicial review by the federal Supreme Court.[22] On a general level, there have been different attempts to provide descriptive and normative conceptualisations of these issues, be it through the theories of constitutional and global pluralism, differentiation, federal theories, or theories of interlegality.[23] But regardless of the specificities of these theoretical approaches, the common thread amongst them is that when norms of different legal orders become incompatible, this should be settled cooperatively between the different actors, rather than through uniformly hierarchical ordering. If the

17 Theodore Konstadinides, 'Constitutional Identity as a Shield and as a Sword: The European Legal Order within the Framework of National Constitutional Settlement' (2011) 13 Cambridge Yearbook of European Legal Studies 195; Pietro Faraguna, 'Constitutional Identity in the EU – A Shield or a Sword?' (2017) 18 German Law Journal 1617; Massimo Fichera and Oreste Pollicino, 'The Dialectics Between Constitutional Identity and Common Constitutional Traditions: Which Language for Cooperative Constitutionalism in Europe?' (2019) 20 German Law Journal 1097.

18 Julian Scholtes, 'Abusing Constitutional Identity' (2021) 22 German Law Journal 534.

19 Sanford Lakoff, 'Between Either/or and More or Less: Sovereignty versus Autonomy under Federalism' 24 Publius 63, Clint Hamilton, 'A Study in Sovereignty: Federalism, Political Culture, and the Future of Conservatism' (Liberty University 2018).

20 Neil MacCormick, 'The Maastricht-Urteil: Sovereignty Now' (2010) 1 European Law Journal 259; Mattias Kumm, 'Who Is the Final Arbiter of Constitutionality in Europe? Three Conceptions of the Relationship Between the German Federal Constitutional Court and the European Court of Justice' (1999) 36 Common Market Law Review.

21 Poland: Judgment K3/21 of the Constitutional Tribunal of 7 October 2021; BVerfG Judgment 2 BvR 859/15 of 5 May 2020. Also see: Marjan Kos, 'The PSPP Judgment of the Bundesverfassungsgericht and the Slovenian Constitutional System' (2021) 2 Central European Journal of Comparative Law 93.

22 See Texas Senate Bill 8 (SB8), allowing a private enforcement of a *de facto* abortion ban in Texas.

23 Jan Klabbers and Gianluigi Palombella (eds), *The Challenge of Inter-Legality* (Cambridge University Press 2019). Also see above (n14).

interplay between legalities within multilevel legal systems produces frictions caused by social, political, or economic diversity reflected in the different levels of the legal orders, they are to be addressed in a dialectical manner, in a rational legal (and sometimes political) discourse between the two conflicting orders. In the EU, this is expressed in the principle of loyal cooperation,[24] but similar guiding principles are present in other multilevel legal orders as well.

The dialectics between the legalities of multilevel legal systems may present themselves in a myriad of different ways. These range from the more obvious and somewhat straightforward questions of the division of competencies, the institutional setup, the different ways in which the institutions of the different levels may interact with each other (external dimension), and how the institutions themselves function (internal dimension), to more boutique questions of specificities of methods of interpretation of laws at the different levels. In essence, the specific nature of the dialectic within a multilevel constitutional system is defined by the normative framework of that specific legal order through which multilevel constitutional systems apply different solutions to reconcile the underlying differences amongst the component units. These solutions can take the form of various legal mechanisms of accommodation, be it mechanisms of legal divergence or mechanisms of legal convergence. The choice between these mechanisms is quintessentially a matter of political or judicial discretion. It is also a choice between a push for unity or an attempt at fostering diversity, depending on whether the underlying value of effectiveness or justified compromise prevails in any given political or judicial context. Legal mechanisms of convergence will serve the goal of unity, while mechanisms of divergence will lead to continued or enhanced diversity.

The Mechanisms of Convergence and Divergence

This brings us to the main purpose of this book. It provides an answer to the question of how the law accommodates diversity between constituent units in multilevel legal systems by identifying and analysing specific legal mechanisms of convergence and divergence through which the law balances and accommodates different conflicting interests in multilevel legal orders. Provided the ever-increasing complexity of national, supranational, international, and global legal regimes, which in itself is a response to increasingly complex global problems in a thoroughly globalised world, answering this question today is more salient than ever. This book aims to unearth important ways in which legal systems can accommodate their inherent diversity today and, above all, tomorrow. With this precise purpose, the book brings together an impressive line-up of junior scholars – it will be their voices that will importantly shape how multilevel legal systems will be able to address the many pressing issues, in Europe and beyond, collectively and effectively. Although it may seem that the issues concerning Europe have captured the most attention of the contributors, the global relevance of the book is

24 Marcus Klamert, The Principle of Loyalty in EU Law (First edition, Oxford University Press 2014).

contextualised in most of the chapters. Most of the chapters in the book are either theoretical and thus globally relevant in nature (Section I of the book), take a broad comparative approach in which they draw on jurisdictions beyond Europe (Sections II and III of the book), or propose and adopt novel intriguing methodologies through which legal convergence and divergence in any multilevel system can be studied (Section III of the book).

In line with this, the chapters that these scholars have contributed set out to explore the dialectics in multilevel systems from three distinct perspectives. On the basis of these perspectives they are organised in three separate sections. The first section provides a theoretical framework, while the second and third sections identify and analyse legal mechanisms of divergence and convergence in multilevel legal systems.

In the first section, the book explores theoretical approaches which contextualise and ground the concrete legal mechanisms through which diversity is accommodated through law in multilevel systems. It examines a variety of theoretical considerations that underpin the balance between convergence and divergence amongst constituent units in multilevel polities: interlegality (Chapter 2), coordination and asymmetry (Chapter 3), and differentiation (Chapter 4). These chapters provide theoretical bases which explain the complex dialectics in multilevel systems and theoretically contextualise the accommodation of diversity through law.

In Chapter 2, Gabriel Encinas combines a discussion of a theoretical approach to accommodation of diversity (interlegality) with an examination of how a concrete legal mechanism (balancing) fits into this theoretical framework, as well as what the implications of accepting interlegality are for the notion of balancing through proportionality in legal decision-making. Indeed, Encinas argues that balancing is closely related to many paradigmatic cases of interlegality and considers interlegality as a counterpart in legal reasoning (*lato sensu*) of legal pluralism. The chapter presents the relation between interlegality and balancing upon a distinction between multilevel settings on the one hand, and horizontal constellations on the other. It explains how interlegality and balancing are congenial: they share the aim of considering all relevant reasons for a decision. Encinas provides a working conceptualization of balancing in practical reasoning on the one hand, and proportionality assessments and other balancing models as its (variably) standardised institutionalizations in legal reasoning, on the other hand. On this basis, a distinction between two possible situations of intertwined legal orders (i.e., multilevel settings and other more horizontal constellations) is made, which leads to the balancing of norms that are sourced from different legal orders. Finally, the Chapter discusses three potential and open challenges related to the notion of interlegal balancing: the nature of jurisdictional collisions and competence norms, the comparability of norms sourced in different legal orders, and the possible criteria for weighting and balancing across legal orders.

Maja Sahadžić starts her analysis in Chapter 3 from the premise that much of the instability in multilevel systems, especially those burdened by identity differences, is caused by the lack of cohesion within the system. This appears to be due to (1) a lack of adaptiveness to the dynamics and complex framework of the system reinforced with (2) insufficient trust among competing realities, and (3) the lack of horizontal and vertical coordination among the levels of government and groups. She argues that the tension between convergence and divergence in these systems implies that the tools for the renegotiation of balance that affect the integrity of the system must include, in the first place, thoughtful coordination between and among the levels of government and groups to properly equalise their mutual relationships to keep the system together. The chapter points out an existing and growing misunderstanding about which federal devices can be consumed to enable cohesion and preserve the stability of the system. Drawing upon research in federalism, it attempts to transform the narratives about constitutional asymmetry as a federal device. To that end, it explores (1) the prospects of using constitutional asymmetry as a federal device and (2) the potential of the concept of dynamic stability based on coordination.

In the final Chapter of the opening section of the book, Marjan Kos asks whether mechanisms of differentiation under EU law may mitigate or prevent constitutional conflicts in the EU multilevel system. In Chapter 4, Kos offers a solution that can accommodate specific national constitutional demands within the framework of EU law: through differentiation, the primacy of EU law and the constitutional sovereignty of Member States may be reconciled. The chapter challenges the idea that an 'ever closer union' can only be achieved via unity and consolidation of national legal orders. Without undermining the core principles on which the EU is built, differentiation in EU law may offer a new theoretical model, more apt to deal with these problems. To show this, Kos examines whether the differences in the constitutional frameworks of the Member States have in the past functioned as justifications behind the existing types of (constitutional) differentiation in EU law; the goal is to ascertain whether differentiation in EU law might be a function of national constitutional demands to any relevant degree. Finally, the chapter discusses whether there is a normative appeal of differentiation as a tool for the accommodation of diversity in EU law.

Moving to Section II of the book, the focus of the chapters shifts away from the theoretical grounding of accommodation of diversity in multilevel systems toward analysing concrete legal mechanisms of convergence and divergence through which this accommodation is conducted. The chapters in Section II focus on the legal mechanism from the perspective of human rights law and constitutional law: these are the areas in which the dialectics within the multilevel systems are most explicit and pertinent. They are the two interrelated areas that are the ground for (constitutional) conflict *par excellence*; (1) it is precisely through the mechanism of constitutional law that diversity is most often accommodated and (2) it is constitutional and human rights law that has the thick normative underpinning that is conducive to the emergence of conflict that needs to be accommodated through mechanisms of divergence and divergence. The chapters in this section discuss the ability of these mechanisms to consolidate the inherent tension between unity and diversity. They evaluate the mechanisms and eventually demonstrate how the mechanisms may be applied across different multilevel systems.

In Chapter 5, Pieter Aertgeerts argues that the adoption of EU legislation not only has the potential to rebalance the relationship between the CJEU and the EU legislature when it comes to shaping EU fundamental rights but also to include national constitutional courts in the shared interpretation of EU fundamental rights. EU fundamental rights legislation can function as a catalyst for what Aertgeerts calls a 'constitutional trilogue' between the EU legislature, the CJEU, and national constitutional courts. This 'constitutional trilogue' is presented as a normatively attractive model for the concretization of the fundamental right to data protection in the multilevel EU legal order. The chapter demonstrates that EU data protection legislation is the foremost example of such a trilogue: it looks at the Austrian, Belgian, Italian, and German courts' case law, applying the Charter as a standard of review under the domestic law of their Member States, precisely by distinguishing the focus on either unity or diversity in the GDPR's provisions. Finally, Aertgeerts argues that EU fundamental rights legislation recognising a certain margin of appreciation for the Member States leads to a higher take-up of the Charter rights at the Member State level.

Jakob Gašperin Wischhoff's contribution aims to explore and accommodate claims of national constitutional identity which are based on the common and shared fundamental rights within the multilevel fundamental rights protection. Throughout Chapter 6, Gašperin Wischhoff raises and explores several questions. First, why should one examine fundamental rights identity claims separately according to its own set of evaluative criteria? Second, what is the significance of multilevel fundamental rights protection concerning identity claims? Third, what is the function of fundamental rights identity claims considering the nature of the intertwined landscape of fundamental rights protection on the national and supranational levels? And finally, does the recent radical turn in German jurisprudence to directly scrutinise and apply the EU Charter in the national constitutional complaint proceedings signal the end of fundamental rights identity claims?

Chapter 7 moves away from the fundamental rights framework to the constitutional setup of EU external action. In his chapter, Thomas Verellen asks how the EU manages convergence and divergence in its external action, a policy area closely connected to the core of state sovereignty. He explores the jurisprudence of the CJEU, showing that the Court eventually implicitly endorsed mixity and was then increasingly asked to resolve issues that mixity brings along. This led to a paradigm shift in the theory of competence allocation in the EU towards a fifty-shades-of-grey approach in which the EU and its Member States could both hold shared competencies to act in overlapping areas. Verellen argues that very recently, in Opinion 2/15, OTIF, and Opinion 1/19, the Court provided some clarifications on the division of labour between the Member States and the EU in areas of shared competence. The chapter traces the very slow emergence of a 'doctrine of shared competence' and sketches its contours. It sets out the rights and obligations the Member States and the EU have in areas of shared competence and offers critical reflections on the strengths and weaknesses of the doctrine. It starts with a hypothesis that the doctrine of shared competence as currently conceived leaves too much to the political discretion of the Member States in the Council, making it too difficult for the EU to independently exercise shared competence, which, in turn, risks undermining the autonomy of EU law.

Pedro Coutinho begins his contribution in Chapter 8 by providing an overview of the Portuguese economic constitution as it was before Portugal's accession to the EU. Coutinho takes this as the departing point for the analysis of the interaction between Portugal's and the European Union's economic constitution and identity. The chapter identifies the key aspects of the EU's economic matrix, showing that it suffers from a mischaracterization as neoliberal. Having established this, the chapter then argues that the relationship between the EU's economic identity and national economic identity is a reciprocal two-way relationship. The Portuguese Constitution, being of a highly ideological content initially, illustrates perfectly the liberalising influence, visible in other states as well, that the EU's economic constitution has had and can have on more state-centred constitutions. In the other direction, the dominant economic constitutional identity – that of the social market economy, combined with a social state – has influenced the EU's economic constitution by dictating the progressive strengthening of the social pillars and by influencing the creation of anti-crises mechanisms that, while absent from the treaties, are present in practice, as evidenced most recently by the COVID-19 economic stimulus package.

The final chapter in Section II of the book examines consensus analysis and demonstrates how this argumentative practice can be used either as a mechanism of convergence or divergence, depending on the way it is used by courts. In its most basic and most prevalent form, consensus analysis is used by courts in multilevel systems when they interpret a legal norm of a higher-level legal order based on how this norm had been interpreted and implemented in lower-level legal orders – the component states. Jaka Kukavica analyses in Chapter 9 consensus analysis as used by the United States Supreme Court, the Court of Justice of the European Union, and the European Court of Human Rights to devise a general typology of consensus analysis as used across different courts. The chapter argues that the establishment of this typology is instrumental to our understanding that consensus may serve either as a converging or diverging mechanism for resolving conflicts in multilevel legal orders; what function it serves will depend on what type of consensus is used by a specific court in an individual case.

In its final Section III, the book shifts the focus away from specific legal areas that are most prone to conflict between unity and diversity and it instead focuses on the subjects that are involved in these conflicts: it offers an institutional view of the legal mechanisms through which accommodation of diversity is governed.

In Chapter 10, Audrey M. Plan discusses inter-institutional dialogue as a way of accommodating diversity in and amongst multilevel systems. She shows that the jurisprudence of the ECJ and the ECtHR displays both convergence (for example, the ECJ acknowledging the rights of businesses to privacy, following the ECtHR), and divergence (for example, on the possible exceptions to EU asylum laws). The trends displayed vary from one issue area to the next, and change through time within each issue area. The chapter explores these dynamic interactions by focusing on the fundamental right of companies to the protection of their business premises, between 1989 and 2015. Using process tracing and triangulation, Plan traces the evolution of the convergence and divergence of both courts on this question and reconstructs the causal pathways leading to this variation. The chapter explains this overlooked variation by demonstrating that the ECJ and the ECtHR engage strategically with each other to safeguard their authority as policymakers within the European judicial and institutional system. It demonstrates that both courts use convergence with each other as a legitimacy-enhancing mechanism, in reaction to threats from domestic courts, governments, and the other European court.

Moving from inter-institutional dialogue to intra-institutional dialogue, Alexander Lazović gives an important view into how analysing intra-institutional dynamics, particularly within Courts, can also help us understand how component units in multilevel systems converge or diverge. Chapter 11 proceeds from the position that the nomination process at the CJEU guarantees equal representation of the Member States within the Court, but it also bears the potential of creating divergence: the judges come from a diverse set of legal systems, have varying degrees of experience in EU law, and can regularly be re-appointed by potentially changing governments who may favour candidates close to their own political outlook. Yet, by and large, the case-law of the Court of Justice remains consistent. The chapter asks why is this so? It argues that both convergence and divergence are crucial for the functioning of the Court. The convergent factors prevent the case-law from becoming incoherent and safeguard expectations of legal certainty, while the factors that facilitate or allow divergence prevent it from becoming calcified and rigid, harming the ability to adapt, the responsiveness to the Member State judicial systems, and the representativeness created by the judicial nomination process. While the Court provides the objective structure of this practice, the judges themselves also influence this structure. The chapter looks at these structural factors at the Court of Justice and how they may cause new-comers to converge around accepted interpretations, adapt to the Court's approach to (EU) law, and form the judges into a cohesive unit.

Chapter 12 looks at multilevel governance in the EU through the prism of deliberative democracy theory and its specific application in the legal regulation of the mechanism of European Citizens Initiative (ECI). Agata Poznańska's main claim is that one of the tools facilitating the complex task of multilevel governance in the EU and further development of the post-national democratic model can be deliberative democracy put into practice. Arguably, the ECI mechanism could perform such a role of being a practical deliberative tool, offering a solution to the unity versus diversity dichotomy of multilevel orders. Since its creation, the ECI has triggered a handful of questions relating to its effectiveness (measured by different variables) but also to the room for reform in its design. The Chapter shows that deliberative democracy theory could provide viable answers. The ECI mechanism can contribute to achieving balanced multilevel governance in the EU, specifically taking the perspective of deliberative democracy as a normative foundation.

Finally, Chapter 13 demonstrates that in the EU, despite the increasing importance and extension of competencies, the implementation and enforcement of EU law still takes place predominantly at the Member State level. Although respecting the constitutional and administrative identities of the Member States, Pieter van Cleynenbreugel argues that this setup poses a significant risk of divergence in the enforcement of otherwise uniform, harmonised, or at least converging supranational substantive law norms. The chapter shows that to address those risks, the EU increasingly imposes requirements on how enforcement authorities have to be organised and on how enforcement activities need to take place. It gives examples of legal instruments in the fields of EU data protection law, EU competition law, and EU utilities regulation. Van Cleynenbreugel identifies and analyses the convergence mechanisms before framing them within more theoretical debates on convergence and divergence in the context of EU's multi-level governance framework. It identifies the emergence of a converging 'independent authority with autonomous enforcement capacities' template, envisaging a converging administrative enforcement space. That space complements the harmonisation or uniformization of substantive laws and is justified by the need to ensure effectiveness in the application of those laws. It further questions whether the effectiveness argument could be considered compatible with the overall constitutional setup of EU multi-level governance. It raises questions as to the legitimacy of those back-door convergence mechanisms and, offering suggestions, calls for a broader debate on the need for administrative convergence within the multilevel EU legal order.

Based on the overview of the chapters, the contributions in the book use a number of theoretical approaches to *accommodating* diversity. The contributions also identify and analyse a number of specific mechanisms of accommodation of diversity via different degrees of *convergence* or *divergence*. These are expressed in the table below. Importantly, accommodation (as a compromise between unity and diversity) may, in fact, include both convergence and divergence and thus could also be explained as a 'supercategory' of convergence and divergence.

Table 1.1 Approaches and mechanisms of convergence, divergence, and accommodation of diversity covered in the book

Theoretical approaches to accommodating diversity	*Mechanisms of accommodation of diversity via degrees of convergence and divergence*
Interlegality	Proportionality
Asymmetry	Distribution of competencies
Dynamic stability	Margin of appreciation
Differentiation	Inter-institutional dialogue
	Intra-institutional dialogue
	Responses to identity claims
	Consensus analysis
	Citizens' initiatives
	Harmonisation
	Derogation clauses
	International cooperation

The *theoretical approaches* that are addressed in the book in more detail are interlegality (Chapter 2), asymmetry (Chapter 3), dynamic stability (Chapter 3), and differentiation (Chapter 4). The *mechanisms* that are addressed in more detail are proportionality (Chapter 2), distribution of competencies, above all shared competencies (Chapters 7 and 8), inter-institutional dialogue (Chapters 5 and 10), intra-institutional dialogue (Chapter 11), responses to identity claims (Chapters 3 and 6), consensus analysis (Chapter 9), citizens' initiatives (Chapter 12), harmonisation (Chapters 4 and 13), derogation clauses (Chapter 4), and international cooperation (Chapter 8). We return to their assessment in the conclusion.

2 The Idea of 'Interlegal Balancing' in Multilevel Settings

Gabriel Encinas

1 Introduction

As part of its notorious *PSPP* judgment of 5 May 2020, the Second Senate of the German Federal Constitutional Court (GFCC) ruled that proportionality, in its full scope and importance, applies just the same to the multilevel division of competences among organs of the European Union and its Member States.[1] Moreover, the very question of the intensity and structure of proportionality analyses was crucial in the GFCC's finding that the *Weiss*[2] judgment of the Court of Justice of the European Union was ultra vires, i.e. beyond the legal scope of competences.

The *PSPP* judgment foregrounded how proportionality analyses take place at the 'interfaces' of legalities, perhaps with a particular intensity within multilevel settings such as the European legal space. More than a few paradigm cases of collisions of legalities have seen proportionality analyses at their interfaces. The *Kadi* judicial saga considered proportionality analyses for norms stemming from the regime of the United Nations Security Council and its implementing directives inside the European legal space.[3] A Chamber of the Second Section of the European Human Rights Court (ECtHR) went arguably further in using its *Bosphorus* doctrine[4] under circumstances reminiscent of *Kadi* in its judgment in *Al Dulimi*,[5] echoing that it could and should review the norms of 'external' legal orders

1 See Judgment of the Second Senate of 5 May 2020 2 BvR 859/15, para 119.
2 See Case C-493/17 *Weiss and Others* [2018] ECLI:EU:C:2018:1000.
3 See Joined cases C-402/05 P and C-415/05 P *Yassin Abdullah Kadi & Al Barakaat International Foundation* v. *Council of the European Union & Commission of the European Communities* [2008] ECR I-6351, paras 326, 355–363, and 367–372; Case T-85/09 *Yassin Abdullah Kadi v European Commission* [2010] ECR II-5177, paras 189–195; Joined Cases C-584/10 P, C-593/10 P and C-595/10 P, *Commision v. Kadi* [2013] ('*Kadi II*'), para 97 (citing the applicability of 'in principle the full review' of the measures).
4 See *Bosphorus Hava Yolları Turizm ve Ticaret Anonim Şirketi v. Ireland* App No 45036/98 (ECtHR, 30 June 2005), paras 155–6.
5 See *Al-Dulimi and Montana Management Inc. v. Switzerland* App no 5809/08 (ECtHR (C), 26 November 2013) paras 120 (finding 'that the protection afforded at international level in this context was not equivalent to that required by the Convention') and 129–35 (conducting an analysis of proportionality). See further Gianluigi Palombella, 'Theory, Realities, and Promises of Inter-Legality: A Manifesto' in Jan

DOI: 10.4324/9781003355762-2

through proportionality analysis where equivalent protection is not found to be provided for.[6] Even the protection of constitutional identity has been argued to be suitable as a robust (but non-exclusive) consideration to be balanced in proportionality analysis in cases of conflict.[7]

The main aim of this chapter is to advocate for the category of 'interlegal balancing', which can be defined as balancing in cases where: (1) obligations stem from norms and reasons of diverse legalities, and (2) a formal, *ex ante* rule to solve such an antinomy is lacking or otherwise inadequate given the circumstances of a case at hand. This chapter will focus upon the uses of interlegal balancing in what we may call multilevel settings – however, interlegal balancing may as well be useful as a structure for similar substantive arguments under less structured, horizontal regime collisions.

The argument is organised as follows. The second section defines 'interlegal balancing' by reference to the ideas of 'interlegality' and 'balancing', accompanied by considerations for their conjunction as 'interlegal balancing'. The third section emphasizes the distinctive features of 'interlegal balancing' in multilevel settings through four main, tentative patterns.[8] The fourth section gathers some limits for 'interlegal balancing'. A conclusion insists on the normative, integrative potential of 'interlegal balancing'.

2 'Interlegality' and 'Balancing' in Interlegal Balancing

2.1 'Interlegality' in Interlegal Balancing

Current legal theory has recently accorded a mainstream position for legal pluralism,[9] ie theories which focus on the diverse legalities which may apply and conflict within one same polity (or 'semi-autonomous' social field, or even one same person).[10] Still,

Klabbers and Gianluigi Palombella (eds), *The Challenge of Inter-Legality* (Cambridge UP 2019), 388–390.

6 A different reasoning was finally provided by the Grand Chamber of the ECtHR in *Al-Dulimi and Montana Management Inc v Switzerland* App no 5809/08 (ECtHR (GC), 21 June 2016). However, in a Concurring Opinion, Judge Pinto de Albuquerque, joined by Judges Hajiyev, Pejchal and Dedov discussed a 'disguised *Bosphorus* solution' (paras 54–56), pointing that '[t]he majority's endorsement of this test is made even clearer by the final lapidary sentence of paragraph 153, which consists in a general comparative assessment of the protection provided by the "access to these procedures" (the Focal Point), on the one hand, and the Convention requirement of "appropriate judicial scrutiny", on the other. The general and abstract tone used is similar to that in *Bosphorus*' (para 55).

7 See below, § 4.3.

8 Although the intertwinement of legalities cannot be fully anticipated, a working typology of 'regularities' 'situations', or 'patterns', of balancing which incorporate norms and normative considerations sourced in more than one legality is offered.

9 See the contributions in Nicole Roughan and Andrew Halpin (eds), *In Pursuit of Pluralist Jurisprudence* (Cambridge University Press 2017).

10 See the definition of legal pluralism in Ralf Michaels, 'Global Legal Pluralism' (2009) 5 Annual Review of Law and Social Science 243.

legal pluralism is sometimes accused of focusing on understanding such overlaps and conflicts, but not on what an appropriate legal answer would be for them. Alexander Somek puts it sharply: 'Pluralists throw up their hands and exclaim 'legally irresolvable conflict' [...] Eventually, the resolution requires judicial diplomacy, that is, deference and accommodation.'[11]

But this need not require a demise of the insights of legal pluralism. Among them, legal pluralism posited its own 'phenomenological counterpart', as De Sousa Santos first characterised interlegality, an 'intersection of different legal orders' which is a constitutive, and not accidental, element of our experience and coexistence under the frame of law.[12] Here, interlegality will be understood as an invitation to account for the question of 'what a *legal solution* would look like if matters were running their course'.[13]

This way, interlegality, in the conception which I adopt,[14] approaches the question of diverse applicable standards sourced in different legalities from a different perspective; namely, from cases at hand and their applicable norms as invoked by the affected parties. Where the received view assumes that criteria of validity and membership within some legal (or doctrinal) system settle the issue, interlegality acknowledges that this move is insufficient, especially where human rights and fundamental principles are involved, leading to artificially isolated judgments which fail to acknowledge the actual complexity of a case.[15] This epistemic and judicial injustice can be avoided, according to interlegality, by taking into consideration all the diverging standards in a substantive judgment, despite their diverse sources.[16] The key is to depart from the facts and the conflicting claims as involved in cases at hand – these will serve as epistemic points of

11 Alexander Somek, 'Monism: A Tale of the Undead' in Matej Avbelj and Jan Komárek (eds), *Constitutional Pluralism in the European Union and Beyond* (Hart 2012), 357. To be fair, some formulations in constitutional pluralism may have approximated this standpoint, such as one of the views held by Neil MacCormick, *Questioning Sovereignty: Law, State, and Nation in the European Commonwealth* (Oxford University Press 1999), 75: 'it is perfectly possible that conflicts will simply go unresolved, or that the solution may be a matter for political rather than legal processes.'

12 See Boaventura de Sousa Santos, 'Law: A Map of Misreading. Toward a Postmodern Conception of Law' (1987) 14(3) Journal of Law and Society 279, 298; cf a critical stocktaking of the concept in Rainer Nickel, 'Interlegalidad' (2015) 8 Eunomía 205.

13 Somek (n 11), 358. *Pace* Somek, what this question requires of us might not necessarily be to 'unearth' monism, but rather to look for some legal reasoning which takes all norms into consideration, in spite of their diverse origins.

14 See the contributions in Jan Klabbers and Gianluigi Palombella (eds), *The Challenge of Inter-Legality* (Cambridge University Press 2019).

15 See Palombella (n 5), 369: 'If conditional upon one particular legality, only in part governing the normative factors at stake, justice shall always remain a lame verdict', and similarly at ibid, 386.

16 Interlegality requires that all relevant legal norms are accounted for, 'considering the reasons and ideas of justice embedded in conflicting legal claims', as put by Jan Klabbers and Gianluigi Palombella, 'Situating Inter-Legality' in Jan Klabbers and Gianluigi Palombella (eds), *The Challenge of Inter-Legality* (Cambridge University Press 2019), 4. Similarly, see Palombella (n 5), 952, on attenuating 'jurisdictional self-containedness, opening the path to a full consideration of the reasons stemming from the diverse legal perspectives involved'.

vantage from which to assess the ensuing rights and duties. In other words, for interlegality, the intertwinement of legalities offers different contributory reasons which must be duly accounted for in an all-things-considered legal decision.

2.2 'Balancing' in Interlegal Balancing

To be sure, accounting for norms with diverse origins in an all-things-considered legal decision is not a simple issue. However, it is akin to 'balancing' judgments, of the sort which are often recurred to in hard cases of adjudication.[17] Balancing judgments first incorporate different counterposed *contributory reasons* to then, at a second step, organize under certain heuristics the justification of a practical decision in a particular case.[18] This contrasts with what for long was taken as the sole, dominating method in legal reasoning, namely, subsumption or syllogistic reasoning. In syllogistic reasoning, there is a major premise which relates certain conditions of application to certain consequences, a minor premise which presents facts, and a conclusion which, given the case, subsumes the facts under the conditions of application and their consequences. In syllogistic reasoning, the preferability of the applicable standard is out of question, but this is crucial for balancing.

A typical model of balancing is the 'structured'[19] type of *proportionality analysis* with sequential stages. These stages are, in short form, the following:[20]

17 *What* exactly may be 'balanced' is partly contextual. In morals, or general practical reasoning, balancing may refer indistinctly to norms, reasons, and values. In law, standing doctrines bear upon the issue. Some authors and some jurisdictions restrict balancing to governmental interferences in rights defined as 'relative', while others extend balancing to interests generally. For discussion, see Matthias Klatt, 'Balancing Rights and Interests: Reconstructing the Asymmetry Thesis' (2021) 41(2) Oxford Journal of Legal Studies 321; cf Duncan Kennedy, 'A Transnational Genealogy of Proportionality in Private Law' in Roger Brownsword, Hans-W Micklitz Leone Niglia and Stephen Weatherill, *The Foundations of European Private Law* (Hart 2011), 190: 'The considerations may be loosely ranked but there are no ontological priorities among them and in private law they include not only the moral considerations often called principles, but also 'policies,' goals, values, rights and even precedents conceived as having differential 'weight.' These are typically arrayed in formulaic pro/con 'argument bites' that are used over and over in legal argument.

18 See Jaap Hage, 'The Justification of Value Judgments: Theoretical Foundations for Arguments about the Best Level to Regulate European Private Law' in Bram Akkermans, Jaap Hage, Nicole Kornet, and Jan M Smits (eds), *Who Does What? On the Allocation of Regulatory Competences in European Private Law* (Intersentia 2015), 84: '"balancing" stands for a logical step in which a conclusion is derived on the basis of three premises. One premise states the contributory reasons that plead for the conclusion. Another premise states the contributory reasons that plead against the conclusion. And a third premise, the "weight-premise", states which of these two sets outweighs the other set.'

19 On this point, see Vicki C Jackson, 'Constitutional Law in an Age of Proportionality' (2015) 124(8) Yale LJ 3094, 3098ff.

20 See ibid, see also a recent exposition in Robert Alexy, 'Constitutional Rights, Proportionality, and Argumentation' in Jan-R Sieckmann (ed), *Proportionality, Balancing, and Rights: Robert Alexy's Theory of Constitutional Rights* (Springer 2021), 2–4.

- *Legitimacy* (whether there is a legal basis for the objective of a decision under review).
- *Suitability* (whether the decision under review can actually advance the selected objectives).
- *Necessity* (whether the least intrusive means regarding the affected right or value were chosen).
- *Balancing*, or *proportionality*, 'in the narrow sense' (a balance among the interference in some right or value and the achievement of other ones).[21]

One must note that each of these aspects admits for alternatives: just as different models for proportionality analysis coexist, proportionality analyses coexist with other methods for balancing.[22] Under interlegal conditions, this alternativity of models is foregrounded and sometimes a volatile point of contention itself.

To anticipate, *interlegal* balancing, as compared to balancing regarding the norms of one single legality, displays a particular intensity in two distinctive features:

a Interlegal balancing involves both substantive (merits-based), and formal (non-merits based) reasons.[23] This occurs with a distinctive intensity given the crucial question of jurisdictional boundaries among the diverse legalities. Formal considerations include provisions and doctrines on jurisdictions, competences, judicial loyalties, deference, subsidiarity, consensus, *inter alia*. For interlegality, judgments should not be merely formal decisions on 'boundary-maintenance'.[24] But it is equally true that interlegal balancing remains barred from purely substantive considerations on rights and principles which would naively assume some 'view from nowhere'.[25] Admittedly, this combination of substantive and formal reasons can occur in quite diverse ways, explicitly or implicitly, either including the formal jurisdictional concerns among the factors

21 As Robert Alexy has masterfully developed, this stage incorporates in relevant cases, some ranking of values in abstract terms and attenuations derived from the degree of uncertainty in available information. See Robert Alexy (n 20), 4ff.

22 For comparisons of proportionality analyses and reasonableness tests, see Mariano Sapag, 'El principio de proporcionalidad y de razonabilidad como límite constitucional al poder del Estado: un estudio comparado' (2008) 17 Díkaion, 157, Duncan Kennedy (n 17), 217ff, Moshe Cohen-Eliya and Iddo Porat, *Proportionality and Constitutional Culture* (Cambridge UP 2013) 10ff, Jackson (n 19). See also the variability of proportionality analyses in Talya Steiner, Andrej Lang, and Mordechai Kremnitzer, 'Comparative and Empirical Insights into Judicial Practice: Towards an Integrative Model of Proportionality' in Mordechai Kremnitzer, Talya Steiner and Andrej Lang (eds), *Proportionality in Action: Comparative and Empirical Perspectives on the Judicial Practice* (Cambridge University Press 2020).

23 On this distinction of merits-based and non-merits-based reasons, see Oddný Mjöll Arnardóttir, 'Rethinking the Two Margins of Appreciation' (2016) 12 European Constitutional Law Review 27.

24 So the formulation in Neil Walker, *Intimations of Global Law* (Cambridge UP), 108, cited in Gianluigi Palombella, 'Inter-Legality: On Interconnections and "External" Sources' (2021) 7(2) The Italian Law Journal 943, 951–2.

25 Jan Klabbers, 'Dystopian Legalities: A Reply to Nico Krisch' (2022) 20(1) 507, 510.

which are balanced,[26] or as considerations which delimit balancing to certain acute cases that threaten human rights and fundamental principles.[27]

b Interlegal balancing alternates with legal categorisations.[28] There is a convergence in using categories to determine the intensity of review: a category is either given or not, and balancing is consequently deployed under fitting degrees of stringency. The underlying reason is to allow the competent authorities to decide in their own scope of legitimacy. In a multilevel context, relevant reasons for subsidiarity are organised through legal categories and doctrines such as the margin of appreciation, *Solange*-style conditionalities, safeguarding constitutional identity, or ultra vires review regarding interdependent goals. Due to the complexity and general scope of 'interlegal balancing', the sequencing in which such categorisations and balancing alternate remains somewhat contingent. What is essential for this alternation is that categorical rules determine the applicability of proportionality analysis.

3 Interlegal Balancing in Multilevel Settings

By multilevel I mean two or more legalities (or regimes) which do not relate because of material interdependence alone, but rather in virtue of institutional design. This is important, as we certainly experience a generalised state of 'regime collisions'[29] or 'crossings'[30] where material interdependence is decisive, even in lieu of formal institutional linkages.[31] In multilevel settings, it is meaningful to

26 See Duncan Kennedy 'Proportionality and "Deference" in Contemporary Constitutional Thought' in Tamara Perišin and Siniša Rodin (eds), *The Transformation or Reconstitution of Europe: The Critical Legal Studies Perspective on the Role of the Courts in the European Union* (Hart 2018).

27 Both possibilities are reminiscent of models to balance what Robert Alexy calls 'formal principles'. See Robert Alexy, 'Formal Principles: Some Replies to Critics' (2014) 12 (3) International Journal of Constitutional Law 511, Thomas Kleinlein, 'Judicial Lawmaking by Judicial Restraint? The Potential of Balancing in International Economic Law' in Armin von Bogdandy and Ingo Venzke (eds) International Judicial Lawmaking (Springer 2012) 287ff.

28 On proportionality and categorisation, see Aharon Barak, *Proportionality: Constitutional Rights and their Limitations* (Cambridge University Press 2012) 502ff.

29 See Andreas Fischer-Lescano and Gunther Teubner, 'Regime-Collisions: The Vain Search for Legal Unity in the Fragmentation of Global Law' (2004) 25 Michigan Journal of International Law 999.

30 See José E Alvarez, 'Beware: Boundary Crossings' in Tsvi Kahana and Anat Scolnicov (eds), *Boundaries of State, Boundaries of Rights* (Cambridge University Press 2016), cf Alec Stone Sweet and Giacinto della Cananea, 'Proportionality, General Principles of Law, and Investor-State Arbitration: A Response to José Alvarez' (2014) 46 NYU Journal of International Law and Politics 911.

31 In contrast to 'multilevel settings', one may speak of more horizontal constellations, for instance, in references from a jurisdictional body of a digital platform (Facebook's Oversight Board) towards Reports of the UN Special Rapporteur, we may also mention the differentiation and collisions of regimes of international law and regimes of global governance. On this latter topic, see Ming-Sung Kuo, 'Resolving the Question of Inter-Scalar Legitimacy into Law? A Hard Look at Proportionality Balancing in

speak of member states and a common order with binding authorities. There are provisions on exclusive, shared, or residual competences among the different legalities. The consent of member states is presupposed, and with it a stable, controllable relation among institutions and a relatively more stable set of procedures for the common construction of concepts, especially through judicial reasoning.

As a tentative and not necessarily exhaustive typology, we could identify four greater 'patterns' or regularities in situations where interlegal balancing as previously defined may occur, at the interfaces of legalities in multilevel settings, namely: (1) in assessing the margin of appreciation and related doctrines; (2) in equivalent protection and related doctrines; (3) in certain conceptions of the protection of constitutional identity; and (4) in the review of *ultra vires* acts whose aims are materially interdependent.

3.1 Interlegal Balancing and Margin of Appreciation

One of the main contexts where balancing occurs regarding norms and normative considerations sourced in more than one legal order is in the dominant doctrine of the margin of appreciation. To be sure, both are not coextensive. The margin of appreciation doctrine enshrines questions which essentially work as an argumentative structure or interface to review, or not review, the decisions of member states in a multilevel setting. Interlegal balancing, as previously defined, implies that norms and normative considerations arising in more than one legality are subject to a review in terms of opting for the preferrable ('all-things-considered') decision. The margin of appreciation may imply balancing, but it may well be delimited into the questions of who decides; when to defer; when is discretion admissible; and so on. In this line of cases, the margin of appreciation helps to assess what Oddný Mjöll Arnardóttir terms 'non-merits reasons', and that might be the essential part of a given decision, instead of an analysis on the merits.[32] This distinction has been drawn usefully by Arnardóttir, (recasting previous contributions, especially by George Letsas[33] and Andrew Legg[34]):

> Defining the two elements of the margin of appreciation, it can be stated that the systemic one is related to *deference to other decision-making bodies for non-*

Global Governance' (2018) 31 Leiden Journal of International Law 793. However, a discussion of interlegal balancing in these more horizontal constellations must be left pending.

32 Although considering all relevant 'non-merits reasons' also implies some general sense of balancing in practical reason, I will leave these cases at one side to focus on 'interlegal balancing', in the sense of combining both substantive and formal considerations.

33 See George Letsas 'Two Concepts of the Margin of Appreciation' (2006) 26 Oxford Journal of Legal Studies 705, on a 'substantive' concept of the margin of appreciation, addressing 'the relationship between individual freedoms and collective goals' and a 'structural' concept based on 'limits or intensity of the review of the European Court of Human Rights' (ibid, 706).

34 See Andrew Legg, *The Margin of Appreciation in International Human Rights Law: Deference and Proportionality* (Oxford University Press 2012)

> *merits reasons*, and that the normative element is related to the Court's *own assessment of merits reasons.* In the former conception the margin of appreciation has a distinct systemic ('structural' or 'procedural') function related to the division of tasks within the European system for the protection of human rights, whereas the latter conception has a normative ('substantive') function and reflects pluralism and normative flexibility in the interpretation and application of Convention rights.[35]

Where the margin of appreciation is amenable to interlegal balancing, we may note that there is not one single structure or 'sequence' for this alternation of the margin of appreciation and interlegal balancing. Sometimes they alternate in 'sequence', but oftentimes they are intertwined. Where sequenced, analysing reasons from consensus, subsidiarity, democratic legitimacy, and other formal, 'non-merits reasons', may take precedence as a sort of 'threshold' or 'enabler' for interlegal balancing, including both 'merits' and 'non-merits' reasons. Where not, interlegal balancing may itself be the way to assess and justify whether the margin of appreciation holds or not to sustain a national decision.[36]

This entanglement of (interlegal) balancing and the margin of appreciation has been present all the way from the beginning of the doctrine. For instance, in the ECtHR's famous *Handyside* judgment, the margin of appreciation was characterised as a consequence of subsidiarity, i.e., the consideration that, 'By reason of their direct and continuous contact with the vital forces of their countries, State authorities are in principle in a better position than the international judge'[37] to assess the concretisation of limitation clauses such as 'the protection of morals' in Article 10 of the European Convention of Human Rights.[38] And, in the case of positive obligations, 'the choice of means is in principle a matter that falls within the Contracting State's margin of appreciation'.[39]

Given that member states enjoy discretion in the implementation of human rights, social ends, and other fundamental principles, balancing is necessary to assess a proper fulfilment of the scope of application of such norms. It is also crucial that these substantive considerations intersect with reasons which may plead for subsidiarity, such as protecting democratic and local decision-making, or the absence of a regional consensus on the level of protection of the substantive norms involved. This impacts legal reasoning. When, in principle, a matter falls inside the margin of appreciation, proportionality analysis is not conducted *ex novo*. Rather, a

35 Arnardóttir (n 23), 53.

36 On this point, cf Arnardóttir (n 23), discussing in turn 'Janneke Gerards' idea that 'procedural review' should always precede 'substantive review', and pointing that 'the Court itself seems to be embracing the doctrine as the mechanism through which to introduce [*the margin of appreciation doctrine*]', citing *Von Hannover v Germany (no 2)* App Nos 40660/08 and 60641/08 (ECtHR, 7 February 2012).

37 *Handyside v The United Kingdom* App. No 5493/72 (ECtHR, 7 December 1976), para 48.

38 ibid.

39 *Fadeyeva v Russia* App. No 55723/00 (ECtHR, 9 June 2005), para 96.

variable intensity of scrutiny is employed, depending on the case. The margin of appreciation doctrine may lead to withholding a full review in terms of proportionality analysis unless 'strong reasons' require the reviewing court 'to substitute its view for that of the final decision' of the local authorities.[40] In such cases, as Arnardóttir notes, 'instead of simply proceeding directly to performing its own review of the proportionality of the contested measure, the Court has created a preliminary step in its analytic approach'.[41]

Finally, the question must be addressed on the applicability of the margin of appreciation in multilevel contexts outside the European legal space. It is hard to deny that the reasons which are made explicit though the margin of appreciation doctrine are universal in nature.[42] After all, legalities always relate under substantive ('merits-based') and formal ('non-merits based') normative considerations. Crucially, this is not always expressed in the language of the margin of appreciation, but oftentimes rather in terms of applicable 'standards of review'.[43]

Now, the generalisation of the margin of appreciation is not uncontested. Discussions of the Inter-American System of Human Rights have voiced a robust opposition to the doctrine. For instance, Laura Clérico forcefully rebuts that the Inter-American Court of Human Rights has rejected calls for deference stemming from 'arguments from lack of regional consensus'.[44] Where the region is marked by systematic human rights violations, applying an 'argument from lack of consensus' would try to appease regional and state interests, but at the cost of relinquishing universal responsibility.[45] In a different sense, Yuval Shany had foreseen that the question on the generalization of the margin of appreciation doctrine hinged upon 'the political need for definitive legal guidance in the more sensitive cases (for instance, use of force cases implicating *jus cogens* norms)'.[46] To my mind, the question regards the essential (if also progressive) scope of protection of human rights which is unfitting for 'non-merits' based reasonings, while in terms of the margin of appreciation, standards of review or deference, more generally. However, this might presuppose, rather than oppose, the generality of the rationale of this doctrine. In other cases, the formal considerations may temper the terms of (interlegal) balancing into more delimited standards of review.

40 *MGN Limited v The United Kingdom* App No 39401/04 (ECtHR, 18 January 2011), para 150, and likewise *Von Hannover v Germany (no 2)* (n 36), para 107.
41 Arnardóttir, 25.
42 See Yuval Shany 'Toward a General Margin of Appreciation Doctrine in International Law?' (2006) 16(5) European Journal of International Law 907.
43 cf Johannes Hendrik Fahner, *Judicial Deference in International Adjudication: A Comparative Analysis* (Hart 2022)
44 Laura Clérico, 'El argumento de la falta de consenso regional en derechos humanos. Divergencia entre el TEDH y la Corte IDH' (2020) 46 Revista Derecho del Estado 57.
45 ibid, 76–7.
46 Shany (n 43), 938.

3.2 Interlegal Balancing and Equivalent Protection

Another core doctrinal area which involves interlegal balancing as previously defined is *equivalent protection* assessments. The core consideration in equivalent protection regards assessing whether a comparable and suitable standard of rights protection and access to justice can be found in 'external' legalities as the ones provided for 'domestically'. This is a complex question involving both formal ('non-merits based') considerations on institutional provisions and remedies, as well as substantive ('merits based') considerations on what a suitable standard of rights protection would be.[47] Insofar as both elements are intertwined in a final judgment, equivalent protection is combined with interlegal balancing.

In the paradigmatic *Solange* I judgment of 1974, the GFCC held that as long as there were no precise catalogue and protection of constitutional rights such as those provided by the German constitution, it would be 'admissible and obligatory' (*zulässig und geboten*) for the national judiciary to exercise its scrutiny over the obligations stemming from the legal order of the European Communities.[48] Finding this state of affairs to be provided for in *Solange* II, the GFCC held that it would not exercise its review so long as the protection of fundamental rights remained in place at the European level.[49]

This logic underlies the 'equivalent protection' doctrine. In its *Bosphorus* judgment,[50] the ECtHR crystallised the doctrine that State actions complying with 'external' obligations would be admissible if these stem from a regime with an equivalent level of protection (as regards both substantive guarantees and mechanisms of access to justice) to those of the European Convention.[51] Then, it would be presumed that such actions are consistent with the obligations under the Convention – but under the case-by-case proviso that such a presumption would be rebutted 'if, in the circumstances of a particular case, it is considered that the protection of Convention rights was manifestly deficient'.[52]

The constitutional vocation to protect human rights must be read in harmony with the efficacy of supranational integration and international cooperation. This is the sense in which, combining substantive concerns (the protection of human rights) with formal considerations (effective integration, cooperation), a balancing judgment must occur which incorporates norms and normative considerations sourced in more than one legality. As a result, the category of 'equivalent protection' usually serves as a threshold for review in terms of proportionality analysis,

47 See Oddný Mjöll Arnardóttir, 'The "Procedural Turn" under the European Convention on Human Rights and Presumptions of Convention Compliance' (2017) 15(1) International Journal of Constitutional Law 9, 34–5.
48 BVerfGE 37, 271 (*Solange* I), para 56.
49 BVerfGE 73, 339 (*Solange* II).
50 *Bosphorus v Ireland* (n 4).
51 ibid, paras 152–8.
52 ibid., para 156.

enshrining efficacy, and the authoritative implementation of obligations as long as the protection of human rights is guaranteed to an equivalent degree.[53]

3.3 Interlegal Balancing and the Protection of Constitutional Identity

The protection of constitutional identity can also imply interlegal balancing. However, *identity review* is not always compatible with interlegal balancing. To see this, we may take avail of a distinction among two senses of the protection of constitutional identity. Giovanni Piccirilli has helpfully distinguished, first, the protection of constitutional identity as enshrined in Article 4(2) TEU, which is interpreted 'as a form of Europeanisation of counter-limits',[54] and, second, 'as a sovereignty claim, in the sense of limiting the primacy and the field of application of EU law in order to reserve specific areas to national law, without comparable parallel restrictions on attaining the same results by domestic legal means.'[55]

Interlegal balancing is compatible with the former sense, i.e., the protection of constitutional identity under a combination of pooled fundamental principles. In contrast, interlegal balancing is barred by the protection of constitutional identity under the logic of sovereignty claims 'without parallel restrictions'.[56] As enshrined in Article 4(2) TEU, the protection of constitutional identity is a (fundamental) factor to be given due consideration.[57] It is a very important but not peremptory, or exclusionary ('non-merits'), reason. As Advocate General Maduro stated in a now classic opinion,[58] constitutional identity 'cannot be understood as an absolute obligation to defer to all national constitutional rules',[59] but instead it is subject to judicial review, ideally through its due incorporation in proportionality analysis.[60] In contrast, as stemming from the idea of sovereignty, the protection of constitutional identity establishes certain provisions behind a 'red line', and away from any balancing.

Further adding to the complexity of the issue, discussions of constitutional identity also include unamendable provisions of constitutions where present, and the particular values and expectations stemming from the history of a constitutional state.[61] There is

53 Further on the topic, see Vassilis P Tzevelekos, 'The Al-Dulimi Case before the Grand Chamber of the European Court of Human Rights: Business as Usual? Test of Equivalent Protection, (Constitutional) Hierarchy and Systemic Integration' (2017) 38 Questions of International Law, Zoom-in 5, cf Arnardóttir (n 42).

54 Giovanni Piccirilli, 'The "*Taricco* Saga": The Italian Constitutional Court Continues Its European Journey' (2018) 14(4) European Constitutional Law Review 814, 827.

55 ibid, 828.

56 ibid.

57 See ibid, 820.

58 Case C-213/07, *Michaniki AE v Ethniko Symvoulio Radiotileorasis and Ypourgos Epikrateias* [2007] ECR I-09999, Opinion of AG Maduro.

59 ibid, para 33.

60 ibid, paras 34–5.

61 For discussion on how constitutional identity oscillates between claims of unamendability, on the one hand, and constitutional culture, on the other hand, see Julian Scholtes 'Abusing Constitutional Identity' (2021) 22 German Law Journal 534, 541ff.

a facet of constitutionalism which buttresses the historical and cultural path dependencies of each polity.[62] This contextualising dimension might be tied to the concept of the sovereignty of nation states, conditional as it may become upon the protection of human rights, but it certainly finds different expressions. One may count here highly stringent protections of certain fundamental rights and organisational principles of state powers (paradigmatic are 'eternity clauses' such as Article 79 (3) of the German Basic Law, which states that '[a]mendments to this Basic Law affecting the division of the Federation into *Länder*, their participation in principle in the legislative process, or the principles laid down in Articles 1 and 20 shall be inadmissible'). But one may otherwise also include concretisations *and limitations* of fundamental rights, and this is where the protection of constitutional identity risks being co-opted[63] (even though no legal or constitutional doctrine is beyond this peril).

In sum, constitutional identity under Article 4 (2) TEU can be part of a proportionality analysis which not only involves fundamental norms from different legalities, but which also incorporates formal reasons (path-dependencies) and substantive concerns. The question of generalisation of constitutional identity into different multilevel settings remains especially thorny, and along the lines of the discussions of the margin of appreciation, the more sensitive cases leave less room for decisions on 'non-merits-based' reasons. In any case, both dimensions of constitutional identity, either under subsumption or balancing, are legitimate expectations in constitutional polities. Constitutional identity stems from the very idea of self-determination in our constitutional states.

3.4 Interlegal Balancing and Ultra Vires *Review regarding Non-Exclusive or Interdependent Aims*

The review of *ultra vires* acts is also not always compatible with interlegal balancing. If the review is strictly formal and upon settled categories, balancing is inadmissible. Everything changes, however, insofar as we find shared, or materially interdependent objectives which make it impossible *ex ante* to resort to conferred competences. In such cases, interlegal balancing is the way to determine whether an act is within or without the material scope of competences.

In the identification of acts which may go beyond conferred competences, it is necessary to incorporate substantive value-laden considerations on fundamental rights and the delimitation of shared goals (i.e., the material scope of a competence) with more formal considerations on jurisdictional standing. On the other hand, this is vexing given that competence norms have a rigid nature which typically seems unfit for balancing, especially with an eye to the principles of legality and conferred powers. Thus, competences include substantive and formal considerations, as well as a typically rather rigid, rule-like character.

62 See e.g. Gary Jeffrey Jacobsohn, *Constitutional Identity* (Harvard University Press 2010), 112ff.

63 On the concept and its potential despite accusations of its proneness to abuse, see Scholtes (n 61).

Under this perspective, a merely formal conflict of jurisdictional claims *as such* is insufficient to merit interlegal balancing. A formal conflict of jurisdictional claims could well arise even without conflicting substantive results,[64] or without any pretension to protect fundamental rights, or it could be resolved by formal rules on applicable law or jurisdiction. Instead, interlegal balancing is useful to account for conflicting substantive ideas of justice which, to be sure, are intertwined with formal claims to competence or jurisdiction. This mixed character must be kept in mind. In the EU, as a 'laboratory of jurisprudential concepts',[65] the conferral of competences ('who decides') is categorical and (generally) prior, and only the material aims, or scope, of competences must be determined under the concepts of subsidiarity and proportionality.

Personal attribution and the fulfilment of established procedures are categorical in nature: they are either satisfied or not. In contrast, the material exercise of the scope of a competence gives room for balancing. Certainly, this cannot eliminate discretion of those concretising (selecting means and policies) the attributions defined in the material scope of competences, especially when the legal definitions are insufficient to 'contain' the material interdependence of the ends involved. To compensate, such discretion must therefore be 'contained' under additional burdens of justification – especially in proportionality analysis. For many, the Treaty on the European Union is paradigmatic of such an understanding in its Art. 5(1), which establishes that subsidiarity and proportionality govern the use, but not the limits, of Union competences. Their limits are 'governed by the principle of conferral'. In this sense, a proportionality assessment may enter the picture only after determining the fulfilment of 'personal' and 'procedural' conditions of competence, i.e., once that it has been decided that an authority is competent, and to ensure that 'Union action shall not exceed what is necessary to achieve the objectives of the Treaties'.[66] As the above cited *PSPP* judgment has shown,[67] in actual practice matters prove to be less clear-cut. Given the well-known intractability of neatly distinguishing monetary from economic policy, and due to the exceptional nature of the PSPP measure,[68] a strict standard of review through proportionality analysis was held as determinant to assess the degree to which the competences of Germany as a Member State were respected – and, as decided by

64 cf Matthias Klatt, 'Balancing Competences: How Institutional Cosmopolitanism can Manage Jurisdictional Conflicts' (2015) 4 (2) Global Constitutionalism 195, 200.

65 The formulation stems from Orlando Scarcello, 'Abriendo el sistema: La actual postura pluralista del Tribunal Constitucional Italiano ante el Derecho de la Unión Europea' in Gabriel Encinas and Miguel Neria (eds), *Ordenamiento jurídico: Fundamentos y apertura* (Derecho Global 2021), 108.

66 Article 5(4) TEU.

67 See Judgment of the Second Senate of 5 May 2020 2 BvR 859/15.

68 A comparable aspect was highlighted in Case C-62/14 *Peter Gauweiler and Others v Deutscher Bundestag* [2015] Opinion of AG Cruz Villalón, ECLI:EU:C:2015:7 para 161: '(…) a review of whether the principle of conferral has been complied with from the perspective of the principle of proportionality (Article 5(4) TEU) is essential in the case of a measure which is presented as unconventional and as being justified on account of exceptional circumstances'.

the GFCC, any latitude was taken to speak against it. Although the merits of the case may be discussed, what is key here is that a balancing judgment becomes legitimate regarding materially interdependent aims (such as monetary and economic policy), as it enables the different epistemic sites to be taken into consideration.

3.5 Intermediate Remarks on Patterns of Interlegal Balancing in Multilevel Settings

Four 'patterns' of interlegal balancing were mentioned: interlegal balancing and the margin of appreciation; interlegal balancing and equivalent protection; interlegal balancing and constitutional identity under an understanding akin to article 4 (2) TEU; and interlegal balancing and ultra vires review regarding materially interdependent objectives. All four of them are instances of balancing/ proportionality analyses which 'alternate' with rather well-known categories and doctrines, and in them we find the incorporation not only of normative considerations stemming from different legal orders, but these normative considerations are both formal and substantive in character.

The main purpose of this section was not to rehearse the finer points of such categories, nor to discuss generally the issue of doctrines which allow contesting multilevel integration under particular cases. Instead, the purpose is to advocate for casting familiar doctrines under the light of interlegal balancing. Under some 'systemic', 'exclusionary' or 'validity' based accounts of legal orders, balancing norms and considerations stemming from more than one legality still sounds rather jarring. The purpose of this chapter is to submit that we already live in a world where interlegal balancing occurs with regularity. The better we understand this concept, the better progress we can make on controlling the arguments and claims we stake. Interlegal balancing is therefore not a utopian abstraction, but a practice in need of further study. It opens views to recognize commonalities among what may seem chaotic engagements.

As regards our 'input' or reference points, we have admittedly taken stock mainly of cases within the European legal space. And yet, as intimated, these four patterns of interlegal balancing can be generalised beyond this context, into other multilevel structures (e.g., the EU and the UNSC, or the Inter-American system of human rights and its Member States).

The main open question here would regard whether interlegal balancing is truly generalisable or whether it accounts for a historical or contextual, European particularity which cannot be transplanted into other contexts. My hunch is that interlegal balancing is generalisable insofar as it can be accounted for in analytical terms. Even if strict doctrines on hierarchy (whether national or otherwise) were adopted, (interlegal) balancing is a conceptual possibility, and it would remain in any case available in a closer sense to the *defeasibility* of primacy, owing, e.g., to considerations from jus cogens norms,[69] owing to the essential importance of the protection of human rights as a

69 Cf the consideration in the judgment in the *Kadi* saga held by the then-Court of First Instance of the European Communities in 2005: 'None the less, the Court is empowered to check, indirectly, the lawfulness of the resolutions of the Security

condition for any authority,[70] or owing to the constitutive dimension of expectations such as access to justice and respect for the rule of law.[71]

4 The Scope of Interlegal Balancing

In this last main section, my intention is to enunciate some necessary nuances and delimitations on interlegal balancing and what I foresee as its main objection. Any attempt at rebuttal or confirmation, however, must be left pending for further works. I will first address the limiting circumstance, which may well obtain, of finding explicit restrictions to interlegal balancing in some legality. I will then address an objection from jurisdictional biases, along with a plea for recasting of objections from incommensurability or incomparability into 'institutional parity'. Finally, I will briefly conjecture some ideas on a more virtuous practice of interlegal balancing.

4.1 Explicit restrictions to interlegal balancing

Nothing impedes a given legality from barring either interlegality, balancing, or interlegal balancing. This may happen variously. Interlegality can be precluded by a state refusing to cooperate in multilevel structures and transnational issues. Proportionality analyses in the judiciary can be precluded by disempowering judges from constitutional judicial review or adopting strict doctrines on categorisation-based reasoning. Interlegal balancing will be precluded by either of both. It can also be hindered by adopting strict system-based doctrines on jurisdiction. Pretty much the same may occur under more immaterial aspects such as legal doctrines and legal culture. Interlegal balancing depends on an environment which is, at least, not overly hostile to its application.

Even in such cases where interlegal balancing were to become precluded, however, a residual but important (arguably: non-waivable) commitment remains from the ideas of interlegality and interlegal balancing. First, respect for interlegality is not a matter of extra-legal aspirations, but it rather flows from the obligation to respect the rule of law; as put by Palombella:

> [...] courts have to live up to their judicial function and have to account for their justice-delivering task, they have to be *accountable* as regards their legal

Council in question with regard to *jus cogens*, understood as a body of higher rules of public international law binding on all subjects of international law, including the bodies of the United Nations, and from which no derogation is possible.' Case T-315/01, *Kadi v. Council & Commission*, 2005 ECR II – 3659, para 226.

70 For this argument regarding the protection of human rights as a check upon the UNSC regime, see Jean L Cohen, *Globalization and Sovereignty: Rethinking Legality, Legitimacy, and Constitutionalism* (Cambridge UP, 2013), 266ff; Dieter Grimm, *Sovereignty: The Origin and Future of a Political and Legal Concept* (Columbia University Press 2015), 126–8.

71 See Gianluigi Palombella, 'Access to Justice: Dynamic, Foundational, and Generative' (2021) 34(2) Ratio Juris 121.

> order, but they are *responsible* courts only in shouldering the entire normative complexity that affects the fate of the people in the issue before their authority.[72]

Before, attention was paid to how Laura Clérico characterised the IACtHR's rejections of 'arguments from lack of consensus' as a matter of responsibility not only to its own member states, but also towards the more universal audience of individuals whose human rights are at stake. A similar consideration belies interlegality. Each jurisdiction, no doubt, is accompanied by its own host of institutional (and informal) biases. Respect for the rule of law, however, can no longer be reduced to a single perspective. Our target audience is not parochial anymore, it is rather a transnational network which becomes conspicuous, e.g., in the diffusion of translated judgments, academic journals and blogs, as well as public scrutiny in the media and informal venues.

Now, even under explicit and unsalvable jurisdictional constraints, courts remain *responsible* in the sense quoted, and this translates into obligations which can be taken up in their legal pronouncements. For argument's sake, let's assume that a case at hand offers both:

(*A*) a correct, interlegal, solution to a case at hand,[73] and
(*B*) a correct solution under a given jurisdiction.

We may further assume that a given deciding authority is somehow explicitly precluded from adopting *A* at the expense of *B*. Even under this scenario, it would be hard to argue that such a deciding authority is barred from even discussing *A*, say, in the way of *obiter dicta*. While we may well foresee many political reasons which might compel a deciding authority to ignore *A*, this would amount to another instance of political pressure and not of conceptual or normative inadmissibility. It remains possible to provide all the details which may be relevant for the affected parties and the publics at large. It would then be up to the public to take all the steps necessary to control their situation.[74]

In this sense, taking all the relevant norms duly into account already serves in 'the search for something beyond particular interests and identity politics, or the irreducibility of difference':[75] it is a reciprocal giving and taking of reasons,

72 Palombella (n 5), 390.
73 To be sure, theories of inter-legality, balancing, or interlegal balancing abstain from claiming that any legal question can receive one right answer. My assumption is that, as in any other practical question, some answers are right, some answers are inadmissible, many other answers are merely admissible, and, unfortunately, some dilemmatic decisions might entail tragic losses.
74 Similarly, albeit formulating the point in terms of a permission inside national constitutional frameworks instead of an obligation in any legal order, see Arnulfo Mateos Durán 'Limits of the *Rechtsstaat* in the Duty to Protect International Fundamental Rights: The Ayotzinapa Committee of Truth' in Nuria Saura-Freixes (ed) *Derechos Humanos, Derecho Constitucional y Derecho Internacional: Sinergias Contemporáneas* (CEPC 2021), 545–6.
75 The formulation stems from Martti Koskenniemi, *The Gentle Civilizer of Nations* (Cambridge University Press 2001), 500.

regardless of the question on whether different interlegal decisions remain admissible. This is not the case if we assume exclusionary, system-based views. This constitutes inter-legality's normative aspect: it is a reasonable expectation for a good faith judgment.

4.2 The problem of fragmentation and jurisdictional perspectivism

According to a forceful objection, in contrast to the context of the constitutional state, balancing becomes hopelessly indeterminate given that there is no common objective standard among diverse legalities. Furthermore, even if a balancing decision were taken, each regime would reach a different decision structurally biased towards its own ends and policy choices, revealing balancing as ineffective regarding the intertwinement of legalities and conflicting norms.

Andreas Fischer-Lescano and Gunther Teubner have formulated one of the earliest and most compelling versions of this objection: 'By virtue of the internal differentiation of global law, however, conflicts judgments are always taken and 'practical concordats' always concluded from the perspective of a specific legal regime'.[76] Along the same lines, Ralf Michaels and Joost Pauwelyn pointed out that 'in the absence of a common, objective standard (available essentially only within a single "system") the value judgments involved in balancing are likely to lead to different results (…)'.[77]

It is true that interlegality, insofar as it claims neither a 'view from nowhere' nor an overarching hierarchy, is always punctual and situated. It can only be taken up by each 'hub',[78] or authority from the intertwined legalities at stake. Therefore, and given that biases are inbuilt into each deciding court or authority, one might worry about the value of interlegality and interlegal balancing if, after all, the problem of diverging decisions is not dispelled.

> We must not lose sight, however, of how interlegal balancing is necessary as a venue for convergence. The idea is that, even if different answers remain available, this will no longer be concealed behind questionable theoretical understandings which exclude and silence applicable legal norms as 'external'. Insofar as the interlegal perspective is assumed in good faith, and even though each court or authority may happen to decide differently, a path opens towards convergence. One same complex of norms will be debated, the same questions on integration will be appreciated. The affected parties will receive a set of arguments and reasons which can be contrasted, accepted, or rejected by the public. All of this is precluded if, on the contrary, a system-based doctrine is invoked, and this seems to be a compelling reason to reverse the burden of

76 Andreas Fischer-Lescano and Gunther Teubner (n 29), 1067.
77 Ralf Michaels and Joost Pauwelyn, 'Conflict of Norms or Conflict of Laws: Different Techniques in the Fragmentation of Public International Law' (2012) 22(3) Duke Journal of Comparative and International Law 349, 368.
78 See Yuval Shany, 'International Courts as Inter-Legality Hubs' in Jan Klabbers and Gianluigi Palombella (eds), *The Challenge of Inter-Legality* (Cambridge University Press 2019).

argument. Certainly, neither system-based doctrines nor interlegality can be said to eliminate the plurality of admissible legal answers. Not even a single legality may do so. However, interlegality allows convergence and argumentative engagement with all the applicable norms invoked by those affected.

Additionally, objections from jurisdictional biases and relativity usually involve some claim of *incommensurability*. Giulio Itzcovich explains such arguments vividly:

> (…) external conflicts between legal orders are unsolvable or irrelevant because, by virtue of the autonomy and authority of the legal order, the norms belonging to different legal orders are incommensurable. (…) the legal orders do not 'communicate' with each other, they do not enter into 'dialogue,' they do not reciprocally 'balance': they claim exclusive authority to solve questions to which they decide to attribute relevance. They uphold a claim to the monopoly of all legally binding statements, because they are an exclusive 'view angle' on their own legality.[79]

However, not only are 'opening' or 'interface norms' conspicuous among legalities,[80] but such incommensurability is itself a false premise.[81] While it is the case that there is no 'comprehensive' catalogue of values among legalities, this remains far from granting that there are *no* common values. Likewise, incommensurability and related notions such as incomparability tend to come loaded with rather heavy theoretical assumptions, but our concern is not *the more theoretical question* of whether two items are comparable. Ultimately, almost any two items can enter comparison under an open-ended 'covering value' or consideration. The interest shifts towards *the more practical questions* of how comparisons are suitable or how

79 Giulio Itzcovich 'Legal Order, Legal Pluralism, Fundaemntal Principles: Europe and Its Law in Three Concepts' (2012) 18(3) European Law Journal 358, 366.

80 On 'interface norms' see Nico Krisch, *Beyond Constitutionalism: The Pluralist Structure of Postnational Law* (Oxford University Press 2010), 285–6. I ventured some condierations for their place as 'necessary' elements of legal orders in Gabriel Encinas, 'Las normas de apertura como elemento necesario del ordenamiento jurídico' in Gabriel Encinas and Miguel Neria (eds), *Ordenamiento jurídico: Fundamentos y apertura* (Derecho Global 2021).

81 In this sense, Armin von Bogdandy and Jürgen Habermas, 'Discourse Theory and International Law: An Interview with Jürgen Habermas' (VerfBlog, 12 March 2013) https://verfassungsblog.de/discourse-theory-and-international-law-an-interview-with-jurgen-habermas/: 'As far as these approaches rely on the contextualist assumption that there are legal languages which form closed, i.e. mutually untranslatable, universes of meaning, they start from a false philosophical premise. (…) Contextualism cannot explain how international courts with justices from different legal traditions ever come to agree on decisions for the same or similar reasons. The jurisdiction of heterogeneously composed international courts provides evidence for the role of principled reasoning; mutual understanding across the gaps between different backgrounds is made easier by recourse to shared principles. Another reason for rejecting the radical versions of legal pluralism is the systematic neglect of needs for legitimation.'

they may contribute to the justification of a challenging decision. In my view, in this context, arguments from 'incommensurability' or 'incomparability' call attention to a particular kind of comparative relation among the norms and considerations of different legalities: *parity*.[82]

4.3 Parity and institutional *parity*

Usually, we think of the relation between two compared items (values, principles) as either 'greater than', 'lesser than', or 'equal to' the other. Ruth Chang calls attention to being 'on a par to' each other as a different comparative relation. In a nutshell, the idea is that parity marks the situation where two compared items are not strictly equal, but none is greater than the other either.[83] Applied to balancing, where there is no clear normative consideration outweighing the other, parity can be identified if small improvements or impairments to either would likely not affect equality, but a chain of them would make one be greater or lesser than the other.[84]

I suspect that there is a particular, institutional sense of parity behind the misgivings on the possibility of a rational choice between different values which are protected by different legalities. This parity may analytically hold in at least two ways. First, the involved reasons would be on a par to each other even if they were part of one same legality: in such a scenario, the presence of jurisdictional constraints or bias (towards 'internal' norms) may either retain this parity or 'tip the scale'. In the second, the involved values are only on a par in virtue of certain jurisdictional constraints or bias: in such a scenario, one of the normative considerations would outweigh the other if they belonged to the same legality.

In this way, in 'institutional parity' a formal jurisdictional 'bound' or 'setting' is revealed as an important but non-exclusionary reason. It enters as a consideration in our practical reasoning, along with the different 'substantive' values (or principles) involved. Cursorily, we obtain a better appreciation of potential covering values that may enable comparison or break parity under interlegality's epistemic shift of attention into avoiding injustice in the circumstances of a case at hand.

4.4 A virtuous application of interlegal balancing?

Finally, it is worth noting that many theories of legal and constitutional pluralism are at risk of having their dearest concepts and doctrines co-opted by dark forces – hence, a move beyond ideal theory is necessary.[85]

Interlegal balancing is a concept which does not need to be exclusive of judges and apex courts. The legislative and the open society of constitutional interpreters

82 On parity, see a recent exposition in Ruth Chang, 'Hard Choices' (2017) 3(1) Journal of the American Philosophical Association 1, 10ff.

83 ibid.

84 ibid, 15.

85 See Julian Scholtes, 'Constitutional Pluralism beyond Ideal Theory' (unpublished draft manuscript on file with the author).

may well engage in fundamental exercises not only of interlegal balancing, but also of interlegal reasoning. That said, one should remain aware that, by and large, judicial, and quasi-judicial bodies remain essentially connected to cases involving the collisions and intertwinements of norms sourced in more than one legal order – and, thus, they are the main actors of interlegal balancing. Balancing and proportionality, as part of judicial review, have known their fair share of debates, from 'countermajoritarian' difficulties to the enactment of a 'juristic state'. These democratic concerns have developed into more 'dialogic' and publicly oriented practices in courts.[86] Interlegality too must be read in intimate proximity to democratic deliberation. Even more reason for interlegal balancing to be kept as close as possible to its publics. The closer the coupling of actors engaged with interlegal balancing to their publics, the lesser the risk of its strategic use, but also of building biases into the decisions.

All of the above decidedly requires judicial virtues, and in particular judicial virtues specifically tailored to interlegality.[87] A judge confronting interlegality requires, in addition to the judicial virtues which apply when judging under one only jurisdiction, to be epistemically humble and open-minded such as to put familiar doctrines and case law under healthy competition; they would also need to be especially sensitive to intersectionalities. As Jan Klabbers puts it, judges confronting interlegality 'will need to encompass the craft, skill, and learning to work across legal spaces',[88] just as they 'will need to consider the question of how a judgment can be justified also in terms recognizable (and preferably acceptable) to other jurisdictions involved',[89] all while potentially receiving pressure from nationalist-biased authorities.[90] Interlegal balancing is threatened by the lack of such virtues, as is the commitment to the rule of law which animates the possibility of discussing interlegal solutions even if these may not be adopted in the final sense of the decision.

5 Concluding Remarks

After recalling some notorious cases which involved interlegal balancing, the theoretical starting point of this chapter has been the relevance of balancing and proportionality for cases of interlegality; in sum, the relevance of interlegal balancing as a technique to take into due consideration all the relevant norms which apply to a case at hand.

Stock was taken of four patterns in which interlegal balancing takes place, working in tandem with the doctrines of: the margin of appreciation, equivalent protection, the review of ultra vires acts (under interdependent objectives), and

86 For discussion, see Seyla Benhabib 'Dialogic Constitutionalism and Judicial Review' (2020) 9(3) Global Constitutionalism 506.

87 See Jan Klabbers, 'Judging Inter-Legality' in Jan Klabbers and Gianluigi Palombella (eds), *The Challenge of Inter-Legality* (Cambridge University Press 2019).

88 ibid, 357.

89 ibid, 358.

90 ibid, 358–9.

the protection of constitutional identity (in a reading amenable to Article 4(2) TEU). The distinctive features of 'working in tandem' with doctrinal categories, and incorporating of formal and substantive normative considerations are characteristic of these four patterns.

Some delimitations were anticipated for the idea of interlegal balancing. The problem of explicit prohibitions and unsalvable constraints was recognised along with a 'residual' but commitment to discuss such possibilities for the publics of a judicial decision; after that, the objections from fragmentation and institutional perspectivism were recast into a possible research agenda on 'institutional parity' and types of jurisdictional biases; finally, some conjectures on factors which may tend to secure a more 'virtuous' employment of interlegal balancing.

To be sure, at the end of the day, one and the same problem may admissibly be solved in different ways, and different legalities may balance differently. What we may realistically expect of interlegal balancing is not more, but also not less, than an incremental convergence through the structuring of discourse and debate in common legal arguments. What a legal order held as self-evident, and as self-evidently justified, ceases to be so: it becomes necessary to account for the respective legal traditions and doctrines. Clearly, the ensuing giving and taking of reasons cannot generate any spontaneous consensus, but it has an integrative vocation as it offers us with a diversity of justifications to discuss, deliberate and collaboratively review.

3 Non-Hierarchical Coordination of Multi-Level Asymmetries for (Dynamic) Stability

Finding the Balance Between Convergence and Divergence

Maja Sahadžić

Investigating in what capacity federal principles can be exploited as a device for addressing stability in multi-level systems is a continuing concern in comparative constitutional law. However, there is an existing and growing misunderstanding about which federal devices can be consumed to preserve the balance between convergence and divergence and enable cohesion. Contemporary research is increasingly attentive to coordination, which is to some extent employed in multi-level systems. Drawing upon research in federalism, this paper attempts to (1) explore the potential of the concept of stability based on coordination and (2) transform the narratives about coordination as a federal device.

1 Where is Stability in Multi-Level Systems?

Over the past few decades, there has been an evolvement in multi-level governance arrangements. The group of existing multi-level constitutional systems (Australia, Austria, Germany, USA) has been expanded to include some less linear forms of multi-level systems. Due to fragmenting forces, some constitutional systems transitioned from mono to multi-level constitutional designs (Belgium, Italy, Spain, UK). Thanks to integrative forces, some multi-level compounds have appeared as a result of a closer alliance (the European Union).[1] Regardless of fragmenting or integrating forces, all of these multi-level systems experience decentralisation[2] or the shift of authority across levels of government.[3] Some decentralisation processes remain low,

1 The rationale behind the change is beyond the subject of this chapter, however, can be consulted here: Alain-G. Gagnon and James Tully, *Multinational Democracies* (Cambridge University Press 2001). Patricia Popelier and Maja Sahadžić (eds), *Constitutional Asymmetry in Multinational Federalism, Managing Multinationalism in Multi-tiered Systems* (Palgrave Macmillan 2019).

2 Hanna Kleider and Simon Toubeau, 'Public policy in multi-level systems: A new research agenda for the study of regional-level policy' 32 Regional & Federal Studies 277, 277.

3 Michael Dobbins, Dennis Niemann and Kerstin Martens, 'Explaining Policy Convergence and Polity Divergence in Federal Systems: German and Swiss Higher Education Revisited' 48 Publius: The Journal of Federalism 607, 610.

DOI: 10.4324/9781003355762-3

some, however, stand high. While their levels are tailor-based to match the system, one of the main ideas behind them is to enable stability.[4] Of course, the concept of legitimacy and its overarching principles certainly remain high on the list of normative goals. However, they have already received considerable attention in contemporary scholarship, unlike the under-researched concept of stability. Importantly, contemporary scholarship indicates that internal risks in multi-level systems extend beyond legitimacy to stability.[5]

Stability, which is essentially based on cohesion, implies continuous *adaptiveness* of the system to satisfy various interests based on *trust* in the fair management of the system.[6] Because this entails necessary interaction and interdependence across levels and actors, stability is then related to *coordination*. However, this also suggests complex relationships and outcomes that may affect stability.

Although a multi-level approach has been successfully applied in many systems[7], multi-level (constitutional and political) systems[8] are, by and large, seen as unstable.[9] This has something to do with their *non-linear evolution* and how the *hierarchy* of such systems is perceived concerning their inner dynamics and complexity.[10] The multiplicity of levels and actors mostly evolve independently and multi-directionally.[11] Their interaction could easily be described as evolving sideways, longways, slantways, or any other way.[12] As a result, the interaction between levels and actors in multi-level systems demonstrates *divergence* (disassociation) as much as it demonstrates *convergence* (interdependence). This is often seen as a cause of instability as it introduces complexities in institutional settings and

4 Jack Jedwab and John Kincaid, 'Introduction and Comparative Observations' in Jack Jedwab and John Kincaid (eds), *Identities, Trust, and Cohesion in Federal Systems* (McGill's-Queen's University Press 2018) 3.

5 Michael Burgess and Franz Gress, 'Symmetry and Asymmetry Revisited' in Robert Agranoff (ed), *Accommodating Diversity: Asymmetry in Federal States* (Nomos 1999) 54.

6 Maja Sahadžić, *Asymmetry, Multinationalism and Constitutional Law, Managing Legitimacy and Stability in Federalist States* (Routledge 2020) 161.

7 Krassimira Stoilova, Todor Stoilov and Alexander Gegov, *Real Time Coordination in Multilevel Systems* (1995) 53.

8 Including federal systems as'governance systems where centers of power and decision making are dispersed across territorial units'. See Francesca Pia Vantaggiato, 'Regulatory relationships across levels of multilevel governance systems: From collaboration to competition' 33 Governance: An International Journal of Policy, Administration, and Institutions 173, 175.

9 Nassera Touati and others, 'Understanding Multilevel Governance Processes through Complexity Theory: An Empirical Case Study of the Quebec Health-Care System' 42 International Journal of Public Administration 205, 207.

10 JD Pearson, 'Multi-Level Control Systems' in P.H. Hammond (ed), *Theory of Self-Adaptive Control Systems* (Springer 1966) 252.

11 Touati and others 207.

12 Sahadžić 128.

13 Filip De Maesschalck and Sergio Gemperle, 'Plural claims to legitimacy: conceptualising legitimacy in hybrid political orders' (ECPR General Conference) 7. Daniel Halberstam, 'Federalism: Theory, Policy, Law' in Andrafi Sajo□and Michael Rosenfeld

decision-making[13] while in reality, instability is rather caused by a lack of adaptiveness to the complex institutional and procedural environments.[14]

On this note, scholarship is torn over the question of whether decentralisation immediately means divergence across levels and actors.[15] Nevertheless, both convergence and divergence of all levels and actors seem to be conditioned as much by centralisation as by decentralisation.[16] Hence, one of the major challenges in governing multi-level systems is then in the right balance of convergence and divergence among the levels and actors to enable stability.

Finally, while the scope of instability that can threaten the bare existence of the system is uncommon, stability still depends on the extent to which the components of the system (levels and actors) are prone to divergence and therefore instability.[17] One of the prominent complicating factors is *asymmetry*. Asymmetry is increasingly used as a federal device in dealing with internal (by rule identity) differences in multi-level systems.[18] In countries, it is linked to decentralising forces leading to fragmentation contained in differences in status, powers, and fiscal matters.[19] In transnational systems such as the EU, it is linked to integrative forces leading to similar if not the same consequences contained in differentiated integration.[20]

(eds), *The Oxford Handbook of Comparative Constitutional Law* (Oxford University Press 2012) 602.

14 Sahadžić 163.

15 See: Kleider and Toubeau 287.

16 Touati and others 205. Some argue that convergence and divergence have underlying factors that explain (de)centralisation processes: sociological (the institutional imitation from other countries), economic (similar reaction to similar strategies), political (influence of political actors on multi-level governance processes). Francesco Palermo and Karl Kössler, *Comparative Federalism* (Hart Publishing 2017) 38.

17 Johanna Schnabel, *Managing Interdependencies in Federal Systems, Intergovernmental Councils and the Making of Public Policy* (Springer 2020) 38.

18 Alain-G. Gagnon, 'Multinational federalism: challenges, shortcomings and promises' Regional & Federal Studies 1, 9 Giuseppe Martinico, 'Asymmetry as an Instrument of Differentiated Integration: The Case of the European Union' 18 European Journal of Law Reform 139, 142. See, also, for example: Maja Sahadžić, 'Can Asymmetrical Constitutional Arrangements Provide an Alternative Answer for the Disputed? Bringing Constitutional Asymmetries into Play in the Middle East Peace Process' 12 Perspectives on Federalism.

19 Sahadžić, *Asymmetry, Multinationalism and Constitutional Law, Managing Legitimacy and Stability in Federalist States* 76. Maja Sahadžić, 'Constitutional asymmetry and equality in multinational systems with federal arrangements' in Eva Maria Belser and others (eds), *The Principle of Equality in Diverse States, Reconciling Autonomy with Equal Rights and Opportunities* (Brill Nijhoff 2021) 46.

20 See, for example: Pieter Van Cleynenbreugel, 'Asymmetry as a Way to Move Forward with Multi-tiered Integration? A Study of Constitutional Asymmetry in the European Union' in Patricia Popelier and Maja Sahadžić (eds), *Constitutional Asymmetry in Multinational Federalism, Managing Multinationalism in Multi-tiered Systems* (Palgrave Macmillan 2019).

2 Asymmetry as an Obstacle to Stability

Typically, asymmetrical solutions are adopted to manage pluralism.[21] However, they have the potential to create divergence by introducing variations in status, powers, and/or fiscal matters for specific levels and actors within a particular multi-level system.[22] As a result, this may complicate the multi-level platform and the relations among the actors which can destabilise parts of the systems or the system as a whole.[23]

Some multi-level systems that incorporate asymmetries as discussed below include Belgium (the Flemish and French regions combined with the Dutch and French linguistic groups), Bosnia and Herzegovina (the Federation of Bosnia and Herzegovina and the Republic of Srpska combined with three constituent peoples, Bosniaks, Croats, and Serbs), Canada (Quebec), Italy (South Tyrol and the Aosta Valley), Indonesia (Aceh and Papua), Iraq (the Kurdistan Region), Malaysia (Sabah and Sarawak in Malaysia) Spain (the Basque Country, Catalonia, and Navarre), the United Kingdom (Northern Ireland, Scotland, and Wales), and many more.

Importantly, in the European Union, an asymmetrical approach has also been introduced for member states that are reluctant about extensive merging.[24] Internal diversity in the European Union seeks the accommodation of diverse interests of the Member States, but it also demands the protection of their asymmetrical rights.[25] This way Member States benefit from the freedom to choose their rhythm in the application of certain rules and policies.

2.1 Status

An asymmetrical *status* appears when a differentiated status is granted to some of the lower-level units of the multi-level system. Asymmetry in status can appear as recognised status at the highest level, power to establish legislative and executive bodies, a specific framework of representation and/or participation in decision-making at the highest level, and/or veto powers.[26]

Transformations in status are typically driven by identity differences.[27] They occur to hold the systems together and preserve the cohesion of the system.

21 Palermo and Kössler 384. Cf Marjan Kos.

22 Sahadžić, *Asymmetry, Multinationalism and Constitutional Law, Managing Legitimacy and Stability in Federalist States* 226.

23 Martinico 143.

24 Giuseppe Martinico, 'A multi-speed EU? An institutional and Legal Assessment' 15 Instituto Affari Internazionali 1, 6.

25 Cf Marjan Kos.

26 Sahadžić, *Asymmetry, Multinationalism and Constitutional Law, Managing Legitimacy and Stability in Federalist States* 79.

27 Michael Burgess, 'The Paradox of Diversity - Asymmetrical Federalism in Comparative Perspective' in Francesco Palermo, Carolin Zwilling and Karl Kössler (eds), *Asymmetries in Constitutional Law, Recent Developments in Federal and Regional Systems* (Academia Europea Bolzano/Europäische Akademie Bozen 2009) 26. Palermo and Kössler 40. Sahadžić empirically establishes the link between asymmetrical arrangements and identity differences. See: Sahadžić, *Asymmetry, Multinationalism and Constitutional Law, Managing Legitimacy and Stability in Federalist States* 73.

Regardless of their holding-together potential, asymmetries also have the potential to contribute to divergence as they expose fractures within the system.[28] (1) If lower levels have formally recognised asymmetrical status in the multi-level system, their capacity for centrifugal episodes is increased (including the extreme ones such as breakaways).[29] This is because of the risk that they will use their status to put forward interests that are not coherent with other levels and actors. For example, so far, the Republic of Srpska in Bosnia and Herzegovina has threatened to organise several independence referendums. (2) Also, an asymmetrical status has the potential to trigger competition across levels and actors which is closely connected with mutual trust.[30] The lack of trust, however, can initiate institutional setbacks and standstills[31] and in effect, undermine overall cohesion.[32] For example, the unsuccessful attempts of Catalonia to (re)negotiate a fiscal framework similar to the Basque Country and Navarre stripped naked the problem of cohesion by challenging territorial solidarity and triggering even the independence referendum.[33]

The conclusion offers itself. While *competition* has the potential to initiate renegotiation of stability, it is also a lack of *adaptiveness* to the demands and institutional disruption that increases the potential for competition. This essentially implies the lack of *coordination* across levels and actors to properly situate the expectations in the management of the system and to intensify interaction across levels and actors.

2.2 Powers

Asymmetrical *powers* occur when specific powers or a specific type or set of powers are granted to some of the lower level units. Asymmetry can appear as an increased or decreased set of powers, assigned specific types of powers, power to opt-in/out,

28 Jan Erk and Lawrence Anderson, 'The Paradox of Federalism: Does Self-Rule Accommodate or Exacerbate Ethnic Divisions?' 19 Regional & Federal Studies 191, 192.

29 See, for example: John McGarry and Brendan O'Leary, 'Federation and Managing Nations' in Michael Burgess and John Pinder (eds), *Multinational Federations* (Routledge 2007). Pau Bossacoma Busquets, *Morality and Legality of Secession, A Theory of National Self-Determination* (Soeren Keil and Eva Maria Belser eds, Palgrave Macmillan 2020).

30 James A. Gardner and Antoni Abad I. Ninet, 'Sustainable Decentralization: Power, Extraconstitutional Influence, and Subnational Symmetry in the United States and Spain' Legal Studies Research Paper Series, 3.

31 Nicholas Charron, 'Government Quality and Vertical Power-Sharing in Fractionalized States' 39 Publius 585, 591.

32 Nicole Bolleyer, Wilfried Swenden and Nicola McEwen, 'A theoretical perspective on multi-level systems in Europe: Constitutional power and partisan conflict' 12 Comparative European Politics 367, 378.

33 Pau Bossacoma Busquets and Marc Sanjaume-Calvet, 'Asymmetry as a Device for Equal Recognition and Reasonable Accommodation of Majority and Minority Nations. A Country Study on Constitutional Asymmetry in Spain' in Patricia Popelier and Maja Sahadžić (eds), *Constitutional Asymmetry in Multinational Federalism, Managing Multinationalism in Multi-tiered Systems* (Palgrave Macmillan 2019) 442.

power to exercise competences at a different speed, and/or differences in the allocation of powers.[34]

Conceptual discussion insists that differences in the distribution of powers may decrease friction and increase cohesiveness.[35] However, this certainly depends on the power-sharing. Strategies of power-sharing that insist on a more centralised framework are more cohesive as they enable more harmonising influence of the highest level.[36] Strategies that involve specific frameworks are less cohesive though. (1) Negotiations between different levels regarding assigned powers imply balancing different interests which often results in differences across levels and actors.[37] Importantly, it also provokes competition and a lack of trust.[38] For example, special regions in Italy apply their own sets of powers, while their distribution varies even between ordinary regions. Because of the lack of institutionalised ways of communication, disputes were triggered before the Constitutional Court.[39] (2) Also, differences in techniques of allocation of powers have the potential to trigger divergence. This is because different levels and actors may have different opinions about how exclusive, shared, and concurrent powers should be allocated. For example, there is a conflict over the management of oil reserves in Iraq, which are located mainly in the Kurdistan Region. Although the highest level presumes that it is in charge, the management is not defined under the exclusive competences but separate provisions. The constitution gives priority to lower levels in case of disputes, hence, the Kurdistan Region claims its primacy.

Importantly, negotiation and bargaining in asymmetrical multi-level systems are essential. There are too many competing levels and actors arguing for their interests and their preferred balance.[40] Under these circumstances, the allocation of powers should be *adapted* continuously since the processes across levels and actors are by rule dynamic. Otherwise, the system will demonstrate a lack of communication channels and complexity and raise issues of *trust*. While this demonstrates that cohesion is undermined, it also indicates that the system lacks *coordination*.[41]

34 Sahadžić, *Asymmetry, Multinationalism and Constitutional Law, Managing Legitimacy and Stability in Federalist States* 79.
35 Arthur Benz, 'Dimensions and dynamics of federal regimes' in Arthur Benz and Jörg Broschek (eds), *Federal Dynamics, Continuity, Change, and the Varieties of Federalism* (Oxford University Press 2013) 73.
36 Nicole Bolleyer, 'Paradoxes of self-coordination in federal systems' in Arthur Benz and Jörg Broschek (eds), *Federal Dynamics, Continuity, Change, and the Varieties of Federalism* (Oxford University Press 2013) 330.
37 Bolleyer, Swenden and McEwen 378.
38 Bolleyer 330.
39 Francesco Palermo and Alice Valdesalici, 'Irreversibly Different. A Country Study of Constitutional Asymmetry in Italy' in Patricia Popelier and Maja Sahadžić (eds), *Constitutional Asymmetry in Multinational Federalism, Managing Multinationalism in Multi-tiered Systems* (Palgrave Macmillan 2019) 299.
40 Mikhail Filippov, Peter C. Ordeshook and Olga Shvetsova, *Designing Federalism: A Theory of Self-Sustainable Federal Institutions* (Cambridge University Press 2004) 53.
41 Bolleyer, Swenden and McEwen 368.

2.3 Fiscal Matters

Finally, asymmetries in fiscal matters occur when differentiated fiscal autonomy is granted to some of the lower level units to match the differences among sub-national entities[42] and redistribute and equalise wealth and fiscal capacities.[43] It can appear in revenue-raising, discretion for taxing powers, spending capacity, budgetary control, and/or reliance on transfers.[44]

While redistributive and solidarity mechanisms that generate cohesive taxing powers and transfers directed to counterbalance discrepancies in wealth and maintain territorial cohesion prove to have cohesive features[45], they still demonstrate shortcomings. (1) Disproportional wealth has the potential to produce levels and actors that are perceived superior, especially if they enjoy wider self-rule based on their wealth. This implies differentiated development and, as a consequence, the lack of territorial cohesion which sparks competition. For example, Papua in Indonesia receives most of the revenues from the country's oil and gas reserves while Bali, Java, Sumatra, and Sulawesi openly express their disagreement with their position within the system.[46] (2) Harmonisation also sparks competition because of the struggle of the superior levels and actors to maintain budget control. This is especially emphasised if there is a lack of social cohesion. For example, Quebec in Canada has sought to redistribute wealth challenging the concept of solidarity that spills over to other levels and groups.[47]

Essentially, the lack of *trust* in asymmetrical multi-level systems originates from imbalanced bargaining power in fiscal matters, especially expenditures that are considered to support stability.[48] Added to this, the expectation of the fair management of the system, and therefore trust will be challenged when social solidarity is not respected. Overall, this implies a lack of appropriate level of *coordination.*

2.4 Asymmetry Needs Cohesion

Multi-level systems are laboratories of diversity.[49] This alone can drive the system apart. Internal restructuring through asymmetrical adjustments in status,

42 Ronald L. Watts, 'A Comparative Perspective on Asymmetry in Federations' Asymmetry Series 2005(4), 5.
43 ibid.
44 Sahadžić, *Asymmetry, Multinationalism and Constitutional Law, Managing Legitimacy and Stability in Federalist States* 79.
45 Watts 5.
46 Simon Butt, 'Provincial Asymmetry in Indonesia: What Is so "Special" About It? A Country Study of Constitutional Asymmetry in Indonesia' in Patricia Popelier and Maja Sahadžić (eds), *Constitutional Asymmetry in Multinational Federalism, Managing Multinationalism in Multi-tiered Systems* (Palgrave Macmillan 2019) 234.
47 André Lecours and Daniel Béland, 'Federalism, nationalist politics, and social policy: How ideas and institutions shape federal dynamics' in Arthur Benz and Jörg Broschek (eds), *Federal Dynamics Continuity, Change, and the Varieties of Federalism* (Oxford University Press 2013) 225.
48 Gerald Pech, 'Coalition governments versus minority governments: Bargaining power, cohesion and budgeting outcomes' Public Choice 1, 4.
49 Cf Agata Poznanska.

powers, and fiscal matters, nonetheless, adds layers of complexity.[50] Evidently, a lack of adaptiveness and trust is a recipe for divergence. To introduce more convergence, the management of these systems preferably includes necessary interaction across levels and actors, vertically and horizontally.[51] Conceptual and doctrinal explanations indicate that more interaction and interdependence are tied to *coordination*.[52] The fundamental puzzle is then how to enable coordination in these systems.

After all, organising parts of any system in such a way as to make sense of governance is a natural inclination.[53] In contemporary multi-level systems, governance is comparable to coordination across multiple levels and actors pursuing a variety of interests to bring more cohesion, and therefore, more stability to the system.[54] As a matter of fact, coordination, understood as a partnership across levels and actors is embedded in the idea of multi-level systems.[55] As such, coordination is, for example, the most important aspect of policymaking.[56] Hence, it is not making sense of governance but making sense of coordination that brings more interaction, and therefore more convergence, across levels and actors.[57] Because, after all, the multiplicity of levels and actors needs to be coordinated[58] to avoid divergence.

3 Coordination for More Convergence

So far, coordination as an instrument and/or mechanism was considered redundant.[59] This is especially true since the traditional scholarship is still influential in advocating the centralised, symmetrical, and hierarchical qualities of multi-level systems and organising all other systems according to those qualities. However, contemporary practice proves the existence of a large number of instruments and mechanisms of coordination.[60] These include making the law[61] and the implementation of the law[62] – both of which are very basic coordinative tools in the search for more convergence. Nevertheless, there is an advanced tool to be considered – the principle of loyalty, mutual consideration, comity, or a term of

50 Benz 73.
51 Palermo and Kössler 210.
52 Sahadžić, *Asymmetry, Multinationalism and Constitutional Law, Managing Legitimacy and Stability in Federalist States* 143.
53 Pearson 252.
54 Yannis Papadopoulos, 'Problems of Democratic Accountability in Network and Multilevel Governance' 13 European Law Journal 469, 469.
55 Palermo and Kössler 16.
56 Vantaggiato 173.
57 Kleider and Toubeau 287.
58 Carol Harlow and Richard Rawlings, 'Promoting Accountability in Multilevel Governance: A Network Approach' 13 European Law Journal 542, 543. Philipp Trein, Eva Thomann and Martino Maggetti, 'Integration, functional differentiation and problem-solving in multilevel governance' 97 Public Administration 339, 343.
59 Palermo and Kössler 209.
60 ibid.
61 ibid.
62 Harlow and Rawlings 543.

similar identification.[63] For example, the Belgian Constitution stipulates that all governments must 'act with respect for federal loyalty to prevent conflicts of interest'.[64] This means that, despite the allocation of powers based on exclusivity, the Constitution defines that the federal structure of Belgium requires cooperation between the authorities based on respect for federal loyalty.[65] Similar provisions, founded merely as federal principles, can be found in Swiss and German constitutions with similar or wider impact. In Spain and Italy, however, it was the Constitutional Court that provided for the duty of loyalty, while in South Africa, these provisions are to be found in specific laws.[66] Interestingly, the United Kingdom does not have these provisions but informal, usually bilateral, agreements to point out what is generically designated as the principle of federal loyalty.[67] Similarly, the duty of loyalty or the principle of loyal cooperation in the European Union requires member states to be at the service of the European Union objectives, while the European Union protects the autonomy of Member States.[68]

Instruments and mechanisms of coordination, however, have been downsized to those that focus on vertical interactions, either top-down or bottom-up.[69] The *top-down coordination* focuses on the central level steering to pull together lower levels and actors in an attempt to synchronise their actions. Due to its controlling nature, it is also referred to as a dirigist form of coordination which can even imply shortcomings in the democratic quality.[70] This steering is especially performed through financial grants. For example, in Switzerland, the top-down approach includes the coordination of personal and corporate taxes that can be levied at federal and cantonal levels and through surcharges applied by cantonal and local

63 Palermo and Kössler 211. Cf Pieter Aergeerts, Pieter Van Cleynenbreugel, and Thomas Verellen.
64 Article 143(1) of the Belgian Constitution. The importance of coordination in Belgium has been especially recognised before the Constitutional Court in the highly publicised case 'VZW Klimaatzaak' from 2015 concerning the insufficient climate policies against climate change. The judgement of the Constitutional Court of Belgium pointed out that various levels knew that climate policies were failing due to the poor coordination within the state. Although powers in Belgium are allocated on the basis of exclusivity, in the Court's opinion, the federal structure of Belgium requires loyal cooperation between the authorities since the constitution defines that all governments must respect federal loyalty. All governments must remain within their powers, but they also must take into account the interests of the other levels and actors. Moreover, the Constitutional Court pointed out that cooperation is an integral part of standard care and diligence. According to the Court, governments cannot hide behind their exclusive powers to evade their obligations.
65 Cf Thomas Verellen.
66 Palermo and Kössler 213.
67 ibid.
68 Eleftheria Neframi, 'The Duty of Loyalty: Rethinking its Scope through its Application in the Field of EU External Relations' 47 Common Market Law Review 323, 323. Cf Pieter Van Cleynenbreugel.
69 Touati and others 207.
70 Papadopoulos 270.

legislation. To avoid overlapping, Switzerland applies the tax collection agreement and bases the collection on a regime of tax harmonisation and entrenches the maximum federal tax rates in the Constitution.[71] The ***bottom-up coordination*** includes a wide range of approaches centred around laws, intergovernmental agreements, and policies initiated by lower levels.[72] For example, in the EU regulators resort to turning existing informal networks into coordination instruments and mechanisms across lower and higher levels, so that lower levels can better formulate and situate their policy demands while higher levels can generate better policies.[73] Nevertheless, because of the fragmentary focus on only one – vertical – direction, the conceptualisation of coordination in multi-level systems (with asymmetrical arrangements) remains oblique.

Partially, this is due to the internal constitutional design[74] (number of levels), institutional diversity[75], political context[76] (such as sub-state identity) that harbours competition and policy diffusion, and difficulties in the application of specific instruments and mechanisms of coordination that make the venture too ambitious.[77] Because of this, higher levels feel compelled to initiate further empowerment to enable the enforcement, while the lower levels perceive it as reductionist – triggering competition.[78] In other words, the coordination remains rather skewed as its application is difficult to enforce. This can be explained by the fact that coordination in multi-level systems requires the involvement of all levels and actors for the purpose of convergence.[79]

Partially, and quite importantly, this is because both top-down and bottom-up approaches insist on the interaction between the central level and lower levels which makes them highly hierarchical. Coordination across levels and actors has been poised by what Palermo and Kössler call supremacy, homogeneity, and subsidiarity clauses that aim at subordinating lower levels.[80] Hierarchy in these systems means a division into levels that are coordinated by one another. And while hierarchy is pertinent to multi-level systems, coordination is a natural concept linked to them that puts levels and actors in interaction and interdependence and allows them to perform.[81] Nevertheless, the direction of interaction and performance is the actual challenge.

The abovementioned implies that hierarchical coordination has reached its limit.[82] Because effective governance depends on coordination and renegotiation

71 Palermo and Kössler 70.
72 Nicole Bolleyer and Tanja Börzel, 'Non-hierarchical policy coordination in multilevel systems' 2 European Political Science Review 157, 157.
73 Vantaggiato 177.
74 Palermo and Kössler 211.
75 Kleider and Toubeau 281.
76 ibid.
77 Bolleyer and Börzel 158.
78 Vantaggiato 177.
79 Palermo and Kössler 40.
80 ibid.
81 Pearson 252.
82 Trein, Thomann and Maggetti 343.

across levels and actors[83], it is crucial to look into *non-hierarchical coordination* that is not entirely unknown but is neglected in the comparative scholarship.[84] For example, this includes the involvement of the Council of Ministers in the Open Method of Coordination in the European Union.[85] Social policies, in particular, are difficult to harmonise due to the present diversity which leaves asymmetries in the field across the member states.[86] Still, the method is based on regular progress monitoring which enables the member states to compare the outcomes of their coordinative efforts. This is because the method is based on 'soft law', meaning no formal enforcement can be triggered.[87] Reiterating what has been already mentioned, governing multi-level systems means rather dynamic and negotiated non-hierarchical interaction among all levels and actors, vertically and horizontally.[88] On the one hand, this *polycentric*[89] approach allows for *convergence* through *adaptiveness* in dealing with the effects of combined multi-levelness and multi-actorness. On the other hand, this implies that the non-hierarchical approach is related to trust as mutual interaction, and consequently, interaction and interdependence rest on mutual *trust* in the management of the system.[90]

4 To Sum Up: What Does All This Mean?

Multi-level systems are not bound to coordinate levels and actors nor to be enthusiastic about coordination.[91] However, if the idea is to hold the system together, the non-hierarchical approach to coordination requires a fundamental rethinking of the present understanding of coordination in multi-level systems. This links to what Harlow and Rawlings call autonomous self-responsibility.[92] To enable the proper density of coordination, a multi-level system has to provide and

83 Katherine A. Daniell and Adrian Kay, *Multi-level Governance, Conceptual Challenges and Case Studies from Australia* (ANU Press 2017) 4.
84 Papadopoulos 470.
85 Bolleyer and Börzel 159.
86 Martinico, 'Asymmetry as an Instrument of Differentiated Integration: The Case of the European Union' 146.
87 Harlow and Rawlings 543.
88 Touati and others 206 This is also in line with the definition of multi-level governance processes. See: Daniell and Kay 6.
89 On the concept of polycentricity, consult: Vincent Ostrom, Charles M. Tiebout and Robert Warren, 'The Organization of Government in Metropolitan Areas: A Theoretical Inquiry' 55 American Political Science Review 831. Paul D. Aligica and Vlad Tarko, 25 Governance: An International Journal of Policy, Administration, and Institutions 237. Ramiro Berardo and Mark Lubell, 'Understanding What Shapes a Polycentric Governance System' 76 Public Administration Review 738.
90 On the same trace, but admittedly cynically, Papadopoulos suggests that mutual interdependence is based on the mutual blackmailing capabilities which can yield disciplining effects. See: Papadopoulos 483.
91 Dobbins, Niemann and Martens 608.
92 Harlow and Rawlings 544.

maintain a platform for the *adaptiveness* of the system.[93] This platform, however, has to embed *coordinative* instruments and mechanisms that have the capacity to support interaction across levels and actors.[94] To reach that, the interaction has to be based on mutual *trust*. Only then the system will display enough convergence that can be properly exploited for *cohesive* purposes. This would then imply that the multi-level system is optimally preserved or, in other words, stable (enough). This does not mean that the argument is that more convergence will lead to more cohesion, and therefore, more stability – although it is certainly hoped-for. It, however, means the argument that the proper density of coordination will be linked to a tailor-made level of convergence considering the particularities of a system.

Importantly, *stability* in multi-level systems is a *dynamic* concept[95] since it is based on the dynamics between convergence and divergence. Striking the same level of balance between convergence and divergence in every multi-level system is certainly not necessary as every system has its own perks.[96] However, the choice of the instrument or mechanism of coordination must be functionally and politically informed.[97] It is also important that the coordination is dense enough.[98] This is because, in dealing with the contradictions of convergence and divergence, coordination is essentially a channel[99] across levels and actors. As such, it has to keep levels and actors close to provide for more cohesive relationships, and stability of the system.[100]

93 Similar: Richard Simeon, 'Adaptability and change in federations' 53 International Social Science Journal 145, 146.
94 Daniel J. Elazar, *Exploring federalism* (University of Alabama Press 2006) 116.
95 On this trace see: Halberstam 598.
96 Bolleyer and Börzel 157.
97 ibid.
98 Based on, but adjusted to properly reflect multiple realities in multi-tiered multi-national systems with asymmetrical features: Simeon 151 Stefan Rummens and Stefan Sottiaux, 'Democratic Legitimacy in the Bund or "Federation of States": the Cases of Belgium and the EU' 20 European Law Journal 568, 573.
99 Arthur Benz, 'Squaring the circle? Balancing autonomy and intergovernmental relations in federal democracy' (International Association of Centers for Federal Studies 2018 Canberra Conference).
100 Drawing from: Saeed Parto, 'Regulatory Dynamics, Institutional Cohesiveness, and Regional Sustainability ' (Doctoral thesis, University of Waterloo 2002) 66.

4 Constitutional Diversity and Differentiation in the EU

What Role for National Constitutional Demands under EU law?

*Marjan Kos**

1 Introduction: Accommodating Constitutional Diversity *via* Differentiation

One of the main characteristics of the European Union (EU) is the diversity of its Member States. Their constitutional setups, reflecting the different values are, by extension, also diverse. The inherent tension present in such a multi-level system inevitably leads to clashes between the Member States' and EU's layers of constitutionalism. The chapter argues that mechanisms of differentiation can accommodate this constitutional diversity and mitigate or prevent conflicts between the national and EU constitutional norms within the framework of EU law. Differential treatment of Member States under EU law reconciles the primacy of EU law and the autonomy of Member States.

Some of the established types of differentiation in EU law already exist to avoid constitutional conflicts between the EU and Member States. Most of political or legal science literature, however, does not specifically analyse the role of national constitutional standards or demands[1] for differentiation in EU law. The predominant narrative explains differentiation as an institutional response to the increasing diversity and divisiveness of the EU, resulting from its widening (repeated accessions) and deepening (increasing competences).[2] The debate revolves around economic able-ness and

* I would like to thank Jaka Kukavica and Maja Sahadžić for their invaluable comments on earlier drafts of this chapter.

1 When discussing national constitutional demands, I mean explicit national constitutional norms, expressed in any relevant source of constitutional law, including the interpretation of those norms by national apex courts.

2 See, for example: Luisa Antoniolli, '"United in Diversity"? Differentiated Integration in an Ever Diverse European Union' in Luisa Antoniolli, Luigi Bonatti and Carlo Ruzza (eds), *Highs and Lows of European Integration: Sixty Years After the Treaty of Rome* (Springer Cham 2019) 85; Bruno de Witte, 'Variable Geometry and Differentiation as Structural Features of the EU Legal Order' in Bruno de Witte, Andrea Ott and Ellen Vos, *Between Flexibility and Disintegration* (Edward Elgar Publishing 2017) 10; Bruno de Witte, 'An Undivided Union? Differentiated Integration in Post-Brexit Times' (2018) 55 Common Market Law Review 227, 227–8; Carlos Closa, 'Flexibility Mechanisms in the Lisbon Treaty' (European Parliament, Policy Department C: Citizens' Rights and Constitutional Affairs 2015) 7; Katharina Holzinger and Frank Schimmelfennig,

DOI: 10.4324/9781003355762-4

political willing-ness to move forward with the integration,[3] which, however, does not tell us much about the role of national constitutions in differentiation. The impact of identity, sovereignty and state powers, which are inherently linked to national constitutions, for differentiation, has been analysed under varying terminologies. *Schimmelfenning* and *Winzen*, for example duscuss constitutional differentiation, contrasting it to its instrumental counterpart.[4] They explain constitutional differentiation as resulting from the deepening of the EU, namely the expansion and transfer of competences vertically. This type of differentiation follows a constitutionalist logic in the sense that it will likely reflect concerns over identity, sovereignty and the nature and powers of the EU.[5] However, their understanding of the 'constitutional' is wide, including ideological commitments or domestic constraints, such as a referendum decision. Similarly, *Tuytschaever*,[6] as before him *Ehlermann*,[7] distinguished between subjective and objective differentiation. The former includes differentiation predicated on constitutional demands, as discussed in this chapter; however, it is also wider. Subjective differentiation is based on political differences,[8] covering disagreements stemming from diverging political interests. Again, this analysis does not look specifically into whether constraints flowing from national constitutions may lie behind these subjective political differences.[9] This shows a common trend where the concrete impact of the legal, especially constitutional reasons behind subjective or political differentiation is generally not explored.[10] The exception to this is an analysis of 'constitutional differentiated

'Differentiated Integration in The European Union: Many Concepts, Sparse Theory, Few Data' (2012) 19 Journal of European Public Policy 292, 299.
Dyson and Sepos speak of widening, deepening and broadening, since they distinguish deepening in institutional and procedural terms from broadening of the policy scope of integration. Kenneth Dyson and Angelos Sepos, 'Differentiation as Design Principle and as Tool in the Political Management of European Integration' in Kenneth Dyson and Angelos Sepos (eds), *Which Europe? The Politics of Differentiated Integration* (Palgrave Macmillan UK 2010) 9, 15.

3 Dominik Hanf, 'Flexibility Clauses in the Founding Treaties, From Rome to Nice' in Bruno De Witte, Dominik Hanf and Ellen Vos (eds), *The Many Faces of Differentiation in EU Law* (Intersentia 2001) 4.

4 Frank Schimmelfennig and Thomas Winzen, 'Instrumental and Constitutional Differentiation in the European Union' 52 Journal of Common Market Studies 354.

5 ibid 363.

6 Filip Tuytschaever, *Differentiation in European Union Law* (Hart 1999) 218–219.

7 Claus-Dieter Ehlermann, 'How Flexible Is Community Law? An Unusual Approach to the Concept of "Two Speeds"' (1984) 82 Michigan Law Review 1274, 1289.

8 If the reason for differentiation are subjective political differences (such as with derogations, exemptions and opt-outs), it has to be authorised in primary law; otherwise, they would be illegal, since they would violate the principle of non-discrimination. See: Tuytschaever (n 6) 122–3.

9 Either constitutional or subjective differentiation, as described above, could be used as super-categories for the type of differentiation discussed in this chapter. Alternatively, Constitutionally predicated differentiation could be analysed as a separate category.

10 Pietro Faraguna, 'Taking Constitutional Identities Away from Courts' (2016) 41 Brooklyn Journal of International Law 491, 532. E.g.: Jiří Přibáň, 'Legal Flexibility, Governance and Differentiated Integration: On Functional Differentiation of EU Law and Politics' in Kenneth Dyson and Angelos Sepos (eds), *Which Europe? The Politics of*

integration' by *Faraguna*. He specifically analysed the role of national constitutional identity in differentiation, focusing particularly on opt-outs.[11]

Building on *Faraguna's* work, the analysis pursued in this chapter assumes a narrower (legal) concept of the 'constitutional', and looks specifically at the possible existence of domestic legal constitutional constraints pushing for differentiation. The aim of the chapter is to address this partial lacuna in the literature and assess to what extent national constitutional demands have fared as motivators behind differentiation. This endeavour helps to show how differentiation can be used to accommodate constitutional diversity within the EU, avoiding constitutional conflicts.[12] This supports the proposal that mechanisms of differentiation should be considered as a principled tool for the accommodation of constitutional diversity and a solution to such constitutional conflicts in the future.

The key argument proposed in this chapter is that without undermining the core EU principles of unity, effectiveness, and equality, differentiation in EU law may offer a theoretical model more apt to deal with the challenge of constitutional diversity. To support this, the chapter proceeds in three steps. Firstly, it offers a definition and short overview of existing differentiation in EU law. Secondly, it analyses differentiation in EU from the perspective of national constitutional demands. It explains the parameters of constitutional conflict, arising from diversity, before delving into the role that national constitutional demands played in the selected cases of differentiation in EU law. The analysis focuses on those instances of differentiation that show preliminary signs of being constitutionally predicated. Thirdly, it provides an evaluation of the normative value of differentiation as a tool for the accommodation of constitutional diversity in EU law before briefly concluding.

2 A Union of Differentiation

Even though differentiation has been a big part of European integration for decades, uniform integration has remained the prevailing norm in the EU.[13] The unity and effectiveness of EU law have been a mantra for the integration.[14] The Court of Justice of the EU (CJEU) played an important role as a custodian of such uniform integration.[15] In simplified terms, according to this view, uniformity of application of EU law

Differentiated Integration (Palgrave Macmillan UK 2010) 26–27; Alkuin Kölliker, 'The Functional Dimension' in Kenneth Dyson and Angelos Sepos (eds), *Which Europe? The Politics of Differentiated Integration* (Palgrave Macmillan UK 2010) 41.

11 Faraguna (n 10) 527 ff.

12 For the definition of a constitutional conflict, see below Section 3.2.

13 Frank Schimmelfennig and Thomas Winzen, *Ever Looser Union? Differentiated European Integration* (Oxford University Press 2020) 2; Dyson and Sepos (n 2) 7.

14 cf Daniel Thym, 'Competing Models for Understanding Differentiated Integration' in Bruno De Witte, Andrea Ott and Ellen Vos, *Between Flexibility and Disintegration* (Edward Elgar Publishing 2017) 56; de Witte, 'Variable Geometry and Differentiation as Structural Features of the EU Legal Order' (n 2) 9.

15 Deirdre Curtin, 'From a Europe of Bits and Pieces to a Union of Variegated Differentiation' (European University Institute 2020) Working Paper 2020/37 7 <https://papers.ssrn.com/sol3/papers.cfm?abstract_id=3607163>. For the most emblematic expressions,

is critical for the continued existence of the EU, especially when talking about the *acquis communautaire.*[16] However, as the integration progressed the EU has also overcome the above-described challenges of diversity by allowing more differentiation among the Member States.[17] This happened to an extent that, somewhat paradoxically, differentiation is now considered an inescapable and empirically a prevalent[18], salient[19], structural[20] feature of the system. The prevalence of differentiation throughout the development of the EU even produced a plethora of different types of differentiated approaches, leading to conceptual and terminological confusion.[21]

Among the many definitions of differentiation (or differentiated integration[22]) in EU law, they all recognise its key feature as the facilitation or accommodation of a degree of difference between the Member States in what would otherwise be common Union policy. EU law gives (or allows) different rights and obligations to the different Member States in different policy areas.[23] This leads to the parallel existence of distinct levels of integration among the Member States.[24] The definition adopted here purposefully includes both differentiation in the narrow sense (*stricto sensu*) and differentiation in the wider sense (*sensu lato*), which I base on *Tuytschaever.*[25] I adopt this broad approach to the concept of differentiation[26] because it shows that mechanisms belonging to either of the two subgroups reflect the common logic of accommodation of diversity.

see: Case 48/71 *Commission of the European Communities v Italian Republic* [1972] ECR 529, para 8 and Case 66/80 *SpA International Chemical Corporation v Amministrazione delle finanze dello Stato* [1981] ECR 1191, para 11.

16 Deirdre Curtin, 'The Constitutional Structure of the Union: A Europe of Bits and Pieces' (1993) 30 Common Market Law Review 17, 46, 67.

17 Richard Bellamy, *A Republican Europe of States: Cosmopolitanism, Intergovernmentalism and Democracy in the EU* (2019) 178–9.

18 ibid 179, 175.

19 Schimmelfennig and Winzen, 'Instrumental and Constitutional Differentiation in the European Union' (n 4).

20 Bruno de Witte, 'The Law as Tool and Constraint of Differentiated Integration' (Robert Schuman Centre for Advanced Studies Research Paper 2019) RSCAS 2019/47 2.

21 For a list of differentiation-related terms in English, French and German, see: Alexander CG Stubb, 'A Categorisation of Differentiated Integration' (1996) 34 JCMS: Journal of Common Market Studies 283, 283–4.

22 This chapter uses the terms as synonyms.

23 cf Kölliker (n 10) 40–1; Richard Bellamy and Sandra Kröger, 'A Demoicratic Justification of Differentiated Integration in a Heterogeneous EU' (2017) 39 Journal of European Integration 625, 628.

24 Christoph M Sielmann, *Governing Difference: Internal and External Differentiation in European Union Law* (1st edition, Nomos 2020) 39.

25 Tuytschaever (n 6) 2–4. The distinction is, despite differences in terminology, maintained elsewhere in the literature as well. See for example Bertolini and Dawson, who make a distinction between 'differentiated integration', meaning 'differences in formal applicability of EU rules across states', which would correspond to differentiation In the narrow sense here, and 'differentiation', which applies to 'informal forms of differentiation, e.g. in the interpretation or the application of rules', which would correspond to differentiation in the wider sense from the present paper. See: Elena Bertolini and Mark Dawson, 'Fundamental Rights as Constraints to and Triggers for Differentiated Integration' (2021) 27 Swiss Political Science Review 637, 638 n 1.

26 *Contra*, see: Thym (n 14) 36–8.

Differentiation in the wider sense covers instances of differentiation, where Member States are not subject to a uniform legal regime. Differentiation applied in this way treats all Member States equally and leaves them an identical margin of discretion, which they may exploit as they prefer.[27] It is sometimes referred to as flexible implementation.[28] Such differentiation is inherent to any multi-level system of divided competences.[29] It occurs when measures adopted by the EU are not aimed at total harmonisation or unification (*e.g.* minimum harmonisation[30]).[31]

Differentiation in the narrow sense is usually equated with the classic tools associated with differentiated integration.[32] It covers instances where EU (primary or secondary) law distinguishes between its addressees. Some Member States are excluded from the scope of application of EU law, or obligations under the law differ between them.[33] Accordingly, it includes situations where a certain margin of discretion is only available to some Member States.[34]

The debate surrounding differentiated integration is far from being novel[35] and ideas of differentiation did not only remain on paper.[36] Variations of differentiation

27 Tuytschaever (n 6) 3. Also see: de Witte, 'An Undivided Union? Differentiated Integration in Post-Brexit Times' (n 2) 228–229.

28 de Witte, 'The Law as Tool and Constraint of Differentiated Integration' (n 20) 1.

29 Tuytschaever (n 6) 2.

30 This type of harmonisation requires all Member States to meet a minimum standard, but allows them to adopt stricter measures: This is likely to result in differences in Member States' legal systems. See, for example: Ellen Vos, 'Differentiation, Harmonisation and Governance' in Bruno De Witte, Dominik Hanf and Ellen Vos (eds), *The Many Faces of Differentiation in EU Law* (Intersentia 2001) 148–149, 153; Schimmelfennig and Winzen, 'Instrumental and Constitutional Differentiation in the European Union' (n 4) 356.

31 For discussions on this form of differentiation, see literature cited in: de Witte, 'Variable Geometry and Differentiation as Structural Features of the EU Legal Order' (n 2) 24 n 43. Also see below, Section 3.3.2.

32 Stubb distinguished between the three main models: variable geometry, multi-speed and à la carte. Stubb (n 21).

33 Tuytschaever (n 6) 2; de Witte, 'The Law as Tool and Constraint of Differentiated Integration' (n 20) 1.

34 Tuytschaever (n 6) 3.

35 Extensive academic literature exists, both in the fields of political (For example: Kenneth Dyson and Angelos Sepos (eds), *Which Europe? The Politics of Differentiated Integration* (Palgrave Macmillan UK 2010); Dirk Leuffen, Berthold Rittberger and Frank Schimmelfennig, *Differentiated Integration* (Macmillan Education UK 2013); Schimmelfennig and Winzen, *Ever Looser Union?* (n 13).) and legal science (For example: Gráinne de Búrca and Joanne Scott, *Constitutional Change in the EU: From Uniformity to Flexibility.* (Bloomsbury Publishing 2000); Bruno de Witte, Dominik Hanf and Ellen Vos (eds), *The Many Faces of Differentiation in EU Law* (Intersentia 2001); Jean-Claude Piris, *The Future of Europe: Towards a Two-Speed EU?* (Cambridge University Press 2011); Matej Avbelj, 'Differentiated Integration – Farewell to the EU-27?' (2013) 14 German Law Journal 191; Giuseppe Martinico, 'Asymmetry as an Instrument of Differentiated Integration: The Case of the European Union' (2016) 18 European Journal of Law Reform 139; Thym (n 14); Sielmann (n 24).).

36 cf Faraguna (n 10) 530–2; Matej Avbelj, 'Revisiting Flexible Integration in Times of Post-Enlargement and Lustration of EU Constitutionalism' (2008) 4 Croatian Yearbook of European Law and Policy 131, 134–8.

were already present in the Treaty of Rome.[37] The Treaty included, among others, limitations on the territorial scope of the Treaty.[38] These were, as noted by *Hanf*, based on political and geographical specifics of the regions, and were, to an extent, based on existing national constitutional (as well as international) law.[39] The Treaty also contained several safeguard clauses, which allow Member States to invoke certain limitative grounds to derogate from their normal Treaty obligations.[40] As is still the case today, it also incorporated derogations to the four freedoms on the grounds of public morality, policy, security, health, etc.[41]

As in time the EU gained in complexity, differentiated integration spread.[42] The use of safeguard clauses was importantly extended by the Single European Act (SEA) with Arts. 100a[43] and 130t TEEC.[44] Subject to specific conditions,[45] these allowed Member States to adopt measures that are more stringent even after harmonisation, which enabled them to protect national constitutional demands. The SEA also inserted Art. 8c TEEC[46] explicitly allowing the differentiated application of harmonisation measures based on economic performance.[47] Importantly, SEA introduced the concept of minimum harmonisation[48] in the fields of social policy (Art. 118a(3) TEEC[49]) and the environment (Arts. 130s, 130t TEEC[50]), which was later also extended to consumer protection (Art. 153 TEC[51]) by the Treaty of Maastricht[52] and public health by the Treaty of

37 Hanf (n 3) 5–9.
38 Tuytschaever (n 6) 7–8; Faraguna (n 10) 527–528. See Art. 227 Treaty Establishing the European Economic Community (TEEC) [1957].
39 Hanf (n 3) 7.
40 Tuytschaever (n 6) 122; Sielmann (n 24) 263–6. The most prominent primary law examples today are Arts. 104(4) and (5) Treaty on the Functioning of the European Union (Consolidated version 2016) (TFEU) [2016] OJ C 202/47.
41 Arts. 36 (goods), 48(3) and (4) (workers), 55–56 (establishment) also in connection with Article 66 (services) TEEC. Ehlermann (n 7) 1280.
42 Faraguna (n 10) 529.
43 Art. 100a TEEC was modified by the Treaty of Amsterdam and became Art. 95 Treaty establishing the European Community (consolidated version 1997) (TEC) [1997] OJ C 340. The content of the Article can now be located in Art. 114 TFEU. cf Tuytschaever (n 6) 83; Bellamy (n 17) 191; de Witte, 'Variable Geometry and Differentiation as Structural Features of the EU Legal Order' (n 2) 11; Claus-Dieter Ehlermann, 'Increased Differentiation or Stronger Uniformity' (European University Institute, Robert Schuman Centre 1995) No. 95/21 8–9; Piris (n 35) 84–5.
44 Now Art. 193 TFEU.
45 These are supervised by the CJEU. For an assessment of the CJEU's (restrictive) role for the use of differentiation, see: Gráinne de Búrca, 'Legal Principles as an Instrument of Differentiation? The Principles of Proportionality and Subsidiarity' in Bruno de Witte, Dominik Hanf and Ellen Vos (eds), *The Many Faces of Differentiation in EU Law* (Intersentia 2001) 141 ff.
46 Now Art 27 TFEU
47 Hanf (n 3) 12; Vos (n 30) 146, 150; Tuytschaever (n 6) 17; Ehlermann (n 43) 8.
48 Tuytschaever (n 6) 19–21; Hanf (n 3) 12; Avbelj (n 36) 132.
49 cf Art. 153(4) TFEU.
50 Now Arts. 192 and 193 TFEU.
51 Now At. 169 TFEU.
52 Vos (n 30) 146–7.

Amsterdam (152(4a) TEC).[53] In 1985, albeit for the time outside the Treaty structure, one of the most common examples of differentiated integration, the Schengen Area, was also created.

The Treaty of Maastricht marks one of the most important and widely discussed changes in the EU's structure, not least due to its differentiation-enabling provisions.[54] It brought opt-outs in favour of Ireland (abortion)[55], the UK (Economic and Monetary Union (EMU), social policy[56]) and Denmark (EMU, Common Security and Defense Policy[57], Justice and Home Affairs (JHA) and citizenship/second home Protocol[58]). In terms of differentiation based on Member States' constitutional demands, the Treaty of Maastricht presented a milestone by including several protocols and declarations, as well as the identity clause in Art. F (1) TEU.[59] These were aimed at addressing specific constitutional aspects of Member States and are discussed in more detail below.

The Treaty of Amsterdam expanded on the novelties of Maastricht.[60] It integrated the Schengen Agreement into the Treaty structure and communitarised the JHA policy area.[61] The UK, Ireland and Denmark had to be excluded to provide the unanimity necessary for the Treaty amendment.[62] Importantly, the Treaty added the provisions on enhanced cooperation[63] (at that time 'closer co-operation'), later developed into what are today Art. 20 TEU and Arts. 326–334 TFEU.

Since the Treaty of Lisbon, differentiation mostly takes the form of derogations from primary law, treaty exemptions (opt-outs) in the Area of Freedom, Security and Justice (AFSJ) and EMU, and *ad hoc* external treaties and agreements among groups of Member States (*inter se* agreements) such as the Fiscal Compact (TSCG) and European Stability Mechanism (ESM). The Treaty also included

53 Hanf (n 3) 12.
54 E.g.: Curtin (n 16); de Witte, 'The Law as Tool and Constraint of Differentiated Integration' (n 20) 3. For an overview of literature, see: Hanf (n 3) 14 n 43.
55 See below, section 3.3.2.
56 For a detailed analysis, see: Curtin (n 16) 51–61; Ehlermann (n 43) 13–14.
57 Recently in 2022, the Danish parliament voted to abolish the opt-out, confirmed on a referendum. See: Ministry of Foreign Affairs of Denmark, 'Danes Vote Yes to Abolish EU Defence opt-out – Here are the Next Steps' <https://via.ritzau.dk/pressemeddelelse/danes-vote-yes-to-abolish-eu-defence-opt-out-here-are-the-next-steps?publisherId=13560888&releaseId=13652552> accessed 11 August 2022.
58 Faraguna (n 10) 544–5, 559 n 271. See the 'Edinburgh Agreement' Council decision: Denmark and the Treaty on European Union [1992] OJ C 348/1.
59 Treaty on European Union (TEU) [1992] OJ C 191/1.
60 For an overview of adopted differentiation measures, see: Tuytschaever (n 6) ch 3.
61 Hanf (n 3) 17 esp. n 56.
62 ibid 17–18.
63 For a comprehensive analysis, see: Robert Böttner, *The Constitutional Framework for Enhanced Cooperation in EU Law* (Brill Nijhoff 2021). For the historical background of enhanced cooperation, see: de Witte, 'Variable Geometry and Differentiation as Structural Features of the EU Legal Order' (n 2) 15. Also see: Tuytschaever (n 6) 49 ff; José M de Areilza, 'The Reform of Enhanced Co-Operation Rules: Towards Less Flexibility?' in Bruno De Witte, Dominik Hanf and Ellen Vos (eds), *The Many Faces of Differentiation in EU Law* (Intersentia 2001) 27.

protocols and derogations to the EU Charter of Fundamental Rights[64], discussed below. Enhanced cooperation was adapted to facilitate its use and put additional emphasis on economic policy and defence (PESCO).[65],[66] Although there are no clear cases of constitutional demands faring prominently concerning enhanced cooperation, this method of differentiation may play a role in the accommodation of constitutional diversity as well.[67] Forms of differentiation in the wider sense, as described above (safeguard clauses, derogations, different harmonisation techniques, the identity clause) remain in place.

3 (Are There) National Constitutional Demands Behind Differentiation in EU Law

The key question in this chapter is whether, and if, to what extent differentiation has been a function of national constitutional diversity. The answer may, first, show that differentiation has already been used (successfully) as a mechanism of accommodation of constitutional diversity in the EU; and second, based on the successfulness of those mechanisms, they can be offered as a more principled solution for accommodating constitutional diversity in the EU in the future (Section 4).

The analysis here follows from the premise that national constitutional claims carry more weight than other subjective or objective[68] differences between Member States. I put forward a formal and a material argument in support this premise. Formally, the constitution (either in the formal or in the material sense) is the highest legal act within every state's hierarchy of norms. Leaving aside the question of the placement of EU law within this hierarchy, this formal placing gives claims from constitutional law additional weight. Substantively, constitutional norms are norms of fundamental importance since they present

64 Charter of Fundamental Rights of the European Union (EU Charter) [2012] OJ C 326/391.

65 Under Art. 42(6) and 46 TEU. Currently, 26 Member States, except for Malta, participate in PESCO. The adoption of EPPO under Art. 86(1) TFEU is an example of a special type of enhanced cooperation.

66 de Witte, 'The Law as Tool and Constraint of Differentiated Integration' (n 20) 3, 7; de Witte, 'An Undivided Union? Differentiated Integration in Post-Brexit Times' (n 2) 239–41.

67 There have been important legal restraints when negotiating some of the measures. For example, when negotiating Council Regulation (EU) No 1259/2010 [2010] OJ L 343/10, implementing enhanced cooperation in the area of the law applicable to divorce and legal separation, Sweden was not open to applying any divorce rules, which would be less liberal than the domestic rules in place. See: Faraguna (n 10) 562–7.

68 On the meaning of subjective and objective differentiation, see above, n 6 and 7. It should be noted here that objective differences which reflect in inability of a specific country to participate in a given policy area is of course a relevant (and strong) claim. Regardless, when compared to claims stemming from constitutional considerations, the main difference is that the latter are not (or are, but to a lesser extent) transitory. In this sense, they may be considered 'stronger'.

manifestations of the key value choices of given societies and a reflection of their collective identity.[69] In this sense, they enjoy the highest level of legitimation and hence carry specific weight. Any consideration of overriding these norms may present an important problem at the level of democratic legitimacy. This shows the normative value of accommodation of national diversity in EU law.

3.1 A Union of Constitutional Diversity

The EU is interwoven with constitutional diversity.[70] The 27 Member States are marked by manifestly different social conditions. Consequently, preferences and interests, not least regarding the future course of the integration, are also diverse.[71] The existence of such asymmetries has been widely recognised in the academic literature.[72] There are essentially two main types: Economic and social on the one hand, and political and cultural value diversity on the other.[73] These expose the underlying pluralism of values in divergent economic and political cultures.[74]

In terms of social and economic development, the starting point of each state is much different: They vary in geography, population, and possession of natural and social capital, which are all reflected in different social and economic preferences.[75] They also diverge importantly in the successfulness of their economies. For the EU, this means that not all states have the same stake in given collective goods (e.g. the internal market, security policy, social policy or the protection of the environment). Costs and benefits of different EU policies may be distributed asymmetrically, meaning that the benefits involved are not valued to the same degree by all Member States.[76] By extension, some Member States may have less incentive for their participation in some of the EU policies and expect differentiated treatment.

69 Joseph HH Weiler, 'On the Power of the Word: Europe's Constitutional Iconography' (2005) 3 International Journal of Constitutional Law 173, 184.
70 Bellamy (n 17) 207 ff.
71 de Witte, 'An Undivided Union? Differentiated Integration in Post-Brexit Times' (n 2) 227.
72 For asymmetries in the field of fundamental rights, see: Leonard FM Besselink, 'The Protection of Fundamental Rights Post-Lisbon: The Interaction between the EU Charter of Fundamental Rights, the European Convention on Human Rights (ECHR) and National Constitutions' 1 4–6. This is also one of the reasons *Martinico* speaks of the European Union as a 'complex legal order': Giuseppe Martinico, 'Asymmetry and Complex Adaptive (Legal) Systems: The Case of the European Union' (2014) 21 Maastricht Journal of European and Comparative Law 281, 288–94. Constitutional diversity in one of the issues addressed by the theory (or theories) of constitutional pluralism.
73 Bellamy (n 17) 179 ff.
74 ibid 3. *Avbelj*, for example, labels these as different 'schemes of justice'. Following Scharpf, they encompass basic differences in national economic conditions, institutions, policy legacies and normative preferences. Avbelj (n 36) 139; Fritz W Scharpf, 'Problem Solving Effectiveness and Democratic Accountability in the EU' (2006) 107 Institut für Höhere Studien 1, 16.
75 cf Bellamy (n 17) 174.
76 ibid 179; Dyson and Sepos (n 2) 9.

In terms of cultural and political differences, there are 24 official languages in the EU. The attribution of importance by European citizens to different values related to family (e.g. marriage, parenting), religion, politics (e.g. freedom, democracy) or society (e.g. solidarity, migration, environment) between the Member States is, despite a general trend of convergence, also still very diverse.[77] Most significant divisions endure over personal freedoms, ethnic tolerance and gender equality.[78] Diverse constitutional setups mirror these differences, often rooted in religious traditions.[79] There is, for example, a great difference in the regulation of abortion[80] between Poland, Malta and until recently Ireland, on the one, and Sweden, France, and Slovenia on the other hand.[81] Similarly, family law regimes, though not necessarily constitutionalised, are also very heterogeneous.[82] Constitutionalised rights reflect different social preferences regarding welfare, privacy, religion etc.[83] Rights are nested in political communities and their particular understanding is 'coloured' by the culture of a political community. This means that even when constitutions protect the same rights, variations in local context may lead to them being interpreted and balanced in different, not always compatible ways.[84] Similar types of political and identity-related differences may also emerge when considering fundamental politico-constitutional (legal and political systems) state structures, e.g. republicanism,[85] as well as electoral systems, the particular

77 For an overview of the data gathered under the European Values Study survey, see: Marga van Zundert, Inge Josephina Petra Sieben and Loek Halman, *Atlas of European Values: Trends and Traditions at the Turn of the Century* (Open Press TiU 2012).
For detailed analyses of the data, see for example: Loek Halman, Wil Arts and Jacques Hagenaars (eds), *The Cultural Diversity of European Unity: Findings, Explanations and Reflections from the European Values Study* (Brill 2003); Wil Arts and Loek Halman (eds), *Value Contrasts and Consensus in Present-Day Europe: Painting Europe's Moral Landscapes* (Brill 2014).
For a more specific recent analysis, see: Plamen Akaliyski, Christian Welzel and Josef Hien, 'A Community of Shared Values? Dimensions and Dynamics of Cultural Integration in the European Union' [2021] Journal of European Integration 1, esp. 4, 11–12.
78 Akaliyski, Welzel and Hien (n 77) 11–12.
79 Bellamy (n 17) 180.
80 See, for example: 'European Abortion Laws: A Comparative Overview' (Centre for Reproductive Rights 2020) <https://reproductiverights.org/wp-content/uploads/2020/12/European-abortion-law-a-comparative-review.pdf> accessed 18 January 2022; 'Abortion Legislation in Europe' (International Planned Parenthood Federation 2021) <https://www.ippfen.org/sites/ippfen/files/2016-12/Final_Abortion%20legislation_September2012.pdf> accessed 18 January 2022.
81 Bellamy (n 17) 119–121. *Fabbrini*, for example, distinguished between four different models of abortion law in EU Member States scaling from a more permissive to a more restrictive regime. As explained below in relation to Ireland, some of the regimes changed in the meantime since the publication of his work. See: Federico Fabbrini, *Fundamental Rights in Europe: Challenges and Transformations in Comparative Perspective* (Oxford University Press 2014) 199–209.
82 Faraguna (n 10) 565 n 295.
83 Bellamy (n 17) 120.
84 ibid 44–45.
85 See, for example, C Case C-208/09 *Ilonka Sayn-Wittgenstein v Landeshauptmann von Wien* [2010] ECR I-13693, esp. paras. 74, 78, 92.

understandings of the separation of powers or the arrangement of local government, which all present themselves in specific constitutional arrangements.[86]

The Member States' legal and constitutional plane reflects this heterogeneity. Alongside the development of the integration, the legal complexity and diversity of the EU grew. The original six Member States were far more homogenous in their legal cultures when compared to the current setup.[87] What emerges is a Union of inherent diversity, which is to an important extent also reflected in national constitutional law. This inevitably leads to conflicts of constitutional norms in a multi-level system such as the EU.

3.2 The Parameters of Constitutional Conflict

The argument in favour of using mechanisms of differentiation to accommodate constitutional diversity in the EU could also be framed in terms of constitutional conflicts between the EU and the Member States. Accommodation of constitutional diversity is the same as solving (actual or potential) constitutional conflicts within the multilevel structure in line with EU law. In this sense, the question is whether the (actual or potential) collisions of (national and EU) constitutional norms have been addressed by employing mechanisms of differentiation.

Constitutional differences among the Member States and between the Member States and the EU produce a potential for constitutional conflict. Such a conflict occurs when a Member State invokes its constitutional standards against the standards of the EU. There are many different procedural venues the Member States can exploit for this purpose. Some of the outstanding examples are discussed in the following parts. The key issue when such a conflict occurs is the tension between the principles of unity and effectiveness of EU law, on the one side, and national constitutional standards that may require special treatment, on the other.[88] By allowing justified divergences[89] based on national constitutional constraints, differentiation could serve as a tool that would enable EU law to retain its primacy. In abstract terms, through differentiation, the primacy of EU law and the constitutional sovereignty of Member States can be reconciled.[90] This may also shed a new perspective on the problems of the legal hierarchy of norms between EU and national rules.[91]

When such a constitutional conflict arises, there are four possible resolutions, depending on the level and the type of solution employed.

The first two options are examples of one of the two systems forcibly prevailing, maintaining a 'conflict' between the two norms. Under the first option, EU law

86 Bellamy (n 17) 174.
87 Faraguna (n 10) 532–4.
88 For an emblematic example, see the quote from the *Melloni* case below, n 144.
89 Although the debate goes beyond the scope of this chapter, it should be noted that any national constitutional demands that would go against the core values of the EU (Art. 2 TEU) or fundamental rights (Art. 6 TEU) cannot be justified. The final say on this would be reserved to the CJEU. See below, n 163, 164, 165.
90 cf Přibáň (n 10) 31.
91 cf de Areilza (n 63) 38.

Table 4.1 Possible solutions for a conflict between EU and national constitutional norms depending on the level at which it arises

Relation Level	*Conflict*	*Accommodation*
EU	**Conflict at the EU level** (option 1) Primacy of EU norm without change in the national constitutional norm: violation of national constitutional law	**Accommodation at the EU level** (option 4) EU law accommodates or adapts to national constitutional demands (by way of differentiation)
National	**Conflict at the national level** (option 2) National constitutional norm prevails over EU law: violation of EU law	**Accommodation at the national level** (option 3) National constitutional norm adapts or changes to correspond to EU law's demand for unity

prevails in line with the doctrine of primacy. The problem of this solution follows from discussions surrounding cases such as Melloni[92] or Taricco I[93] where the CJEU required that the EU norms override national constitutional standards.[94] Under the second option, the national constitutional norm may prevail. This is the position of some national constitutional courts with more recent examples including the PSPP decision by the BVerfG[95] or the Polish Constitutional Tribunal judgment o the status of EU law;[96] however, this is incompatible with the EU legal order. The second pair of solutions is associated with 'accommodation'. Under the third option, the national constitutional norm is changed. This is not foreign to EU integration, since many Member States had to change their constitutions to join the EU, and even, later on, adapted their constitutional system to the demands of EU law.[97] Under the fourth option, EU law adapts to the national demands. This is where differentiation, as defined above, has a role to play. One of the solutions for conflict resolution is to allow one or several Member States to deviate from the common standard by EU law itself due to the existence of national constitutional demands. This last option reconciles the primacy of EU law with the national constitutional claim by accommodating the latter under EU law.

92 Case C-399/11 *Stefano Melloni v Ministerio Fiscal* [2013] ECLI:EU:C:2013:107.
93 Case C-105/14 *Ivo Taricco and Others* [2015] ECLI:EU:C:2015:555.
94 Taricco could also be an example of the national norm prevailing over EU law, had the CJEU not changed its interpretation of the latter in Taricco II. See: Case C-42/17 *M.A.S. and M.B.* [2017] ECLI:EU:C:2017:936. Generally on the case, see: Marjan Kos, 'The Relevance of National Identity in European Union Law and Its Potential for Instrumentalisation' (2019) 79 Zbornik Znanstvenih Razprav 41.
95 BVerfG, 2 BvR 859/15, 5 May 2020. See: Marjan Kos, 'The PSPP Judgment of the Bundesverfassungsgericht and the Slovenian Constitutional System' (2021) 2 Central European Journal of Comparative Law 93.
96 Polish Constitutional Tribunal, K 3/21, 7 October 2021.
97 For a comprehensive study on national constitutional amendments with a view to EU membership, see: Anneli Albi and Samo Bardutzky (eds), *National Constitutions in European and Global Governance: Democracy, Rights, the Rule of Law: National Reports* (TMC Asser Press 2019).

3.3 Is Differentiation Used to Manage Constitutional Diversity?

The examples of differentiation in EU law discussed above present only a small part of the multitude of instances of differentiation in EU law. Due to the sheer volume, it would be an impossible task to analyse all of them from the perspective of their constitutional footing. To narrow the analysis, I, therefore, focus on 'suspect' policy areas, which are most prone to constitutional clashes, such as foreign and security policy (including defence), interior policies (especially justice and home affairs, asylum, citizenship, fundamental rights) and economic and monetary policy.[98] Specific examples include the rights of citizens, social security, non-discrimination, family law, parts of environmental policy, energy policy and property rights.[99]

3.3.1 Examples of Differentiation in the Narrow Sense

Under differentiation in the narrow sense (*stricto sensu*), we find examples where EU law (primary or secondary) excludes some Member States from the scope of application of EU law or provides differing obligations between them.[100] The most prominent examples are opt-outs to the EU Charter and from the Area of Freedom, Security and Justice (AFSJ), as well as examples from secondary law,[101] such as the establishment of the European Public Prosecutor's Office (EPPO)[102] or procedural rights in criminal proceedings.[103]

98 The categorisation is based on Policy areas in European integration, as defined in: Schimmelfennig and Winzen, *Ever Looser Union?* (n 13) 61, 193 Table A4.1. cf Dirk Leuffen, Berthold Rittberger and Frank Schimmelfennig, *Differentiated Integration: Explaining Variation in the European Union* (Palgrave Macmillan 2013) 253–254.

99 Faraguna (n 10) 561, 573–4.

100 Tuytschaever (n 6) 2.

101 Frank Schimmelfennig and Thomas Winzen, 'Differentiated EU Integration: Maps and Modes' (European University Institute 2020) Working Paper 2020/24 16 ff.

102 Council Regulation (EU) 2017/1939 of 12 October 2017 implementing enhanced cooperation on the establishment of the European Public Prosecutor's Office [2017] OJ L 283/1. Currently, five Member States do not participate: Ireland and Denmark have an opt-out to AFSJ, Poland and Hungary refused due to sovereignty concerns, while Sweden questioned the necessity of its establishment, but plans to join at a later date. See: Edit Inotai and others, 'Democracy Digest: Hungary and Poland Refuse to Join EU Justice League' *Balkan Insight* (4 June 2021) <https://balkaninsight.com/2021/06/04/democracy-digest-hungary-and-poland-refuse-to-join-eu-justice-league/> accessed 16 November 2021. For an analysis of national parliamentary concerns regarding the establishment of EPPO, see: Diane Fromage, 'The Second Yellow Card on the EPPO Proposal: An Encouraging Development for Member State Parliaments?' (2016) 35 Yearbook of European Law 5.

103 Denmark and Ireland do not participate (fully) due to the opt-out. See: Cornelia Riehle and Allison Clozel, '10 Years After the Roadmap: Procedural Rights in Criminal Proceedings in the EU Today' (2020) 20 ERA Forum 321; European Commission, 'New Rules and Guarantees in Criminal Proceedings Now Apply Across the EU' (*European Commission*, 11 June 2019) <https://ec.europa.eu/commission/presscorner/detail/en/IP_19_2910> accessed 16 November 2021.

Imprints of constitutional arguments are spread across some of the above-described examples of differentiation, however, clear connections are hard to establish. Partially this is because the text of the documents adopted does not explain the reasons for a differentiated approach. These usually only emerge from the political discussion preceding the adoption of a legal instrument. Additionally, the problem is also due to the challenge of distinguishing between different types of subjective reasons for differentiation, discussed above: it is not always clear whether a claim by a Member State is due to a national constitutional demand or merely a transient political preference.[104]

Regardless, in terms of their constitutional contingency, two examples stand out. The first was Protocol no. 17,[105] or the so-called 'Grogan' Protocol. It provided that nothing in the Treaties shall affect the application in Ireland of Article 40.3.3 of the Constitution of Ireland.[106],[107] The latter, until it was amended in 2018, dealt with the prohibition of abortion in Ireland.[108] It was a response to the Grogan judgment[109] of the CJEU, where the Court held that the medical termination of pregnancy constituted a service under Art. 60 of the Treaty.[110] Despite the Court allowing the ban on the dissemination of information about abortion clinics in the UK under the public policy exemption, Ireland negotiated a permanent exemption under EU law. To appease the ensuing public outcry in Ireland, a clarifying Declaration was added to the Final Act of the Conference in May 1992 three months after the conference.[111] Additionally, the Constitution was also changed to explicitly guarantee the right to travel abroad for an abortion and to provide information about abortion services overseas.[112] The Constitution was later fundamentally changed in 2018 to remove the ban,[113] but the exemption remains. This Protocol represents the

104 One way of distinguishing between the two would be to look at the transitory nature of the demand: If the demand is a political whim, it should disappear when the government changes; if it is constitutional, it should endure.

105 Now: Protocol (No 35) on Article 40.3.3 of the Constitution of Ireland [2017] OJ C 202/320.

106 This was amended by the Eight Amendment of the Constitution of Ireland, Adding a sub-section to section 3 of Art. 40, which until 2018 read: 'The State acknowledges the right to life of the unborn and, with due regard to the equal right to life of the mother, guarantees in its laws to respect, and, as far as practicable, by its laws to defend and vindicate that right.'

107 Faraguna (n 10) 542–4.

108 For the legal regulation of abortion in Ireland before the 2018 change, see: Fabbrini (n 81) 206–9.

109 Case C-159/90 *The Society for the Protection of Unborn Children Ireland Ltd v Stephen Grogan and others* [1991] ECR I-4685.

110 Now Art. 57 TFEU.

111 For a more thorough discussion on the circumstances surrounding the adoption of the Protocol, see: Curtin (n 16) 48–51.

112 Fabbrini (n 81) 207, 211–2.

113 For an overview of developments leading to the change in 2018, see: David Kenny, 'Abortion, the Irish Constitution, and Constitutional Change' (2018) 5 Revista de Investigações Constitucionais 257.

most obvious example of differentiation in EU law, motivated by national constitutional demands.

Another example that belongs to the same category is Protocol no. 7, annexed to the 2003 Accession Agreement concerning Malta. The protocol provides that 'Nothing in [the Treaties] shall affect the application in the territory of Malta of national legislation relating to abortion.'[114] As follows from the above, Malta, and until recently Ireland, were the two countries with the most restrictive stance on abortion and both succeeded in negotiating an exemption from EU law related to that issue.[115] Additionally, Ireland brokered another exemption post-Lisbon. It refers to the protection of the right to life, family and education, as safeguarded by the Irish constitution, as well as including exemptions from taxation and security and defence.[116]

The second constitutionally relevant category of differentiation is represented by the exemptions to the EU Charter by the UK and Poland[117] under the Treaty of Lisbon included in Protocol no. 30.[118] The provisions aim at limiting the application of the EU Charter in the two countries. These limitations have been assigned limited success in the academic literature[119] and the CJEU ruled that the Protocol does not call into question the applicability of the Charter in the UK or Poland.[120] Regardless, the reasons behind the opt-out are interesting for this chapter. As far as the UK is concerned, the request for an opt-out was foremost a political manoeuvre, intended for the Euro-sceptic audience.[121] At the same time, officials expressly acknowledged that it is actually 'not an opt-out'. In the background though, there may also have been deeper constitutional

114 Protocol No 7 on abortion in Malta [2013] OJ L 236/947.

115 In the case of Malta, the prohibition is only entailed in ordinary legislation. Debates have been ongoing regarding the constitutionalisation of the prohibition. See, for example: Philip Leone Ganado, 'PN, PD Pledge Anti-Abortion Constitutional Amendment This Year' (*Times of Malta*, 20 May 2019) <https://timesofmalta.com/articles/view/pn-pd-pledge-anti-abortion-constitutional-amendment-this-year.710508> accessed 14 September 2022.

116 Protocol on the concerns of the Irish people on the Treaty of Lisbon [2013] OJ L 60/131.

117 Also see: Declaration by the Republic of Poland on the Charter of Fundamental Rights of the European Union (no. 61) [2016] OJ C 202/358. The Czech Republic initially also wanted to join the opt-out, however the request was later removed and only a Declaration attached to the Treaty. See: Declaration by the Czech Republic on the Charter of Fundamental Rights of the European Union (no. 53).

118 Faraguna (n 10) 548–51.

119 S Peers, 'The "Opt-out" That Fell to Earth: The British and Polish Protocol Concerning the EU Charter of Fundamental Rights' (2012) 12 Human Rights Law Review 375; Faraguna (n 10) 549–550; Catherine Barnard, 'The "Opt-Out" for the UK and Poland from the Charter of Fundamental Rights: Triumph of Rhetoric over Reality?' in Stefan Griller and Jacques Ziller (eds), *The Lisbon Treaty*, vol 11 (Springer Vienna 2008); Fabbrini (n 81) 19 n 81, 240–1.

120 Case C-411/10 and C-493/10 *N. S. v Secretary of State for the Home Department and M. E. and Others v Refugee Applications Commissioner and Minister for Justice, Equality and Law Reform* [2011] ECLI:EU:C:2011:865, para 119.

121 Barnard (n 119) 258, 277–81.

concerns[122] with regards to the right to strike,[123] which is treated differently under UK law.[124] The concern was the incorporation of social and economic rights in the same document as civil and political rights, based on the distinction between positive and negative rights, preferring to refer to the latter group as principles.[125] As far as Poland is concerned, the Protocol has to be read together with a separate Declaration to the Treaty regarding the social rights contained in the EU Charter.[126] The reason for the opt-out was apparently not the development of social and labour rights, but the fear of further developments mainly in the field of family law, specifically concerning same-sex couple regulation.[127] This follows from Poland's declaration to the Charter as well.[128]

3.3.2 Examples of Differentiation in the Wider Sense

As defined above, differentiation in the wider sense (*sensu lato*) entails cases where Member States are not subject to a uniform legal regime within the scope of EU law. It occurs when measures adopted by the EU are not aimed at total harmonisation[129] or unification. It includes cases where Member States are allowed to deviate from the common standard, for example *via* safeguard clauses included in primary[130] or secondary law,[131] minimum

122 Faraguna (n 10) 550–1 n 229.
123 cf Fabbrini (n 81) 145–63.
124 In the UK, trade unions only enjoy immunity from tort actions and there is no 'right to strike' as such. cf Barnard (n 119) 269–71.
125 ibid 260 n 9. Aslo see: Fabbrini (n 81) 239.
126 Declaration by the Republic of Poland concerning the Protocol on the application of the Charter of Fundamental Rights of the European Union in relation to Poland and the United Kingdom (no. 62) [2016] OJ C 202/358.
127 Faraguna (n 10) 551; Barnard (n 119) 276; Fabbrini (n 81) 239. The relevant provision is Art. 18 of the Constitution of the Republic of Poland: 'Marriage, being a union of a man and a woman, as well as the family, motherhood and parenthood, shall be placed under the protection and care of the Republic of Poland."'Constitution of the Republic of Poland of 2 April 1997 r. 2009 [Constitution] art. 18 (Poland).
128 'The Charter does not affect in any way the right of Member States to legislate in the sphere of public morality, family law, as well as the protection of human dignity and respect for human physical and moral integrity.' Declaration (no. 61), above, n 117.
129 For a categorisation of the methods of harmonisation, see: Catherine Barnard, *The Substantive Law of the EU: The Four Freedoms* (4th ed, Oxford Univ Press 2013) 656–66; Bruno de Witte, L Ad Geelhoed and Jan Inghelram, 'Legal Instruments, Decision-Making and EU Finances' in Paul JG Kapteyn and others (eds), *The law of the European Union and the European Communities: with reference to changes to be made by the Lisbon Treaty* (4th rev ed, Kluwer Law International 2008) 316–20. cf Vos (n 30) 148–9.
130 E.g. Art. 114(4) – (10), 153(4), 169(4) or 193 TFEU. See: Thym (n 14) 36–7.
131 One such example is the Directive 2003/88/EC of the European Parliament and of the Council of 4 November 2003 concerning certain aspects of the organisation of working time (Working Time Directive) [2013] OJ L 299/9, setting high standards of social protection, while simultaneously allowing for derogations. cf de Witte, 'Variable Geometry and Differentiation as Structural Features of the EU Legal Order' (n 2) 19 n 28; Thym (n 14) 37; Vos (n 30) 153–4.

harmonisation,[132] derogations from fundamental market freedoms[133] or specific internal market provisions.[134] Member States continue to exercise their competence, provided that they act in conformity with their Treaty obligations.[135]

There are countless examples of differentiation defined in this sense. Here, I would draw attention only to two important venues of judicially induced differentiation that may offer such accommodation, namely derogation clauses and the identity clause.

Derogation clauses are clauses in EU law acts that allow Member States to derogate from what is otherwise a common EU rule that applies equally to all Member States. The most important examples are the derogations from the market freedoms, based on exemptions of public health, public security, public policy etc.[136] The room for manoeuvre left to Member States to differentiate is limited by the requirement to respect EU law and is supervised by the CJEU, which makes it the key actor in condoning the respect for national constitutional diversity.[137] In its case law, the CJEU sometimes showed openness to constitutional claims from Member States. There are at least two very well-known constitutionally-permeated internal market-related examples. The first is the Schmidberger case, where the CJEU accepted that freedom of expression and assembly, as protected by the Austrian constitution (and ECHR), may be invoked as a legitimate aim to derogate from market freedoms.[138] This shows the potential for the differentiation of national constitutionally based arguments within the four freedoms, which was soon after famously accepted in the Omega case. There, the CJEU sanctioned Germany's plea for special protection accorded to human dignity under the German Basic Law as a derogation from Treaty obligations. This case adds to the point that even if there exist different standards in different Member States, derogations may

132 E.g. the non-discrimination directives. For a detailed discussion, including on the problems concerning this type of minimum standards, briefly discussed below as well, see: Eleanor Spaventa, 'Should We "Harmonize" Fundamental Rights in the EU? Some Reflections about Minimum Standards and Fundamental Rights Protection in the EU Composite Constitutional System' (2018) 55 Common Market Law Review esp. 1009 ff.

133 E.g. Art. 36 TFEU.

134 Thym (n 14) 37 n 40.

135 Tuytschaever (n 6) 3–4. cf Francesco de Cecco, 'Room to Move? Minimum Harmonization and Fundamental Rights' (2006) 43 Common Market Law Review 9, 9.

136 These are expressed in Arts. 36 (goods), 52(1) (workers), 62 in connection with 52(1) (services) and 63(1)(b) and 45(3) TFEU (capital and establishment).

137 Tuytschaever (n 6) 12–13; Eleanor Spaventa, 'Federalisation Versus Centralisation: Tensions in Fundamental Rights Discourse in the EU' in Michael Dougan and Samantha Currie (eds), *50 Years of the European Treaties: Looking Back and Thinking Forward.* (Bloomsbury Publishing 2009) 13; Michael Dougan, 'Judicial Review of Member State Action under the General Principles and the Charter: Defining the "Scope of Union Law"' (2015) 52 Common Market Law Review 1211, 1215–1216. For the role of CJEU's interpretation in harmonisation measures, see: de Búrca (n 45).

138 Case C-112/00 *Eugen Schmidberger, Internationale Transporte und Planzüge v Republik Österreich* [2003] ECR I-5659, para 69 et. seq. cf Dougan (n 137) 1215 n 54.

still be in line with EU law.[139] It is a paradigmatic example of how strong national constitutional claims should be accommodated within EU law if respect for constitutional diversity is taken seriously. Although in some high-profile cases, such as in Taricco II, the CJEU has accepted this,[140] it is still not the prevailing approach. As cases such as AGET Iraklis,[141] Melloni,[142] and Alemo-Herron[143] show EU standards may still also function as a ceiling to potential higher national constitutional (esp. fundamental rights) standards; the CJEU may opt for a unified EU standard.[144] Of course, importance has to be given to the type of competence of the EU in a concrete case,[145] as well as the type of measure that is chosen by the EU to regulate the issue (no regulation, minimum or total harmonisation[146]).[147]

139 Case C-36/02 *Omega Spielhallen- und Automatenaufstellungs-GmbH v Oberbürgermeisterin der Bundesstadt Bonn* [2004] ECR I-9609 esp. paras 31, 37–9. On the difference between the Court's decisions in *Schmidberger* and *Omega* in relation to the extent of deference left to the Member States, see: Spaventa (n 137).
Also see: Case C-88/03 *Portuguese Republic v Commission of the European Communities (Azores)* [2003] ECR I-7115, Case C-145/04 *Kingdom of Spain v United Kingdom of Great Britain and Northern Ireland (Gibraltar)* [2006] ECR I-7917 and Case C-379/87 *Anita Groener v Minister for Education and the City of Dublin Vocational Educational Committee* [1989] ECR I-3967. Faraguna (n 10) 509.

140 Kos (n 94) 51–3.

141 Case C-201/15 *Anonymi Geniki Etairia Tsimenton Iraklis (AGET Iraklis) v Ypourgos Ergasias, Koinonikis Asfalisis kai Koinonikis Allilengyis* [2016] ECLI:EU:C:2016:972.

142 C-399/11 *Melloni* (n 92).

143 Case C-426/11 *Mark Alemo-Herron and Others v Parkwood Leisure Ltd* [2013] ECLI:EU:C:2013:521.

144 The most clear expression is provided by the quote from *Melloni*, para 60: '[W]here an EU legal act calls for national implementing measures, national authorities and courts remain free to apply national standards of protection of fundamental rights, provided that the level of protection provided for by the Charter, as interpreted by the Court, and the primacy, unity and effectiveness of EU law are not thereby compromised.'
For an analysis, arguing that the choice on when a uniform standard of fundamental rights should be enforced is actually up to political institutions, see: Koen Lenaerts, 'EU Values and Constitutional Pluralism: The EU System of Fundamental Rights Protection' [2015] Polish Yearbook of International Law 135.

145 The connection between the scope of application of EU law in the field of fundamental rights and EU competence is clear, for example from Art. 6(1) TFEU or Art. 51(1) EU Charter.

146 See, for example, Case C-291/12 *Michael Schwarz v Stadt Bochum* [2013] ECLI:EU:C:2013:670. In connection with that case, Lenaerts argued that since the regulation in question set a uniform standard, Member States would not be allowed to introduce higher standards, as long as the regulation complied with the EU Charter. This is also how Leanerts explains the CJEU's Judgment in *Melloni*: Since the EAW expresses a legislative consensus reached at the EU level, which complies with the EU Charter, the EU is allowed to set a unified standard of the protection of fa fundamental right and value diversity is ruled out. Lenaerts (n 144) 147, 150–1. On the discussion of the approach of the German Federal Constitutional Court, see: Aertgeers Chapter 5, Gašperin Chapter 6.

147 Spaventa (n 132); de Cecco (n 135); Francesco de Cecco, 'Minimum Harmonization and the Limits of Union Fundamental Rights Review: TSN and AKT' (2021) 58 Common Market Law Review.

Generally, however, the above case law shows that EU law may block national derogating measures both when one speaks of national derogations from internal market primary law, as well as of national measures related to areas of full or even minimum harmonisation.

Additionally, I would stress the possible role that a specific 'derogation clause', namely the identity clause from Art. 4(2) TEU, the centrepiece for the protection of pluralism, may play for differentiation based on constitutional demands. This article could be used as a proxy for the most fundamental national constitutional claims.[148] It could function as a cross-cutting mechanism, applicable, albeit to varying degrees, in all the different areas of EU competence and applying to all the different EU measures selected in a specific case. It could operate either as a self-standing basis for derogation or as an interpretative device coupled with other differentiation-enabling provisions. The fact that this is possible is already reflected to some extent in CJEU's case law, namely in Runevič,[149] Sayn Wittgenstein,[150] Bogendorff von Wolffersdorff,[151] as well as, though without direct references to the clause, Taricco II.[152]

4 Principled Constitutional Differentiation: Differentiation as a Tool of Accommodation of Constitutional Diversity?

The argument pursued in this chapter challenges the idea that an 'ever closer union' can only be achieved *via* unity and consolidation of national legal orders, with *effet utile* posited as the holy grail of integration.[153] To retain the existing level of European integration and possibly extend it further, constitutional conflicts between the two systems need sufficient resolution mechanisms. Unifying measures may produce a backlash and therefore a certain degree of respect for national constitutional diversity is necessary. This would make the EU more resilient since the Member States would be more willing (or less unwilling) to commit to the common goals. Without undermining the core EU principles of unity, effectiveness and equality, differentiation in EU law as understood here may offer

148 Kos (n 94) 48–51.

149 Case C-391/09 *Malgožata Runevič-Vardyn and Łukasz Paweł Wardyn v Vilniaus miesto savivaldybes administracija and Others* [2011] ECR I-3787.

150 Case C-208/09 *Sayn-Wittgenstein* (n 85).

151 Case C-438/14 *Nabiel Peter Bogendorff von Wolffersdorff v Standesamt der Stadt Karlsruhe and Zentraler Juristischer Dienst der Stadt Karlsruhe* [2016] ECLI:EU:C:2016:401.

152 C-42/17 *M.A.S. and M.B* (n 94).

153 On the importance of the *effet utile* principle for EU law, see: Thym (n 14) 56; Schimmelfennig and Winzen, *Ever Looser Union?* (n 13) 2; de Witte, 'Variable Geometry and Differentiation as Structural Features of the EU Legal Order' (n 2) 9; Dyson and Sepos (n 35) 7; Curtin (n 16) 46, 67; Ehlermann (n 7) 1288. Generally on the principle, see: M Elvira Mendez-Pinedo, 'The Principle of Effectiveness of EU Law: A Difficult Concept in Legal Scholarship' (2021) 11 Juridical Tribune 5; Urška Šadl, 'The Role of Effet Utile in Preserving the Continuity and Authority of European Union Law: Evidence from the Citation Web of the Pre-Accession Case Law of the Court of Justice of the EU' (2015) 8 European Journal of Legal Studies 18.

a theoretical model more apt to deal with the challenge of constitutional diversity. It does not implicate the complete overriding of *effet utile* but merely tips the balance between principles to the side of national constitutional demands. This could be done effectively by extending the application of the mechanisms of differentiation discussed above.

When it comes to differentiation in the narrow sense, we see that it is already well in place in EU law. Even though the idea that national constitutional provisions could allow Member States to obtain exemptions to EU law was in the past presented as the opening of Pandora's box,[154] no such reality transpired. Moreover, even coupled with all the other forms of differentiation that exist in EU law, they do not seem to have a pronounced centrifugal effect on European integration. Considering that some of the integrating measures could not be adopted without differentiation, it could even be argued that differentiated integration had a centripetal effect on the EU as a whole. Considering all the above, differentiation in the narrow sense can be seen as an effective mechanism to address national constitutional diversity under EU law. The limitation of these mechanisms is, that they are mostly limited to periods of Treaty revisions. Additionally, as noted above, the substance of EU law concessions was in the past problematic from the point of view of retaining minimum fundamental rights standards under EU law and ECHR.

Differentiation in the narrow sense occurs when constitutional demands are already apparent and can be accommodated in advance when adopting an act of primary or secondary legislation. In terms of its versatility, here, differentiation in the wider sense has an important advantage. It can also be approved by primary or adopted through secondary law, which demands action on behalf of the EU. The competent institution can anticipate a possible collision and provide for an appropriate mechanism of accommodation in advance. However, this type of differentiation also entails the implementation and application of EU law in concrete cases, meaning that it can be employed without an explicit change in EU law, anytime a national constitutional demand arises (differentiated application[155] or implementation[156]). This is especially valuable since clashes of constitutional-level norms, discussed in this paper, may sometimes only materialise later on, especially in concrete cases.[157] As mentioned above, when for example considering fundamental rights, the culture of the political community marks their understanding. This means that even when Member States acknowledge the same rights, variations in local context may lead to them being interpreted and balanced in different, not always compatible ways.[158] This means that the result of balancing may be different in different contexts depending on the factual circumstances of a

154 Curtin (n 16) 49.
155 Ehlermann (n 7) 1279, 1281–5.
156 de Witte, 'The Law as Tool and Constraint of Differentiated Integration' (n 20) 1.
157 The fact that judicial dialogue, as a mechanism of differentiation, fostered the emergence of differentiation has already been established on the example of ASFJ with the introduction of the 'systemic deficiency' test. See: Bertolini and Dawson (n 25) 645.
158 Bellamy (n 17) 44–45; Faraguna (n 10) 525–6.

specific case. As poetically framed by *Faraguna*, dissonances regarding basic constitutional principles would in most cases be linked more to the musical execution than the composition of a musical score.[159]

The paradigmatic example of how national constitutional demands may be accommodated under these mechanisms is the abovementioned case Omega. This is especially so since there do not seem to be any significant negative repercussions of such accommodation for the *effet utile* principle. I have also offered the identity clause from Art. 4(2) TEU as a proxy for the most fundamental national constitutional demands under EU law. *Faraguna* argued that differentiated integration is already used as a non-judicial tool to respect national constitutional identities. In his view, the identity clause should be interpreted as a legal obligation to differentiate for the purpose of the protection of national constitutional identity.[160] In this sense, it should be understood as a legal tool entailing an obligation to adopt different measures of differentiation in the wider sense. He suggests a cross-cutting application of the identity clause, detached from its limitation to the judicial sphere. What I would add to his argument is that also the reverse should be true. The underlying idea of differentiation, which is, as shown above, already prevalent in many parts of the EU legal framework as an inherent part of the integration, should be assumed in the judicial sphere to a greater extent as well. Considering the openness of European integration to differentiation based on national constitutional demands, the CJEU should also adopt an open attitude towards differentiation. Since this approach is already adopted in other areas of EU law, it should *a fortiori* be extended to the field of national constitutional claims which carry specific weight.

As follows, the role of the CJEU is extremely important for differentiation in the wider sense. Once the legal framework for differentiation is established, the CJEU executes its supervisory role on the application of derogations by Member States. Their scope is dependent on the stringency of the CJEU's interpretation of EU law and its acceptance of and openness towards national constitutionally-based arguments. The Court has in the past often opted for a restrictive interpretation[161], having in sight *effet utile* of EU law.[162] One of the aims of this chapter is to show that this should be changed in the direction of more lenience towards the Member States. I advocate for a more principled adoption of mechanisms of differentiation. We see that differentiation is already a prevalent feature in EU law. Such accommodation of diversity should especially be adopted when national deviations from the common EU standard stem from national constitutional demands. The practice is not new to EU law and it should be more pronounced in the CJEU's approach if it is to take national constitutional diversity seriously.

This proposed argument leaves some important questions open though. Perhaps the most important among them are the limits of acceptable differentiation.

159 Faraguna (n 10) 526. He notes that the situation is somewhat different when national constitutional particularities exist in the specific Member States.

160 ibid 494–5.

161 Tuytschaever (n 6) 12–13.

162 cf Koen Lenaerts, 'The Role of National Constitutions in EU Law: From Shared Values to Mutual Trust and Constructive Dialogue' (2018) 73 Pravnik 5, 11.

When arguing in favour of recognising national constitutional diversity in EU law, the latter also draws some red lines. As discussed elsewhere, national constitutional claims under any of the mechanisms discussed here can only be accommodated if they respect the values[163] from Arts. 2 and 6 TEU[164], including the principle of non-discrimination.[165]

5 Conclusion

The above-discussed demands for differentiation based on national constitutional requirements cannot *a priori* be deemed illegitimate. As noted by *Bellamy* in his republican intergovernmentalist account of differentiated integration, the rationale behind these demands is the fact that the different *demoi* of Member States have already developed their own constitutional and juridical orders that reflect the distinctive and diverse public cultures of their citizens.[166] National constitutions are a reflection of the values of the polity and the collective identity of the people.[167] This leads us back to the initial normative claim that constitutional diversity within the EU needs to be accommodated to preserve or perhaps even strengthen its legitimacy. One way of doing that is to use the mechanisms already well in place within the EU legal order, gathered here under the umbrella term of differentiation. I subscribe to *Faraguna's* argument that European integration calls for a more central role of differentiated integration which can serve as an efficient instrument of preventive neutralisation of conflicts between EU law and national constitutional demands.[168] Additionally, when employed in line with the underlying idea of accommodation of diversity, these mechanisms can also be used in concrete cases where conflicts of constitutional norms arise.

As shown in this chapter, differentiation has become an important feature of EU law. It has been deemed acceptable in various policy areas and for both objective and subjective reasons. Based on the arguments presented in this paper, I believe that legitimate national constitutional claims for differentiation can and should therefore seriously be considered within EU law. As follows from the discussion, these mechanisms have already played an important role in accommodating national constitutional diversity and could be used for that purpose in the

163 On the nature of values from Art. 2 TEU, see: Saša Zagorc and Marjan Kos, 'European Values and National Constitutions: Bringing the EU Charter in from Uncharted Waters' in Federica Casarosa and Madalina Moraru (eds), *The practice of judicial interaction in the field of fundamental rights: the added value of the charter of fundamental rights of the EU* (Edward Elgar Publishing 2022).

164 It should never lead to the lowering of fundamental rights standards in the EU beyond the minimum provided by the ECHR. For fears of the opposite raised by the Amsterdam revision, see: Curtin (n 16) 49.

165 cf Bellamy (n 17) 192, 199; Kos (n 94). Especially with regards to the relationship between Arts. 2 and 4(2) TEU, see: C-156/21 Hungary v Parliament and Council, paras. 124–127, 232–4.

166 Bellamy (n 17) 192.

167 Weiler (n 69) 184.

168 Faraguna (n 10) 526–7.

future. Some of the types of differentiation in the wider sense that are more adaptable to constitutional conflicts that emerge in specific cases are particularly useful in that regard. Exemptions granted to legitimate national constitutional concerns in specific cases should not be considered as the opening of Pandora's box and an inherent threat to the unity and effectiveness of EU law. In some cases, accommodating strong constitutional concerns within EU law would even bolster the legitimacy of EU law and consequently the EU itself. It is perhaps high time to start looking at the EU as a mature legal order, which does not need to insist on uniformity for the sake of its preservation anymore. It may be that a better answer to Euroscepticism would be to show more openness to considering the accommodation of diversity, as presented in this paper. Though this plea aims at the EU as a whole, the role of the CJEU will be crucial to achieving this.

5 Between Unity and Diversity

EU Data Protection Legislation as a Catalyst for a Constitutional Trilogue

Pieter Aertgeerts

1 Introduction

Just like in other areas of EU law, potential divergences between the EU and its Member States also exist in the field of fundamental rights. In order to better understand the relationship between the EU and its Member States in the field of EU fundamental rights, and the different institutions involved in shaping them, this chapter conceptualises the relationship between these institutions as a 'constitutional trilogue' between the EU legislature (Parliament and Council), the Court of Justice of the European Union (CJEU) and constitutional courts. This chapter illustrates the workings of such a constitutional trilogue through a case study of the field of EU data protection law. It will focus, more precisely, on the connection between EU data protection legislation, the CJEU's case law on the subject, and the reception in the case law of three constitutional courts (the Austrian *Verfassungsgerichtshof*, the Italian *Corte costituzionale* and the German *Bundesverfassungsgericht*). More broadly, the constitutional trilogue, as presented in this chapter, could function as a generalised mechanism of convergence and divergence, ensuring both the unity of EU fundamental rights legislation and accommodating diversity between the Member States to understand other EU fundamental rights policies better.

As for the field of EU data protection law, the EU legislature has given specific expression to the fundamental right laid down in the Charter of Fundamental Rights (CFR) with the adoption of various pieces of legislation. This mainly comprises the General Data Protection Regulation (GDPR),[1] which entered into force in 2018 and replaced the Data Protection Directive (DPD),[2] and is complemented by more specialised legislation, such as the ePrivacy Directive.[3] As will be shown in this chapter, on a horizontal (intra-EU) level, a mutual dialogue takes

1 Regulation (EU) 2016/679 of 27 April 2016 on the protection of natural persons with regard to the processing of personal data and on the free movement of such data, and repealing Directive 95/46/EC [2016] OJ L 119/1.

2 Directive 95/46/EC of 24 October 1995 on the protection of individuals with regard to the processing of personal data and on the free movement of such data [1995] OJ L 281/31.

3 Directive 2002/58/EC of 12 July 2002 concerning the processing of personal data and the protection of privacy in the electronic communications sector [2002] OJ L 201/37.

DOI: 10.4324/9781003355762-5

place between the EU political institutions which have given specific expression to a fundamental right, through the adoption of legislation, and the CJEU which further interprets these pieces of legislation in line with the fundamental right to data protection as laid down in primary law in Article 16 TFEU and Article 8 CFR.

Throughout the years, the CJEU has interpreted the scope of application of these different pieces of EU data protection legislation very broadly. Since the main piece of legislation is a Regulation (the GDPR), it thus directly impacts a vast array of situations in the Member States. Therefore, constitutional courts are also necessarily confronted with cases relating to data protection and have to deal with the interpretation of EU data protection legislation and the right to data protection in their jurisprudence. Thus, on a vertical (EU-Member State) level, a mutual dialogue could also take place between the EU institutions mentioned above and constitutional courts, if the latter explicitly engage with these EU norms. Constitutional courts could also leave the interpretation of these norms (and thus the right to data protection) to the CJEU or, even if they do engage, could interpret these norms in divergent manners if they would not liaise with the CJEU. The interpretation of the right to data protection, as given expression in a Regulation with a clear general intent of harmonisation, should, however, be understood in a generally uniform manner.

Therefore, convergence between constitutional courts could be attained if they explicitly engage with EU data protection legislation and the right to data protection *and* cooperate with the CJEU as the centralised interpreter of these norms. In recent years it has become evident that a rising number of constitutional courts increasingly engage with precisely these norms, fearing a decline of influence on their interpretation. These courts want to include themselves in the interpretative process of EU fundamental rights legislation with such vast ramifications.

As such, EU data protection legislation forms the catalyst for what I term a 'constitutional trilogue' between the EU legislature, the CJEU and constitutional courts, who all three together shape, interpret and give expression to a fundamental right in a generally converging manner. In limited areas, EU data protection legislation leaves open certain margins for more divergent national interpretations of the right to data protection, which are guarded in a collaborative exercise between the actors mentioned above. In terms of their respective power in the constitutional trilogue, however, it has yet to be seen to what extent the constitutional courts can persuade the CJEU or the EU legislature to change course in their case law or legislation, in case they would like them to do so.

Section 2 will introduce the metaphor of 'constitutional trilogue', which functions as a normatively attractive model to understand the concretisation of the right to data protection under EU law. Section 3 will show how the CJEU draws the line between the application of the Charter and/or national constitutional rights to Member State action, which is based on the EU legislature's choice to require more unity or allow more diversity in the relevant fundamental rights standards. Finally, section 4 will show how constitutional courts actively take up their position in the constitutional trilogue with regard to EU data protection legislation. The chapter will conclude that the metaphor of a constitutional trilogue could also function as a normatively attractive model to understand the concretisation of other EU fundamental rights for which the EU legislature is competent to adopt legislation.

2 A Case of Communicating Vessels: A Constitutional Trilogue on Fundamental Rights in the EU Context

2.1 The Horizontal Axis: A Constitutional Dialogue Between Courts and Legislatures as Applied to the EU Context

Most authors agree that both the judiciary and the legislature should be involved in fundamental rights decision-making and interpretation, but disagree on the extent to which one or the other should be able to trump the other institution.[4] Certain authors propose the thesis that the legislature is the most appropriate institution to advance fundamental rights since, in light of essential disagreements on social justice, the democratic representativeness of the political institutions accords particular legitimacy to legislation.[5] Other authors argue that judicial review of legislation is necessary in order to protect citizens' individual rights against the risks involved in majority rule.[6] These writings exist on a continuum, though: authors who stress the particular authority that we should accord legislation do not necessarily completely rule out judicial review of legislation.[7] Similarly, authors who advocate a decisive role for the judiciary in protecting fundamental rights recognise that both courts and legislatures should be enlisted in the protection of fundamental rights.[8]

An interesting metaphor in this regard, which proves useful in the EU context, is the concept of 'constitutional dialogue', developed mainly in Canadian constitutional doctrine.[9] In order to bridge the gap between proponents and

4 Richard H Fallon, 'The Core of an Uneasy Case For Judicial Review' (2008) 121 Harvard Law Review 1693; Rosalind Dixon, 'The Core Case for Weak-Form Judicial Review' (2017) 38 Cardozo Law Review 2193.

5 Jeremy Waldron, *Law and Disagreement* (Oxford University Press 1999); Richard Bellamy, *Political Constitutionalism: A Republican Defense of the Constitutionality of Democracy* (Cambridge University Press 2007); Martijn van den Brink, 'Justice, Legitimacy and the Authority of Legislation within the European Union' (2019) 82 The Modern Law Review 293.

6 John Hart Ely, *Democracy and Distrust* (Harvard University Press 1980); Fallon (n 4).

7 Robert A Dahl, *Democracy and Its Critics* (Yale University Press 1991); Philip Pettit, *On the People's Terms: A Republican Theory and Model of Democracy* (Cambridge University Press 2012).

8 Fallon (n 4).

9 Peter W Hogg and Allison A Bushell, 'The Charter Dialogue Between Courts and Legislatures (Or Perhaps the Charter of Rights Isn't Such A Bad Thing After All)' (1997) 35 Osgoode Hall Law Journal 75.

opponents of judicial review and to overcome the 'counter-majoritarian difficulty',[10] Hogg and Bushell advanced judicial review as only constituting part of a constitutional dialogue between courts and legislatures.[11] Under the model of constitutional dialogue, judicial review does not function as a 'judicial veto over the democratic process'.[12] Instead it operates 'as an opportunity for dialogue between the legislature and the judiciary over how public policy objectives and human rights commitments could be adequately balanced.'[13] The judiciary and the legislature thus share responsibility for constitutional interpretation, with neither having the final authority over the other.[14] As such, '[t]he court-legislature dialectic is centred on the critical evaluation of the legislative specification of a constitutional right.'[15]

According to Dawson, the EU may prove 'a fertile breeding ground' for the concept of constitutional dialogue.[16] Firstly, the constitutional dialogue might mediate the different national traditions of judicial review.[17] Secondly, in light of the political diversity of the Union, the CJEU might do well to involve the legislature in the resolution of conflicts between EU legislation and constitutional rights, since the legislature might be better placed to take into account different interests and consider alternative solutions.[18] Thirdly, in light of the high level of constitutionalisation of the EU legal order, the CJEU has to resolve many conflicts between different values or rights in the Treaties, and since fundamental rights are not 'de-politicised concepts', it might be normatively attractive to involve the legislature as well in joint constitutional interpretation.[19]

Nevertheless, Dawson concludes that the institutional structure of the EU 'limits the incentives necessary for legal and political actors to constitutionally engage'.[20] Firstly, the EU legislature does not always possess the necessary competence under the Treaties to adopt measures responding to the CJEU.[21] Secondly, the CJEU does not always make the reasons for its decisions explicit, making it difficult for the legislature to know how it can respond to the CJEU.[22] Thirdly, the CJEU does not have clear institutional incentives to engage with the

10 Alexander Bickel, *The Least Dangerous Branch: The Supreme Court at the Bar of Politics* (Yale University Press 1986).
11 Hogg and Bushell (n 9) 79.
12 Mark Dawson, 'Constitutional Dialogue between Courts and Legislatures in the European Union: Prospects and Limits' (2013) 19 European Public Law 369, 373.
13 ibid.
14 Grégoire CN Webber, 'The Unfulfilled Potential of the Court and Legislature Dialogue' (2009) 42 Canadian Journal of Political Science 443, 454.
15 ibid 453.
16 Dawson (n 12) 370.
17 ibid 377–8.
18 ibid 378–81.
19 ibid 382–4.
20 ibid 369.
21 ibid 386–88.
22 ibid 388–90.

legislature, even more so since an 'override' of its decisions is very difficult in practice.[23]

However, as far as EU data protection law is concerned, the reasons mentioned above seem less problematic for constitutional dialogue to work in a meaningful manner. It is clear that the EU legislature has a specific competence to adopt data protection rules based on Article 16 TFEU. Moreover, although criticism has been levelled against the sometimes opaque reasoning of multiple CJEU judgements relating to data protection, in some instances the CJEU has been very specific as to where the EU legislature (or other EU institutions) did not adequately justify its measures or has given hints as to how the political institutions could address these shortcomings. For example, the judgements *Digital Rights Ireland*[24] and *Schrems*[25] contain a detailed list of shortcomings inherent in the Data Retention Directive (DRD) and the Commission's Safe Harbour Decision.[26] The last inhibiting aspect, surrounding the lack of clear institutional incentives to engage with the legislature, might also be also problematic in the data protection context. For a constitutional dialogue between the CJEU and the EU legislature to work within the field of EU data protection law, the willingness of the CJEU to engage would prove of singular importance.

2.2 The Vertical Axis: Inserting Constitutional Courts Into a Constitutional Trilogue

The willingness of constitutional courts to engage, however, also proves of singular importance since the mutual relationship between the CJEU and the EU legislature is not the only relevant relationship that has to be assessed when it comes to elaborating fundamental rights through legislation at EU level. In their respective roles, constitutional courts are confronted with EU legislation and EU fundamental rights within the scope of EU law. They have to enforce EU law (and its concomitant fundamental rights protection) in light of the primacy of EU law.

Some authors have been sceptical about the involvement of constitutional courts with EU fundamental rights. For example, Komárek has argued that, notwithstanding efforts to 'politicise' fundamental rights at the EU level, no proper deliberative mechanism, comparable to the one in national constitutional democracies, exists at the EU level.[27] Therefore, embracing EU fundamental rights

23 ibid 390–4.

24 Joined Cases C-293/12 and C-594/12 *Digital Rights Ireland and Others* [2014] ECLI:EU:C:2014:238.

25 Case C-362/14 *Schrems* [2015] ECLI:EU:C:2015:650.

26 Commission Decision of 26 July 2000 pursuant to Directive 95/46/EC of the European Parliament and of the Council on the adequacy of the protection provided by the safe harbour privacy principles and related frequently asked questions issued by the US Department of Commerce [2000] OJ L 215/7.

27 Jan Komárek, 'Why National Constitutional Courts Should Not Embrace EU Fundamental Rights' in Sybe de Vries, Ulf Bernitz and Stephen Weatherill (eds), *The EU Charter of Fundamental Rights as a Binding Instrument: Five Years Old and Growing* (Hart Publishing 2015) 87–8.

would undermine the constitutional courts' role in their national constitutional democracy. One might disagree, however, with this characterisation of the EU's political process. In the example of the fundamental right to data protection, legislation was adopted at the EU level to implement that fundamental right through more precise rules. The GDPR came into force after prolonged negotiations between the European Parliament (which directly represents the Union's citizens) and the Council (which consists of representatives of each Member State at the ministerial level). Numerous civil society organisations could also make their interests known to the EU's political institutions. As such, a fundamental right was shaped and further elaborated at the EU level through a distinctly political process.[28] Moreover, constitutional courts would be obliged to obey the CJEU rulings in any case, in light of the primacy of EU law, even if they would not recognise the Charter as a standard of review. It is therefore preferable for constitutional courts to include themselves in the constitutional trilogue by referring preliminary questions to the CJEU, which would give them the opportunity to signal their concerns or interpretations of EU (fundamental rights) legislation to the CJEU.

It is therefore argued that constitutional courts should also engage in interpretation of EU law, and *a fortiori* of EU fundamental rights. It should not be forgotten that 'Europeanization has reshaped courts performing constitutional adjudication and continues to do so' and that this 'transformative process' has further accelerated since the Charter became legally binding.[29] As correctly stated by Rauchegger:

> it is not practicable to dissect national measures that are determined by EU law neatly into their EU and their national elements and to assign their review in light of the Charter and their review in light of national fundamental rights to the ordinary and the constitutional judiciary respectively.[30]

When constitutional courts use the Charter as a standard of review, they can thus combine the review of national measures in light of both national and EU fundamental rights. In that way, constitutional courts would take up their mandate as courts of Union law, just like ordinary courts.[31] Furthermore, just like for ordinary

28 For a behind-the-scenes look at the GDPR negotiations, see the documentary *Democracy: Im Rausch Der Daten* (directed by David Bernet, 2015).

29 Armin von Bogdandy, Christoph Grabenwarter and Peter M Huber, 'Constitutional Adjudication in the European Legal Space' in Armin von Bogdandy, Christoph Grabenwarter and Peter M Huber (eds), *The Max Planck Handbooks in European Public Law: Volume III: Constitutional Adjudication: Institutions* (Oxford University Press 2020) 4.

30 Clara Rauchegger, 'National Constitutional Courts as Guardians of the Charter: A Comparative Appraisal of the German Federal Constitutional Court's Right to Be Forgotten Judgments' (2020) 22 Cambridge Yearbook of European Legal Studies 258, 275.

31 For an analysis of the 'Simmenthal' mandate of national constitutional courts, see Monica Claes, *The National Courts' Mandate in the European Constitution* (Hart Publishing 2006) 452–64.

courts, this is not *a priori* a problematic mandate for them to take up, since '[l]ike ordinary court judges, constitutional court judges can wear two hats simultaneously. They can be judges of EU law and judges of national law at the same time.'[32]

Therefore, it is argued that constitutional courts should be included in the deliberative process surrounding EU fundamental rights legislation. Since it will be a specific piece of EU legislation that will bring a national measure within the scope of EU law, the constitutional courts' interpretation of EU law in that regard will concentrate on the relevant piece of EU legislation rather than on EU primary law, such as the Charter or general principles of EU law.[33] The focus on EU legislation will thus make it possible for the conversation between the Member State and the EU level to take place in a manner which is more respective of the different actors' roles and responsibilities and, in particular, the political nature of the concretisation of a fundamental right through legislation.

The deliberative process set out in Section 2.1 should thus be modified into a constitutional *trilogue*, where the EU fundamental rights legislation forms the catalyst for the constitutional trilogue, and in which the EU legislature, the CJEU and constitutional courts all shape and elaborate the interpretation of the fundamental right to data protection at EU level from their respective roles. A good example is the series of judgements by constitutional courts that declared national implementing measures implementing the DRD unconstitutional and ultimately led to the annulment of the DRD itself. This created a feedback loop of political negotiations on new harmonised data retention rules and numerous new preliminary references by apex courts.[34]

Two final remarks are in order here. Firstly, in terms of their respective power in the constitutional trilogue, it has yet to be seen to what extent the constitutional courts can persuade the CJEU or the EU legislature to change course in their case law or legislation, in case they would like them to do so. In the end, the constitutional courts would have to cede ground to the CJEU as the ultimate interpreter of EU law. However, when constitutional courts directly engage with EU fundamental rights, it could enhance their standing with the CJEU and convince the latter to take into account any potential concerns. It should be noted here that constitutional courts have already successfully demonstrated this power since, according to received wisdom, '[t]he formulation of [EU] protection for

32 Rauchegger (n 30) 276.

33 I thank Elise Muir for this point. For the sake of completeness, it should be noted that there can also be instances of interpretation of fundamental rights taking place exclusively at the level of primary law, when there is no 'implementation' of fundamental rights through EU legislation. In those cases, national measures could fall within the scope of EU law by, for example, derogations from primary law. However, as this chapter specifically deals with instances where the EU legislature has given specific expression to a fundamental right through secondary law, those situations will not be covered in this chapter.

34 Edoardo Celeste, 'The Court of Justice and the Ban on Bulk Data Retention: Expansive Potential and Future Scenarios' (2019) 15 European Constitutional Law Review 134.

fundamental rights was prompted by the constitutional courts of some Member States, especially by the *Bundesverfassungsgericht*.'[35]

Secondly, the metaphor of a constitutional trilogue could be broadened with other involved actors. For example, in the case of EU legislation that does not envisage total harmonisation, national parliaments have a role to play when making use of their discretion in implementing EU law. A good example is, again, the aforementioned series of judgements by different constitutional courts that declared their national legislatures' implementing measures implementing the DRD to be unconstitutional. In that regard, '[i]n the [constitutional] courts' view, national legislators did not make use of the implementation discretion in a responsible way for such a sensitive matter as data protection'.[36] Although national parliaments could indeed be seen as relevant actors in this regard, they are not included in this chapter since they cooperate, in general, in a less directly dialogic manner with the other actors involved. In the same manner, one could also include the European Court of Human Rights (ECtHR) in the analysis, where the ECtHR could play the role of a 'common reference point' for the CJEU and the constitutional courts.[37] This chapter, however, focuses solely on the impact that legislation giving specific expression to an EU fundamental right has on the judicial actors of the EU legal order: the CJEU as the ultimate interpreter of EU law, and constitutional courts in light of their position 'at the intersection between legal orders'.[38]

3 The Scope of Application of EU Fundamental Rights With Regard to Member States in the Case Law of the CJEU: Between Unity and Diversity

As for the field of EU data protection law, the EU legislature has given specific expression to the fundamental right to data protection enshrined in Article 8 CFR with the adoption of various pieces of EU data protection legislation. The pieces of secondary legislation that concretise the fundamental right have an extensive scope of application, both in their statutory language and as interpreted in the case law of the CJEU. The broad scope of application of secondary EU data protection law also impacts the scope of application of the right to data protection in the Charter. Pursuant to Article 51(1), first sentence CFR, the Charter also applies to the Member States 'when they are implementing Union law'. Accordingly, the

35 Koen Lenaerts and Piet Van Nuffel, *EU Constitutional Law* (Tim Corthaut ed, Oxford University Press 2021) 660–661. See also G Federico Mancini and David T Keeling, 'Democracy and the European Court of Justice' (1994) 57 The Modern Law Review 175, 187.

36 Darinka Piqani, 'The Role of National Constitutional Courts in Issues of Compliance' in Marise Cremona (ed), *Compliance and the Enforcement of EU Law* (Oxford University Press 2012) 145.

37 Jan Podkowik, Robert Rybski and Marek Zubik, 'Judicial Dialogue on Data Retention Laws: A Breakthrough for European Constitutional Courts?' (2021) 19 International Journal of Constitutional Law 1597.

38 von Bogdandy, Grabenwarter and Huber (n 29) 6.

broad scope of application of EU data protection law and of the fundamental right to data protection also impacts Member State action. This section will show how the CJEU draws the line between the application of the Charter and/or national constitutional rights to Member State action, which is based on the EU legislature's choice to require more unity or allow more diversity in the relevant fundamental rights standards.

In general, the Charter applies to all situations governed by EU law, since, as the CJEU clarified in *Åkerberg Fransson*, the applicability of EU law entails the applicability of the Charter rights.[39] In that way, the Charter forms the 'shadow' of EU law.[40] Throughout the years, a suite of scholars has attempted to categorise the CJEU's case law concerning the application of EU fundamental rights.[41] In general, the Charter applies to the Member States in two broad situations: where Member States adopt measures to comply with the obligations set by EU law[42] and where Member States derogate from EU law.[43] In practice, however, multiple cases hover in a grey zone where it is not immediately clear whether Member States are indeed implementing EU law.[44] Therefore, in the *Iida* case, the CJEU provided national courts with non-exhaustive and non-cumulative criteria, which may be taken into account to assess the (in)applicability of the Charter.[45]

However, '[o]nce it is established that a national measure implements EU law, and hence the Charter applies, the question arises whether national law may provide for a higher level of protection of fundamental rights.'[46] In its case law concerning Article 51 and Article 53 CFR, the CJEU has 'embraced a pluralist model of fundamental rights protection' in which it focuses on the EU legislature as the institution that sets a uniform EU-wide standard or allows diversity for the Member States.[47] On the one hand, where EU law entirely determines the way in which the Member States must act, the Charter displaces the application of national fundamental rights.[48] On the other hand, as the CJEU held in *Åkerberg*

39 Case C-617/10 *Åkerberg Fransson* [2013] ECLI:EU:C:2013:105, paras 19 and 21.
40 Koen Lenaerts and José Antonio Gutiérrez-Fons, 'The Place of the Charter in the EU Constitutional Edifice' in Steve Peers and others (eds), *The EU Charter of Fundamental Rights: A Commentary* (Hart Publishing 2014) 1567–8.
41 Michael Dougan, 'Judicial Review of Member State Action under the General Principles and the Charter: Defining the "Scope of Union Law"' (2015) 52 Common Market Law Review 1201.
42 Case 5/88 *Wachauf* [1989] ECLI:EU:C:1989:321.
43 Case C-260/89 *ERT* [1991] ECLI:EU:C:1991:254.
44 Allan Rosas, 'Five Years of Charter Case Law: Some Observations' in Sybe de Vries, Ulf Bernitz and Stephen Weatherill (eds), *The EU Charter of Fundamental Rights as a Binding Instrument: Five Years Old and Growing* (Bloomsbury Publishing 2015) 18.
45 Case C-40/11 *Iida* [2012] ECLI:EU:C:2012:691, para 79.
46 Koen Lenaerts, 'The Role of the EU Charter in the Member States' in Michal Bobek and Jeremias Adams-Prassl (eds), *The EU Charter of Fundamental Rights in the Member States* (Hart Publishing 2020) 26.
47 Lenaerts and Gutiérrez-Fons (n 40) 1591.
48 Daniel Sarmiento, 'Who's Afraid of the Charter? The Court of Justice, National Courts and the New Framework of Fundamental Rights Protection in Europe' (2013) 50 Common Market Law Review 1267, 1289.

Fransson and *Melloni*, national authorities and courts remain free to apply national standards of fundamental rights protection when reviewing a national measure which is 'not entirely determined by EU law', provided that the level of protection provided for by the Charter, as interpreted by the Court, and the primacy, unity and effectiveness of EU law are not thereby compromised.[49] Thus, Article 53 CFR operates dynamically, depending on the specific features of the relevant legislative framework.[50] It could operate as a minimum 'floor' of fundamental rights protection, allowing the Member States to apply higher national standards of fundamental protection, or it could require the EU standard to be applied, without the possibility of applying higher national standards of fundamental rights protection.[51]

A broad distinction can be made between the two poles of total harmonisation and minimum harmonisation. The judgements of *Melloni*[52] and *M.A.S. and M.B.*[53] can clarify these poles.[54]

In *Melloni*, the CJEU held that Article 53 CFR does not allow a Member State to apply a higher national standard of fundamental rights protection to make the surrender of a person convicted *in absentia* conditional upon the conviction being open to review in the issuing Member State.[55] The European Arrest Warrant Framework Decision (EAWFD)[56] constitutes a harmonisation of the conditions of execution of a European arrest warrant in the event of a conviction rendered *in absentia*.[57] Thus, allowing a Member State to apply a higher national standard of fundamental rights protection under Article 53 CFR, would cast doubt on the uniformity of the standard of fundamental rights protection as set by the EU legislature.[58]

In contrast to *Melloni*, the judgement in *M.A.S. and M.B.* (also known as *Taricco II*) is a good example of a case where national courts can apply national standards of fundamental rights protection in areas that are not fully harmonised by EU law.[59] The limitation rules applicable to criminal proceedings relating to

49 *Åkerberg Fransson* (n 39), para 29; Case C-399/11 *Melloni* [2013] ECLI:EU:C:2013:107, para 60.
50 François-Xavier Millet, 'How Much Lenience for How Much Cooperation? On the First Preliminary Reference of the French Constitutional Council to the Court of Justice' (2014) 51 Common Market Law Review 195.
51 Aida Torres Pérez, 'Constitutional Dialogue on the European Arrest Warrant: The Spanish Constitutional Court Knocking on Luxembourg's Door' (2012) 8 European Constitutional Law Review 105, 117.
52 *Melloni* (n 49).
53 Case 42/17 *M.A.S. and M.B.* [2017] ECLI:EU:C:2017:936.
54 These cases are also used as distinguishing examples by Lenaerts (n 47) 28–32.
55 *Melloni* (n 49), paras 46 and 64.
56 Council Framework Decision 2002/584 of 13 June 2002 on the European arrest warrant and the surrender procedures between Member States [2002] OJ L 190/1, art 4a(1).
57 *Melloni* (n 49), para 62.
58 ibid para 63.
59 Daniel Sarmiento, 'To Bow at the Rhythm of an Italian Tune' (*Despite our Differences*, 5 December 2017) <https://despiteourdifferencesblog.wordpress.com/2017/12/05/to-bow-at-the-rhythm-of-an-italian-tune/> accessed 22 March 2022.

VAT had not been harmonised by the EU legislature at the time of the main proceedings. Therefore, the CJEU held that Italy was, at that time, free to provide that in its legal system, those rules form part of substantive criminal law and are thereby subject to the principle that offences and penalties must be defined by law.[60] National courts should disapply the limitation rules if they were to deter the effective penalisation of VAT fraud. However, in disapplying those limitation rules, the national courts have to ensure that the fundamental rights of persons accused of committing criminal offences are observed.[61] They remain free, in that respect, to apply national standards of fundamental rights protection as long as the level of protection provided for by the Charter, and the primacy, unity and effectiveness of EU law are not thereby compromised.[62]

4 The Case Law of Constitutional Courts Engaging with the Charter: A Janus-Faced Evolution

As seen in the previous section, since the Charter also applies to the Member States 'when they are implementing Union law', according to Article 51(1), first sentence CFR, the broad scope of application of EU data protection law and of the fundamental right to data protection also impacts Member State action. This section will therefore analyse the application of the EU fundamental right to data protection to action by the Member States and the role that three constitutional courts (the Austrian *Verfassungsgerichtshof* (VfGH), the Italian *Corte costituzionale* (CC) and the German *Bundesverfassungsgericht* (BVerfG)) have played in the constitutional trilogue. These constitutional courts have been chosen for the case study since, among the different constitutional courts of the Member States, they have most clearly laid out their way of engaging with EU fundamental rights in their recent jurisprudence. The workings of a nascent constitutional trilogue between the EU legislature, the CJEU and constitutional courts will be further explained in this regard.

In recent years, several constitutional courts have explicitly engaged with the applicability of EU fundamental rights as a standard of review under their respective domestic law. The VfGH, the CC and the BVerfG delivered judgements precisely on the application of the EU fundamental right to data protection as a standard of review under their respective domestic law. These courts are keen on including themselves in the process of European integration undertaken via legislation giving specific expression to Charter rights. They explicitly adopt EU fundamental rights within their own domestic judicial review standards whenever cases are covered both by national fundamental rights and Charter rights. As Sarmiento noted in 2013, 'Åkerberg Fransson and Melloni have set the basic rules for a new framework of fundamental rights in Europe.'[63] These constitutional courts clearly reckon with the implications of this post-Charter European fundamental

60 *M.A.S. and M.B.* (n 53), paras 44–5.
61 ibid para 46.
62 ibid para 47.
63 Sarmiento (n 48) 1269.

rights landscape. The full potential of a constitutional trilogue between the CJEU, the EU legislature and the constitutional courts is, however, still to be realised to a deeper extent. The constitutional courts could do so when they start engaging more deeply with the content of EU legislation giving expression to Charter rights and sending preliminary references to Luxembourg whenever necessary.

4.1 The Austrian Constitutional Court: Acting as a Pioneer Among Constitutional Courts

In 2012, the VfGH was the first constitutional court to recognise that the Charter rights could be considered as a domestic standard of review. In that regard, it was EU legislation giving specific expression to the right to data protection enshrined in Article 8 CFR that formed the catalyst for the engagement of the VfGH with EU fundamental rights. Although most references by the VfGH to the Charter are characterised as 'mere name-dropping',[64] there are promising signs that it is willing to engage in a deeper analysis of EU legislation giving specific expression to the fundamental right to data protection.

In the reasoning of its 2012 judgement, the VfGH focused on its position within Austrian constitutional law, acting as a 'monopolist' court within a Kelsenian system of centralised constitutional review. According to the VfGH, 'it would be contrary to the notion of a centralised constitutional jurisdiction provided for in the Austrian Federal Constitution if the Constitutional Court were not competent to adjudicate on largely congruent rights such as those contained in the [Charter].'[65] Therefore, based on the principle of equivalence, the Charter rights may also be invoked as constitutionally guaranteed rights before the VfGH. Moreover, they may constitute a standard of review within their scope of application.[66] This is so, according to the VfGH, 'if the guarantee contained in the [Charter] is similar in its wording and purpose to rights that are guaranteed by the Austrian Federal Constitution'.[67] It would have to be decided on a case-by-case basis which of the Charter rights are comparable to rights guaranteed by the Austrian Federal Constitution (including ECHR rights) to constitute a standard of review for proceedings before the VfGH.[68] As will be seen below, the BVerfG follows a very comparable reasoning in its *Right to be Forgotten I and II* judgements.

Since then, the VfGH has declared Article 8 CFR to be a right comparable to constitutionally guaranteed rights in Austria, and thus also a constitutionally guaranteed right on its own, in a judgement in which it referred a request for a preliminary ruling to the CJEU about the DRD.[69] This judgement clearly shows

64 Rauchegger (n 30) 271.
65 VfSlg 19.632/2012 (2012) ECLI:AT:VFGH:2012:U466.2011, para 34 (official translation).
66 ibid para 35.
67 ibid para 35 (official translation).
68 ibid para 36.
69 VfSlg 19.702/2012 (2012) ECLI:AT:VFGH:2012:G47.2012; VfSlg 19.892/2014 (2014) ECLI:AT:VFGH:2014:G47.2012.

that the VfGH actively included itself in the constitutional trilogue by communicating to the CJEU the problems it saw in the DRD as adopted by the EU legislature. Notably, the VfGH considered that the DRD could only be implemented in Austrian law in a manner that would infringe on the fundamental right to data protection as enshrined in §1 DSG 2000 (a right with constitutional rank). The VfGH would thus be precluded from reviewing the national implementing measures against the standard of §1 DSG 2000, given the primacy of the DRD over the domestic right to data protection.[70]

The fact that the VfGH sent a request for a preliminary ruling to the CJEU in the case that ultimately led to the *Digital Rights Ireland and Seitlinger and Others* judgement shows that it intends to take a constructive position vis-à-vis EU fundamental rights. It is well-known that the VfGH is one of the more active constitutional courts when it comes to submitting preliminary references under Article 267 TFEU.[71] Even more so, however, it is the content of its preliminary questions that shows a clear interest to engage with the EU data protection law framework. Thus, the VfGH is eager to take up its position in the constitutional trilogue and is genuinely interested in the interpretation of EU fundamental rights legislation in light of the Charter.

After the CJEU declared the DRD invalid in *Digital Rights Ireland and Seitlinger and Others*,[72] the VfGH felt free again, in response to the CJEU, to use §1 DSG 2000 and Article 8 ECHR as standards of review for the Austrian data retention measures.[73] It considered that if the national legislator adopts provisions interfering not only with a Charter right but also with a constitutionally guaranteed right at the national level, when acting within its margin of appreciation in implementing EU law, it would review these national provisions primarily in light of the constitutional right. However, this only applies under the assumption that the latter has the same scope of application as the Charter right and that its limitations for interferences correspond to those of the Charter right or foresee even stricter conditions. The VfGH found that this was indeed the case for Article 8 ECHR as well as for § 1 DSG 2000.[74] In those matters where the national legislator has discretion in implementing EU law, the level of protection is unaffected by the Charter, according to the VfGH.[75] The reasoning by the VfGH here mirrors the CJEU's judgements in *Åkerberg Fransson* and *Melloni* very closely: it also focuses on the degree of diversity that is allocated to the Member States by the EU legislature in the relevant piece of EU legislation.

70 VfSlg 19.702/2012 (n 69), para 3.2.
71 Monica Claes, 'Luxembourg, Here We Come? Constitutional Courts and the Preliminary Reference Procedure' (2015) 16 German Law Journal 1331, 1338.
72 Joined Cases C-293/12 and C-594/12 *Digital Rights Ireland and Seitlinger and Others* [2014] ECLI:EU:C:2014:238
73 VfSlg 19.892/2014 (n 69), para 2.2.4.
74 ibid para 2.2.8.
75 ibid para 2.2.9.

4.2 The Italian Constitutional Court: Trying to Follow in the Footsteps?

The CC has also explicitly engaged with EU fundamental rights in its case law in the last few years. Most references to the Charter are still very limited in nature, though, and there has not yet been a deeper engagement with EU legislation giving expression to the right to data protection, in contrast to the VfGH. Moreover, in comparison to the VfGH and the BVerfG, it does not always seem to follow the CJEU's *Åkerberg Fransson* and *Melloni* case law. Therefore, the CC would do well to engage more directly with the CJEU. There are promising signs that it is willing to use the preliminary reference procedure to push for a constitutional trilogue with the CJEU and EU legislature, as can be witnessed from the '*Taricco* saga' and in a more recent case outside the field of data protection law mentioned below.

At first, the CC seemed to be focused on its role in the centralised system of constitutional review in Italy by holding that in cases of 'dual preliminarity' (*doppia pregiudizialità*) in the field of fundamental rights protection (the situation in which a national law potentially infringes both the Italian Constitution and the Charter), lower court judges would be obliged to submit a request for a preliminary ruling first to the CC whenever the scope and content of a Charter right overlap with a right enshrined in the Constitution.[76] In these cases, the CC would decide its judgement in light of constitutional provisions, and only, if applicable, in light of EU provisions as well, in accordance with whichever system is most appropriate to the specific case.[77] Although the CC itself referred to the 2012 judgement of the VfGH as containing an analogous line of reasoning, there is a difference with the VfGH's approach (and with the CJEU's case law). Namely, the CC did not differentiate between situations of total and partial determination by EU law (i.e. whether the Member States have a margin of discretion or not).[78]

A little over a year later, the CC seemed to act more friendly towards EU law by being less strict on the priority of the question of constitutionality: it stressed more explicitly that its own involvement in a given case does not preclude the ability of ordinary courts to submit any question they deem necessary to the CJEU.[79] The added value of this case, compared to the earlier 2017 case, was the claim that national law also contradicted EU legislation intimately connected with rights in the Charter, specifically, the DPD. As the CC itself put it:

> [t]he principles laid out by the [DPD] are marked, indeed, by a singular connection with the relevant provisions of the [Charter], not only in the sense that they provide it with detail or implement it, but also in quite the opposite sense that they

76 Corte costituzionale 269/2017 (2017) ECLI:IT:COST:2017:269, para 5.2. Pietro Faraguna, 'Constitutional Rights First: The Italian Constitutional Court fine-tunes its "Europarechtsųfreundlichkeit"' (*Verfassungsblog*, 14 December 2018) <https://verfassungsblog.de/constitutional-rights-first-the-italian-constitutional-court-fine-tunes-its-europarechtsfreundlichkeit/> accessed 30 March 2022.

77 Corte costituzionale 269/2017 (n 76), para 5.2.

78 Rauchegger (n 30) 272.

79 Corte costituzionale 20/2019 (2019) ECLI:IT:COST:2019:20, para 2.3.

> constituted the 'model' for those rules and, therefore, they can be used as evidence of their nature, as expressed in the Explanations relating to the [Charter].[80]

Therefore, this case gave the CC an ideal chance to take a more active position in the constitutional trilogue by referring a preliminary reference to the CJEU on the interpretation of EU data protection legislation. However, it did not take this chance and even misinterpreted EU data protection legislation and Article 8 CFR when it negated the direct effect of the right to data protection because of the origin of the right in the provisions of, inter alia, the DPD.[81] The CC would do well to involve the CJEU via preliminary references to get a correct interpretation of the right to data protection and the relationship between primary and secondary law in that regard. This would be just like the VfGH was eager to do it in its preliminary reference to the CJEU in 2012.

Through its doctrine, the CC clearly showed that it wants to have a direct say on the interpretation of EU law and EU fundamental rights. By extending its judicial review under domestic law to all instances in which the scope and content of a right in the Constitution overlap with a Charter right, the CC could indeed extensively adjudicate cases concerning the interpretation of rights laid down in the Charter and/or in secondary EU law.[82] Nevertheless, these judgements do not present a clear-cut picture of a constitutional court entirely keen on including itself in a conversation with the EU legislature and the CJEU. For example, the criterion it uses to decide on the application of Charter rights is quite vague: it will base its ruling on constitutional provisions and EU law if applicable, 'according to whichever system is most appropriate to the specific case'.[83] In the 2019 judgement, the CC decided to express its own evaluation of the challenged national provisions above all in light of constitutional provisions and only 'as supplemented by the principles of European extraction'.[84] Moreover, the CC did not contemplate the possibility of submitting a request for a preliminary ruling to the CJEU.[85] If it had done so, it could have entered into a conversation with the CJEU to try to persuade the CJEU to interpret Article 8 CFR and the relevant provisions of the DPD in harmony with the constitutional traditions common to the Member States. Therefore, one cannot interpret the CC's approach, as of yet, as engaging in a complete dialogue with the CJEU through the preliminary reference procedure.

80 ibid para 2.1 (unofficial translation).

81 ibid para 2 (unofficial translation). Oreste Pollicino and Giorgio Repetto, 'Not to be Pushed Aside: the Italian Constitutional Court and the European Court of Justice' (*Verfassungsblog*, 27 February 2019) <https://verfassungsblog.de/not-to-be-pushed-aside-the-italian-constitutional-court-and-the-european-court-of-justice/> accessed 30 March 2022.

82 ibid.

83 Corte costituzionale 269/2017 (n 76), para 5.2; Corte costituzionale 20/2019 (n 79), para 2.1.

84 Corte costituzionale 20/2019 (n 79), paras 2.3 and 3.1 (unofficial translation).

85 Pollicino and Repetto (n 81).

In a more recent case outside of the field of data protection law, however, the CC undertook a direct judicial dialogue by using the preliminary reference procedure.[86] The factual situation and the reasoning by the CC, in this case, are very similar to the 2012 judgement of the VfGH referred to above.[87] Just like the VfGH, the CC stated that national legislation implementing EU law could violate provisions of the Constitution, which meant that a finding of unconstitutionality risked creating a conflict with EU law.[88] In addition, it argued that the EU legislation in question was ambiguous and, under a certain interpretation, could even be incompatible with Articles 47 and 48 CFR.[89] Therefore, 'in the aforementioned spirit of loyal cooperation between national and European courts in establishing common levels of protection of fundamental rights (an objective of primary importance in matters subject to regulatory harmonisation such as the one under examination),' the Court decided the following. It was necessary to request clarification from the CJEU on the exact interpretation and possibly the very validity of the EU legislation at issue before ruling on the question of constitutionality.[90] This case demonstrates that the CC could follow the same trajectory when similar cases would arise with regard to EU data protection legislation or other EU fundamental rights legislation and that these pieces of legislation could thus trigger a constitutional trilogue with the CJEU and the EU legislature.

4.3 The German Federal Constitutional Court: Fully Taking Up its European Mandate

The traditional approach of the BVerfG to EU fundamental rights used to be a strict separation between the application of EU and national fundamental rights.[91] Their respective spheres of influence were strictly demarcated on the basis of complete or partial determination of a national measure by EU law. If a national measure was completely determined by EU law, the BVerfG considered that it had no jurisdiction since these cases were to be reviewed in light of EU fundamental rights, for which it was not competent.[92] If a national measure was only partially determined by EU law, the BVerfG considered that it had jurisdiction and reviewed these cases solely in light of the German *Grundgesetz* (Basic Law, BL).[93] The Charter did not constitute a standard of review in the case law of the BVerfG.

86 Corte costituzionale 117/2019 (2019) ECLI:IT:COST:2019:117.
87 VfSlg 19.702/2012 (n 69).
88 Corte costituzionale 117/2019 (n 86), para 9.
89 ibid para 9.
90 ibid para 10.
91 Rauchegger (n 30) 261. See also Daniel Thym, 'Separation versus Fusion – or: How to Accommodate National Autonomy and the Charter? Diverging Visions of the German Constitutional Court and the European Court of Justice' (2013) 9 European Constitutional Law Review 391.
92 Rauchegger (n 30) 262.
93 ibid.

With this strict separation approach, the BVerfG had made itself irrelevant in areas completely determined by EU law, which would only continue in the near future because of the broad scope of application of the Charter and EU legislation.[94] However, in the second 'Right to be forgotten' case (*RBTF II*), the BVerfG changed direction. Instead of declaring the constitutional complaint (*Verfassungsbeschwerde*) inadmissible, it decided, for the first time, to conduct a fundamental rights review on the basis of EU fundamental rights in a case of fully harmonised EU law.[95] In this way, the BVerfG left its focus on 'separation' behind in favour of 'fusion'.[96] From now on, the BVerfG has also actively inserted itself into a constitutional trilogue with the EU legislature and the CJEU by directly engaging with EU fundamental rights legislation. References for preliminary questions to the CJEU, whenever necessary, would complete the picture of a court that wants to influence the interpretation of EU fundamental rights.

In *RTBF II*, the matter at hand (a claim against a search engine operator to dereference personal data) is governed by fully harmonised EU data protection law. The adoption of the GDPR as a regulation confirms the objective of full harmonisation.[97] The Charter constitutes the sole standard of review in the case of fully harmonised EU law, whereas BL rights are inapplicable since their application would run counter to the objective of full harmonisation.[98] By applying the Charter as the standard of review in cases of fully harmonised EU law, the BVerfG fully 'exercises its responsibility with regard to European integration' (*Integrationsverantwortung*) under the BL.[99] The BVerfG acknowledges the need to cooperate closely with the CJEU in the correct interpretation of EU fundamental rights legislation by stating that it will request a preliminary ruling from the CJEU where necessary.[100] The BVerfG notes that it will consider referrals to the CJEU to a far greater extent in cases of full harmonisation of EU law, where it applies the Charter as the relevant standard of review. This is contrasted with cases where the Charter applies in addition to the BL, but where the BVerfG conducts its review based on the BL rights.[101]

The BVerfG showed that it clearly grappled with the CJEU's *Åkerberg Fransson* and *Melloni* case law by stating that the extent of harmonisation of EU legislation should be assessed correctly since the determination of whether to apply the BL rights or the Charter as the standard of review essentially hinges on the distinction between fully harmonised EU law and EU law that affords the Member States

94 ibid 264.
95 Daniel Thym, 'Friendly Takeover, or: The Power of the "First Word". The German Constitutional Court Embraces the Charter of Fundamental Rights as a Standard of Domestic Judicial Review' (2020) 16 European Constitutional Law Review 187, 195.
96 Thym (n 91).
97 BVerfG 1 BvR 276/17 (2019) ECLI:DE:BVerfG:2019:rs20191106.1bvr027617, paras 40–41.
98 ibid paras 42–4 and 46.
99 ibid paras 53–4.
100 ibid para 68.
101 BVerfG 1 BvR 16/13 (2019) ECLI:DE:BVerfG:2019:rs20191106.1bvr001613, paras 43–5.

more diversity.[102] In that respect, the relevant provisions of EU law and the legislative context and objective of the piece of legislation of which they form part should be examined.[103] Whether the piece of EU legislation constitutes a directive or a regulation can be a relevant element but does not in itself lead to a definitive conclusion, since regulations can still contain provisions affording the Member States latitude and directives can set definitive and binding standards.[104] The central assessment is whether the specific provisions of EU law seek to accommodate diversity or whether they generally pursue the aim of uniform application of the law.[105] As to the solution to this specific case, the BVerfG reasonably concluded that a request for a preliminary ruling from the CJEU was not necessary since the relevant issues had already been clarified in CJEU case law.[106] It has been argued that the BVerfG deviated from the CJEU's case law by requiring a balancing exercise between the rights to privacy and data protection, on the one hand, and the rights to freedom of expression and information, on the other hand.[107] However, the CJEU had in fact already recognised the necessity of a balancing exercise for the processing of requests for dereferencing, one month and a half before the BVerfG decided its *RTBF I and II* cases.[108]

In *RTBF I*, the processing of personal data was carried out for journalistic purposes and fell under Article 85(2) GDPR, which allows the Member States to provide for exemptions or derogations to specific GDPR provisions, and thus does not constitute fully harmonised EU law.[109] The BVerfG concluded that the BL rights constitute the primary standard of review when the case concerns EU law that is only partially harmonised.[110] In such cases, the BVerfG applies the BL rights as the primary standard of review, irrespective of whether the Charter is also applicable.[111] Here again, the BVerfG places itself in line with the CJEU case law, which recognises that national authorities and courts remain free to apply national fundamental rights standards within the Charter's scope of application, provided that the level of protection of the Charter as interpreted by the CJEU and the primacy, unity and effectiveness of EU law are not compromised.[112]

The BVerfG is the constitutional court that engages most intensely with the CJEU's *Åkerberg Fransson* and *Melloni* case law. It argues that by deciding on the

102 ibid para 77.
103 ibid paras 78–9.
104 ibid para 79.
105 ibid para 80.
106 ibid paras 137–138. Case C-131/12 *Google Spain and Google* [2014] ECLI:EU:C:2014:317; Case C-507/17 *Google (Portée territoriale du déréférencement)* [2019] ECLI:EU:C:2019:772; Case C-136/17 *GC and Others* [2019] ECLI:EU:C:2019:773.
107 Paul Friedl, 'A New European Fundamental Rights Court: The German Constitutional Court on the Right to Be Forgotten' (2020) 5 European Papers 447, 457.
108 *GC and Others* (n 106), para 59.
109 BVerfG 1 BvR 16/13 (n 101), para 74.
110 ibid paras 41 and 74.
111 ibid paras 41–2 and 45.
112 *Åkerberg Fransson* (n 39), para 29; *Melloni* (n 49), para 60.

degree of harmonisation of EU legislation, the EU legislature lays out the framework for the application of the fundamental rights of the Member States, striking a 'federal balance' between the EU and the Member States.[113] In scenarios where EU legislation provides for diversity, Article 53 CFR allows cases to be resolved on the basis of national constitutional rights (unlike in the case of fully harmonised legislation).[114] The 'floor' of the Charter should, at minimum, be respected. Still, here the BVerfG relies on the presumption that the BL rights simultaneously ensure the level of protection of the Charter, as interpreted by the CJEU, which it develops from the Charter's basis in the constitutional traditions common to the Member States.[115] It is possible to rebut the presumption that the BL rights guarantee the level of protection of the Charter where, in exceptional cases, there is 'specific and sufficient indication' to the contrary.[116] If that is the case, national measures implementing EU law should also be reviewed in light of the Charter.[117] The BVerfG explicitly notes that it will request a preliminary ruling from the CJEU in case this would give rise to unresolved questions regarding the Charter's interpretation.[118]

Thus, the First Senate has clearly taken account of the continuous Europeanisation and constitutionalisation of fundamental rights protection in Europe. It thus creates for itself a more direct line of communication with the CJEU, and its approach has been met with the approval of CJEU President Lenaerts.[119] Nevertheless, some potential risks do remain. For example, it will have to be seen how thoroughly the presumption of equivalent protection in the BL will be assessed in cases where EU legislation may indeed provide a higher standard of fundamental rights protection than the level of protection guaranteed by the BL. In the field of data protection law, a thorough analysis of EU data protection legislation would be necessary in order not to circumvent its level of protection. As of the *RTBF I and II* cases, the BVerfG has used its methodology towards the application of EU fundamental rights as a standard of review in two more cases related to EU data protection law. The Court limited itself to a relatively short analysis of the ePrivacy Directive and the CJEU's case law in that regard. However, the fact that the BVerfG undertook an analysis of the level of protection under the ePrivacy Directive (in comparison to the level of protection provided under national law) bodes well for the conclusion that it is willing to scrutinise the wording and context of EU legislation for concrete and sufficient indications of a higher level of protection.

113 BVerfG 1 BvR 16/13 (n 101), para 53.
114 ibid para 54.
115 ibid paras 55–6.
116 ibid paras 66–7 and 69.
117 ibid para 72.
118 ibid para 72.
119 Koen Lenaerts, 'No Member State Is More Equal than Others' (*Verfassungsblog*, 8 October 2020) <https://verfassungsblog.de/no-member-state-is-more-equal-than-others/> accessed 30 March 2022.

The BVerfG could also open up a risk of disparate treatment of harmonised EU law, if it is not accompanied by the requisite number of requests for a preliminary ruling in case of doubt. Without preliminary references, the BVerfG would be free to decide for itself whether a certain piece of EU law provides the Member States with discretion. If different national courts were to interpret the discretion afforded to the Member States in other ways, the application of fundamental rights to the same piece of EU law could be differentiated from Member State to Member State. This conclusion is all the more relevant considering that harmonisation takes place on a continuum and not in a black-and-white, either/or constellation.[120] The BVerfG and other constitutional courts should thus be advised to put the cherry on top of their 'EU law-friendly' jurisprudence and be willing to frequently refer to the CJEU preliminary questions as to the scope of harmonisation of concrete pieces of EU law. In that way, the willingness to apply different sets of fundamental rights would also be accompanied with the necessary unity in fundamental rights application in those instances where the EU legislature preferred to set a uniform standard.

5 Conclusion

This chapter has shown that EU data protection legislation can form the catalyst for what I term a 'constitutional trilogue' between the EU legislature, the CJEU and constitutional courts. In this trilogue all three types of institutions together shape, interpret and give expression to a fundamental right in a generally converging manner. In limited areas, EU data protection legislation leaves open certain margins for more divergent national interpretations of the right to data protection, which are guarded in a collaborative exercise between the aforementioned actors. However, it has yet to be seen to what extent the constitutional courts have the power to persuade the CJEU or the EU legislature to change the course of their case law or legislation.

This chapter concludes that the metaphor of a constitutional trilogue could also function as a normatively attractive model to understand the concretisation of other EU fundamental rights, subject to the competence of the EU legislature (for example, with respect to legislation concerning various social rights and the prohibition of discrimination). In those areas of EU law, different pieces of EU fundamental rights legislation with various levels of harmonisation have been interpreted by the CJEU at the invitation of both lower and constitutional courts.[121] It remains to be seen to what extent this case law depends on the specifics of the competence(s) at issue or whether this case law could be extended to

120 Mattias Wendel, 'The Two-Faced Guardian - Or How One Half of the German Federal Constitutional Court Became a European Fundamental Rights Court' (2020) 57 Common Market Law Review 1383, 1406.

121 Case C-609/17 *TSN* [2019] ECLI:EU:C:2019:981. This judgement has been confirmed in Case C-177/18 *Baldonedo Martín* [2020] ECLI:EU:C:2020:26. A similar case, regarding discrimination on the grounds of religion, is Joined Cases C-804/18 and C-341/19 *WABE and Müller Handels* [2021] ECLI:EU:C:2021:594.

more policy areas.[122] At least where the EU enjoys the competence to adopt legislation giving expression to fundamental rights, its added value is that it can function as a mechanism requiring unity or accommodating diversity in the standards of fundamental rights protection between the Member States. In that way, EU legislation makes it possible for the constitutional trilogue between the Member State and the EU level to take place in a manner which is more respective to the different actors' roles and responsibilities and, in particular, the political nature of the concretisation of a fundamental right through legislation.

122 Francesco De Cecco, 'Minimum Harmonization and the Limits of Union Fundamental Rights Review: TSN and AKT' (2021) 58 Common Market Law Review 187, 199.

6 Forgetting Identity Claims

The New Constitutional Paradigm in Multilevel Fundamental Rights Standards

Jakob Gašperin Wischhoff

1 Introduction

In light of the red thread of the book, the chapter explores convergences and divergences in the field of multilevel fundamental rights protection in the European Constitutional 'Verbund'.[1] In an attempt to navigate an ever-closer European harmonisation and the protection of national constitutional diversity, the accommodation of various fundamental rights standards puts forward the pivotal challenge of the European multilevel system.[2] On the one hand, unifying European legislation increasingly requires some form of common and shared fundamental rights standards under the EU Charter, going beyond mere minimal protection. On the other hand, the protection of national constitutional idiosyncrasies is often accompanied by the highly volatile concept of national identity,[3] which is to be understood here as unique *interpretations* of fundamental rights, potentially undermining the primacy of EU law and its unified and effective application.

The chapter firstly explicates and contextualises the landscape of national and supranational fundamental rights standards together with national (constitutional) identity claims. It analyses the disputed scope of fundamental rights application and critically demonstrates how minimum protection may become the final norm. Second, the chapter engages with the concept of identity in general, questioning the suitability of national identity's application in constitutional law from various angles. The following section then highlights an alternative approach adopted by the German Federal Constitutional Court (hereinafter: 'BVerfG'). The BVerfG held that the EU Charter could be directly applied as the only standard of fundamental rights review in national proceedings as long as the legislation in question had been fully harmonised under EU Law. This can be characterised as a

1 Andreas Voßkuhle, 'Multilevel Cooperation of the European Constitutional Courts: Der Europäische Verfassungsgerichtsverbund' (2010) 6 European Constitutional Law Review 175.

2 Dieter Grimm, 'The Various Faces of Fundamental Rights' in David Dyzenhaus, Jacco Bomhoff and Thomas Poole (eds), *The Double-Facing Constitution* (Cambridge University Press 2020) 426.

3 Federico Fabbrini and András Sajó, 'The Dangers of Constitutional Identity' (2019) 25 European Law Journal 457. Julian Scholtes, 'Abusing Constitutional Identity' (2021) 22 German Law Journal 534.

DOI: 10.4324/9781003355762-6

paradigm shift in our understanding of the multilevel fundamental rights protection in the EU and could indicate the end of identity claims. Finally, the chapter normatively scrutinises and evaluates the suggested change of paradigm of the BVerfG.

2 National and Supranational Fundamental Rights Standards

This section contextualises the challenges and open questions of the multilevel fundamental rights protection in the Union and its Member States.[4] It first explores the European constitutional design of fundamental rights protection together with identity claims (Section 2.1). Moreover, it explicates the disputed scope of fundamental rights application (Section 2.2). Finally, it demonstrates how minimum protection can become the final norm (Section 2.3).

2.1 Multilevel Constitutional Design of Fundamental Rights Protection

The European Union is commonly regarded as a Community of values[5] in light of its commitment to democracy, the rule of law, human dignity, equality and respect for human rights. The CJEU just recently stated that:

> Article 2 TEU is not merely a statement of policy guidelines or intentions, but contains values which [...] are an integral part of the very identity of the European Union as a common legal order, values which are given concrete expression in principles containing legally binding obligations for the Member States.[6]

However, the national constitutional identity argument and the resisting national apex courts,[7] most notably the German BVerfG with its *Solange I* jurisprudence,[8] prompted the ECJ to resourcefully invent the protection of fundamental rights at the Community level. In the cases of *Stauder*,[9] *Internationale Handelsgesellschaft*[10] and

4 Due to the specific focus of the questions posed, the ECHR will not be taken into account.

5 Matteo Bonelli, 'From a Community of Law to a Union of Values' (2017) 13 European Constitutional Law Review 793. Jan Wouters, 'From an Economic Community to a Union of Values: The Emergence of the EU's Commitment to Human Rights' in Manfred Nowak and others (eds), *The European Union and Human Rights Law and Policy* (Oxford University Press 2020).

6 Case C-156/21 *Hungary v European Parliament and Council of the European Union* [2022] ECLI:EU:C:2022:97 para 232.

7 William Phelan, 'The Role of the German and Italian Constitutional Courts in the Rise of EU Human Rights Jurisprudence: A Response to Delledonne & Fabbrini' (2020) TRiSS-WPS-02-2020 TRiSS Working Paper Series <https://papers.ssrn.com/sol3/papers.cfm?abstract_id=3617248> accessed 19 August 2022.

8 BVerfGE 37, 271 *(Solange I)*.

9 Case 29–69 *Erich Stauder v City of Ulm* [1969] ECR 419, ECLI:EU:C:1969:57.

10 Case 11–70 *Internationale Handelsgesellschaft* [1970] ECR 1125, ECLI:EU:C:1970:114.

Nold[11], the ECJ established the protection of fundamental rights as a part of general principles of EU law[12] while openly acknowledging that its derivative source is dependent on Member States' legal cultures and common constitutional traditions.[13]

After a gradual but continuous development of fundamental rights protection in the Union,[14] the current EU Charter of Fundamental Rights finally[15] also formally became part of EU primary law.[16] Yet, the multilevel protection of fundamental rights remains designed and interpreted ambiguously. While Article 53 of the Charter promises not to affect any standard or level of protection elsewhere,[17] the Court's interpretation in *Melloni* prohibits the application of higher national standards when the subject matter is fully harmonised by EU law – thus possibly affecting higher national standards.[18] Moreover, the Charter concurrently protects in two distinctive ways. First, as the only and fully adequate protection in fully harmonised areas. Second, as the minimum level of protection in non-fully harmonised areas. That in itself already bears a risk of contradicting standards.[19] The constitutional tensions relating to fundamental rights standards thus continue to exist. And once again, and in the absence of a more predictable and concretised mechanism for accommodating different (national and supranational) standards of protection, identity claims continue to functionally undertake that role.

2.2 The Scope of Fundamental Rights Application – A Disputed Matter

An additional challenge is the disputed scope of the application of fundamental rights. In a nutshell, there are two distinct cases where the EU Charter ought to

11 Case 4–73 *Nold* [1974] ECR 491, ECLI:EU:C:1974:51.

12 The argument was first made by Walter Hallstein in parliamentary discussions. Paul Craig and Gráinne de Búrca, *EU Law: Text, Cases, and Materials* (6th edition, Oxford University Press 2015) 365.

13 Damian Chalmers, Gareth Davies and Giorgio Monti, *European Union Law: Text and Materials* (4th edition, Cambridge University Press 2019) 237.

14 Case C-540/03 *European Parliament v Council of the European Union* [Grand Chamber, 2006] ECR I-5769, ECLI:EU:C:2006:429, para 58. Case C-173/9 *Broadcasting, Entertainment, Cinematographic and Theatre Union (BECTU) v Secretary of State for Trade and Industry* [2001] ECR I- 4881, ECLI:EU:C:2001:81, Opinion of AG Tizzano, para 27.

15 Although in 1953 the European Community wanted to include the Convention for the Protection of Human Rights and Fundamental Freedoms into the Statute, which was rejected by France, the Community nevertheless rejected Francoist Spain's EU membership due to different ideological commitments.

16 Daniel C Thomas, *The Limits of Europe: Membership Norms and the Contestation of Regional Integration* (Oxford University Press 2021).

17 Article 53 EU Charter fully corresponds to the wording of Article 53 ECHR, but the drafters 'overlooked' a different role of the Union which at times has to provide the only fundamental rights protection, not just minimum standards.

18 Case C-399/11 *(Melloni) Stefano Melloni v Ministerio Fiscal* [Grand Chamber 2013] ECLI:EU:C:2013:107, para 63, 65.

19 Eleanor Spaventa, 'Federalisation versus Centralisation: Tensions in Fundamental Rights Discourse in the EU' in M Dougan and S Currie (eds), *50 Years of the European treaties: looking back and thinking forward* (Hart Publishing 2009) 29.

apply. First, when the Member States are *implementing* Union law. Second, when national legislation *falls within the field* or *scope* of Union law.[20]

Before the EU Charter formally came into force, the CJEU had extensively defined its jurisdiction concerning fundamental rights protection.[21] For example, in *Grogan*,[22] the Court stated that it had jurisdiction 'to assess the compatibility of that legislation with the fundamental rights [...] where national legislation *falls within the field of application* of Community law' (emphasis added).[23] Moreover, in the *ERT*[24] case, it similarly decided that 'where such rules do *fall within the scope of* Community law', European fundamental rights apply (emphasis added).[25] Henceforth, the ECJ firmly established its jurisdiction to scrutinise the subject matter through the lens of EU fundamental rights every time the relevant national legislation 'falls within the field or scope of application of the EU laws'.

The constructed jurisdiction is, however, exceedingly general and far-reaching. A lot of frustration from the Member States, as well as critique from legal scholars, relate precisely to a too widely construed European jurisdiction.[26] Accordingly, the EU Charter introduced a more limited scope of fundamental rights application.[27] Article 51 (1) EU Charter states that EU fundamental rights apply only when the Member States are 'implementing Union law'. Henceforth, the *scope of the application* was replaced by the *implementation*.

Yet, the CJEU has not given up its previously defined broader jurisdiction. Due to the Explanations,[28] soft law which provides guidance relative to the interpretation of the EU Charter,[29] 'the requirement to respect fundamental rights [...] is only binding on the Member States when they act *in the scope of* Union law' (emphasis added).[30] Moreover, the Explanations directly refer to the cases such as *Wachau*,[31]

20 See the chapter in this volume by Aertgeerts.
21 Xavier Groussot, Laurent Pech and Gunnar Thor Petursson, 'The Scope of Application of Fundamental Rights on Member States' Action: In Search of Certainty in EU Adjudication' [2011] The Eric Stein Working Papers <https://papers.ssrn.com/abstract=1936473> accessed 19 August 2022.
22 Case C-159/90 (*Grogan) The Society for the Protection of Unborn Children Ireland Ltd v Stephen Grogan and others* [1991] ECR I-04685, ECLI:EU:C:1991:378.
23 ibid para 31.
24 Case C-260/89 *(ERT) Elliniki Radiophonia Tiléorassi AE and Panellinia Omospondia Syllogon Prossopikou v Dimotiki Etairia Pliroforissis and Sotirios Kouvelas and Nicolaos Avdellas and others.* [1991] ECR I-02925, ECLI:EU:C:1991:254.
25 ibid para 42.
26 Michal Bobek, *Viking, Laval and Beyond* (Mark R Freedland and Jeremias Adams-Prassl eds, Hart Publishing 2015).
27 Michael Dougan, 'Judicial Review of Member State Action under the General Principles and the Charter: Defining the "Scope of Union Law"' (2015) 52 Common Market Law Review 1205.
28 Explanations relating to the Charter of Fundamental Rights, OJ C 303, 14.12.2007, 17–35.
29 Article 52 (7) of the EU Charter.
30 Explanations relating to the Charter of Fundamental Rights, OJ C 303, 14.12.2007, 17–35.
31 Case 5/88 *(Wachauf) Hubert Wachauf v Bundesamt für Ernährung und Forstwirtschaft* [1989] ECR 02609, ECLI:EU:C:1989:321.

ERT,[32] and *Annibaldi*,[33] which all specifically established the broader application of fundamental rights.[34] The scope of application of fundamental rights remains a disputed matter among scholars, subject to dissent and controversy,[35] while the CJEU continues to apply the same jurisdiction as construed at the beginning.

2.3 Three Levels of Fundamental Rights Protection – Turning Minimum Protection into a Final Norm

The last challenge concerns the concurrent coexistence of minimum and fully adequate levels of protection of fundamental rights in multilevel constitutional systems. One may observe the levels of protection from three perspectives.

First, from the perspective of the Member States, national constitutional systems usually consider themselves adequate and self-sufficient. However, the systems of protection and the adjudicative outcomes in the 27 Member States are considerably diverse.

Second, when national laws are fully harmonised by EU law, usually in the form of a Regulation, the CJEU interprets the EU Charter as the only standard of protection. Nevertheless, not as the minimum standard, but as the adequate standard of protection. Yet, these standards cannot fully overlap with *all* the national standards.[36] That logically derives from the fact that the national fundamental rights adjudications considerably differ. A typical example is the well-known landmark *Melloni* decision, where the CJEU firmly rejected the Spanish Constitutional Tribunal's suggestion, that the Member States should be able to apply their higher national standards, if they provide higher protection than the one awarded by the CJEU under the EU Charter.[37]

Finally, in the areas of law which have not yet been fully harmonised, only minimum protection of fundamental rights is provided. Concurrently the Member States are allowed to apply their own (higher) national standards of fundamental rights protection, as stated in the *Åkerberg Fransson* decision. Where the matter falls 'within the scope of European Union law,' but 'in a situation where the action of the Member States is not entirely determined by European Union law,' Member States 'remain free to apply national standards of

32 Case C-260/89 *(ERT) Elliniki Radiophonia Tiléorassi AE and Panellinia Omospondia Syllogon Prossopikou v Dimotiki Etairia Pliroforissis and Sotirios Kouvelas and Nicolaos Avdellas and others.* [1991] ECR I-02925, ECLI:EU:C:1991:254.

33 Case C-309/96 *(Annibaldi) Daniele Annibaldi v Sindaco del Comune di Guidonia and Presidente Regione Lazio* [1997] ECR I-07493, ECLI:EU:C:1997:631.

34 Koen Lenaerts, 'Exploring the Limits of the EU Charter of Fundamental Rights' (2012) 8 European Constitutional Law Review 375.

35 Eleanor Spaventa, 'Should We "Harmonize" Fundamental Rights in the EU? Some Reflections about Minimum Standards and Fundamental Rights Protection in the EU Composite Constitutional System' (2018) 55 Common Market Law Review.

36 Francesco de Cecco, 'Room to Move? Minimum Harmonization and Fundamental Rights' (2006) 43 Common Market Law Review.

37 Case C-399/11 *(Melloni) Stefano Melloni v Ministerio Fiscal* [Grand Chamber 2013] ECLI:EU:C:2013:107.

protection of fundamental rights', provided that the level of protection due to the Charter and the primacy, unity and effectiveness of the EU law are not thereby compromised.[38]

The described system is generally known among legal scholars.[39] What is largely overlooked, however, are the *consequences* of these double standards of protection. This sub-section demonstrates only one of the most problematic outcomes. Namely, how even the minimum protection in non-fully harmonised legislation might turn into an ultimate (final) standard.[40]

When thinking about the problem of combining the European minimum protection of fundamental rights with higher national standards, one should consider the following. A particular standard for a fundamental right often results from a balancing exercise between two or more colliding or conflicting rights. For example, the scope of privacy is often counter-balanced by the question of security stand. Labour and social protection stand in conflict with the freedom to conduct business and freedom of speech with personality rights. Hence the question of whether minimum protection of a particular fundamental right is possible without determining the scope and limits of its opposing right. The case *AGET Iraklis*[41] might help us to understand the above-raised query better.

According to the Collective Redundancies Directive,[42] workers enjoy minimum protection against collective lay-offs. However, the Directive specifically states that the Member States may afford additional higher protection to workers.[43] Accordingly, the Greek legislator provided more extensive regulation in favour of the workers. Specifically, before authorising (some of the) collective redundancies, the Ministry of Labour would have to consider factors such as the market conditions, the situation of the company, and the interests of the national economy.[44]

In the case at hand, the Greek Ministry of Labour refused to authorise the projected redundancies of AGET Iraklis because 'there was no plan for relocating the workers concerned to other plants belonging to AGET Iraklis',[45] combined with the existence of a high unemployment rate in the state. Moreover, 'the

38 Case C-617/10 *(Åkerberg Fransson) Åklagaren gegen Hans Åkerberg Fransson* [Grand Chamber 2013] ECLI:EU:C:2013:105, para 21, 29.

39 Eleanor Spaventa, 'Federalisation versus Centralisation: Tensions in Fundamental Rights Discourse in the EU.' in M Dougan and S Currie (eds), *50 Years of the European treaties: looking back and thinking forward* (Hart Publishing 2009).

40 Eleanor Spaventa, 'Should We "Harmonize" Fundamental Rights in the EU? Some Reflections about Minimum Standards and Fundamental Rights Protection in the EU Composite Constitutional System' (2018) 55 Common Market Law Review.

41 Case C-201/15 *(AGET Iraklis) Anonymi Geniki Etairia Tsimenton Iraklis (AGET Iraklis) v Ypourgos Ergasias, Koinonikis Asfalisis kai Koinonikis Allilengyis* [Grand Chamber 2016] ECLI:EU:C:2016:972.

42 Council Directive 98/59/EC on the approximation of the laws of the Member States relating to collective redundancies [1998] OJ 225/16 and corrigendum OJ 2007 59/84.

43 ibid section IV art 4 (3) and art 5.

44 Law (N.) 1387/1983 Control of Group Dismissals and Other Provisions (FEK A' 110/18–19.8.1983), art 5(3).

45 Case C-201/15 *AGET Iraklis* [Grand Chamber 2016] ECLI:EU:C:2016:972, para 17.

projected redundancies had not been substantiated by concrete and detailed evidence, and [that] the arguments relied on by AGET Iraklis appeared too vague.'[46]

The decision was challenged before the CJEU, which found the measures in question to be 'liable to impede the exercise of freedom of establishment or render it less attractive'.[47] Furthermore, under the EU Charter, 'the establishment of a regime imposing a framework for collective redundancies, such as the regime at issue [...], entails a limitation on the exercise of the freedom to conduct a business enshrined in Article 16 of the Charter'.[48] Accordingly, the CJEU decided that the required authorisation was contrary to EU law due to the vagueness of the established conditions for exercising the discretionary power in question.

To sum up, although the Directive only established the minimum level of protection, the fact that it conflicted with the freedom to conduct business enabled the CJEU to determine the relationship between two conflicting fundamental rights. Effectively, the minimum European labour standard of protection became the ultimate standard.

3 Constitutional Identity as Protection of National Fundamental Rights Standards

The above-described challenges of multilevel fundamental rights protection stand in correlation with (certain types of) claims of national constitutional identity. To protect national interpretations of fundamental rights, Member States occasionally claim they are part of their constitutional identity. This section first examines whether the requirement of the Union pursuant to Article 4 (2) TEU to respect national identities intends to encapsulate the issue of fundamental rights *interpretation* (Section 3.1). Moreover, it analyses the national judicial practice as to how national identity claims relate to fundamental rights in particular. Identity claims refer to the general commitments to fundamental rights,[49] their idiosyncratic national interpretations,[50] or even specific and unique constitutional rights[51] (Section 3.2). Finally, national constitutional identity is a much broader phenomenon than its specific relation to fundamental rights. Accordingly, I argue here that one should treat and evaluate identity claims concerning fundamental rights as a separate and normatively specific issue (Section 3.3).

3.1 European Identity Clause and Fundamental Rights Standards – Going Beyond

If a claim of national constitutional identity is to be 'successful' in challenging EU law, the CJEU must accept it. Hence, national constitutional identity requires

46 ibid para 18.
47 ibid para 48.
48 ibid para 69.
49 Corte Costituzionale 1146/1988 [1988] (Italian Constitutional Court) para 2.1.
50 C-42/17 *(Tarico II) Criminal proceedings against M.A.S. and M.B.* [Grand Chamber 2017] ECLI:EU:C:2017:936.
51 Case C-159/90 *(Grogan) The Society for the Protection of Unborn Children Ireland Ltd v Stephen Grogan and* others [1991] ECR I-04685, ECLI:EU:C:1991:378.

participation on both levels, national and supranational. Only national authorities are to determine and/or interpret the meaning of respective national identities. In the same way, the CJEU alone is competent to interpret the Treaties, whereby Article 4 (2) TEU articulates the meaning and the scope of national identity. Accordingly, does the cited European identity clause encapsulate (national) fundamental rights *standards* as part of national identity?

The meticulous reading of the European identity clause suggests no recourse to specificities of national *interpretations* of fundamental rights.[52] De Witte supports that view. He argues that 'Article 4(2) TEU does not refer to fundamental rights as a component of constitutional identity, and the Court of Justice tends to steer from dealing with fundamental rights questions in the language of national constitutional identity.'[53]

Moreover, when the BVerfG yielded to review EU law in *Solange II* due to sufficient protection of fundamental rights on the level of the Union – previously carried out in the name of constitutional identity – it never demanded that fundamental rights standards both at a national and at a European level be *the same* to recognise the primacy of EU law over national, even constitutional law. On the contrary, the BVerfG has explicitly recognised that the standards of protection will naturally differ. However, the decisive point is that the essence of fundamental rights is not hollowed out.[54] Fundamental rights protection at the Union level is regarded as *essentially equivalent* to national fundamental rights protection. The BVerfG has explicitly stated that it 'will no longer review the Community law against the national *standards* of fundamental rights; especially since the essence of fundamental rights is generally guaranteed by the ECJ (emphasis added).'[55] In the same decision, the BVerfG also wrote that the adherence of the Union to the ECHR, which guarantees only minimum protection of fundamental rights, although not formally binding, in principle already satisfies the conditions which the German Basic Law demands.[56]

To sum up, while the general *commitment* to fundamental rights may plausibly constitute national constitutional identity (and the lack of it even justified the refusal of the EU primacy principle by the BVerfG), the specific national *interpretations* or *standards* of fundamental rights cannot.

52 Article 4 (2) TEU merely states: 'The Union shall respect the equality of Member States before the Treaties as well as their national identities, inherent in their fundamental structures, political and constitutional, inclusive of regional and local self-government. It shall respect their essential State functions, including ensuring the territorial integrity of the State, maintaining law and order and safeguarding national security. In particular, national security remains the sole responsibility of each Member State.'

53 Bruno De Witte and Diane Fromage, 'National Constitutional Identity Ten Years on: State of Play and Future Perspectives' (2021) 27 European Public Law 420.

54 BVerfGE 73, 339 *(Solange II)* para 363.

55 ibid para 388.

56 ibid para 386.

3.2 National Identity as Fundamental Rights Commitments, Procedural Levels of Protection, Idiosyncratic Interpretations, and Unique Fundamental Rights

Despite the suggested scholarly interpretation of the European identity clause above, the CJEU's case law, as well as some of the more recent claims of national constitutional identity by the apex courts, occasionally suggests otherwise.

First, Member States often argue that the general commitment to fundamental rights forms part of their national constitutional identity.[57] The German eternity clause,[58] Czech eternity clause,[59] or Italian Controlimiti doctrine[60] exemplify this. In that sense, identity as a general commitment to fundamental rights could only be plausible if the Union manifestly disregarded its own duty to respect fundamental rights.[61] Identity in that regard plays a role as the ultimate guardian of liberal values. Mere reasonable disagreement on the *interpretation* of fundamental rights does not fulfil that standard.[62]

Second, identity claims can serve to secure the concrete *procedural* level of fundamental rights protection in general. For example, the Czech Constitutional Court has argued that 'no amendment to the Constitution can be interpreted in such a way that it would result in limiting an already achieved procedural level of protection for fundamental rights and freedoms.'[63] Hence, the Czech eternity clause or the identity of a constitution protects not only the general commitments to, but also the concrete *procedural level* of protection of, fundamental rights. In that light, one can also observe an Italian *Taricco* saga. Articulated as national constitutional identity, Italy argued that the statute of limitations in Italian criminal law constitutes a matter of material rather than procedural law. Accordingly, it is subsumed under the principle of legality, which prohibits any retroactive action in criminal law.[64]

57 Luke Dimitrios Spieker, 'Framing and Managing Constitutional Identity Conflicts: How to Stabilize the *Modus Vivendi* between the Court of Justice and National Constitutional Courts' (2020) 57 Common Market Law Review.

58 Sabine Blömacher, *Die Menschenwürde als Prinzip des deutschen und europäischen Rechts: Kohärenz der Konzepte?* (1st edition, Duncker & Humblot 2016). BVerfG - 2 BvE 2/08 - *(Lisbon Decision)* [2009].

59 Ústavní soud Pl. ÚS 19/08 [2008] *Treaty of Lisbon I* (The Constitutional Court of Czechia) paras 109, 215.

60 Corte Constituzionale 1146/1988 [1988] (Italian Constitutional Court) para 2.1.

61 Luke Dimitrios Spieker, 'Defending Union Values in Judicial Proceedings. On How to Turn Article 2 TEU into a Judicially Applicable Provision' in Armin von Bogdandy and others (eds), *Defending Checks and Balances in EU Member States: Taking Stock of Europe's Actions* (Springer 2021).

62 BVerfG - 2 BvR 859/15 - *(PSPP)* [2020]. Case C-493/17 *(Weiss) Proceedings brought by Heinrich Weiss and Others* [2018] ECLI:EU:C:2018:1000.

63 Ústavní soud Pl. ÚS 36/01 [2002] *Euro-Amendment* (The Constitutional Court of Czechia) para 10. David Kosař and Ladislav Vyhnánek, 'The Constitutional Court of Czechia' in Armin von Bogdandy, Peter Huber and Christoph Grabenwarter (eds), *The Max Planck Handbooks in European Public Law: Volume III: Constitutional Adjudication: Institutions* (2020) 166.

64 C-42/17 *(Taricco II) Criminal proceedings against M.A.S. and M.B.* [Grand Chamber 2017] ECLI:EU:C:2017:936.

Third, national constitutional identity can relate to human dignity. Human dignity may be understood as the normative general guiding principle among the fundamental rights or a concrete right with a specific idiosyncratic meaning. For example, whereas the EU itself complies with human dignity, as articulated in Article 1 of the EU Charter and Article 2 TEU as the common foundational value, in the *Omega* decision, the CJEU nevertheless accepted the German claim that the particular German *interpretation* of human dignity justified disapplication of the respective EU norms.[65]

In addition, and apart from the issues of national language(s),[66] which should be treated as a separate phenomenon, concrete constitutional norms or principles might be seen as part of national identity. For example, the French principle of secularism (*la laïcité républicaine*, freedom of conscience as distinct from the right to manifest religion or belief),[67] the former constitutional protection of the right to life in Ireland,[68] or the Romanian claim (supported by the Latvian Government), and refused by the CJEU, that marriage only between the persons of the opposite sex forms part of national identity.[69]

3.3 Treating Fundamental Rights Identity Claims Differently

Contrary to the suggested interpretation of Article 4 (2) TEU, excluding fundamental rights (standards), the above-cited examples show that in practice fundamental rights often connect with claims of national identity. I argue here that one should examine and evaluate these types of identity claims separately.

Identity claims in general cover a wide variety of issues. From general commitments to democracy and the rule of law[70] to political and constitutional structures,

65 Case C-36/02 *(Omega) Omega Spielhallen- und Automatenaufstellungs-GmbH v Oberbürgermeisterin der Bundesstadt Bon* [2004] ECR I-09609, ECLI:EU:C:2004:614.

66 C-391/09 *(Runevič-Vardyn) Malgožata Runevič-Vardyn and Łukasz Paweł Wardyn v Vilniaus miesto savivaldybes administracija and Others* [2011] ECLI:EU:C:2011:291, para 84. Decision no. 2004–505 DC of 19 November 2004 *The Treaty establishing a Constitution for Europe* (French Constitutional Council). François-Xavier Millet, 'Constitutional Identity in France: Vices and – Above All – Virtues' in Christian Calliess and Gerhard van der Schyff (eds), *Constitutional Identity in a Europe of Multilevel Constitutionalism* (Cambridge University Press 2019) 149.

67 François-Xavier Millet, 'Constitutional Identity in France: Vices and – Above All – Virtues' in Christian Calliess and Gerhard van der Schyff (eds), *Constitutional Identity in a Europe of Multilevel Constitutionalism* (Cambridge University Press 2019) 149.

68 PROTOCOL on the concerns of the Irish people on the Treaty of Lisbon, Official Journal L 060, 02/03/2013 P. 0131–0139. [Add: Marjan Kos]

69 Case C-673/16 (*Coman) Relu Adrian Coman and Others v Inspectoratul General pentru Imigrări and Ministerul Afacerilor Interne* [Grand Chamber 2018] ECLI:EU:C:2018:385, para 42.

70 Helle Krunke, 'Constitutional Identity in Denmark: Extracting Constitutional Identity in the Context of a Restrained Supreme Court and a Strong Legislature' in Christian Calliess and Gerhard van der Schyff (eds), *Constitutional Identity in a Europe of Multilevel Constitutionalism* (Cambridge University Press 2019).

essential elements of a state, security, migration, fiscal policy,[71] national sovereignty,[72] territorial integrity,[73] protection of languages,[74] religious questions,[75] and many others. However, ***fundamental rights identity claims*** (hereinafter: 'FR identity claims') deserve special scholarly attention due to their specific normative foundation.

First, in contrast to other insurmountable differences, FR identity claims are often shallow constitutional disagreements revolving around shared basic liberal constitutional commitments. Moreover, occasional idiosyncratic interpretations and tolerance towards constitutional interpretations can hardly undermine the principle of primacy, effectiveness and unity of EU law. Finally, the constitutional *interpretation* of fundamental rights is subject to change by its very nature. Even the highest courts err. Contrary to some understandings of identity as sameness[76] – which grants the argument of identity an additional normative strength – idiosyncratic interpretations of fundamental rights as national identity are subject to constant and continuous change by their very nature.

In addition, one may perceive FR identity claims as a mechanism to mitigate potentially conflicting multilevel fundamental rights standards. In that sense, the argument of identity undertakes a different, more functional[77] role to navigate the constitutional tensions. I call it the *functional aspect of identity*, which counterbalances the increasing European trajectory of unification and harmonisation of fundamental rights standards. The national apex courts are occasionally better suited to determine the concrete considerations of conflicting fundamental rights, locally more sensitive to the specificities of the respective community, and with a higher democratic legitimacy. In light of the foregoing, it would be unwise to

71 PROTOCOL on the concerns of the Irish people on the Treaty of Lisbon, Official Journal L 060, 02/03/2013 P. 0131–0139.

72 Trybunał Konstytucyjny Ref. No. K 32/09 [2010] *Treaty of Lisbon* (Polish Constitutional Tribunal) para 38. Anna Śledzińska-Simon and Michał Ziółkowski, 'Constitutional Identity in Poland: Is the Emperor Putting On the Old Clothes of Sovereignty?' in Christian Calliess and Gerhard van der Schyff (eds), *Constitutional Identity in a Europe of Multilevel Constitutionalism* (Cambridge University Press 2019).

73 José Martín Y Pérez de Nanclares, 'Constitutional Identity in Spain: Commitment to European Integration without Giving Up the Essence of the Constitution' in Christian Calliess and Gerhard van der Schyff (eds), *Constitutional Identity in a Europe of Multilevel Constitutionalism* (Cambridge University Press 2019) 238.

74 Case C-379/87 *(Groener) Anita Groener v Minister for Education and the City of Dublin Vocational Educational Committee* [1989] ECR 03967, ECLI:EU:C:1989:599.

75 C-414/16 *(Egenberger) Vera Egenberger v Evangelisches Werk für Diakonie und Entwicklung eV* [Grand Chamber 2018] ECLI:EU:C:2018:257.

76 Pietro Faraguna, 'Constitutional Identity in the EU–A Shield or a Sword?' (2017) 18 German Law Journal 1617, 1625. Tímea Drinóczi, 'Constitutional Identity in Europe: The Identity of the Constitution. A Regional Approach' (2020) 21 German Law Journal 105, 112. Michel Rosenfeld, *The Identity of the Constitutional Subject: Selfhood, Citizenship, Culture, and Community* (1st edition, Routledge 2009). Gary Jeffrey Jacobsohn, *Constitutional Identity* (Harvard University Press 2010).

77 Kassandra Wetz, *Funktionen von Verfassungsidentität Als Gerichtliches Konzept in Der Europäischen Union*, vol 18 (1st edn, Mohr Siebeck 2021).

force the same standards developed by the CJEU on all the Member States. FR identity claims thus have the potential to open a dialogue where one settles the right equilibrium between the 'ever closer Union' and national diversity.

In conclusion, the special nature of FR identity claims requires that we give them special consideration, and in turn raises the following question: Is this special type of identity claim the best way how to navigate multilevel FR standards, or does the connection of fundamental rights and identity rather create more problems than it promises to solve?

4 Going Astray? Identity Terminology as Part of the Problem

This section highlights three main – and often-overlooked – problems of identity terminology in constitutional law. First, the original meaning of (national) identity as a relational concept (Section 4.1). Second, the relationship between identity and change (Section 4.2). Finally, how the concept of identity introduces the highly problematic hierarchy of rights (Section 4.3).

4.1 The Overlooked Meaning of Identity as a Relational Concept

What is identity, national and/or constitutional? For Rosenfeld, '[s]elf-identity can connotate sameness or selfhood'.[78] Analogously, national constitutional identity is 'based on the dynamic interaction between projections of sameness and images of selfhood.'[79] Aristotelian constitutive understanding conflates the identity of a nation and a state (polis), being at odds with the contemporary liberal understanding of constitutionalism.[80] Anderson sees communal identity as socially constructed, imagined, 'because the members of even the smallest nation will never know most of their fellow members.'[81] Fukuyama argued that national identity could be embodied in formal laws and institutions, language, but it also extends into the realm of culture and values, the stories that people tell about themselves or their shared historical memories.[82] According to Weiler, '[o]ur constitutions are said to encapsulate fundamental values of the polity and this, in turn, is said to be a reflection of our collective identity as a people, as a nation, as a state, as a community, or as a union.'[83] What is more, for Jacobsohn:

78 Michel Rosenfeld, *The Identity of the Constitutional Subject: Selfhood, Citizenship, Culture, and Community* (1st edition, Routledge 2009) 27.
79 ibid.
80 Aristotle, *The Politics of Aristotle* (Ernest Barker tr, Oxford Univ PR 1962) 98–9.
81 Benedict Anderson, *Imagined Communities: Reflections on the Origin and Spread of Nationalism* (Revised ed edition, Verso 2016) 6.
82 Francis Fukuyama, 'Why National Identity Matters' (2018) 29 Journal of Democracy 5, 8.
83 JHH Weiler, 'On the Power of the Word: Europe's Constitutional Iconography' (2005) 3 International Journal of Constitutional Law 173, 184.

> a constitution acquires an identity through experience, that this identity exists neither as a discrete object of invention nor as a heavily encrusted essence embedded in a society's culture, requiring only to be discovered. Rather, identity emerges *dialogically* and represents a mix of political aspirations and commitments that are expressive of a nation's past, as well as the determination of those within the society who seek in some ways to transcend that past. It is changeable but resistant to its own destruction, and it may manifest itself differently in different settings.[84]

The above-mentioned 'definitions' of national constitutional identity carry an almost poetic aura; they are highly abstract, paradoxical and inexplicable for *legal* practice. The best alternative way to comprehensively understand the meaning of national constitutional identity would be to analyse judicial practice throughout the Union and its member States, establish a pattern of the given meanings, and create a legal definition. Yet, the diversity of the case law makes a coherent account of identity a difficult and highly disputed task.[85]

I argue that the use of identity terminology in constitutional law is unsuitable for legal practice. Mainly because the genuine meaning of national identity cannot be appropriately transplanted into *describing* the essentials of a constitution. Judicial practice is firmly embedded in language and its meaning. Even constitutional concepts, which by their very nature are general and open to interpretations, are subject to the inescapable gravity of their linguistic meaning. Accordingly, to my best understanding, identity requires an agent capable of creating a relation to an identifiable subject. Identity is a relational and reflexive concept.[86] A car, an object, or a legal text cannot have an identity. Only an agent itself can determine its own identity. And a court cannot and should not attribute an identity to a legal text. Because ascribing an identity to the constitutional text, which clarifies what is at the core of the collective political agency of the constitutional community, is a missed attempt of either of the following two endeavours. Either the courts describe what is the essence or core of a constitution – analysing and interpreting it. If so, naming it 'the essential elements' of a constitution brings more clarity and sense than covering it up with the undeterminable terminology of identity. Alternatively, the courts aim to identify the *national identity* of the people as reflected in the constitution – national constitutional identity. That comes close to Weiler's definition above.

84 Gary Jeffrey Jacobsohn, *Constitutional Identity* (Harvard University Press 2010) 7.

85 Martin Nettesheim, 'Wo "endet" Das Grundgesetz? Verfassungsgebund Als Grenzüberschreitender Prozess' (2012) 51 Der Staat 313, 316. Fabbrini and Sajó (n 4) 471. Michel Rosenfeld, 'Constitutional Identity' in Michel Rosenfeld and András Sajó (eds), *The Oxford Handbook of Comparative Constitutional Law* (Oxford University Press 2012) 773.

86 CJF Williams, 'Is Identity a Relation?' (1979) 80 Proceedings of the Aristotelian Society 81. William James, *The Principles of Psychology, Vols. 1–2* (Combined edition, CreateSpace Independent Publishing Platform 2017). The basic idea of reflexivity in human selfhood – how the 'I' encounters and makes sense of itself (the 'Me').

The problem of this second attempt is twofold. National identity is a multitude of 'imagined'[87] narratives which are impossible to articulate in one coherent account,[88] making it legally relevant and maintaining a liberal commitment to individuality. Second, national constitutional identity is currently understood also as covering 'fundamental political structures' which have little to do with the national identity of the people. Hence, national constitutional identity cannot be only a legal reflection of people's national identity.

Accordingly, the concept of national constitutional identity creates misplaced expectations rooted in the genuine meaning of the word identity as a relational concept.[89] Due to the incoherent case law,[90] one misses a sufficiently consistent legal definition of national constitutional identity. Furthermore, scholars have been unable to develop a coherent account of this elusive term. Accordingly, in my opinion, one would be better advised to omit it from the European constitutional acquis.

4.2 Identity and Changeability

Why do the apex courts apply the terminology of national constitutional identity against the application of EU law instead of simply arguing that a certain subject matter presents an essential and sensitive constitutional matter which should be treated deferentially or deserve special care – without calling it identity?

One part of the answer can be found in the terminology of Article 4 (2) TEU, which introduced the jargon of identity.[91] The issue of changeability provides the second part of the answer.[92] Not all Member States interpret their own national constitutional identities as unchangeable elements of their constitutional systems. In that sense, the identity argument can be a constructive input which only signals a specific national sensitivity in an open dialogue with the CJEU. However, while the Court respects national identities under Article 4 (2) TEU in principle, that obligation is not absolute[93] and is subject to proportionality and balancing against

87 Benedict Anderson, *Imagined Communities: Reflections on the Origin and Spread of Nationalism* (Revised edn, Verso 2016).

88 Omar Dahbour, 'National Identity: An Argument for the Strict Definition' (2002) 16 Public Affairs Quarterly 17.

89 Jakob Gašperin Wischhoff, 'A Plaidoyer Against the Sisyphean Endeavour to Imagine the Constitutional Identity for the EU' in de Poorter and others (eds), *European Yearbook of Constitutional Law 2023: A Constitutional Identity for the EU?*, vol 4 (TMC Asser Press 2023) Forthcoming.

90 Fabbrini and Sajó (n 4) 471.

91 Strictly speaking; identity has been introduced already by its predecessor, Article F (1) of the Maastricht Treaty and later Article 6 (3) of the Amsterdam Treaty.

92 'Identity only becomes an issue when it is in crisis, when something assumed to be fixed, coherent and stable is displaced by the experience of doubt and uncertainty.' Kobena Mercer, *Welcome to the Jungle: Identity and Diversity in Postmodern Politics* (Routledge 1994) 43.

93 C-357/19 (*Euro Box) Euro Box Promotion and Others* [Grand Chamber 2021] ECLI: EU:C:2021:1034, para 249.

other principles and rules in the equation. The Court recently stated in *Euro Box* in relation to potential exceptions to the primacy principle that the Member States are 'unable to rely on a unilateral measure, whatever its nature'.[94] Ultimately, the Court can reject an identity claim. In that sense, the argument of identity loses its absolute strength and cannot stand against the primacy of EU law.

The scenario is different, though, when the Member States interpret their national constitutional identity as a subject immune to change;[95] an example of this would be the eternity clauses and their further judicial interpretations.[96] The unchangeability (eternity or unamendability) of a constitution makes identity claims powerful national tools. It puts the Member States on an equal footing with the EU and challenges the principle of primacy. Because even if the CJEU refuses to allow the disapplication of EU law due to a national identity claim, Member States can argue that they simply *cannot change* the respective unchangeable constitutional norm which conflicts with the EU law – as interpreted by the respective apex courts.

Nevertheless, in these circumstances, designating a matter as a question of national constitutional identity creates serious consequences which might be at odds with the principle of democratic reversibility.[97]

To explain further, as long as national constitutional identity does not go beyond a general commitment to fundamental rights, its unchangeability protects the ideological essence of its democratic system. Yet, it loses the meaningful function – demanding an exception to disapply the EU law – in relation to the Union with which it shares these commitments. However, when one declares a specific *interpretation* or *standard* of fundamental rights as a matter of identity, that irreversibly hinders further development of constitutional adjudication and/or constitutional amendment. Declared as identity, constitutional norms and subsequent constitutional adjudication can no longer adjust or amend the initial interpretation. For example, when the BVerfG interpreted the German (unchangeable) constitutional identity as consistsing of the principle of democracy which presupposes, *inter alia*, the national control of fiscal decisions, military, and social policy,[98] it became extremely difficult to change this interpretation by the new composition of the Court or by a constitutional amendment. After all, it was declared an eternal identity that cannot be changed. Accordingly, a proclamation of identity can take away the strength of a constitutional system – to retain the ability to adapt and respond to the challenges of time. As we know, even

94 ibid.
95 Spieker (n 74) 374.
96 Monika Polzin, 'Constitutional Identity, Unconstitutional Amendments and the Idea of Constituent Power: The Development of the Doctrine of Constitutional Identity in German Constitutional Law' (2016) 14 International Journal of Constitutional Law 411.
97 Jakob Hohnerlein, *Recht Und Demokratische Reversibilität*, vol 36 (1st edn, Mohr Siebeck 2020).
98 BVerfG, 2 BvE/08, (*Lisbon Decision*) para 249, 252.

the highest judicial decisions change over time – today's certainties will likely be the sediments of the contingent tomorrow.[99]

4.3 Hierarchy of Constitutional Fundamental Rights

Declaring something as a matter of national constitutional identity also creates a type of 'constitutional hierarchy'. If one fundamental right or its judicial expression qualifies itself as belonging to the constitutional identity while others do not, a qualitative difference can be identified between them. In simple terms, designating a matter as part of the constitutional identity elevates it within a constitution.[100]

Constitutional hierarchy is not entirely new.[101] As mentioned above, several constitutions prohibit an amendment of certain parts of a constitution – the so-called unconstitutional constitutional amendment.[102] In some cases, this is expressly stated in the constitution, and in other cases, similar doctrines are developed by the judiciary. The referred differentiation aims to protect the liberal essence of a constitution, its backbone, in light of the commitments to human rights, democracy, the rule of law, or the separation of powers. It protects a constitutional system from deteriorating into an ideologically different system, such as an autocratic system of governance. Whereas such qualification of *general* constitutional norms may be normatively justified (although not without inner contradictions),[103] the elevation of concrete *interpretations* or *standards* of fundamental rights as identity creates bigger tensions.

Judicial constitutional adjudication requires judges to perform balancing exercises. When faced with two or more opposing fundamental rights, they have to determine whether the restrictions of said rights are proportionate, necessary, and appropriate in the real case in front of them. The specificities of the concrete cases co-determine the outcomes. Henceforth, there is no absolute and given ponderation among the concrete fundamental rights *per se*. Qualifying some of them as part of the national constitutional identity may severely distort the nature of constitutional adjudication. In my opinion, identity in relation to fundamental rights creates more problems than it promises to solve.

99 Ronald Dworkin, *Taking Rights Seriously* (Harvard University Press 1978) 215.
100 Although the legal consequences of such qualification are not entirely clear.
101 Cesare Pinelli, 'Theories Concerning the Hierarchy of Norms' in Rainer Grote and others (eds), *Max Planck Encyclopedia of Comparative Constitutional Law* (Oxford University Press 2016).
102 Yaniv Roznai, *Unconstitutional Constitutional Amendments: The Limits of Amendment Powers* (Oxford University Press 2019).
103 Christoph Möllers, '5: "We Are (Afraid of) the People": Constituent Power in German Constitutionalism' in Martin Loughlin and Neil Walker (eds), *The Paradox of Constitutionalism: Constituent Power and Constitutional Form* (Oxford University Press 2008). Adrienne Stone, 'Unconstitutional Constitutional Amendments: Between Contradiction and Necessity' (2018) 12 ICL Journal 357.

5 An Alternative Change of Paradigm: Directly Applying the EU Charter And the End of Fundamental Rights Identity Claims

The following case law addresses both of the previously outlined challenges. The lack of a consistent and foreseeable constitutional design as to multilevel fundamental rights standards, and as a consequence, the problematic adherence to identity claims to manage constitutional conflicts. The section shortly outlines two recent landmark decisions of the BVerfG, *Right to Be Forgotten* I[104] and II,[105] which signal a significant paradigm change (Section 5.1).[106] Furthermore, it critically explores the potential consequences of the cited case law for FR identity claims as well as for the new trajectory of European fundamental rights standards (Section 5.2).

5.1 To Be Forgotten, One and Two

In the case Right to be Forgotten I,[107] the BVerfG addressed the matter of fundamental rights standards in the context of a national constitutional complaint concerning legislation which was *not* fully harmonised by Union Law.[108] The question raised was whether the BVerfG could apply its national standards of fundamental rights protection, although the matter 'falls within the scope of the EU law'.

The Complainant had murdered two people on the high seas in 1981, a story extensively covered by the media. In 1999 the magazine *Spiegel Online* decided to make its entire archive of articles available online. In 2002, when the Complainant had been released from prison and was trying to reintegrate into society and start a new life, every Google search of his name quickly revealed his notorious past. The Complainant argued that after all these years, his right to personality (*Persönlichkeitsrecht*) entitled him to at least some protection regarding his name; particularly the right to be forgotten.

The subject matter fell within the scope of EU law but was not fully regulated by EU law, which allows the Member States some leeway as to concrete legislative conditions of the freedom of expression and information, including the processing of personal data for journalistic purposes ('media privilege').[109] The BVerfG decided that national standards of protection, as guaranteed by the German Basic Law, were applicable.[110]

104 BVerfG - 1 BvR 16/13 - (*Right to be Forgotten I)* [2019].
105 BVerfG - 1 BvR 276/17 - (*Right to be Forgotten II)* [2019].
106 See the chapter by Aertgeerts.
107 BVerfG - 1 BvR 16/13 - (*Right to be Forgotten I)* [2019].
108 The same question was addressed by CJEU in the Case C-617/10 (*Åkerberg Fransson) Åklagaren gegen Hans Åkerberg Fransson* [Grand Chamber 2013] ECLI:EU:C:2013:105, para 29.
109 Article 85, Regulation (EU) 2016/679, General Data Protection Regulation, OJ L 119, 2016/88.
110 BVerfG - 1 BvR 16/13 - (*Right to be Forgotten I)* [2019] para 46. 'The application of German fundamental rights as the primary standard of review also implies their interpretation in light of the Charter'.

The second decision, the Right to be Forgotten II,[111] introduced a true novelty. It addressed the question of the constitutional complaint relating to the fully harmonised legislation by EU law.[112] In this context, the BVerfG ruled that it would no longer scrutinise potential fundamental rights violations against the Basic Law, but would apply the EU Charter as the only relevant yardstick. It stated that it 'cannot be assumed that the Charter, insofar as uniform fundamental rights protection is to apply in all Member States to fully harmonised EU law, corresponds with the Basic Law and is congruent with its guarantees in all details'.[113] An interpretation of fully harmonised EU law in light of the fundamental rights of the Basic Law would thus run the risk of prematurely applying to EU law the standards developed domestically – this would then imply that these standards would also have to apply to the other Member States.

Accordingly, 'the relevant standard of review does not derive from the fundamental rights of the Basic Law, but solely from EU fundamental rights.'[114]

5.2 European Fundamental Rights Standards and the End of Fundamental Rights Identity Claims?

Both decisions can be seen as a constructive proposal addressing the interplay between various fundamental rights standards. Yet, without denying the powerful voice of the BVerfG, the suggested new paradigm is still predominantly a national (German) approach. Although the apex courts of Spain and Austria have already examined questions regarding the applicability of the EU Charter as the relevant yardstick (*Prüfungsmaßstab*) in national constitutional proceedings,[115] the outcome has not been as clear as the above-cited German decisions.

However, the proposed change of paradigm is not without its own problems. Three main points will be made in this respect. As long as the new approach remains solely the German solution, not followed by the other Member States, national constitutional complaint based on the EU Charter does not extend to all European citizens. This leads to an unequal status among EU citizens, although bound by the same EU rules.[116] Moreover, the approach by the BVerfG of

111 BVerfG - 1 BvR 276/17 - (*Right to be Forgotten II)* [2019].

112 The same question was addressed by CJEU in the Case C-399/11 *(Melloni) Stefano Melloni v Ministerio Fiscal* [Grand Chamber 2013] ECLI:EU:C:2013:107, paras 56–58.

113 BVerfG - 1 BvR 276/17 - (*Right to be Forgotten II)* [2019] para 45.

114 ibid para 42.

115 Verfassungsgerichtshof (VfGH) U466/11 ua [2012] ECLI:AT:VFGH:2012:U466.2011 (Austrian Constitutional Court).

116 A potential solution could be to create a new procedural remedy in the form of a common 'European individual complaint' in front of any national apex court, but directly pertaining to the EU Charter – an improvement perhaps to be seen in the future.

directly *applying* the EU Charter raises the question of transparency of national case law applying the EU Charter, as well as regarding equal application or interpretation of EU law. Finally, it has the inherent potential of enabling national apex courts to assume the role of *de facto* interpreters of the EU Charter, which is reserved for the CJEU only.

Moreover, how does the above-described case law relate to FR identity claims? The suggested paradigm change may signal the end of FR identity claims, or at least a significant decline.

When areas of the law are not fully harmonised, Member States may directly apply their own fundamental rights standards. Hence, their national constitutional identity relating to idiosyncratic national fundamental rights standards cannot be challenged – because EU law is reviewed only and directly against the national standards. FR identity claims thus make no sense.

Otherwise, when areas of the law are fully regulated by EU law, the apex courts would directly apply the EU Charter. Accordingly, national fundamental rights (standards) would no longer be applicable as the yardstick of constitutionality. Hence, because national standards would no longer be relevant for constitutional review, the apex courts would have no reason to claim that these national standards have to be applied – in the name of national constitutional identity.

The described change of paradigm leaves us with numerous questions, one of them concerning the BVerfG's attestation in the EAW[117] decision to carry out the identity review in the name of human dignity and fundamental rights. Will the BVerfG maintain this line of reasoning despite the new 'right to be forgotten' paradigm and highly disputed[118] reasoning in the said decision? For example, the BVerfG itself acknowledged that the admissibility in EAW stands in contrast with the 'past jurisprudence declaring inadmissible both constitutional complaints and referrals in specific judicial review proceedings that assert a violation of fundamental rights under the Basic Law by secondary Community law or Union law respectively.'[119] However, even though in the identity review the BVerfG scrutinised EU law against German fundamental rights, it also heavily relied on fundamental principles as enshrined in Article 6 TEU and reflected in the EU Charter.[120] Accordingly, the new 'right to be forgotten framework' can close that chapter on the German identity review, focusing onwards directly and solely on human dignity and fundamental rights as guaranteed directly under the EU Charter. Alternatively, fundamental rights identity review may remain a tacit possibility, along the lines of the comment of the former president of the BVerfG, that the 'emergency brake mechanisms' are most effective if they do not have to be applied.[121]

117 BVerfG - 2 BvR 2735/14 - (*EAW*) para 49, 53.
118 Mathias Hong, 'Human Dignity, Identity Review of the European Arrest Warrant and the Court of Justice as a Listener in the Dialogue of Courts: Solange-III and Aranyosi' (2016) 12 European Constitutional Law Review 549.
119 ibid para 49, 53.
120 ibid para 93, 98, 102, 104.
121 Voßkuhle (n 2) 195.

In my opinion, the new framework offers and enables the possibility to consign the identity review of EU law in the name of national fundamental rights (interpretations) to the past. The question remains, however, whether one sufficiently recognises the damaging nature of identity claims. The lack of transparency, diverse national understandings of identity, identity's confusing terminology, assumptions of unchangeability and democratic irreversibility, and the introduction of a constitutional hierarchy and its immense potential for abuses, to name a few.[122] Only then would one be motivated enough to use the potential of the new paradigm in light of the right to be forgotten. If not, and in the absence of a more suitable mechanism,[123] national claims of constitutional identity may carry on to mitigate the conflicts between the Union and the Member States.[124]

Finally, this new framework offers both diversity and collective unity without adhering to FR identity claims. In the first scenario, while allowing the application of diverging national standards, the Union remains committed to nurturing national diversities without forcing the Member States to apply the same standards. As the BVerfG lucidly stated, 'differences in domestic fundamental rights frameworks reflect factual differences between the Member States resulting from various factors, including country-specific historical experiences.'[125] The diversity of the Member States, also concerning fundamental rights standards, constitutes the value of the Union.[126] Nurturing diversity enriches reality and offers a multitude of solutions that most adequately address a particular community's linguistic, cultural, historical, and political characteristics.

In the second scenario, applying the EU Charter by all national apex courts could enhance the judicial dialogue and the best practices competition, inviting all Member States to cooperate in shaping the interpretation of the common standards of the EU Charter, led by the CJEU. However, one should not overlook the motivation of the apex courts to be seen as equal interlocutors with the CJEU.[127] That inclination has an inherent danger of taking control over the development of the European legal system. Moreover, it would question the

122 Fabbrini and Sajó (n 4) 466, 469. Gašperin Wischhoff (n 111). Scholtes (n 4). Gábor Halmai, 'Abuse of Constitutional Identity. The Hungarian Constitutional Court on Interpretation of Article E) (2) of the Fundamental Law' (2018) 43 Review of Central and East European Law 23. Pietro Faraguna and Tímea Drinóczi, 'Constitutional Identity in and on EU Terms' (*Verfassungsblog*) <https://verfassungsblog.de/constitutional-identity-in-and-on-eu-terms/> accessed 22 August 2022. Christoph Schönberger, 'Identitäterä' (2015) 63 Jahrbuch des öffentlichen Rechts der Gegenwart. Neue Folge (JöR) 41.

123 See the chapter by Kos. Pietro Faraguna, 'Taking Constitutional Identities Away from the Courts' (2016) 41 Brooklyn Journal of International Law.

124 Wetz (n 98).

125 BVerfG - 1 BvR 276/17 - (*Right to be Forgotten II)* [2019] para 44.

126 Spaventa, 'Should We "Harmonize" Fundamental Rights in the EU?' (n 53).

127 Christoph Grabenwarter and others, 'The Role of the Constitutional Courts in the European Judicial Network' (2021) 27 European Public Law. Faraguna (n 148).

effectiveness and the unity of the Union law as well as the equality of the Member States.[128]

In addition, while identity claims, in general, will likely exist in the future, the above-suggested paradigm has the potential to at least eliminate the least convincing *type* of identity claims. Namely, claims of national constitutional identity as idiosyncratic fundamental rights standards or specific fundamental rights interpretations. If at all, I argue that the FR identity claims should only serve to protect the general commitment to liberal constitutional principles and values. Used in that way, they can mutually guarantee for the Member States and the Union that the basic principles of constitutionalism are respected.

6 Conclusion

The multilevel landscape of fundamental rights among the Union and its Member States occasionally creates constitutional disputes, partially explained by the historical development of fundamental rights protection in the Union and a contemporary European constitutional design and its interpretation. To overcome these tensions, Member States apply the highly volatile terminology of national constitutional identity when faced with challenges of diverging and converging fundamental rights standards. The matter is complex, and it cannot be solved simply with one stroke of the pen.

The chapter constructively explicates the new approach of the German Constitutional Court, directly applying the EU Charter as the sole standard of review in areas fully harmonised by EU legislation. This shift could signal the decline of fundamental rights identity claims while embracing the diversity of national constitutional standards. Moreover, it can serve as a new framework for thinking about various idiosyncratic fundamental rights standards. The chapter shows that despite the intellectually innovative and constructive solution of the BVerfG, the outcome does not come without its challenges and contradictions. The final accommodation of the above-described tensions remains a disputed subject in the future.

Finally, the chapter conveys two messages. First, one should be cautious when applying identity arguments related to fundamental rights. They are subject to inner contradictions and prone to abuse.[129] Second, even if one desires a coherent and unified world of fundamental rights norms, the European multilevel landscape is too complex for that.[130] The European motto of 'united in diversity' is a reminder of that value.

128 Koen Lenaerts, 'No Member State is More Equal than Others' (*Verfassungsblog*) <https://verfassungsblog.de/no-member-state-is-more-equal-than-others/> accessed 22 August 2022.

129 Monica Claes, 'National Identity and the Protection of Fundamental Rights' (2021) 27 European Public Law.

130 Mattias Kumm, '9 The Moral Point of Constitutional Pluralism: Defining the Domain of Legitimate Institutional Civil Disobedience and Conscientious Objection' in Julie Dickson and Pavlos Eleftheriadis (eds), *Philosophical Foundations of European Union Law* (Oxford University Press 2012).

7 Convergence and Divergence in EU External Action

The Very Slowly Emergent Doctrine of Shared Competence[1]

Thomas Verellen

1 Introduction

The tension between unity and diversity lies at the heart of the European integration project.[2] It is reflected in constitutional principles such as those of subsidiarity and conferral; it is visible in the institutional setup of the EU in which precisely those actors that value diversity most strongly – the Member States – are also those that shape the EU's common policies and actions; it is visible in the fact that EU laws are made by the EU institutions but their implementation is typically left to the Member States; and it is reflected in the fact that the EU Treaties ask the EU institutions to do lots of things, but the financial means necessary to enable the EU to do those things remain, to an important extent, under Member State control.

The tension between unity and diversity is particularly pronounced in the sphere of the EU's foreign relations. In contrast to the United States Constitution, the EU Treaties did not extinguish the external sovereignty of its member units. EU Member States existed *qua* sovereign states before the entry into force of the Rome Treaty in 1958 and they continued to exist thereafter – reason for which Alan Dashwood refers to the EU as a 'federation of sovereign states.'[3] The EU Treaties set up a system in which the EU institutions and the Member States can both act externally. This makes sense in historical terms: the European Economic Community's (EEC) mandate extended only to a limited number of areas, most of which were connected to the establishment of the internal market. Outside of

1 This chapter was written during a short stay at the Université de Moncton in Moncton, Canada, in June 2022. I am grateful to Professor Serge Rouselle for his hospitality, to the Belgian American Educational Foundation for its generous financial support, and to the editors for their invitation to contribute to this volume. The title of the chapter is a nod to an article by Robert Schütze: 'Supremacy Without Pre-Emption? The Very Slowly Emergent Doctrine of Community Pre-Emption' (2006) 43 Common Market Law Review 1023.

2 See e.g. Koen Lenaerts, 'Constitutionalism and the Many Faces of Federalism' (1990) 38 American Journal of comparative law 205, 263.

3 Alan Dashwood, 'EU Constitution – What Will Really Change, The' (2004) 7 Cambridge Yearbook of European Legal Studies 33, 47.

DOI: 10.4324/9781003355762-7

these areas, Member States retained their ability to act independently, as sovereign states do.

The very fact that both the EU and its Member States can act externally, including through the conclusion of international agreements, creates a risk of conflict. How to avoid or resolve conflicts between EU and Member State external action? How to ensure that EU policy objectives (unity) can be attained without the pursuit of those objectives excessively constraining the autonomy of the Member States as they conduct their own foreign policies (diversity)? How to ensure, in other words, that a balance is found between convergence and divergence as the EU and the Member States both engage in foreign relations? As we will see, EU law – and in institutional terms: the Court of Justice (hereafter also: the Court) – has addressed these questions differently over time. In this chapter, I sketch how exactly it has done so and how until this day the Court struggles to preserve and enforce the balance between unity and diversity which the Treaties envisaged.

I will sketch the balance between unity and diversity in EU foreign relations by offering an account of how the Court of Justice has pursued two strategies to avoid and if necessary resolve conflicts between the EU institutions – most often the Commission – and the Member States in the foreign policy sphere. First, a strategy of conflict avoidance through exclusivity. Under this approach – in the comparative federalism literature sometimes referred to as one of dual federalism[4] – the EU is allocated exclusive competences to conclude international agreements. Issues outside of the scope of these exclusive competences remain with the Member States. Under this approach, addressing conflicts is a matter of putting issues and policy areas in either one of two boxes: the EU box or the Member State box. It is an approach practiced also in Belgium, where both the federal and member unit governments can conclude international agreements and each policy issue falls within the exclusive jurisdiction of only one level of government. Second, a strategy of conflict avoidance through the imposition on the Member States of obligations to act and not to act. Under this approach, the EU and the Member States both hold shared competences to act externally, but Member States must exercise their powers in such a way that they do not jeopardise the ability of the EU to act effectively.

In the first two decades since the Court of Justice started addressing questions on the EU's authority to act externally, the Court embraced the first approach. In more recent case law, the second approach has become predominant – even though the first approach has created path dependencies that continue to influence EU foreign policy-making to this day. In Sections 3 and 4 of this chapter, I sketch how the Court of Justice moved from the first approach to the second. In Sections 5 and 6, I have a closer look at the difficulties EU law faces today in avoiding and if necessary resolving conflicts between EU institutions and Member States in a paradigm of shared as opposed to exclusive external EU competences.

4 Robert Schütze, *From Dual to Cooperative Federalism: The Changing Structure of European Law* (Oxford University Press 2009) 290.

We will see that, despite the shift from a world of exclusive competences to one of shared competences, there is much continuity in the EU's foreign affairs constitution: in the past as today, the EU Treaties prioritise the full effectiveness of EU law, including EU decision-making rules. Before making the above argument, however, first a few more words on the nature of the challenge the EU faces: in an open federation in which both levels of governance can act externally it is particularly challenging to balance unity and diversity (Section 2).

2 The Challenge: Balancing Unity and Diversity in an Open Federation

In comparative terms, the EU has a particularly open 'foreign affairs constitution.'[5] As mentioned, both the EU and its Member States have international legal personality, and both levels of governance can conclude international agreements and engage in external representation. This can be contrasted with 'closed' federations such as Canada and the U.S. In both of these federal unions, only the federal government has the constitutional authority to conclude international agreements. The justification is both constitutional and international: the constitution allocates the power to make treaties exclusively to the federal government, because only the federal government holds external sovereignty, and the power to make treaties – just like the power to make war or to maintain diplomatic relations – is a necessary concomitant of that sovereignty. In the U.S., Supreme Court Justice Sutherland put it this way:

> As a member of the family of nations, the right and power of the United States in that field are equal to the right and power of the other members of the international family. Otherwise, the United States is not completely sovereign. The power to acquire territory by discovery and occupation … the power to expel undesirable aliens … the power to make such international agreements as do not constitute treaties in the constitutional sense … none of which is expressly affirmed by the Constitution, nevertheless exist as inherently inseparable from the conception of nationality. This the court recognised, and in each of the cases cited found the warrant for its conclusions not in the provisions of the Constitution, but in the law of nations.[6]

5 On the concept of the 'open' federation, see generally Bardo Fassbender, *Der offene Bundesstaat: Studien zur auswärtigen Gewalt und zur Völkerrechtssubjektivität bundesstaatlicher Teilstaaten in Europa* (Mohr Siebeck 2007). The term 'foreign affairs constitution' is routinely used in the U.S. to refer to the constitutional rules and principles that govern the interactions of the United States with the outside world. See e.g. PJ Spiro, 'Globalization and the (Foreign Affairs) Constitution' (2002) 63 Ohio State Law Journal 649. It is used in the EU context e.g. in Robert Schütze, *Foreign Affairs and the EU Constitution: Selected Essays* (Cambridge University Press 2014).

6 *U.S. v. Curtiss-Wright Export Corporation*, 299 U.S. 304 (1936), Sutherland J, 318. For an application of a similar theory in the Canadian context, see Reference Re: Offshore Mineral Rights, [1967] S.C.R. 792, at 816, where the Supreme Court held that the federal Crown has jurisdiction over the seabed because 'it is Canada which is

It is not surprising that the framers of the EU Treaties did not take the path of a wholesale transfer of the power to make treaties to the EU. The EU is after all not a 'state', while the EU Member States are exactly that: sovereign states. From the vantagepoint of Member State capitals, to suggest that only the EU should be able to make international agreements would have come down to the Member States accepting the loss of a core component of their statehood, i.e. the power to conclude international agreements.[7]

That said, the above 'sovereign state' argument which holds that *only* the federal government can make treaties because *only* the federal government is the holder of external sovereignty ultimately begs the question of why in many federations only the federal level of governance has international legal personality and the necessary constitutional authority to conclude international agreements. After all, in Belgium, mentioned earlier, both the federal government and the member units of the federation can conclude international agreements.[8] And in Switzerland, cantons also hold certain, albeit limited, treaty-making powers.[9] The experience of these two federations suggests there is nothing inherent in the concept of external sovereignty that prevents it from being divided between levels of governance. International law in fact acknowledges this reality. On the question of whether member units of a federal state may make treaties, the International Law Commission's Draft articles on Responsibility of States for Internationally Wrongful Acts refer back to the domestic constitution of the federal state.[10]

As a matter of international law, it is thus up to the drafters of the constitution to decide how the powers to engage in foreign relations are to be allocated. And surely, in many – but not all – federal states these powers reside at the federal level. Centralising treaty making powers at the federal level of governance has an important advantage: conflicts between the federal and member unit governments can be kept 'in-house'. To take the example of Canada: in Canada only

recognised by international law as having rights in the territorial sea adjacent to the Province of British Columbia.'

7 Alan Dashwood, 'Why Continue to Have Mixed Agreements at All?' in Jacques HJ Bourgeois, Jean-Louis Dewost and Marie-Ange Gaiffe (eds), *La Communauté européenne et les accords mixtes: quelles perspectives?* (Peter Lang Pub Incorporated 1997) 96.

8 Jan Velaers, '"In foro interno et in foro externo": de internationale bevoegdheden van gemeenschappen en gewesten' in Godfried Geudens and Frank Judo (eds), *Internationale betrekkingen en federalisme: Staatsrechtconferentie 2005 - Vlaamse Juristenvereniging* (Uitgeverij Larcier 2006).

9 Fabrice Filliez, 'La participation des Cantons à la politique extérieure de la Suisse', *L'action extérieure des entités subétatiques: Approche comparée Europe Amérique du Nord* (Presses universitaire de Louvain 2008) 86–8.

10 Art. 4 of the Articles on the Responsibility of States for Internationally Wrongful Acts, in Report of the International Law Commission on the Work of its Fifty-Third Session, UN Doc. A/56/10, chap. V (2001), AOR 56th Sess. Supp. 10. See also Gleider Hernández, 'Federated Entities in International Law: Disaggregating the Federal State?' in Duncan French (ed), *Statehood and Self-Determination* (Cambridge University Press 2013) 510.

the federal government can make treaties.[11] As a consequence, only Canada's federal government will be held internationally responsible for non-compliance with Canada's international obligations. As a consequence, it does not matter whether the non-compliance was caused by Canada's federal government or by one or several of its provincial or territorial governments.[12] The same point can be made about other 'closed' federations such as Germany, the U.S. or Australia.

Not so in the European Union. The EU and its Member States may incur conflicting international obligations as both levels of governance hold competences to conclude international agreements. Different types of conflicts can be imagined. A Member State may have been a party to an international agreement with a third country that predates its accession to the European Union. (Think, for example, of the European Convention on Human Rights to which all EU Member States were a party before they established the then EEC.) Or a Member State may decide to conclude a new international agreement after having become a member of the EU – as Member States did, for example, when they concluded bilateral investment agreements (BITs) with one another. Absent adequate conflict resolution mechanisms, in both of these hypotheses Member States risk being caught between conflicting international obligations: those towards the third country or countries concerned, and those towards the EU.[13] The converse may also occur: the EU may conclude an international agreement that conflicts with an agreement a Member State had previously concluded with a third country. (The BIT Poland had concluded with Canada in 1990 and which would have conflicted with CETA, the EU-Canada trade agreement which provisionally entered into force in 2017, would offer an example.) Or a conflict may arise between a treaty and internal legislation. The example is hypothetical, but take Ireland: Ireland could adopt a statute barring entry into the Irish Republic of goods from Northern Ireland. If this were to occur, the Irish statute would be in breach of the Northern Ireland Protocol, which is part of the EU-UK Withdrawal Agreement, an international agreement to which the EU is a party but which binds Ireland as well by virtue of the agreement's incorporation into EU law.

As the above examples demonstrate, when both levels of governance can act externally, conflicts between exercises of authority by those levels of governance

11 See Thomas Verellen, 'Federalism and Foreign Affairs in Canada and the European Union: The Search for Equal Autonomy' (2016) 5 Cambridge Journal of International and Comparative Law 306.

12 Canada's constitution does not provide for a federal 'treaty implementing power' as exists in the United States following that country's Supreme Court's ruling in *Missouri v Holland* (252 U.S. 416 (1920)). Instead, the power to implement treaty obligations remains divided as set out in Canada's Constitution Act, 1867. See here *Attorney General for Canada v Attorney General for Ontario ('Labour Conventions')*, [1937] A. C. 326 (1937).

13 Note that the solution offered by the abovementioned draft articles (note 10) whereby the federal state remains liable for non-compliance by member units with international obligations incurred by those member units does not apply to the EU-Member State relationship as the EU as the EU is not a state.

can arise. To be clear, such risks exist in 'closed' and 'open' federations alike. An international agreement concluded by the federal government can clash with a domestic member unit statute not only in the EU but also in, say, the U.S. In that federal union, states cannot conclude international agreements. They do however often have the authority to enact statutes on issues covered by international agreements to which the U.S. is a party. Nevertheless, resolving conflicts can be more complicated in 'open' federations. For as soon as international legal obligations vis-à-vis a third country are at play, the conflict is no longer contained within the domestic legal system. Instead, its resolution may have a domestic constitutional aspect as well as an international legal component, and for the conflict to be resolved both legal orders must align.

The problem, however, is that international law and domestic law do not necessarily align. They constitute separate legal orders. As a general rule, international law is not interested in the domestic constitutional structures of states.[14] What matters is compliance and *pacta sunt servanda*. And to make matters worse, international agreements do not always offer solutions enabling states (or the EU) to avoid or resolve conflicts with one another.[15] When they do not, conflicts such as those described earlier may give rise to international legal responsibility. To avoid international responsibility, drafters of constitutions are well advised to set up mechanisms to avoid rather than resolve conflicts. This is where the domestic 'foreign affairs constitution' comes in. As mentioned, the Court of Justice has strived to avoid conflicts between internal norms and international legal obligations incurred by either the EU or the Member States from arising in two ways: initially through exclusivity, and more recently through loyalty obligations within a framework of shared competences. In the following I look at each in turn.

3 The Early Decades: Avoiding Conflicts Through Exclusivity

The Treaty of Rome, the founding treaty of the EEC, had little to say on foreign relations. Only a few of its provisions enabled the EEC to conclude international agreements, and the Treaty was largely silent on how conflicts between EEC norms and Member State international agreements were to be resolved.[16] Given the scarcity of Treaty text, questions were bound to be asked to the Court of Justice. In 1971, in what coincidentally was the very first annulment action brought by the Commission against the Council, the Court was asked to assess the legality of a set of Council conclusions.[17] In these conclusions, the Council had decided the Member States rather than the EEC should conclude an international agreement on the working conditions of truckers known as the European Road Transport Agreement (ERTA). The Commission disagreed with the

14 See Arts. 27 and 46 VCLT.

15 Art. 30.8 CETA, for example, provides that pre-existing BITs such as the abovementioned Canada-Poland BIT shall be replaced by CETA.

16 See however Art. 234 of the Rome Treaty (current Art. 352 TFEU).

17 Case 22/70, *Commission v Council ('ERTA')*, EU:C:1971:32.

Council. It considered the issues covered by the ERTA to fall under the exclusive competence of the EEC. For this reason, the EEC rather than the individual Member States should conclude the agreement, the Commission concluded.

The Court agreed with the Commission. In a judgment which in terms of its significance for the development of the EU's constitutional framework is as important as *Van Gend en Loos* and *Costa v ENEL*, the Court held that

> each time the Community, with a view to implementing a common policy envisaged by the Treaty, adopts provisions laying down common rules, whatever form these may take, the Member States no longer have the right, acting individually or even collectively, to undertake obligations with third countries which affect those rules.[18]

In this case, the Court considered that the EEC had indeed laid down common rules in the form of a set of regulations that governed working conditions in the road transport sector within the EEC. Moreover, the scope of the pre-existing EU rules was defined differently from that of the ERTA, which meant that the ERTA could indeed 'affect' the pre-existing common rules. For these reasons, the Court concluded that the Member States had lost the authority to conclude the ERTA, and only the EEC could conclude the agreement.

But why this far-reaching a conclusion? Why is it that the EEC acquires an external competence – and an *exclusive* external competence at that – whenever the EU adopts internal common rules? The ERTA principle, as the principle introduced in the *ERTA* case became known, is a conflict prevention mechanism.[19] By precluding Member States from incurring international obligations on issues on which the EU has legislated internally, conflicts between EU rules and Member State international obligations do not arise and complex issues of international responsibility can be avoided. The Court turned to the principle of sincere cooperation in search of a normative foundation for the new doctrine – not coincidentally the same basis the Court referred to in *Costa* to support the Court's claim that EU law has primacy over conflicting (internal) Member State law[20], and, as we will see, also the foundation of

18 ibid para. 17.

19 In this sense, see Geert De Baere, *Constitutional Principles of EU External Relations* (Oxford University Press 2008) 71; Piet Eeckhout, 'Bold Constitutionalism and Beyond' in Miguel Maduro and Loic Azoulai (eds), *The Past and Future of EU Law: The Classics of EU Law Revisited on the 50th Anniversary of the Rome Treaty* (Hart 2010) 219. The same can be said of the Art. 218 TFEU opinion procedure, which allows the Court to review whether proposed EU agreements comply with existing EU law. See here Marise Cremona and Jaka Kukavica, 'Common Commercial Policy and the Determination of Exclusivity: Opinion 1/75 (Local Cost Standard)' in Graham Butler and Ramses Wessel (eds), *EU External Relations Law. The Cases in Context* (Hart 2022) 50–52.

20 Case 6/64, *Costa v ENEL*, EU:C:1964:66, 593–594. See also Timothy Roes and Geert De Baere, 'EU Loyalty as Good Faith' (2015) 64 International and Comparative Law Quarterly 829, 837; Marise Cremona, 'EU External Competence – Rationales for Exclusivity' in Sacha Garben and Inge Govaere (eds), *The Division of*

the duty of sincere cooperation that governs the exercise of shared competences. In *ERTA*, the Court of Justice thus opted for a strategy of conflict avoidance through exclusivity: whenever a risk of a conflict between a Member State international commitment and a pre-existing EU norm arises, the EU acquires an exclusive external competence on the issue(s) covered by a proposed international agreement. I have referred to this doctrine as one of pre-emption, after the U.S. legal doctrine according to which state law yields to federal law in the event of a conflict.[21] It has also been referred to as one of 'subsequent exclusivity',[22] 'supervening exclusivity'[23], or simply 'ERTA-type exclusivity.'[24]

ERTA-type exclusivity can be distinguished from *a priori* exclusivity.[25] The EU holds an *a priori* exclusive external competence when the Treaties expressly characterise the EU's competence as exclusive. This is the case for a limited number of policy areas of which the common commercial policy is arguably the most important one for our present purposes.[26] Here too, it was the Court of Justice which made it clear that the EEC's competence to engage in external trade policy was an *exclusive* competence, and it was only in later rounds of Treaty reform that the exclusive nature of the competence was recognised in the Treaty text.[27] In Opinion 1/75, issued in November 1975, on whether export credits could be considered part of the EU's trade policy competence, the Court categorically ruled out the possibility of concurrent (or shared) competences:

Competences between the EU and the Member States: Reflections on the Past, the Present and the Future (Hart 2017) 143.

21 Thomas Verellen, 'The ERTA Doctrine in the Post-Lisbon Era: Note under Judgment in Commission v Council (C-114/12) and Opinion 1/13' (2015) 21 Columbia Journal of European Law 383. Similarly see Cremona, 'EU External Competence – Rationales for Exclusivity' (n 20) 145; Piet Eeckhout, 'Exclusive External Competences: Constructing the EU as an International Actor' in Court of Justice of the European Union (ed), *The Court of Justice and the Construction of Europe: Analyses and Perspectives on Sixty Years of Case-law* (T M C Asser Press 2013) 627. On preemption in the U.S., see generally William W Buzbee, *Preemption Choice: The Theory, Law, and Reality of Federalism's Core Question* (Cambridge University Press 2008).

22 Robert Schütze, 'The European Community's Federal Order of Competences: A Retrospective Analysis' in M Dougan and S Currie (eds), *50 Years of the European Treaties: Looking Back and Thinking Forward* (Hart 2008) 74.

23 Eleftheria Neframi, 'Article 216(1) TFEU and the Union's Shared External Competence in the Light of Mixity: Germany v. Council (COTIF)' (2019) 56 Common Market Law Review 489, 502.

24 Laurens Ankersmit, 'Requiring "Unity First" in Relations with Third States: The Court Continues ERTA-Doctrine in Opinion 1/13' (*European Law Blog*, 20 October 2014) <https://europeanlawblog.eu/2014/10/20/requiring-unity-first-in-relations-with-third-states-the-court-continues-erta-doctrine-in-opinion-113/> accessed 23 June 2022.

25 De Baere (n 19) 39; Cremona, 'EU External Competence—Rationales for Exclusivity' (n 20) 136.

26 Art. 3(1) TFEU.

27 Art. 3(1)(e) TFEU.

> [The common commercial policy] is conceived ... in the context of the operation of the Common Market, for the defence of the common interests of the Community, within which the particular interests of the Member States must endeavour to adapt to each other.
>
> Quite clearly, however, this conception is incompatible with the freedom to which the Member States could lay claim by invoking a concurrent power, so as to ensure that their own interests were separately satisfied in external relations, at the risk of compromising the effective defence of the common interests of the Community.[28]

As the above citation suggests, as in *ERTA*, in Opinion 1/75 the Court of Justice was concerned with possible conflicts between Member State and EU external action. That said, when compared to *ERTA*, the Court is interested in a somewhat different type of conflict. In *ERTA*, the relationship between pre-existing EU common rules and a proposed Member State international agreement was at issue. In Opinion 1/75, there were no pre-existing common rules. Instead, the conflict lay in the future: the Court is concerned about potential future conflicts between Member State external actions and actions yet to be undertaken by the EU that may arise. In this sense, the conception of 'conflict' on which the Court relied in Opinion 1/75 is thus broader and more forward-looking than that at work in *ERTA*.[29] The Court developed the point a bit further down on the same page of the opinion, where it held:

> To accept that the contrary were true [i.e. that Member States did hold a concurrent power to conduct trade policy] would amount to recognising that, in relations with third countries, Member States may adopt positions which differ from those which the Community intends to adopt, and would thereby distort the institutional framework, call into question the mutual trust within the Community and prevent the latter from fulfilling its task in the defence of the common interest.[30]

Both ERTA-type and *a priori* exclusivity, then, are mechanisms to avoid conflicts from arising between Member State international commitments and EU rules (and policies). By precluding Member States from acting externally, the above-mentioned risk of conflict is foreclosed. In terms of constitutional theory, this approach aligned with the theory of a transfer of sovereignty within limited fields articulated by the Court in *Van Gend*[31], albeit that in the external sphere the

28 Opinion 1/75 ('Local Cost Standard'), EU:C:1975:145, 1363–4.
29 Emphasising the concern for external unity, see Cremona, 'EU External Competence – Rationales for Exclusivity' (n 20) 139., and again in Marise Cremona, 'Internal Differentiation and External Unity' in Fabian Amtenbrink and others (eds), *The Internal Market and the Future of European Integration* (1st edn, Cambridge University Press 2019).
30 ibid.
31 Case 26/62, *Van Gend en Loos*, EU:C:1963:1, 12.

Court replaced conflict *resolution* through primacy with conflict *prevention* through exclusivity.[32]

4 The Slow Emergence of a Doctrine of Shared Competence

While most Member States accepted the principle that the EU can hold both *a priori* and subsequent exclusive external competences, many Member States disagreed with the Commission on the scope of those exclusive competences. These disagreements continue until this day. For example, in Opinion 2/15 on the EU-Singapore free trade agreement, the Court further clarified the contours of the EU's common commercial policy competence.[33] It concluded that most but not all provisions of the agreement fell within the EU's exclusive external competence – either its *a priori* exclusive competence to conduct a common commercial policy, or an ERTA-type exclusive competence. Over 20 years earlier, the Court had reached a similar conclusion when it was asked to opine on the EU's competence to accede to the WTO agreements.[34] In Opinion 1/94, the Court held that under the Treaty rules that were in force at the time, several components of the WTO agreements were covered neither by the EU's *a priori* exclusive competence to conduct a common commercial policy nor by ERTA-type exclusivity.

Opinion 1/94 as well as Opinion 2/15 illustrate an important point: only rarely will an international agreement be covered entirely by EU exclusive competence.[35] I see three explanations for this fact.

First, the list of *a priori* exclusive competences is short, and amongst the areas of exclusive competence only the common commercial policy is relevant for the EU's foreign relations.[36] And while the Court has adhered to a broad interpretation of the scope of the common commercial policy, that scope is not limitless. In Opinion 1/94, for example, the Court made clear that under the Treaties as they then stood, the treatment of nationals of non-Member States on crossing the external borders of Member States did not fall within the scope of the common commercial policy.[37] Similarly, in Opinion 2/15 the Court concluded that non-direct foreign investment fell outside of the scope of the common commercial policy.[38]

Second, at times the Court of Justice has adhered to a fairly restrictive interpretation of what it means for Member State international commitments to 'affect'

32 In this sense, see Marise Cremona, 'EU External Relations: Unity and Conferral of Powers' in Loïc Azoulai (ed), *The Question of Competence in the European Union* (Oxford University Press 2014) 68.: '[T]he approach to both express and implied competence was based on conceptions of effectiveness and unity, and in the initial cases the Court assumes that unity requires a transfer of competence and therefore exclusivity.' Highlighting how the Court could have opted to extend the primacy principle to the external sphere, see Eeckhout (n 19) 219.
33 Opinion 2/15 ('EUSFTA'), EU:C:2017:376.
34 Opinion 1/94 ('WTO'), EU:C:1994:384.
35 In this sense, see also Eeckhout (n 21) 634.
36 Art. 3(1) TFEU.
37 Opinion 1/94 ('WTO'), EU:C:1994:384, para. 46.
38 Opinion 2/15 ('EUSFTA'), EU:C:2017:376, para. 243.

common rules in the meaning of the ERTA principle. This restrictive approach was visible in particular in Opinion 1/94, where the Court seemed to suggest an ERTA effect could be triggered only if the common rules concerned completely harmonised a given area.[39] But arguably it is visible also in more recent case law, in which the Court emphasises how ERTA-type exclusivity can be recognised only on the basis of a 'comprehensive and detailed' analysis of the relationship between the envisaged international agreement and the EU law in force.[40]

Third, and perhaps most importantly, the scope of many of the contemporary international agreements to which the Member States or the EU wish to become a party is much broader than that of earlier agreements such as the ERTA. The ERTA was a narrowly tailored agreement on the working conditions of truckers. Compare that to the WTO agreements, which aimed to set up an ambitious set of multilateral trading rules covering not only tariffs on goods, but also services and intellectual property rights. Or compare the ERTA to the more recent 'second generation' trade agreements such as CETA, which contain chapters on sustainable development, labour rights, investment, competition policy, and so forth. The wider the agreement, the less likely that it will be covered in its entirety by either *a priori* or ERTA-type exclusive competence.

As it became increasingly obvious that not all areas in which the EU was active externally fell within the scope of EU exclusive competence, a new constitutional question became salient: What is the status of those areas not covered by EU exclusive competence? How to characterise those areas in legal terms? If a competence is not exclusive to the EU, does it necessarily follow that it is exclusive to the Member States?

The Court seemed to answer the last of the above questions in the positive. In Opinion 1/94, mentioned earlier, it held that the competence to conclude the GATS was 'shared' between the EU and its Member States.[41] For this reason, the EU and the Member States had to 'jointly' conclude the GATS by means of a mixed agreement.[42] In Opinion 1/94, 'shared' meant that the competence needed to conclude the agreement at issue was not entirely held by the EU, but that parts of the necessary competence had not yet been 'transferred' to the EU, either through the allocation of an *a priori* exclusive competence or through an ERTA effect. There was no room in the Court's analysis in Opinion 1/94 for the possibility that the EU has a competence to act externally outside of the *a priori* or ERTA exclusivity scenarios. This was visible, in particular, in the way the Court conflated 'shared' with 'joint' competence – 'joint' referring to the joint

39 Opinion 1/94 ('WTO'), EU:C:1994:384, para. 96.

40 See e.g. Opinion 1/13 ('Hague Convention'), EU:C:2014:2303, para. 74.

41 Opinion 1/94 ('WTO'), EU:C:1994:384, para. 46.

42 For readers not familiar with the concept: a mixed agreement is an international agreement to which, in addition to one or several third countries, both the EU and one, several or all Member States are a party. On mixed agreements, see generally Christophe Hillion and Panos Koutrakos (eds), *Mixed Agreements Revisited: The EU and Its Member States in the World* (Hart 2010).

conclusion by the EU and the Member States of a mixed agreement.[43] Or as Nanette Neuwahl noted in a 1996 contribution: 'The notion of "*shared* competence" serves to stress that the entire life of a (projected) mixed agreement is the *joint* affair of the Community and the Member states.'[44]

In Neuwahl's account, as in that of the Court, there was no space for a shared competence understood as a concurrent competence whereby the EU and the Member States *both* hold competences to act independently of one another in the *same* area. Rather, in keeping with the categorical approach that characterised *ERTA* and Opinion 1/75, external competence fit into one out of two boxes: the EU box or the Member State box. And while the Court did speak the language of shared competence in Opinion 1/94, shared competence did not constitute a distinct competence category. Rather, the term 'shared' competence had to be read in the context of a specific international agreement: if the agreement fell only in part within the scope of the EU's exclusive competence, the competence to conclude the agreement was shared between the EU and the Member States. Because competence was shared, joint EU-Member State action was necessary to conclude the agreement.

The equation of 'shared' competence with 'joint' action has continued to haunt the case law of the Court for quite a while. As recently as 2017, in Opinion 2/15 the Court seemed to suggest that in those areas of the EU-Singapore trade agreement that fall outside of the scope of the EU's exclusive competence but within the scope of EU shared competence, the EU and the Member States *must* act jointly by concluding a mixed agreement.[45] (The Court held, for example, that 'Section A of Chapter 9 of the envisaged agreement [which falls within a competence shared between the EU and the Member States] cannot be approved by the European Union alone.'[46]) It was interesting to note, then, that in a judgment issued only a couple of months after Opinion 2/15, in the case of *COTIF*, the Court made the following statement, directly referring to what it had said earlier in Opinion 2/15:

> Admittedly, the Court found … that the relevant provisions of the agreement concerned, relating to non-direct foreign investment, which fall within the shared competence of the European Union and its Member States, could not be approved by the Union alone. However, in making that finding, the Court did no more than acknowledge the fact that … there was no possibility of the required majority being obtained within the Council for the Union to be able to exercise alone the external competence that it shares with the Member States in this area.[47]

43 Opinion 1/94 ('WTO'), EU:C:1994:384, para. 105.
44 Nanette A Neuwahl, 'Shared Powers or Combined Incompetence: More on Mixity' (1996) 33 Common Market Law Review 667, 667. Italics added.
45 Opinion 2/15 ('EUSFTA'), EU:C:2017:376, paras 243–4.
46 ibid para. 243.
47 Case C-600/14, *Germany v Council ('COTIF')*, EU:C:2017:935, para. 68.

In this paragraph, the Court clearly confirmed that the competence division is not black or white (exclusive EU versus exclusive Member State competence) but that there is also grey (shared EU competence), and that the EU can act autonomously also within the scope of its shared competence.[48] In so ruling, the Court contradicted a submission made by Germany according to which in areas of shared competence the European Union cannot exercise a competence externally when it has not already made use of its competence internally.[49] Germany had argued firmly within the contours of the categorical paradigm that underlay the Court's *ERTA* ruling. If EU competence is necessarily exclusive, and if it is allocated either directly by the Treaties (*a priori* exclusivity) or emerges gradually as the EU adopts internal common rules (ERTA-type exclusivity), it follows that outside of the *a priori* and ERTA exclusivity scenarios, the EU lacks external competence altogether.

By so clearly dismissing Germany's theory, the Court in *COTIF* put an end to the ambiguity that surrounded shared competence as a distinct competence category in the EU's 'foreign affairs constitution': when the EU holds a shared competence, it can exercise that competence independently from the Member States. This has an important political consequence: whereas an EU-only agreement can likely be concluded by means of a qualified majority vote in the Council, mixity often implies unanimity-based decision-making. Prior to *COTIF*, it was often made to appear as if mixity – i.e. the practice of concluding mixed agreements – was a constitutional necessity. Whenever a proposed agreement did not fall entirely within the scope of the EU's exclusive competence, mixed or joint EU-Member State action was the only permissible option. Mixity was, to use the typology introduced by Allan Rosas, always *mandatory* and never *facultative*.[50] In *COTIF*, the Court made clear that in many instances, mixity is in fact facultative rather than mandatory, and that mixity is often the result of a political choice by the Member States in the Council.

COTIF makes plain that the EU now lives in a world of shared rather than exclusive external competence. As a general rule, EU external competence is shared. This means the Council may choose to exercise EU external competence, or it may opt not to do so. Solely when EU external competence is exclusive, only the EU may act, and Member State action is not an option. As often some aspects of a proposed international agreement will fall within the scope of the EU's

48 Advocates-General and commentators had been arguing that EU external competence could be non-exclusive for quite a while. See e.g. Opinion of AG Wahl in Opinion 3/15 ('Marrakesh Treaty'), EU:C:2016:657, para. 119 and De Baere (n 19) 62. And the Court itself had implicitly confirmed the possibility that competences be non-exclusive by distinguishing in its analysis between the question of the existence of competence and that of its nature. See e.g. Opinion 1/13 ('Hague Convention'), EU:C:2014:2303, paras 67 and 69.

49 Case C-600/14, *Germany v Council ('COTIF')*, EU:C:2017:935, para. 37.

50 See generally Allan Rosas, 'The European Union and Mixed Agreements' in Alan Dashwood and Christophe Hillion (eds), *The General Law of E.C. External Relations* (Sweet & Maxwell 2000).

exclusive external competence – either *a priori* or of the ERTA-type – EU action will typically be needed to conclude the agreement. Whether the Member States join the EU, or whether the EU exercises the additional shared competence needed to conclude the agreement, is a political choice for the Council to make.[51] If the Council decides to exercise EU shared competence, the agreement can be concluded as an EU-only agreement.[52] If it does not, the Member States must supplement EU exclusive competence to enable the EU to conclude the agreement. In this universe, mixed or joint action thus tends to be *facultative*. Only when the EU lacks competence altogether will mixity be *mandatory*. This does not happen very often, however, considering the wide scope of the EU's shared competence.[53] As a consequence, in many if not most cases, mixity is the result of a political choice by the Member States in the Council.

5 Avoiding Conflicts in a World of Shared Competences: The Duty of Sincere Cooperation

In the above I discussed how the EU Treaties dealt with conflicts between EU and Member State external actions in the early decades: by characterising EU competences as exclusive, conflicts could be avoided as Member States did not have the necessary competence to act in the first place. In a world of shared competences, this strategy of conflict avoidance is no longer readily available. How, then, are conflicts between the EU and the Member States addressed in a world of shared competences—a world in which *both* the EU and the Member States hold competences to conclude international agreements on the same issues?

To avoid and if necessary resolve conflicts in a world of shared competences, the Court of Justice turned to a concept well known to German constitutional lawyers: that of *Bundestreue* or federal loyalty.[54] The EU's own federal loyalty principle – the duty of sincere cooperation – imposes procedural and in some instances substantive obligations on Member States. Member States first and foremost owe the EU institutions – and in particular the Commission – information. Whenever they consider acting externally on an issue on which the Commission has put in motion a decision-making process, individual Member States must coordinate and consult with the Commission. This is the lesson of the *Inland Waterways* cases. These two infringement proceedings were brought by the Commission after Germany and Luxembourg had unilaterally concluded

51 Neframi (n 23) 506.

52 This happened e.g. with the EU-UK Trade and Cooperation Agreement, which was concluded as an EU-only agreement.

53 In this sense, see Allan Rosas, 'Exclusive, Shared and National Competence in the Context of EU External Relations: Do Such Distinctions Matter?' in Inge Govaere and others (eds), *The European Union in the world: essays in honour of Marc Maresceau* (Brill 2014) 33–4.

54 In the German context, see generally Patricia Egli, *Die Bundestreue: eine rechtsvergleichende Untersuchung* (Dike 2010).

bilateral international agreements with a number of Central and Eastern European countries to regulate traffic on inland waterways.[55] As Germany and Luxembourg were concluding these agreements, the Commission was busy negotiating a multilateral agreement with the same countries. The Court considered that Germany and Luxembourg had violated their duty of sincere cooperation vis-à-vis the EU by failing to cooperate and consult with the Commission as they proceeded to ratify and implement the above bilateral agreements.

In addition to procedural duties, the duty of sincere cooperation also imposes substantive obligations on Member States. In *PFOS*, the Commission had asked the Court of Justice to assess whether Sweden had violated its duty of sincere cooperation by submitting to an international body a proposal to include Perfluorooctane sulfonic acid (PFOS) on a list of toxic chemicals.[56] In contrast to *Inland Waterways*, this was a case of mixed rather than EU-only external action as both the EU and all Member States were members of the international body at issue. As in *Inland Waterways*, however, in *PFOS* a single Member State also acted unilaterally while a decision-making process at EU level was ongoing. At the time Sweden made its proposal, the Council was considering what position the EU should take within the international body. The Court held that by submitting the proposal, Sweden had violated its duty of sincere cooperation. The Court made it clear that Sweden was required not only to coordinate and consult with the Commission, but also to refrain from acting altogether.[57]

Inland Waterways and *PFOS* demonstrate the extent to which the duty of sincere cooperation restricts the autonomy of Member States to act unilaterally once some form of concerted action is in the making at EU level. As some commentators have pointed out, the obligations the duty of sincere cooperation imposes on the Member States are not all that different from those imposed on them by the EU Treaties when the Treaties characterise a given issue as falling under the EU's exclusive competence.[58] In both instances, Member States are under an obligation not to act to avoid conflicts from arising between EU and Member State external action.

That said, there are at least two important differences between the duty of sincere cooperation as it operates in a world of shared competences and the obligations it imposes on Member States when EU external competence is exclusive. First, the threshold for the obligation not to act to take effect is higher under the duty of sincere cooperation as compared to the doctrine of exclusivity. As the Court made clear in *PFOS*, only when Member State actions are likely to *harm* EU policy are Member States precluded from acting. In *PFOS*, Sweden's actions were 'likely to compromise the principle of unity in the international representation of the Union and its Member States and weaken their negotiating

55 Case C-433/03, Commission v Germany ('Inland Waterways'), EU:C:2005:462 and Case C-266/03, Commission v Luxembourg ('Inland Waterways'), EU:C:2005:341.

56 Case C-246/07, *Commission v Sweden ('PFOS')*, EU:C:2010:203.

57 ibid para. 91.

58 See in particular Marise Cremona, 'Extending the Reach of the AETR Principle: Comment on Commission v Greece' (2009) 34 European Law Review 754.

power with regard to the other parties to the Convention concerned', the Court held.[59] This can be compared to the ERTA requirement that, for ERTA-type exclusivity to arise, a Member State international commitment must merely be likely to 'affect' pre-existing common rules. Such 'affectation' can take the form of a conflict, but something less than a conflict may also trigger an ERTA effect. Second, under the duty of sincere cooperation Member States are not obliged to refrain from acting forever. As Advocate General Poiares Maduro suggested in *PFOS*, they should refrain from acting at least until the EU decision-making procedure has come to an end.[60] But after that point, arguably Member States are again free to act.

As far as the scenario of one or a couple of Member States 'going at it alone' is concerned, the EU Treaties thus send a relatively clear message to the Member States: talk to the Commission (*Inland Waterways*), and do not act when your action(s) risk(s) harming EU policies that are either in the making or that have already been decided upon (*PFOS*). As is the case for EU exclusive competences, the approach is one of conflict avoidance rather than conflict resolution. Not unlike the constitutional arrangements in Belgium, where the constitution effectively obliges all governments to negotiate until a consensus is reached, the EU Treaties oblige Member States and the EU institutions to consult and cooperate. By doing so, potential conflicts can be identified and prevented before they materialise.

6 Coming Full Circle: The Autonomy of EU Law as a Conflict Resolution Mechanism in a World of Shared Competence

The duty of sincere cooperation thus imposes significant limitations on the autonomy of Member States to act externally in an effort to avoid conflicts between EU and Member State external action from materialising. That said, once a conflict has in fact materialised, the duty of sincere cooperation has little to offer. As a constitutional principle operating within the confines of the EU legal order, it cannot undo the international legal consequences of the Member State(s)' unilateral action. In the case of *PFOS*, for example, Sweden had put in motion a decision-making process at international level the outcome of which would be binding on the EU and all EU Member States, regardless of the Court of Justice's findings in the infringement proceedings brought by the Commission.[61]

International law limits the reach of the duty of sincere cooperation also in other ways. Let us return to the scenario of the negotiation and conclusion of a

59 ibid 104.

60 Opinion of AG Poiares Maduro in Case C-246/07, *Commission v Sweden ('PFOS')*, EU:C:2009:589, para. 49.

61 Case C-246/07, *Commission v Sweden ('PFOS')*, EU:C:2010:203, para. 100. See also Geert De Baere, '"O, Where Is Faith? O, Where Is Loyalty?" Some Thoughts on the Duty of Loyal Co-Operation and the Union's External Environmental Competences in the Light of the PFOS Case' (2011) 36 European Law Review 405, 409; Marcus Klamert, *The Principle of Loyalty in EU Law* (Oxford University Press 2014) 114.

mixed agreement. In this scenario, the EU and the Member States negotiate and conclude an international agreement together: the EU is a party, as are all Member States. In this process, the latter act as sovereign states in addition to their role as Member States in the Council. Under international law, Member States *qua* sovereign States cannot be forced to express their consent to the proposed international agreement.[62] As a consequence, in some instances Member States hold a *de facto* veto power over the conclusion of mixed agreements by the EU. This is the case, in particular, where a mixed agreement requires all parties to have ratified the agreement before it enters into force. CETA is a good example: while it can be provisionally applied, its entry into force hinges on the prior ratification by all parties, which means: Canada, the EU, and all Member States.[63] By contrast, other agreements – typically multilateral agreements – do not require all parties to have ratified the agreement before it can enter into force. For such agreements, individual Member States do not hold a veto power as it is permissible under international law for the EU to conclude the agreement without all Member States being on board. The mixed agreement would then become an *incomplete* mixed agreement, i.e. a mixed agreement to which the EU and some but not all Member States are parties.

In a 2021 opinion on the Istanbul Convention on women's rights, the Court clarified that incomplete mixity does indeed offer a way out of the deadlock in which the EU may find itself when the Council wants to conclude a bilateral mixed agreement, but one or several Member States refuse to do so. In Opinion 1/19, the Court held that nothing can stop a majority of Member States in the Council from forcing a vote, and a qualified majority of Member States from enabling the Council to adopt a decision to conclude the agreement on behalf of the EU.[64] EU law is autonomous, the Court held, and applies to the exclusion, if necessary, of any other law.[65] Likewise, and contrary to the submission made by France[66], it would seem, the duty of sincere cooperation does not require the EU to wait for a common accord amongst the Member States to materialise before exercising its external competence. Following the same logic, the duty of sincere

62 Art. 51 VCLT. On this point, see also Thomas Verellen, 'On Hybrid Decisions, Mixed Agreements and the Limits of the New Legal Order: Commission v Council ('US Air Transport Agreement') (2016) 53 Common Market Law Review 741, 754; Guillaume Van der Loo and Ramses A Wessel, 'The Non-Ratification of Mixed Agreements: Legal Consequences and Solutions' (2017) 54 Common Market Law Review 735, 745.

63 Art. 30.7(2) CETA. The provisional application of those parts of CETA within the EU's exclusive competence significantly limits the practical impact of the lack of formal entry into force of the agreement. However, provisional application *ad infinitum* should be avoided both for reasons of legal certainty (each party can unilaterally terminate an agreement's provisional application) and for reasons of democratic legitimacy (provisional application can be decided by the executive without involvement of the legislature – in the EU's case the European Parliament).

64 Opinion 1/19 ('Istanbul Convention'), EU:C:2021:198, para. 274.

65 ibid para. 231.

66 ibid para. 187.

cooperation does not oblige the Member States to ratify a mixed agreement either. For such an interpretation of the duty would run counter the above-mentioned international legal principle that states cannot be coerced to express their consent to an international agreement.

In the final analysis, then, the duty of sincere cooperation finds its limits in the autonomy of EU law on one side, and the sovereignty of the Member States on the other.[67] This is noteworthy as it is possible to imagine an alternative reality in which the EU Treaties would constitutionally require the EU and the Member States to act jointly, on the basis of unanimity, to conclude any and all mixed agreements. This is in fact the path taken in Belgium, where the constitution requires the different Belgian governments to set up institutional frameworks to negotiate and conclude mixed agreements on a consensual basis. In the Belgian framework, mixity always implies unanimity, and absent unanimity no external action can be undertaken. Not so in the EU, where the Court of Justice has thus made clear that the duty of sincere cooperation imposes real legal obligations on the Member States and, to a lesser extent, on the EU institutions, but the duty of sincere cooperation cannot preclude the EU from exercising its own competences, if necessary independently from the Member States.

Despite the shift from a world of exclusive competence to one of shared competence, there is a lot of continuity between recent opinions such as Opinion 1/19 on the one hand, and earlier rulings such as *ERTA* and Opinion 1/75 on the other. At the time of *ERTA* and Opinion 1/75, conflicts between EU and Member State external action were avoided through exclusivity. Today, conflicts are avoided through the duty of sincere cooperation (*PFOS*) and resolved through the autonomy principle (Opinion 1/19). Both in the past and today, the constitutional framework privileges the full effectiveness of EU law – both substantive common rules as in *ERTA* and procedural rules as in Opinion 1/19 – over the external autonomy of the Member States. To be sure, recent case law does not explicitly refer to the need to ensure that the EU is capable of defending the 'common interests' of the EU, which the Court did invoke in Opinion 1/75, mentioned earlier. Yet, by affirming that the EU can independently conclude a mixed agreement even in the absence of a common accord amongst the Member States, the Court of Justice demonstrates it is as committed to ensuring that the EU is capable of acting autonomously today as it was at the time of Opinion 1/75.

In this sense, we have indeed come full circle. When the Court concluded in Opinion 1/94 that the competence to conclude the WTO agreements was shared between the EU and its Member States, it added that 'in a framework of shared competence, close cooperation between the Member States and the EU institutions, both in the process of negotiation and conclusion and in the fulfilment of

67 On how the autonomy of EU law and the sovereignty of Member States may very well be two sides of the same coin, see Thomas Verellen, 'European Sovereignty Now? A Reflection on What It Means to Speak of "European Sovereignty"' (2020) 5 European Papers 307, 310.

the commitments entered into, is needed.'[68] This phrase seemed to announce a profound shift in the structure of the EU's foreign affairs constitution, from a paradigm in which conflicts are avoided and resolved through hierarchy, to one in which levels of governance are co-equal and institutions and governments resolve conflicts by working together in a spirit of loyalty.[69] Cases such as *Inland Waterways* and *PFOS* seemed to confirm this paradigm shift as the Court of Justice started to transform an abstract *principle* of sincere cooperation into a *duty* of sincere cooperation that imposes real legal obligations on the Member States. The Lisbon Treaty's reformulation of the duty as a duty that applies not only to the Member States, but also to the EU institutions, gave further credence to the paradigm shift thesis.[70]

Opinion 1/19 makes clear that the abovementioned transformation should not be overstated.[71] Today, as in the past, the Court of Justice is committed to preserving the full effectiveness – and thus the autonomy – of the EU Treaties. While in the past it did so through exclusivity, today the duty of sincere cooperation fulfils a similar role in avoiding conflicts from arising between EU and Member State external action. And when conflicts do arise, they are resolved in favour of the EU Treaties.

7 Conclusion

In this chapter, I sketched how the tension between unity and diversity that characterises the European integration project presents itself with a particular intensity in the context of the EU's foreign relations. I explained how in the EU – an 'open' federation in which both levels of governance have competences to act externally – conflicts between EU and Member State external action are either avoided or resolved. The approach to conflict prevention and resolution has shifted over time. In early decisions such as *ERTA* and Opinion 1/75, the Court of Justice articulated a doctrine of exclusivity. By characterising issues as falling under EU exclusive competence, the Member States were precluded from acting. This would in turn, the thinking went, avoid conflicts from materialising.

68 Opinion 1/94 ('WTO'), EU:C:1994:384, para. 108.

69 See here the somewhat optimistic assessment of the Court's case law on the duty of sincere cooperation prior to *PFOS* as an approach that is more in keeping with the EU's pluralist DNA in Christophe Hillion, 'Mixity and Coherence in EU External Relations: The Significance of the "Duty of Cooperation"' in Christophe Hillion and Panos Koutrakos (eds), *Mixed agreements revisited: the EU and its member states in the world* (Hart 2010).

70 Art. 4(3) TEU.

71 See similarly also Case C-28/12, *Commission v Council ('US Air Transport Agreement')*, EU:C:2015:282 in which the Court of Justice annulled a so-called 'hybrid act.' In this case, the Court rejected the argument that the duty of sincere cooperation required the EU and the Member States to merge decision-making procedures so as to protect the unity in the international representation of the EU and the Member States. I discuss the case in Verellen, 'On Hybrid Decisions, Mixed Agreements and the Limits of the New Legal Order: Commission v Council ('US Air Transport Agreement') (n 65).

In more recent decades, the Court of Justice acknowledged the existence of broad areas of non-exclusive or shared competence. What it meant for an issue to fall within 'shared' competence remained ambiguous for a long period of time. Not that long ago, however, the Court clarified that in areas of shared competence both the EU and the Member States may act externally, independently from one another. To avoid conflicts in this world of shared competences, the duty of sincere cooperation imposes obligations to consult and cooperate on the EU institutions and the Member States. These obligations may in some cases go as far as to preclude Member States from acting altogether, thus somewhat narrowing the gap between the obligations on Member States in areas of shared and exclusive competence.

Whereas the duty of sincere cooperation may thus impose on Member States a 'duty to remain silent'[72], individual Member States cannot preclude the EU from acting if the requirements to act set out in the EU Treaties – in particular the voting rules in the Council – are met. At this juncture, the autonomy principle remerges as the contemporary, somewhat more light-touch, cousin of the exclusivity doctrine through which conflicts between Member State and EU decision-making rules are resolved rather than prevented. Today as well as in the past, the EU foreign affairs constitution constrains the external autonomy of Member States while protecting that of the EU. What matters, for the Court of Justice, is that the EU is constitutionally well-equipped to act autonomously on the international stage.

In this sense, through the principles of exclusivity, sincere cooperation and autonomy the EU's foreign affairs constitution privileges unity over diversity in an effort to construct the EU as a foreign policy actor in its own right.[73] This does not mean Member State diversity is not protected in EU foreign policy making. It clearly is: Member States are represented in the Council, which is the main decision-maker in EU foreign relations.[74] Crucially, however, from the vantagepoint of the EU Treaties as interpreted by the Court of Justice, this protection takes place within the confines of the EU legal order, rather than through the involvement of Member States acting alongside the EU on the international stage as sovereign states in their own right.

72 Andrès Delgado-Casteleiro and Joris Larik, 'The Duty to Remain Silent: Limitless Loyalty in EU External Relations?' (2011) 36 European Law Review 524.

73 See here Robert Post, 'Constructing the European Polity: ERTA and the Open Skies Judgments' in Miguel Maduro and Loic Azoulai (eds), *The Past and Future of EU Law: The Classics of EU Law Revisited on the 50th Anniversary of the Rome Treaty* (Bloomsbury Publishing 2010).

74 In this sense, the Council acts as a significant political safeguard of the EU's foreign relations federalism. See here Thomas Verellen, *Foreign Relations Federalism* (Oxford University Press 2023) ch 6.

8 A Convergence Movement Between the European Union's Economic Constitution and National Economic Constitutions – Lessons from the Portuguese Case

Pedro Coutinho

1 Introduction

The relationship between national constitutional identities and the European Union's constitutional identity is often seen as a one-way street. This would be the case even prior to accession to the European Union, where conditions to be met certainly require compatibility with the EU's fundamental rules and, in most cases, changes to national constitutions and, therefore, to national constitutional identities. Once the accession procedure is complete, the principle of primacy of EU law would ensure that the EU's constitutional identity would inexorably keep encroaching on national ones, leading up to a point where national constitutional identities are, essentially, absorbed by the EU's.

There is certainly some truth to this narrative. The EU's constitutional identity, particularly regarding the economy, has considerably impacted national constitutional identities. However, it is argued in this chapter, this does not constitute the whole truth. While national constitutional identities are themselves diverse, they have at their core some fundamental commitments – the welfare state, for example – that, slowly but steadily, have been shaping the EU's constitutional identity.

In this chapter, we will attempt to demonstrate – using the example of the Portuguese Constitution – that the relationship between the EU's constitutional identity and national ones is more complex than a simple top-to-bottom imposed change. This relationship is, in fact, a more complex process of mutual influences that has resulted in a convergence movement.

2 A Brief Overview of the Portuguese Constitution in 1976

It is worthwhile to look at the Portuguese Constitution as it was in its original version due to its particular history and origins. The current Portuguese Constitution dates back to 1976 and is the product of the revolution of 1974 that overthrew the autocratic dictatorship that ruled Portugal from around 1926. Due to the particular happenings and chain of events that followed the overthrow of the dictatorship, the Constitution of 1976, in particular the part addressing the economy, is, in my own

DOI: 10.4324/9781003355762-8

opinion, more the legacy of the revolutionary period than the product of the will of the people that elected the constituent assembly that wrote and approved the Constitution. This is the case because the writing of the Constitution was conditioned, both *de facto* – by the revolutionary events and by the military's control of the situation – and *de jure* – by agreements signed between the political parties and the military power. In a sense, it was not genuinely the will of the people expressed through their representatives, something which ultimately contributed to a mismatch between the constitutional text and constitutional reality.

While the Constitution presented, as most of the doctrine stresses,[1] a compromise between different schools of thought and ideologies – as it happens frequently in such cases, like the Italian and Spanish constitutions, that also represented ruptures with dictatorial pasts[2] – these different ideologies are present in different degrees in different parts of the Constitution. While liberal thought is dominant in most aspects of fundamental rights, the economic part of the Constitution enshrined much of the Marxist-Leninist economic principles that had shaped the revolutionary period between 1974 and 1976.[3] This happened because the transition period between the overthrow of the regime and the entry into force of the new Constitution – known as the PREC, an acronym for On-going Revolutionary Process – was, in the economic field, marked by extensive occupations and nationalisations of companies in almost every economic sector – from banking to beer – as well as an 'agrarian reform', promoted by the provisional governments. This 'pre-constitution', as it became known, was largely received or incorporated by the later constitutional text, mainly due to the fact that pacts signed between the military power and the political parties included a general clause that guaranteed the revolutionary *acquis*, but also because of political and practical difficulties in reversing the *status quo*.

Thus, the economic constitution had as its main aim bringing about a 'classless society' and the 'transition to socialism'[4], via collectivisation (i.e. the collective appropriation of the means of production), nationalisations, expropriations (in some cases, expressly without payment of compensation), a planned economy, almost exclusively public economic initiative, and agrarian reform. Private property that was deliberately excluded from the catalogue of fundamental rights and merely accepted temporarily, while the transition to socialism was not completed, and, in typical

1 See, for instance, Guilherme d'Oliveira Martins, "Compromisso político, económico e social" in Maniel Afonso Vaz *et. al., Jornadas nos quarenta anos da Constituição da República Portuguesa*, (Universidade Católica Editora, 2017) 248; Paulo Alves Pardal, 'A Constituição Económica Portuguesa' in Luís Silva Morais (coord.), *Direito da Economia*, (Vol. I, AAFDL Editora 2020) 107; and Guilherme d'Oliveira Martins and António L. Sousa Franco, *A Constituição económica portuguesa–- ensaio interpretativo* (Almedina 1993) 140.

2 In the Italian case, the Constitution dates from 1948, formalising the cut with Mussolini's fascism. In the Spanish case, the Constitution dates from 1978, and was the result of a transition to democracy from Francisco Franco's dictatorship.

3 JC Vieira de Andrade, 'As grandes opções constituintes em matéria de direitos fundamentais', in Manuel Afonso Vaz *et al.* (coord.), 57.

4 Purposes enshrined in what were then articles 1 and 2 of Constitution.

Marxist-Leninist fashion, economic and social rights were subordinated to collective appropriation and economic progress.

As I have explained elsewhere,[5] the Portuguese economic constitution was characterised by four main identifying traits: 1) a marked aversion to the free market and to private property - visible in the basic option for collectivisation,[6] as well as in the mechanisms for State intervention in prices;[7] 2) a view that public economic initiative should be the driving force of the economy – evident in the reduced role for private initiative and the extensive sectors where public initiative was exclusive;[8] 3) it set out a planned economy;[9] 4) it defined as a main goal the repression of monopolies.[10]

So, as evidenced, the original text of the Portuguese constitution was not only intensely ideological, both in its use of language – those were times of 'semantic colonisation'[11] – and in the fundamental choices it made, but also intensely programmatic, setting out a detailed programme for any government to follow, with significant compression of the democratic principle. It worked, in short, as a 'guide-book that points the way',[12] that could be characterised as a directive constitution.[13]

It soon turned out that such a constitutional text was at odds with constitutional reality,[14] as the economic constitution was, to quote Shakespeare, 'more honoured in the breach than in the observance'. It was largely ignored, in its socialist teleology, by the governing political forces, which seemed more intent on avoiding and mitigating the more pungent aspects of the economic constitution, through a strategic use of legislation,[15] which was mostly validated by the Constitutional Commission – the predecessor of the Constitutional Court.

5 Pedro Coutinho, *A Constituição Económica Portuguesa – À luz da globalização e da integração europeia* (AAFDL Editora 2021), 122 ss.
6 Article 80.
7 Article 109.
8 Article 85.
9 Article 91.
10 Article 81 g).
11 Jorge Miranda, *Da revolução à Constituição* (Principia 2015), 280.
12 Orlando de Carvalho, 'The Constitution of the Republic of Portugal and ownership of the means of production' (1981) LVII Boletim da Faculdade de Direito da Universidade de Coimbra, 222.
13 A concept theorised in Portugal by JJ Gomes Canotilho, in his work *Constituição dirigente e vinculação do legislador* (Coimbra Editora 1982).
14 These two elements forming, along with constitutional culture, the three elements that make up the tridimensionality of constitutional law. According to Professor Manuel Afonso Vaz, only by perceiving these three elements and their interaction can we grasp the constitutional phenomenon and constitutional normativity as a whole. Cf. Luís Heleno Terrinha, 'The tridimensionality of constitutional law', in Rita Lobo Xavier *et al.* (org.), *Constitucionalismos e contemporaneidade – Estudos em Homenagem ao Professor Doutor Manuel Afonso Vaz*, (Universidade Católica Editora 2020) 615.
15 Legislation regarding the delimitation of private initiative, the agrarian reform and compensation in cases of nationalisation was distinctly more liberal-minded than the constitutional text seemed to want – or allow.

From this brief introduction we can draw two important points. Firstly, that the Portuguese economic constitution has a very particular history. And secondly, more importantly, that constitutional reality tends to impose itself over the constitutional text when the two do not match. It is also relevant to state that the national economic identity – a set of fundamental values, principles and rules pertaining to the economy, historically and culturally contingent – is a part of the constitutional reality but, provided that the Constitution is a normative one, it is also influenced and conditioned by the Constitution, in a two-way process. This is not to say that, in general, constitutional texts are irrelevant. That is not the case, as they certainly condition, at the very least from a formal perspective, the actions of political powers. However, where the gap between constitutional text and constitutional reality is abysmal, the latter tends to impose itself. If a constitution seeks to be truly normative, in the sense of Karl Lowenstein's ontological classification,[16] an alignment between text, reality and culture is necessary.

But let us let us for now leave the Portuguese Constitution aside and have a look at the EU's economic constitution.

3 The Mischaracterisation of the European Union's Economic Model: Is It Really 'Neoliberal'?

Quite often, particularly in political speech but also in some legal doctrine[17], the European Union's (EU) economic Constitution is presented as an enemy of national economic policies. The alleged reason for this is the 'neoliberalism' embedded in the Treaties, the EU's constitution, economic and otherwise. This embedded neoliberalism, it is argued, leads to a sanctification of the market and free competition and, consequently, to deregulation. This neoliberalism at EU level is then, within the framework of such theory, enforced or imposed upon Member States. This is a view that I do not share and which I believe rests on several misconceptions and on a mischaracterisation of the EU's economic constitution. If we are to affirm a role for national economic constitutions, then this narrative has to be disproven.

The first misconception is the simple understanding of what neoliberalism is. If we look at what the proponents of the EU's economic constitution as neoliberal believe it is, we inevitably find that their concept of neoliberalism implies a blind belief in the invisible hand of the market, complete absence of state intervention in the economy, be it direct intervention – as a *'player'* or *'actor'* – or indirect intervention – such as regulation through agencies or legislation – and the inexistence of social and welfare policies. It is, I think, quite plain to see that this alleged

16 Karl Loewenstein, *Political Power and the Governmental Process* (University of Chicago Press 1957), 147.

17 For example, Hagen Schulz-Forberg and Bo Strath, *The political history of European integration – the hypocrisy of democracy-through-market* (Routledge, 2010) 2; António Avelãs Nunes, 'A Europa está toda errada. É preciso passá-la a limpo' in Fernando Alves Correia *et al.* (coord.), *Estudos em homenagem a António Barbosa de Melo* (Almedina 2013), 83.

neoliberalism is in fact a description of 19th-century liberalism, with its 'Nightwatchman State' model. There is nothing 'neo', nothing new to this 'neoliberalism.' This reading, in my view, serves to illustrate the abuse of normative potential that economic constitutions are prone to, in favour of a certain ideology.[18]

True or real neoliberalism, or, more appropriately, ordoliberalism, does not fit in this description of what its critics believe the EU's economic constitution to be. It is, so to speak, more refined and sophisticated than mere 19th-century liberalism.

Ordoliberalism originated in Germany, beginning in the 1930s and, while it was, as the name suggests, based on liberal ideas and a liberal conception of the market, it distinguishes itself from simple *laissez-faire, laissez-passer* policy. While ordoliberals believe that the market is by definition the best mechanism for resource allocation, they strongly believe that it can only do so when protected from market abuse. In a nutshell, ordoliberals believe that the market should be isolated and protected from power, be that power public or private. If not, the market becomes an instrument for tyranny and abuse. This much was stated by Franz Böhm:

> Within society itself, no power groups should be formed which would make it possible for others, individually or as groups, to be subjugated and exploited. The populace should be protected against this danger by the system of price competition, by the absence of social privileges and by the need to ensure a fair system by which services or assets could be subject to voluntary exchange agreements to ensure equivalent payment.[19]

In ordoliberalism, then, the State is highly active and interventionist (through legislation and regulation) in the insulation of the market from power and abusive use.

For some authors, the reason for the perceived association of the EU's economic constitution with ordoliberalism stems from the fact that the very concept of economic constitution is of German origin and owes a lot to ordoliberal thinkers.[20] Kaarlo and Klaus Tuori note that only 'beginning in the 1990s did the term "economic constitution" gain wider currency in scholarly discourse outside Germany, and only then did it start to escape from the confines of market-liberal economic thought and receive more neutral connotation.'[21] The underlying argument seems to be that, due to the fact that the term 'economic constitution' was ideological charged, the simple fact the EU explicitly had one associated with ordoliberlism. It is, however, not true that the term was only discussed outside

18 As pointed out by Marco Dani, *Economic Constitutionalism(s) in a time of uneasiness – comparative study on the Economic Constitutional Identities of Italy, the WTO and the EU* (NYU School of Law 2005) 16.

19 Franz Böhm, 'Rule of law in the market economy' in Alan Peacock and Hans Willgerodt (eds), *Germany's Social Market Economy: origins and evolution* (Macmillan 1989) 58.

20 Kaarlo Tuori and Klaus Tuori, *The Eurozone crisis – A constitutional analysis,* (Cambridge University Press, 2014) 13.

21 Idem.

Germany after the 1990s. In Portugal, it has been in use since the early 1970s,[22] and, for the reasons outlined above, it was one of the most discussed topics through the 1970s and 1980s, and certainly not in an ordoliberal way.

Another reason that might lead to the conclusion that the EU is not, in its framework and from the onset, ordoliberal, is the fact that some scholars who believe it to be so refer to a 'neoliberal turn' in the 1970s or 1980s.[23] Naturally, one would assume that for those the EU was not neoliberal before said turn. However, the turn was merely one of policies, rather than of the EU's economic constitution.

Notwithstanding, it is easy to see why some would be tempted to consider the EU's economic constitution as ordoliberal, as the basic idea of preventing market abuse is a fundamental aspect of competition policy and the protection of the free-market at EU level. So, it is true, some aspects can be found where there is a connection between some characteristics of ordoliberalism and the EU's economic constitution.

However, to invoke a few contact points and overlapping areas between neoliberalism and the EU's economic constitution in order to characterise the latter as neoliberal is an oversimplification. As Miguel Poiares Maduro states, the 'original concern of ordoliberals – with political values rather than economic concerns – has however been replaced on some present-day conceptions of ordoliberalism within the European Union, with a concern for the value of efficiency. Initial ordoliberal claims for social justice and the equitable distribution of resources (…) are to a great extent ignored by contemporary authors, who prefer to emphasise the efficiency and classical 'laissez-faire' goals of ordoliberals.'[24] Therefore, this oversimplification is one that can only be done if we ignore some crucial aspects of the EU's economic matrix, as well as key aspects of ordoliberalism.

Moreover, as Pedro Madeira Froufe rightly pointed out:

> the Union has never seen competition as an absolute goal. (…) A policy of competition has always been part of the Union, assuming that the competition itself is an instrument at the service of wider goals of economic policy and/or of goals of non-economic nature (such as the promotion and the defence of employment, technological development or protection of large interests of consumers).[25]

22 Vital Moreira, *Economia e Constituição: para o conceito de constituição económica*, (Faculdade de Direito da Universidade de Coimbra 1974).

23 Kolja Möller, 'Struggles for law: global social rights as an alternative to financial market capitalism' in Poul F Kjaer, Gunther Teubner, Alberto Febbrajo (coord.), *The Financial Crisis in Constitutional Perspective* (Hart Publishing 2011), 306; Michael A Wilkinson, 'Constitutional pluralism: Chronicle of a death foretold' (2017) 23 European Law Journal, 226.

24 Miguel Poiares Maduro, *We, the Court – the European Court of Justice, the European Economic Constitution and Article 30 of the EC Treaty* (Bloomsbury Publishing 1998) 152 and 153.

25 Pedro Madeira Froufe, 'Economic Constitution of the European Union, before and after Lisbon (between the principle of Competition and the "Social Market Economy")' (2017) 3 UNIO-EU law journal 1, 112.

While, prior to the great economic and financial crisis from 2007 onwards, a substantial amount of deregulation was observed (particularly in the financial and banking sectors), such deregulation was the result of policies brought about and implemented by political officials based on political manifestoes and programmes. Such deregulation was not, however, the result of the EU's economic constitution. Therefore, to invoke such deregulation to state that the European Union's economic model is, by default, deregulatory and neoliberal would be untruthful. Indeed, there is, and there must be, a distinction between the policies enacted by politicians within the framework of the Treaties and the economic model itself. It is one thing to admit that, in accordance with the democratic principle, the Treaties allow for some degree of deregulation. It is completely different from stating that the Treaties mandate such deregulation. As Miguel Poiares Maduro puts it, 'The constitutionalization of the Treaty of Rome, the subjectivation of free movement rules and the spill-over effects of market integration rules into all national regulatory areas has in part led, unintentionally or otherwise, to a 'political deficit', and to deregulatory consequences at the national level that support economic liberal constructions of the Treaty of Rome and the European Economic Constitution. However, (...) no such concept of the European Economic Constitution has been adopted by the Court.'[26] Similarly, Clemens Kaupa states that the 'significant influence of neo- or ordoliberals on the Treaty of Rome, or the fact its architecture corresponds to a certain degree to their programme, does not allow the conclusion that it also should, from a normative perspective, be interpreted along such ideological lines.'[27]

Even more significantly, the EU's economic constitution goes far beyond mere competition policy, and includes several key aspects incompatible with ordoliberal thought – even when correctly understood. These include many social and welfare policies and intervention that is not aimed at maintaining healthy competition but at the promotion of other goals, such as fostering and preserving a high standard of living or correcting geographical economic asymmetries and promoting social and territorial cohesion. One example would be the Common Agricultural Policy, which is essentially an extensive subsidy scheme,[28] something profoundly at odds with ordoliberal thought. Other examples include the numerous circumstances where the Treaties allow for a deviation from market rules, in order to promote social or non-economic goals. This is the case of paragraph 3 of Article 107 of the TFEU. It is also the case of services of general economic interest, which will be mentioned below. These instruments are neither aimed at insulating the market from powers and influences, nor at ensuring the normal functioning of the market. Thus, they are not congruent with an ordoliberal framework. Therefore, in my view, construing the EU's economic constitution as neo- or ordoliberal visibly

26 Maduro, 158.

27 Clemens Kaupa, *The pluralist character of the European economic constitution* (Hart Publishing 2016), 21. Contrarily, *vide* Christian Joerges, 'What is left of the European Economic Constitution?' (2004) EUI working paper LAW, No. 2004/13, 14 ss.

28 James Dinnage and John Murphy, *The constitutional law of the European Union* (2nd edn, LexisNexis 2008) 445 and 446.

contradicts the Treaties. The particular mixture of the four freedoms and competition policies, on one side, and social and welfare policies and intervention, on the other, identifies the EU's economic constitution as a complex and plural model that resulted from a compromise between liberal economic ideas (certainly inspired, as well, by ordoliberals) and interventionist thought.[29]

It must also be said that an ordoliberal reading of the European Union's economic constitution is not compatible with the shared values of Member States. While ordoliberalism is of theoretical interest and some aspects of it are, or can be, an influence in the interpretation of certain policies – namely, competition policy – ordoliberalism as a whole never really took hold anywhere. Not in Germany, where it originated, nor anywhere else in the EU. This is relevant because whatever the EU's economic identity is, it is surely composed of common ground and shared values of national economic identities of Member States. And, while these are certainly variable in decisive aspects, for example with the role of the State in the economy traditionally being stronger in the south (Italy, Portugal, Spain, Greece, etc) and weaker in the north (Belgium, Netherlands, Finland, etc), no national identity includes ordoliberalism. So it would be very peculiar if we were to consider that the EU's economic constitutional identity – built upon the economic identities of Member States – is ordoliberal while no national economic identity espouses it, and even more peculiar if we were to consider that Member States, Masters of the Treaties, would shape them based on an economic model not espoused by any Member State's identity or constitution.

Another point worth mentioning is that when we refer to the EU's economic constitution and identity and to the Treaties we are in fact talking about 'living documents' that evolve through time to adapt to the particular historic circumstances of the moment. This much has been stated by the Court of Justice of the European Union in its CILFIT decision:

> every provision of Community law must be placed in its context and interpreted in the light of the provisions of Community law as a whole, regard being had to the objectives thereof and to its state of evolution at the date on which the provision in question is to be applied.[30]

If one compares the dispositions and rules of the initial Treaty of Rome to today's treaties, we will inevitably find that the first ones are markedly more liberal than the second ones. Does this mean that the EU's economic model has radically changed and that the commitment to the social state was not present from the beginning? If we read the context, it does not – notwithstanding an increasing depth of social measures and policies resulting from the convergence movement we will look at further on. At the time of the Treaty of Rome, state intervention in the economy was at its peak[31], still as a result of European states having to take

29 Tuori and Tuori, 16.
30 Case 283/81, paragraph 25.
31 Kaupa, 78.

control of the economy due to World War II and its aftermath. That is the reason why the Treaty of Rome assumes a more liberal nature: to prevent Member States from falling into the temptation of adopting protectionist measures. However, if we look closely, we will find that this liberal nature does not contend with the presence of elements of the social state model already at the Treaty of Rome. Firstly, the non-intervention rules set in the Treaty have numerous derogation possibilities, in favour of non-economic objectives (as we can see, for example, with the derogation of the prohibition of state aid). Further indicators that the EU's initial treaty was already concerned with the welfare state include the pre-ambulatory references to social and economic progress, harmonious development and correction of asymmetries between regions as well as the substantive social provisions, regarding, for example, living conditions of workers and equality of payment for men and women. These examples, which are reinforced when we look at preparatory documents such as the Spaak Report, or when we consider the thought of the EU's 'founding fathers', such as Jean Monet, serve to illustrate, in my view, that from the beginning the European project was committed to the model of the social state, which is not surprising given that it is the dominant model of the national economic identities of Member States. Thus, the economic identity of the EU is built from the national economic identities and, so, must largely respect them.

A crucial point that is indicative of the respect that the EU accords national economic identities and economic constitutions are the provisions regarding Services of General Economic Interest. Within the framework of the EU's economic constitution, each Member State largely retains the freedom to determine what it considers should be a Service of General Economic Interest (SGEE).[32] This is an extremely important aspect, as classifying something as a SGEE allows for the derogation of competition and state aid rules. Naturally, each state will determine what are its SGEE according to its own national economic identity and the role of the state in the economy resulting from the national economic identity, the Constitution, and political options of the moment. So, the regime of SGEE, extant from the Treaty of Rome, is a mark of the respect and deference of the EU's economic constitution to national economic identities.

Another point that tends to be overlooked when the EU's economic constitution is discussed is that the concrete policies implemented are not a direct result of the treaties. Like any economic constitution, the EU's economic constitution sets out goals to be achieved and, sometimes, loosely mentions some of the means used to achieve those goals. But the specific policies and ways to reach the goals are defined by the EU's political institutions. The composition of these institutions (namely, the Commission, the Council and the European Parliament) is determined by the peoples' vote. Therefore, what concrete actions are taken are dictated by political options, based on the democratic principle. Such is the case, also, at the national level: elected officials determine economic policy, within the framework

32 Grith Skovgard Olykke and Peter Molgaard, 'What is a service of general economic interest?' (2016) 41 European Journal of Law and Economics.

and the obligations of the national Constitution. So, even if it could be argued that, at times, the EU's action is 'neoliberal' – in the wrong sense of the word – such neoliberalism would be not so much the result of the EU's economic constitution *per se*, but of the political choices of the citizens and of their elected representatives. It is also relevant to point out, particularly with regard to action with the Council, that when national representatives deliberate on measures regarding economic policies they are bound to their own constitutions – that is to say, in this regard, to their own national economic constitutional identity – and should, therefore, seek to act in the Council in accordance with its purposes. As such, national economic constitutional identities are institutionally represented at EU level.

All this leads to the conclusion that when we look at the EU's economic model we see that, while it is committed to a social market economy, it is also a plural model. As Clemens Kaupa puts it:

> in negative terms, this means that we cannot assume that European law has to be interpreted on the basis of any specific socio-economic worldview; in positive terms it means that a multitude of socio-economic projects may be pursued within the framework of the Treaty.[33]

That is to say, a model that allows for the 'tuning' of economic, social and fiscal policies according to the political preferences of the people in each historic moment, but always, and it is important to stress this, within the framework of the Treaties, which is a commitment to the social state.

4 The Interaction Between the Portuguese Economic Constitution and the EU's Economic Constitution – A Two-Way Process

So how do the two points mentioned so far connect with each other? Thus far, I have mostly described the initial points of a relationship: the initial text of the Portuguese Constitution in 1976 and the founding Treaty of Rome with its economic model. Let us now see how they influenced each other's development.

The present state of the Portuguese economic constitution is radically different from the highly ideological and socialist initial text. It corresponds to what was already at the time, in 1976, the constitutional reality. That is a social market economy: a model that regards the market as a good rule, but not as an absolute rule; a model where the economy is regarded as means to an end, which is social wellbeing and thus dictates wealth redistribution through taxation and generous social rights.

Although there have been further constitutional revisions, including some that touched upon details of the economic constitution, the current Portuguese economic constitution is largely the result of the constitutional revisions of 1982 and 1989. These revisions de-ideologised the constitutional text and brought it into match with the constitutional reality of a social market economy. These

33 Kaupa, 337.

constitutional revisions removed the socialist teleology and metanarrative, introduced private economic initiative as a fundamental right, and strengthened private property by removing some of its constitutional limitations – such as the possibility of expropriation without compensation and the merely transitional tolerance of private property – removed the principle of the irreversibility of nationalisations, removed the subordination of social rights to collective appropriation, and introduced many other changes that protected the pillars of a social market economy. At the same time, the constitution provides ample ground for a plurality of political options, respecting the democratic principle within the economic options.

But other than just national constitutional reality, the revision procedures were also dictated by what was then the European Economic Community (EEC). Portugal wanted to accede to the EEC, which was impossible with a programmatic socialist economic constitution, largely incompatible with the European one. This was one of the hindrances of the accession process, which started with a formal request in 1977. The first revision procedure was finished in 1982, following which Portugal joined the EEC, in 1986. The 1989 revision then completed the constitutional text's route towards matching with the real economic constitution.

This interaction or articulation shows the influence that a strong economic constitution such as the EU's can have on national constitutions. Already prior to the revisions, the constitutional reality was far more liberal, or market-minded, than the constitutional text. This while still allowing for a significant role for the State and its intervention, both direct and indirect, in accordance with the traditional role of the State in southern European countries. Simply put, the market aspects of the constitutional economic identity and reality, beyond the text, imposed themselves and found their way into the text. This contributed the wider constitutional reality. Portugal being a part of Western Europe and desiring to accede to the EEC exerted considerable pressure to adapt the Constitution.

It must be said that while the Portuguese case is not, in this aspect, unique – other countries had to amend their constitutions before accession to the EU or as a consequence of it – it is useful in demonstrating the considerable influence that the EU's economic model can exert on national economic identities. As a result of this influence, not only were constitutional changes brought about, but a national economic model that was exclusively state-centred has become less so.

It would, however, be wrong to say that this is a one-way relationship, and that only the EU's economic constitution influences national ones. There are, in my view, two fundamental elements that allow us to conclude that national constitutional identities also influence the EU's constitutional identity and economic constitution.

The first one is the progressive reinforcement of social goals and policies in the Treaties. While the degree and methods may vary significantly (from the German Grundgesetz's social clause, from which derive a wide range of socio-economic rights, to the extensive catalogue of economic, social and cultural rights protected by the Portuguese Constitution), it is fair to say that all Member States' constitutions enshrine some sort of commitment to the social state. This is a defining feature of every national economic identity, a truly European matrix or 'European social model.'[34]

As we have mentioned before, the commitment to the social state also occurs at the EU level, from the very beginning, the Treaty of Rome – derogation of state-aid rules in favour of social goals; correction of territorial asymmetries; harmonious development, etc. Further treaties clarified and deepened the commitment, through the broadening of social goals and mechanisms for their attainment.

Firstly, the Single European Act of 1986 introduced in the Treaties provisions regarding workers' health, safety and labour conditions,[35] as well as strengthening social cohesion measures. Secondly, the Treaty of Maastricht introduced what is now Article 175 TEU. This article's content demanded that 'the formulation and implementation of policies and activities of the internal market must take into account, and contribute to the achievement of, the policy objectives of economic and social cohesion.'[36] It became, therefore, clear that the market was perceived as means to an end, that end being social well-being. Along the same lines, Maastricht created the Cohesion Fund, to contribute to the correction of territorial asymmetries. Amsterdam and Nice reiterated the goal. Finally, the Treaty of Lisbon truly constitutionalised this commitment, by enshrining the concept of social market economy in article 3 of the TEU. All introduced changes in the Treaties strengthened the social pillars of the EU, emphasising its commitment to the social market economy. These changes were, at least partially, the result of national calls for further social action by the EU, so that Member States could fulfil their own constitutions and due to something that, already in 1976, Ulrich Scheuner had identified:

> It is, however, clear that within the legal orders of the Member States there exists a certain agreement regarding the common adoption of a mixed economic system, combining free exchange and intervention. (…) This is also the case regarding the legal, or in any case, factual guarantee of the economic and professional freedom of the individual. The Member States are also in agreement in basically leaving the fixing of the level of prices and wages to the market or to the free collective bargaining of the parties.[37]

34 Froufe, 112.

35 It seems pertinent to note, here, the importance that labourers' right have in an economic constitution. The first constitution to contain a full and coherent socio-economic project, the Weimar Constitution of 1919, took particular care with workers' rights, as did, for example, the Italian Constitution of 1948. Even before that, the Mexican Constitution of 1917 – a precursor to the concept of economic constitution, while generally not considered an economic constitution, due to the lack of a global view on the economy – regulated exhaustively certain aspects of labour law.

36 Robert Lane, 'New Community competences under the Maastricht Treaty' (1993) Vol. 30. Common Market Law Review, 962.

37 Ulrich Scheuner, 'Report by Ulrich Scheuner' in Paul Kapteyn (ed.), *The economic law of the Member States in an economic and monetary union* (A.W. Sijthoff 1976) 53.

It is the agreement, this core of shared values that shapes the EU's economic constitutional identity and makes it match with that of Member States.

The second one relates to anti-crises mechanisms. Notwithstanding the advances in the EU's institutional architecture, particularly relating to the Economic and Monetary Union, it is now clear that the EU's economic constitution had a serious flaw,[38] as the EMU, like the Euro – designed as a 'fair weather currency'[39] – worked well in times of economic growth but lacked instruments to deal with generalised recession.[40] Not only were these instruments unavailable at EU level but more: because of certain provisions in the EU's economic constitution – such as the no bail-out clause, or the prohibition of state-aids – Member States found themselves deprived of many anti-crisis mechanisms, in particular those Member States that adopted the Euro, as they could not use the traditional devaluation of their currency in order to boost exports. As result, Member States gave up significant powers, in the economic domain, without the introduction of an EU-level mechanism that would ensure an equivalent effect, that is adequate anti-recession tools. This flaw in the design of the EU's economic constitution was painfully evident during the financial and economic crisis that began in 2007. That absence of mechanisms to counteract crises and inject money into the economy forced EU institutions to adopt rather creative solutions to in order to achieve goal while, simultaneously, respecting the 'no bail-out clause'. Such mechanisms were found, such as the Outright Monetary Transactions scheme, and the creation of the European Stability Mechanism, the European Financial Stabilisation Mechanism, as well as an overhaul of the Economic and Monetary Union, operated by the 'Six pack' and the 'Two pack'.

While, on the one hand, these changes highlight the pluralist character of the EU's economic constitution,[41] on the other hand, the fact that they overcame legal challenges placed against them,[42] clarifies that the EU's economic constitution does significantly limit the range and of measures that can be adopted in a crisis scenario. This means that a wide range of measures are susceptible of being adopted, including more interventionist ones. This brought the array of measures that can be adopted at EU-level closer to that which can be adopted at Member States level, in accordance with their own constitutions. Thus, a flaw

38 To some authors, the structural flaws of Maastricht are to blame for the euro-zone crisis. See James Caporaso and Min-Hyung Kim, 'The Maastricht Treaty at twenty: a Greco-European tragedy?' in Thomas Christiansen and Simon Duke (eds), *The Maastricht Treaty: second thoughts after 20 years* (Routledge 2013) 91 and 98.

39 Cf. Bergsten and JF Kirkegaard, *The coming resolution of the European crisis*, online article of the Peterson Institute for International Economics, available at www.ciaonet.org/pbei/iie/0024277/f_0024277_19801.pdf

40 Giandomenico Magione, *Rethinking the Union of Europe post-crisis* (Cambridge University Press 2014) 29.

41 Kaupa, 336.

42 Pringle Case (C-370/12), where the European Stability Mechanism's conformity to the Treaties was challenged, and Gauweiler (C-62/14), where the conformity of European Central Bank's Outright Monetary Transaction scheme was challenged.

was corrected and the EU's economic identity brought to match national economic identities.

It is reasonable to argue that changes that occurred during the 'learning moment' that was the economic and financial crisis of 2007 onwards and its aftermath significantly changed the EU's approach to the recession brought about by the COVID-19 pandemic. Notwithstanding the fact that anti-crises mechanisms were devised, these mechanisms imposed, through the 'strong conditionality' required for the activation of the European Stability Mechanism and the European Financial Stability Mechanism, significant austerity[43] upon countries that required assistance. The measures adopted to comply with said conditionality 'capable of affecting social rights of people at large', but tended to 'hit harsher on the most vulnerable groups and individuals.'[44] Therefore, it highlighted 'the contradiction between an existing system of domestic social and welfare policies, on the one hand, and the substantive transfer of decisions on economic and financial policies, on the other hand, now even outside the EU legal and institutional framework.'[45]

By contrast, the EU's response to the current crisis consists of a €750 billion package, Next Generation EU, more than half of which consists of grants, and only the remaining part of loans. Equally significant, when viewed in the like of convergence of identities, is the fact that the main source of funding for this package will be EU-issued bonds.

More and more, it is plain to see, EU institutions tend to mimic the responses to crisis typical at national level (certainly typical in western European States), thus bridging the gap in the anti-crises tools and increasing the overlap of national economic constitutional identities of Member States, all committed to the social market economy and socially interventionist, with the EU's own economic constitutional identity.

These changes have not, thus far materialised in change to the Treaties, as, given their relevance, they should. They do, however, represent a deep change in the EU's material or real economic constitution, if not the formal. And they have been brought about not only by the previous experiences of dealing with crises, but also by pressure from Member States who saw themselves deprived of anti-crisis measures with no compensating mechanisms at EU level, something that they realise can put social market national models, and, therefore, national constitutional identities, at risk.

So, what we have here is a convergence movement that perfectly illustrates the two-way relationship between the EU's economic constitution and its economic identity and national economic constitutions and identities. Convergence, it must be said:

43 Francisco Pereira Coutinho, 'Austerity on the loose in Portugal: European judicial restraint in times of crisis' (2016) 8 Perspectives on Federalism 3, 111.

44 Giovanni Guiglia, 'Italian Constitutional Court and social rights in times of crisis: in search of a balance between principles and values of contemporary constitutionalism' in Catarina Santos Botelho, Luís Terrinha and Pedro Coutinho (eds), *Constitutionalism in a Plural World* (Universidade Católica Editora 2018) 244.

45 ibid.

does not mean dismissal of the original diversities but, more sophisticatedly, incorporation and re-elaboration of the principles or solutions devised in other ECIs within the original and unaltered legal frameworks.[46]

As result of this progressive adaption and incorporation of differences, on the one side, the EU's economic constitution moderates certain tendencies for excessive State intervention and, potentially, protectionism, at the national level. On the other, the national constitutional identities and economic constitutions' commitment to the social market economy dictate a strengthening of the EU's social action and 'constitutionalisation' of those policies and action in the treaties.

5 Conclusions

In conclusion, we can say that the design of the EU's economic constitution is that of the constitution of a social market economy. This is not surprising, as the social market economy, notwithstanding some variation, is dominant in the constitutions of Member States, and is a key component of national economic identities. The inherent tension between national economic identities and constitutions, on one side, and the EU's own economic constitution and identity serves to maintain a balance between them: the European economic constitution prevents protectionism and excessive state intervention in the economy at the national level, while the national economic identities prevent excessively liberal tendencies from taking hold at EU level.

This tension, as is evident when we consider the case of the Portuguese Constitution, can also bring about formal changes to constitutional texts. However this does not necessarily happen in a top-down fashion – that is, the EU's economic constitution provoking changes in national constitutions – but, collectively, can happen from the bottom up, as I believe was the case with the reinforcement in the treaties of the social pillars, dictated by the Member-State's constitutions collective commitment to the social market economy, as well as the case with the introduction of anti-crisis mechanisms.

But, notwithstanding these useful tensions between identities, the EU's economic model is designed to allow for leeway and respect national economic constitutions and, thus national economic identities. That is visible when we consider the derogation possibilities present in many rules and the question of SGEE.

46 Dani, 59.

9 Towards a General Typology of Consensus Analysis

From Entrenching Divergence to Constituting Convergence

Jaka Kukavica[1]

1 Introduction

On 2 September 1974, Ehrlich Anthony Coker escaped a Georgia penitentiary where he had been serving a sentence for murder, rape, kidnapping, and aggravated assault. Soon after his escape, Coker broke into the house of the Carver family; he robbed Mr Carver at knifepoint, stealing his money and the keys to the family car, tied him up in the bathroom, and proceeded to rape and abduct Mrs Carver. Soon after, Mr Carver had managed to break free and inform the authorities; they promptly tracked down the stolen car with Coker behind the wheel, finding Mrs Carver still alive. Coker was prosecuted and sentenced to death for non-homicidal rape. His conviction was upheld by the Supreme Court of Georgia and Coker brought his case to the United States Supreme Court (SCOTUS). In a 7–2 ruling, SCOTUS overturned Coker's death penalty, deciding that capital punishment for non-homicidal rape violates the Cruel and Unusual Punishment Clause of the Eighth Amendment. In reaching this conclusion, the majority leaned heavily on what the states themselves thought of the matter. It wrote that '[t]he current judgment with respect to the death penalty for rape is not wholly unanimous among state legislatures, but it obviously weighs very heavily on the side of rejecting capital punishment as a suitable penalty for raping an adult woman.'[2]

In doing so, the Court used what is known in US constitutional law as the national consensus doctrine, whereas SCOTUS would interpret a norm of the federal constitution – the Eighth Amendment – based on how the states understand and had implemented that provision in their state law. Other highest courts in multilevel legal systems use similar interpretative methods, too. The European Court of Human Rights (ECtHR) regularly employs the European consensus doctrine in interpreting the European Convention on Human Rights (ECHR) when it gauges the views of states parties to the ECHR to interpret its provisions. Similarly, the Court of Justice of the European Union (CJEU) gives meaning to

1 I would like to thank Urška Šadl, Gabor Halmai, Mathias Siems, Marjan Kos, and Julian Scholtes for their comments on earlier drafts. I also thank Miha Homšak for his kind help with calculating the number of possible permutations of consensus analysis. All mathematical errors remain his and his alone.

2 *Coker v Georgia*, 433 U.S. 584 (1977) at 596.

DOI: 10.4324/9781003355762-9

EU human rights norms by examining if a right forms part of 'constitutional traditions common to the Member States'. Across different institutional and structural contexts, consensus analysis, much like the one SCOTUS performed in *Coker*, influences the outcomes of cases regarding 'delicate moral and ethical questions', to borrow the wording of the ECtHR. Be it abortion, artificial insemination, voting rights of prisoners, LGBT and Roma rights, or the death penalty, courts across different multilevel legal systems have decided on these issues through consensus analysis.

Consensus analysis is also important for systemic and structural reasons. Employing it in their decision-making, not only can courts change, affect, and literally end human lives, but they can also influence how multilevel legal systems accommodate the diverse views of their constituent states. Through consensus, courts can either entrench the pre-existing divergences between the constituent units, or constitute a converging force themselves. Going back to *Coker*, SCOTUS decided that because the majority of states were against capital punishment for non-homicidal rape, the federal constitution should be interpreted in line with that consensus. This decision bared the minority of outlier states from continuing to deliver capital sentences and brought them in line with the majority through a federal constitutional mandate. Consensus analysis, as the driving argumentative force behind that decision, thus constituted a convergence as it forced states to follow a single (federal) standard and did not allow states to diverge from it. Conversely, if SCOTUS had found that there was no consensus against capital punishment for non-homicidal rape amongst the states and, as a result, the federal constitution did not enjoin states from using it, this would entrench the pre-existing divergences between the states. It would confirm that federal (constitutional) law does not impose a unified view on the states but instead permits them to come to divergent solutions to the problem at hand.[3]

And yet, despite the fact that courts have influenced the lives of hundreds of millions of people in very personal and intimate ways through consensus analysis, and despite the fact that it has an important role in how courts accommodate diversity in multilevel legal systems, there has not yet been a comprehensive study of consensus analysis as a method in the abstract, devoid of a specific systemic context. There is abundant literature on the applications of consensus analysis within a specific jurisdiction, as well as some attempts at a comparative treatment of courts' approaches.[4] In addition, many system-specific typologies of consensus

3 For such situation regarding the death penalty in general, and the effect it had on the reasoning of SCOTUS regarding the constitutionality of the death penalty, see *Gregg v Georgia*, 428 U.S. 153 (1976), at 179–84.

4 See, for instance, Panos Kapotas and Vassilis P Tzevelekos, 'How (Difficult Is It) to Build Consensus on (European) Consensus' in Panos Kapotas and Vassilis P Tzevelekos (eds), *Building Consensus on European Consensus: Judicial Interpretation of Human Rights in Europe and Beyond* (Cambridge University Press 2019), particularly Part III (Chapters 15–18); Hanneke Senden, *Interpretation of Fundamental Rights in a Multilevel Legal System: An Analysis of the European Court of Human Rights and the Court of Justice of the European Union* (Intersentia 2011); Conor O'Mahony and

have been developed.[5] But few, if any at all, have attempted to transcend the dependence of their analyses on a specific systemic context and to examine consensus analysis in the abstract. This chapter aims to begin to fill this gap.

It makes this contribution by setting up the groundwork for future more in-depth inquiries of consensus outside a specific systemic context through building a general typology of consensus analysis. It constructs this typology inductively, by generalising common traits of consensus from the consensus-related case law of various courts, as well as the legal commentary on those courts. Building such a general typology of consensus analysis is important because, for one, it opens up consensus to a more comparative rather than institutionally self-contained criticism and analysis. It also allows for a better and more encompassing contextualisation of consensus. It shifts the focus away from the systemic and institutional specificities towards the method in the abstract and its underlying methodologies, normativities, and peculiarities. In line with this, such a shift can also inform our understanding of how consensus analysis affects the processes of convergence and divergence between states across multilevel systems, as well as enable us to appreciate how courts can use consensus to accommodate diversity in complex legal systems more generally.

The chapter identifies four typological dimensions that define consensus analysis in the abstract and sketches out ways in which this typology can shed light on our understanding of the accommodation of converging and diverging forces in multilevel systems. Section 2 discusses bases of consensus as the first typological variable. Section 3 discusses levels of generality of consensus. Section 4 focuses on temporality of consensus, while Section 5 delves into automaticity of consensus. Section 6 concludes.

2 Bases of Consensus

The bases of consensus are the central element of consensus analysis. They concern the fundamental question of what consensus is, and on the basis of what

Kanstantsin Dzehtsiarou, 'Evolutive Interpretation of Rights Provisions: A Comparison of the European Court of Human Rights and the US Supreme Court' (2013) 44 Columbia Human Rights Law Review 309; Christopher McCrudden, 'Using Comparative Reasoning in Human Rights Adjudication: The Court of Justice of the European Union and the European Court of Human Rights Compared' (2013) 15 Cambridge Yearbook of European Legal Studies 383.

5 For extensive typological treatments of European consensus as used by the ECtHR, see Kanstantsin Dzehtsiarou, *European Consensus and the Legitimacy of the European Court of Human Rights* (Cambridge University Press 2015) 39–55; Jens T Theilen, *European Consensus between Strategy and Principle: The Uses of Vertically Comparative Legal Reasoning in Regional Human Rights Adjudication* (Nomos Verlagsgesellschaft 2021) 23–31; Lawrence Helfer, 'Consensus, Coherence and the European Convention on Human Rights' (1993) 26 Cornell International Law Journal 133, 139. For a fairly comprehensive typology of approaches to consensus by SCOTUS, see Ian P Farrell, 'Strict Scrutiny Under the Eighth Amendment' (2013) 40 Florida State University Law Review 853, 858–883; Robert J Smith, Bidish J Sarma and Sophie Cull, 'The Way the Court Gauges Consensus (and How to Do It Better)' (2014) 35 Cardozo Law Review 2397, 2402–18.

factors it is established. It tells us what evidence courts use when they make consensus-related arguments and what they reference when they examine if a consensus exists on a given issue. This typological dimension has been named differently by different courts and commentators in different institutional contexts. For instance, literature discussing European consensus of the ECtHR has settled on the terms 'sources of consensus' and 'elements of consensus'. SCOTUS and its commentators, on the other hand, have consistently been using 'objective indicia' of consensus to reference this typological dimension. In the CJEU context, no consistent terminology is established. This chapter uses the term 'bases of consensus' to unite all these naming conventions under a single umbrella term. If it uses the specific terms 'sources of consensus', 'elements of consensus', or 'indicia of consensus,' it uses them interchangeably.

Across different multilevel systems and institutional contexts, courts have used a wide range of sources to discern the (non)existence of consensus. It is precisely on the basis of indicia of consensus that we can distinguish between the *core* meaning and the *peripheral* meanings of the consensus analysis method as a whole.[6]

Under the core meaning of consensus, courts establish consensus on the basis of legislation of the constituent units on the disputed issue, or the practices prevalent in the constituent units. In the context of the Council of Europe (CoE), for instance, the former would refer to the ECtHR gauging consensus by examining how an issue is regulated by the laws of states parties to the ECHR; in the domestic US constitutional context, it would refer to SCOTUS using state laws on the disputed issue as the basis for establishing the existence of consensus. Examples of different courts using consensus analysis in this way abound.[7] Consider, for instance, the decision of the CJEU in *D and Sweden* v. *Council*, in which the Court leaned heavily on the different meanings of 'registered partnership' and 'marriage' in the domestic laws of the EU Member States in ruling that the term 'married official' in EU Staff Regulations does not cover individuals in registered partnerships.[8] Discerning consensus on the basis of practices of constituent units would entail a similar exercise, with the exception that a court – SCOTUS, for instance – would not examine state laws but state practices

6 For the introduction of the idea of a 'core' meaning of consensus, see Kapotas and Tzevelekos (n 4) 7.

7 For the many examples in the jurisprudence of the EctHR, see Dzehtsiarou (n 5) 40–5; Luzius Wildhaber, Arnaldur Hjartarson and Stephen Donnelly, 'No Consensus on Consensus? The Practice of the European Court of Human Rights' (2013) 33 Human Rights Law Journal 248, 253; Helfer (n 5) 139 and the case law contained therein. For the examples in the jurisprudence of SCOTUS, see Jaka Kukavica, 'National Consensus and the Eighth Amendment: Is There Something to Be Learned from the United States Supreme Court?' in Panos Kapotas and Vassilis P Tzevelekos (eds), *Building Consensus on European Consensus: Judicial Interpretation of Human Rights in Europe and Beyond* (Cambridge University Press 2019) 370–85 and the case law contained therein.

8 Joined cases C-122/99 P and C-125/99 P *D and Sweden v Council* [2001] ECLI: EU:C:2001:304 paras 34–39.

or policies.[9] It would not examine whether state penal laws permit the imposition of the death penalty as a matter of law, but it would examine whether state attorneys are pushing for the death penalty to be imposed, whether juries actually sentence individuals to death, and whether those sentences are actually being executed. In other words, the court would not examine penal laws, but penal policies and practices of constituent states.

Courts have been quite innovative in adding layers to this core understanding of consensus and developing further peripheral meanings of it. An impressively lengthy list of bases of consensus that have been referenced by courts can be assembled. Various national and international courts have thus discerned consensus on the basis of international treaties,[10] decisions of international tribunals,[11] regional law,[12] international or regional soft law,[13] internal soft law,[14] foreign legal orders,[15] trends in the laws of constituent units,[16] international trends,[17] the margin by which laws of constituent units are passed by legislatures,[18] judges'

9 See, for instance, *Gregg v Georgia*, 428 U.S. 153 (1976) at 179–82; *Woodson v North Carolina*, 428 U.S. 280 (1976) at 289–95; *Coker v Georgia*, 433 U.S. 584 (1977) at 593–6; *Enmund v Florida*, 458 U.S. 782 (1982) at 789–97; *Thompson v Oklahoma*, 487 U.S. 815 (1988) at 823–31.

10 See Dzehtsiarou (n 5) 45–9; Wildhaber, Hjartarson and Donnelly (n 7) 253–4; Helfer (n 5) 139 and the case law contained therein.

11 See Dzehtsiarou (n 5) 49; Wildhaber, Hjartarson and Donnelly (n 7) 254–5 and the case law contained therein.

12 This corresponds to sources that are neither internal to a system, nor international in nature, but are nonetheless closely connected to a system in question. In the context of the CoE and the ECHR, EU law would fall within the meaning of regional law. And vice versa, within the EU context, the ECHR would qualify as regional law. In the context of the USA, NAFTA, for instance, could qualify as regional law. See Dzehtsiarou (n 5) 49 and the case law contained therein.

13 See, for instance, *Karner v Austria* App no 40016/98 (ECtHR, 24 July 2003), para 36, in which the ECtHR referred to a resolution of the European Parliament.

14 This corresponds to soft law instruments that are internal to a particular system. For instance, within the context of the CoE and the ECHR, this would mean CoE regulations and recommendations. However, a reference to a CoE regulation or recommendation made by SCOTUS would better be characterised as international soft law. See Dzehtsiarou (n 5) 48; Wildhaber, Hjartarson and Donnelly (n 7) 256; Helfer (n 5) 139 and the case law contained therein.

15 Wildhaber, Hjartarson and Donnelly (n 7) 255–6, n 79–80 and the case law contained therein. As Wildhaber et al. explain, the ECtHR has mostly looked for inspiration to extra-European liberal and democratic common law jurisdictions, such as the USA, Canada, South Africa, Australia, and Israel; For equivalent references made by SCOTUS, see Youngjae Lee, 'International Consensus as Persuasive Authority in the Eighth Amendment' (2007) 156 University of Pennsylvania Law Review 63.

16 *Babar Ahmad and Others v the United Kingdom* App nos 24027/07, 11949/08, 36742/08, 66911/09 and 67354/09 (ECtHR, 10 April 2012) para 242; *Atkins v Virginia*, 536 U.S. 304 (2002) at 315.

17 *Christine Goodwin v the United Kingdom* App no 28957/95 (ECtHR, 11 July 2002), para 85.

18 *Atkins v Virginia*, 536 U.S. 304 (2002) 316.

perception of social consensus,[19] scientific developments and the views of experts,[20] statements of religious authorities,[21] and polling data.[22] This typology of bases of consensus is also demonstrated in Table 9.1 below.

Some authors, in developing their system-specific, most often ECHR-specific typologies, have attempted to group some of the above bases together to form discrete categories of consensus. Helfer, for instance, has identified legal consensus, expert consensus, and European public consensus as the three overarching categories of consensus used by the ECtHR.[23] Dzehtsiarou, on the other hand, has identified four 'types' of consensus from the various bases used by the ECtHR: consensus based on comparative analysis of laws and practices of states parties to the ECHR; consensus based on international treaties; expert consensus; and internal consensus within a single state.[24] While engaging in such a categorising and clustering exercise may have been useful for their analytical purposes, the

Table 9.1 Bases of consensus used by domestic and international courts across institutional contexts

Bases of consensus	
Core meaning	Laws of constituent units
	Practices of constituent units
Peripheral meanings	International treaties
	Decisions of international tribunals
	Regional law
	International soft law
	Regional soft law
	Internal soft law
	Foreign legal orders
	Trends in laws of constituent units
	International trends
	Margin by which legislation of constituent units is passed
	Judges' perception of social consensus
	Scientific developments and the views of experts
	Statements of religious authorities
	Polling data

19 *Winterwerp v the Netherlands* App no 6301/73 (ECtHR, 24 October 1979), para 37.
20 *Atkins v Virginia*, 536 U.S. 304 (2002) 316; *Sutherland v the United Kingdom* App No 25186/94 (ECtHR, 1 July 1997); *B. v France* App no 13343/87 (ECtHR, 25 March 1992), para 48.
21 *Atkins v Virginia*, 536 U.S. 304 (2002) 316.
22 ibid 317.
23 Helfer (n 5) 139.
24 Dzehtsiarou (n 5) 38–9.

purpose of this chapter is precisely the opposite: it is to deconstruct consensus analysis as a method into its smallest constituent elements and abstracting them from the various institutional contexts in which they are used.

Before proceeding, however, the nature of this volume calls for a brief excursus concerning Dzehtsiarou's 'internal consensus within the respondent state' and the reasons for its omission from this typology. By internal consensus, Dzehtsiarou refers not to consensus *amongst* states that comprise a multilevel system, but rather to consensus *within* a single state; this internal consensus is established based on declarations of the respective national parliament, perceived internal consensus, and the results of potential national referenda.[25] It is highly reminiscent of the national identity clause of Article 4(2) TEU in EU law.[26] Through referring to any member state's individual national identity, the national identity clause, much like 'internal consensus within the respondent state', generally serves as a shield for individual member states against encroachments of EU law. It provides a legal justification for a member state to depart from the common standards that have been agreed on and made their way into EU law.[27] Conversely, consensus analysis is an intrinsically communitarian legal standard and gives courts a justificatory device through which they can ensure a measure of unity between the legal orders of constituent units. Whereas identity clauses and internal consensus promote diversity by granting constituent states the right to depart from common positions, consensus analysis permits courts to promote unity by prohibiting such departures from the common positions of constituent units. One is a unifying standard in accordance with which those states that are out of line with the general consensus are more likely to be found in breach of their constitutional or international obligations, while the other can be used by the same outlier state to justify its unorthodox position. Due to the inherently different nature of 'internal consensus' to consensus analysis, the former should therefore not be included in the general typology of the latter.

Having established this, we can now proceed to a more detailed discussion of both bases that constitute the core meaning of consensus: (i) laws and (ii) practices of constituent units.

2.1 Laws of Constituent Units

At first sight, 'laws of constituent units' as basis of consensus may seem self-explanatory; the existence of consensus is based on a comparative analysis of domestic laws of constituent units, be it constitutional provisions, statutes, or

25 ibid 49–55.

26 See also Chapters 4 and 6 in this volume.

27 See, for instance, Armin von Bogdandy and Stephan Schill, 'Overcoming Absolute Primacy: Respect for National Identity under the Lisbon Treaty' (2011) 48 Common Market Law Review 1417. For more on the national identity clause of Article 4(2) TEU, see Elke Cloots, *National Identity in EU Law* (Oxford University Press 2015). For similar uses of 'internal consensus' by the ECtHR, see *A, B and C v Ireland* App no 25579/05 (ECtHR, 16 December 2010).

other sources of law within the relevant states.[28] However, there is more than meets the eye, and references to domestic laws raise a number of important (methodological) questions. More specifically, such references raise three additional typological considerations that need to be considered to fully understand laws of constituent units as a basis for consensus: (i) how many states suffice for a court to find the existence of consensus; (ii) which states should be counted by the court and, finally, (iii) which states are actually counted by the court?

Examining these questions, as well as the conceptual problems that they raise, is more than just a theoretical or a mere taxonomical exercise. It is important because different answers to these questions can result, and often do, in different outcomes in concrete cases before courts. How precisely courts conduct consensus analysis thus has an important effect on how consensus accommodates diversity amongst the states that comprise a multilevel system. By varying the way they employ the method – for instance by changing how many states are needed in favour of a particular solution for consensus to exist – courts can make consensus either a device that leans more towards entrenching divergences, or a device that by imposing a uniform standard on the basis of consensus constitutes a convergence.

2.1.1 How Many States Are Required?

This typological concern refers to the question of when the threshold of 'consensus' is reached. What is the required majority of constituent units – states – in favour of a particular solution for a court to recognise the existence of consensus? Is it a simple majority? Perhaps a qualified majority? Something in between? Unanimity of all states, except for the respondent state, in cases in which there is one?[29] Thus far, to the best of my knowledge, no empirical research has been conducted in any of the legal systems in which highest courts use consensus analysis with the aim of determining how many states those courts require to find consensus to exist, though some things are clear. Not only across different courts, but also within the jurisprudence of a single court, there are significantly divergent approaches from case to case as to the majority required.[30] Moreover, particularly in the context of the ECtHR, there is a strong agreement amongst commentators that using the expression 'consensus' to denote consensus analysis is fundamentally inappropriate because it implies unanimity amongst the states, which is almost

28 Note that this includes cases in which courts engage in consensus analysis that is unsubstantiated and opaquely reasoned; that is cases in which the comparative legal analysis underlying consensus analysis is not explicit in the judgment. See, for instance, *Tyrer v the United Kingdom* App no 5856/72 (ECtHR, 25 April 1978), para 31; Case 136/79 *National Panasonic (UK) Limited v Commission* [1980] ECLI:EU:C:1980:169, para 18.

29 For a criticism of the state-counting approach while disregarding the percentage of the population that lives in an individual state, see Roderick M Jr Hills, 'Counting States' (2009) 32 Harvard Journal of Law & Public Policy 17, 21.

30 Senden (n 4) 395.

never required by the Court.[31] Furthermore, in this same context, some authors argue that the ECtHR has been unclear as to the percentage of states whose views must converge for the Court to be satisfied that consensus had been reached[32] and that determining the percentage in the abstract would have been impossible.[33]

But regardless of these system-specific intricacies, it is important, for our purposes, to simply acknowledge that the majority of states required for consensus to gain normative value is a crucial typological consideration in studying consensus analysis across specific institutional contexts. It is particularly important in the study of consensus as a mechanism through which diversity is accommodated as the different majorities required fundamentally alter consensus' nature in that respect. Generally put, the smaller the required majority, the more convergence constituting consensus analysis will be; an agreement between fewer states will be necessary for a court to impose a unified standard on all constituent units. Conversely, the more qualified the required majority, the more divergence-entrenching consensus becomes; an agreement between a larger number of states is needed for consensus to be recognised and a uniform standard to be imposed by a court.

2.1.2 Which States Count?

From a conceptual perspective, the question of which states should count in consensus analysis is even more fundamental and primary than the question of the required majority. The latter tells us the numerator, while the former tells us the denominator; it tells us what the sample of constituent units amongst which we are seeking for consensus is. Much similar to the question of the required majority, different answers to this question can result in different outcomes of cases, which, in turn, can change the nature of consensus as a mechanism of accommodation.

There has been a lot of discussion, particularly in the USA, regarding which states should count in assessing consensus; there, the discussion has been whether all states or just those for which a particular issue arises should be counted?[34] Eighth Amendment jurisprudence of SCOTUS is demonstrative of this issue. In *Roper* v. *Simmons*, SCOTUS had to decide whether sentencing underaged offenders to death was barred by the Eighth Amendment. The methodological dilemma faced by SCOTUS in surveying the state of national consensus was whether to take into account only the positions of US states that permit the death penalty, thereby substantially narrowing down the sample, or whether laws of all US states should be taken into account. The core of the disagreement on this issue between the majority and the dissenters in *Roper* may be summed up through this passage by Justice Scalia: 'That 12 States favour *no* executions says something about the consensus against the

31 Wildhaber, Hjartarson and Donnelly (n 7) 257; Dzehtsiarou (n 5) 12.
32 Helfer (n 5) 140.
33 Wildhaber, Hjartarson and Donnelly (n 7) 258–9.
34 For more, see Tonja Jacobi, 'The Subtle Unraveling of Federalism: The Illogic of Using State Legislation as Evidence of an Evolving National Consensus' (2006) 84 North Carolina Law Review 1089, 1125–31.

death penalty, but nothing – absolutely nothing – about consensus that offenders under 18 deserve special immunity from such a penalty.'[35]

Scalia's argument is that it is not possible to infer from a categorical position against the death penalty of the 12 states what their position is on the special nature of culpability of minors. Put differently, Justices disagreed whether *argumentum a fortiori* can be applied when assessing consensus. In one of the few papers that have dealt with this issue, Dzehtsiarou and O'Mahony advocated for what they called an 'inclusive approach', according to which positions of all states should be considered when analysing the existence of consensus.[36] Only exceptionally, according to them, 'if the evidence indicated that the absence of relevant laws in an individual state was a result of that state genuinely not having considered the issue at hand, rather than a conscious decision to not regulate the issue,'[37] we could adopt the *a fortiori* exclusive approach.

However, the distinction between an inclusive approach, where all constituent units are counted in conducting consensus analysis, and the Scalian exclusive approach, under which only states 'for which the issue arises' should be considered, creates a false dichotomy. There is a third approach that can be discerned from the jurisprudence of consensus-employing courts.[38] I shall simply refer to it as the 'specific approach'.

What the 'specific approach' entails can be best demonstrated with the ECtHR case of *Lekić* v. *Slovenia*.[39] At the heart of the dispute in *Lekić* were the provisions of the Financial Operations of Companies Act 1999 (FOCA) passed by the Slovenian legislature.[40] On the basis of FOCA, Slovenia struck a significant number of companies off the registry and 'introduced a "non-rebuttable" presumption that the members of a struck-off company were deemed to have undertaken joint and several liability for any outstanding debts of the company.'[41] Members could exonerate themselves from any liability only by proving that their role in the company was a passive one. After one of the members of one of the affected companies failed to do so, he brought his case to Strasbourg, arguing that Slovenia had violated his right to peaceful enjoyment of his possessions from Article 1 of Protocol 1 of the ECHR. In rejecting his claim, the ECtHR explained that FOCA was introduced in a particular context in which 'thousands of companies, which had been created under the legislation of the former Socialist Federal Republic of Yugoslavia, existed only on paper and, moreover, had large debts, but no assets.'[42] The ECtHR also explained that 'the FOCA was introduced in response to a

35 See *Roper*, 611 (Scalia. J., dissenting).
36 O'Mahony and Dzehtsiarou (n 4).
37 ibid 346.
38 To paraphrase the famous philosopher Slavoj Žizek: 'There is a third pill!'
39 *Lekić v Slovenia* App no 36480/07 (ECtHR, 11 December 2018).
40 *Zakon o finančnem poslovanju podje*tij (ZFPPod), Official Gazette RS, nos. 54/99, 110/99, 93/02 – odl. US, 117/06 – ZDDPO-2, 31/07, 33/07 – ZSReg-B, 58/07 – odl. US in 126/07 – ZFPPIPP.
41 *Lekić v Slovenia* App no 36480/07 (ECtHR, 11 December 2018), para 27.
42 ibid para 114.

serious and widespread problem in post-socialist Slovenia extending to no less than 6,500 companies and undermining some of the basic conditions which the companies had to satisfy in a free-market economy.'[43]

As the Court made clear, the situation that gave rise to the case was highly specific to the post-Yugoslav context in which newly independent countries were making a transition from a centrally planned economy to a free-market system. It was within this specific context that the ECtHR decided that the admittedly wide-sweeping measures of FOCA were justified under the ECHR. Therefore, it could be argued that in conducting consensus analysis in *Lekić*, only laws of those CoE member states that have undergone a transition from a communist to a capitalist economic system should be relevant to the analysis. In fact, when conducting the comparative survey, the Court examined laws of all ex-Yugoslav states and the majority of the states that were surveyed were indeed ex-communist states.[44]

To put the lesson of *Lekić* into the abstract, the third 'specific approach' comprises of cases that originated from a very distinct factual substratum that only applies to a limited part of the constituent units and does not lend itself to the applicability of *argumentum a fortiori*. When discussing laws of which constituent units should count in establishing consensus, the first way in which the dichotomy between inclusive and exclusive approaches is false is that it overlooks these *Lekić*-like special cases. Therefore, there are not just two, but three approaches to defining what states are relevant in ascertaining consensus: the inclusive approach (all states count), the *a fortiori* exclusive approach (rejecting *a fortiori* inferences, only states that adopted a specific position on the specific issue count), and the special approach (only states that share a specific factual context count).

2.1.3 Which States are Actually Counted?

But even identifying the three approaches does not yield the full picture; there is a second way in which the hitherto established dichotomy between the inclusive and the *a fortiori* exclusive approach is false. This is because the preceding discussion was only concerned with domestic laws of what constituent units are *relevant* for discerning consensus. However, it said nothing about domestic laws of which states are *actually considered* by courts in deciding any given case. Therefore, within each of the approaches – the inclusive, the exclusive, and the specific – there are three sampling options a court could follow when deciding which states' laws to *actually* examine. First, a court can examine domestic laws of all of the relevant constituent units. Second, it can examine the laws of a statistically representative sample of the relevant constituent units. Finally, it can analyse a statistically unrepresentative sample of the relevant constituent units. Therefore, in discussing which states count in establishing consensus, there are not only two approaches, as is commonly discussed in literature. Instead, there are nine distinct approaches: three in defining which states are *relevant* for the consensus inquiry,

43 ibid para 116.
44 ibid para 56.

and three options under each of the approaches as to how many states' laws are *actually* surveyed by courts. This is presented in Table 9.2 below.

Table 9.2 Different approaches to counting legislative positions of states as bases of consensus

How to count states?	
Which states count?	*Which states are actually counted?*
Inclusive approach	All states
	Statistically representative sample
	Statistically unrepresentative sample
Exclusive approach	All states
	Statistically representative sample
	Statistically unrepresentative sample
Specific approach	All states
	Statistically representative sample
	Statistically unrepresentative sample

As noted above, the decision which of these nine approaches to follow is not mere theoretical fetishism. Each of the approaches changes consensus analysis as a method dramatically, and it changes how cases are decided. Going back to SCOTUS and its decision in *Roper*, Scalia's insistence on following the exclusive approach, and the majority's insistence on adopting the inclusive approach, was not only a matter of constitutional doctrine but also a matter a practical consequence. Were Scalia's theory to carry the day, the Court would not have been able to find consensus against sentencing minors to death;[45] it would therefore be more likely to find capital punishment of minors constitutional and thereby further entrench the existing divergences in sentencing policy amongst states. Conversely, as the majority's inclusive approach prevailed, SCOTUS was able to find a consensus against the death penalty for minors and found such punishment unconstitutional. In so doing, consensus acted as a converging force through which the Court was able to impose a uniform standard on capital punishment across all 50 states.

2.2 Practices of Constituent Units as a Separate Source

Legal commentary on consensus analysis, especially in Europe, has taken 'laws and practices of constituent units' as a unitary singular basis of consensus, even though they are not one and the same. This approach overly simplifies how consensus works, and it blurs the lines between the different bases of consensus that are better examined separately. It is an unavoidable fact that the law can be applied, practised, and administered in various different ways, especially when discretion is

45 See *Roper*, 609–11 (Scalia. J., dissenting).

built into it by design.[46] Indeed, the evergreen distinction between 'law in books' and 'law in action' is predicated on this fact.

The distinction between, and the importance of separately examining consensus on the basis of legislation and practices shines through most explicitly in the USA, where most consensus-related case law concerns the constitutionality of certain types of punishment, historically most often the death penalty. In this context, the distinction between the two bases is the distinction between criminal law and sentencing policy. SCOTUS not only looks at whether states permit, in their criminal legislation, the death penalty (consensus on the basis of laws of constituent units), but also if the states still execute the death penalty and if the juries still sentence people to death (consensus on the basis of practices of constituent units). For instance, in *Gregg* v. *Georgia*, the Court rejected the idea that the death penalty was unconstitutional *per se*.[47] When examining national consensus, SCOTUS demonstrated that '[t]he legislatures of at least 35 States have enacted new statutes that provide for the death penalty for at least some crimes [...]'.[48] The Court then separately analysed the sentencing practices, stating that:

> the actions of juries in many States [...] are fully compatible with the legislative judgments [...] as to the continued utility and necessity of capital punishment in appropriate cases. At the close of 1974, at least 254 persons had been sentenced to death [...] and, by the end of March, 1976, more than 460 persons were subject to death.[49]

In the same way, SCOTUS has treated state laws and state practices separately in every national consensus case after *Gregg*.[50]

Making the distinction between consensus on the basis of laws and on the basis of practices is important because the two raise different normative considerations and methodological issues. As pertaining to consensus on the basis of laws of constituent states, some of these have been raised in the preceding paragraphs. All of them apply equally to counting states on the basis of practices as well. However, there are some methodological questions that are unique to them, for instance what inferences and conclusions, if any, can be drawn from state practices. This can again be illustrated with relation to jury decisions and sentencing policy in the USA. Does the rarity of a sentencing practice mean that there is a consensus that it should not be used, or that it should be used, well, rarely? In *Stanford* v. *Kentucky*, Justice Scalia wrote that rarity:

46 Frederick Schauer, 'The Convergence of Rules and Standards' (2003) 2003 New Zealand Law Review 303, 304–11.
47 *Gregg v Georgia*, 428 U.S. 153 (1976).
48 ibid 179–80.
49 ibid 182.
50 See, for instance, *Woodson v North Carolina*, 428 U.S. 280 (1976) at 289–95; *Coker v Georgia*, 433 U.S. 584 (1977) at 593–6; *Enmund v Florida*, 458 U.S. 782 (1982) at 789–97; *Thompson v Oklahoma*, 487 U.S. 815 (1988) at 823–31.

> does not establish [...] that the death sentence for offenders under 18 is categorically unacceptable to prosecutors and juries. To the contrary, it is [...] overwhelmingly probable, that the very considerations which induce petitioners and their supporters to believe that death should never be imposed on offenders under 18 cause prosecutors and juries to believe that it should rarely be imposed.[51]

From a more practical standpoint, maintaining the typological distinction between legislation and practices of constituent units as bases of consensus is useful because a court may refer only to one; or only to the other; or to both bases in a single decision. They can lead to contradicting conclusions, or they can work in unison. Such different dynamics can obviously affect how consensus analysis is conducted, and what conclusions courts draw from it, therefore affecting whether consensus acts as converging or diverging mechanism of accommodation of diversity.

Acknowledging the differences between the two bases of consensus also allows for a more detailed and precise discussion of normative and dogmatic dimensions and effects of consensus analysis across different institutional contexts.

3 Level of Generality of Consensus

Moving from the question of what types of evidence courts seek when making arguments from consensus – that is what are the bases of consensus – we move to the question of what precisely is the object of consensus. Consensus on what does a court examine? What is the question a court asks to define to scope of its comparative inquiry? Generally, two approaches to these questions have been recognised depending on the level of abstraction at which courts assess consensus: consensus at the level of legal rules, and consensus at the level of legal principles.[52]

Whenever a court is searching for a consensus at the level of legal rules, the level of abstraction is low. Consensus is sought on a relatively specific issue and, generally, it will be more difficult to find as compared to a consensus at a higher level of abstraction.[53] *M.C.* v. *Bulgaria*,[54] a case decided by the ECtHR, examined the existence of consensus at an extremely low level of abstraction, i.e. at the level of a legal rule. The Court assessed whether physical resistance of a victim was a constitutive part of the definition of rape in domestic criminal statutes of CoE states when it decided that the incrimination contained in the Bulgarian criminal code was not in line with how other ECHR state parties defined rape in their criminal

51 *Stanford v Kentucky*, 492 US 361 (1989) at 374.

52 See, for instance, Jens T Theilen, 'Levels of Generality in the Comparative Reasoning of the European Court of Human Rights and the European Court of Justice: Towards Judicial Reflective Equilibrium' in Panos Kapotas and Vassilis P Tzevelekos (eds), *Building Consensus on European Consensus: Judicial Interpretation of Human Rights in Europe and Beyond* (Cambridge University Press 2019) 402–403.

53 Dzehtsiarou (n 5) 15–16.

54 *M.C. v Bulgaria* App no 39272/98 (ECtHR, 4 December 2003).

law at the time.[55] Obviously, examining whether a specific element of a crime is included in the definition of an offence in national criminal codes is perhaps as close to seeking a consensus on the level of legal rules as one could imagine.

Conversely, consensus at the level of legal principles means that the level of abstraction is high, courts are searching for consensus on relatively broad and loosely defined questions. Because of this, consensus at the level of principles is generally easier to find. The jurisprudence of the CJEU is emblematic of this approach: rather than looking for convergence on legal rules, the CJEU would typically examine whether an issue forms part of the hopelessly opaque standard of 'constitutional traditions common to the Member States'.[56] Similarly, the ECtHR has also taken a similar approach in some of its cases. In *D.H. and Others* v. *the Czech Republic*,[57] for instance, the Court found that there exists a consensus on an abstract level that the Roma 'require special protection' which 'also extends to the sphere of education,'[58] without going into details as to what that consensus might be more specifically.

Regardless of this analytically helpful dichotomy between consensus at the level of legal rules and principles, however, we should acknowledge that different levels of abstractness are not discrete categories. Instead, they exist on a spectrum. As a result, most cases may not fit neatly into one of the two categories but might lie somewhere in between. Take a hypothetical example of the recognition of same-sex marriage. On a spectrum from legal rules to principles on this issue, a consensus-seeking court may compare, for instance, (i) what specific procedures are prescribed by states for same-sex couples to obtain a marriage certificate; (ii) what specific rights are afforded to them; (iii) whether or not states permit marriages by same sex couples; (iv) whether or not states offer a legal recognition of a same-sex relationship in any way, be it through marriage, civil unions, or a registration of a partnership; (v) whether or not states enumerate sexual orientation as a suspect category in their definition of the prohibition of discrimination; (vi) whether or not states extend the scope of the prohibition of discrimination to all family law issues; or (vii) whether or not the states' domestic laws include the right to equal treatment and the prohibition of discrimination.

Finally, much like with the typological dimensions discussed above, an understanding of levels of generality as typological category is important for understanding how consensus can be used by courts either as a divergence entrenching or convergence constituting mechanism. As noted, by redefining the object of consensus as a specific question of a rule, or an abstract question of a principle, courts can manipulate the likelihood of them finding the existence of consensus: it is easier to find on the level of principles than on the level of rules. Simply by

55 ibid para 156.

56 See Case 11/70 *Internationale Handelsgesellschaft mbH v Einfuhr- und Vorratsstelle für Getreide und Futtermittel* [1970] ECLI:EU:C:1970:114. See also Article 52(4) of the Charter of Fundamental Rights of the European Union [2009] OJ C 326.

57 *D.H. and Others v the Czech Republic* App no 57325/00 (ECtHR, 13 November 2007).

58 ibid para 182.

redefining the question, courts can thus affect the likelihood of reaching a certain outcome in a case, which, in turn, determines whether the lack of consensus entrenches the status quo, or the existence of a consensus constitutes a converging force for all the constituent units of a system.

4 Temporality of Consensus

Courts have not only examined whether consensus on an issue exists, but also whether consensus is recent or long-standing. Recency of consensus is thus another typological variable of consensus that has been relevant in the decision-making processes of courts and in debates surrounding consensus. Most often, the recency argument has been used by courts or dissenting minorities to disqualify or diminish the weight that consensus analysis should play in the case and in determining its outcome, thereby also affecting how consensus would accommodate the diverse views held by states. A dissenting opinion of Justice Scalia in *Atkins* v. *Virginia* raises the issue well and gives a glimpse at this discursive use of the argument:

> a major factor that the Court entirely disregards is that the legislation of all 18 States it relies on is still in its infancy. The oldest of the statutes is only 14 years old; five were enacted last year; over half were enacted within the past eight years. Few, if any, of the States have had sufficient experience with these laws to know whether they are sensible in the long term. It is myopic to base sweeping constitutional principles upon the narrow experience of [a few] years.[59] [citations omitted]

In his dissent, in which Justice Thomas and Chief Justice Rehnquist joined, Scalia scolded the *Atkins* majority for basing their decision – that sentencing an intellectually disabled person to death was unconstitutional – on national consensus that was too recent at the time. Consensus, in their view, should have been long-standing in order to justify the foreclosure of diversity in approaches to this issue amongst the states, as well of democratic contestation, and mandate a convergence by basing a norm of constitutional law on the views of a (recent) majority.

Although recency of consensus might seem like a rather straightforward category at first, things get blurred when recency and longevity of consensus, on the one hand, and trends in the laws of constituent units as a basis of consensus, on the other hand, are discussed side by side. Trends as basis of consensus form an important part of the argumentative practice and courts rely on them regularly in deciding whether a consensus exists or not.[60] When they do so, courts declare that an (emerging) consensus exists based not on a certain majority of states taking a particular view, but instead on there being a trend, a steady shift in favour of that view amongst the states. Because trends have an inherent temporal component to

59 *Atkins v Virginia*, 536 U.S. 304 (2002) at 344 (Scalia. J., dissenting).
60 See *supra* n 16 and 17.

them – they establish the existence of 'consensus' on the basis of how positions of states have changed through time – the difference and the relationship between them and the perspective of temporality of consensus – its recency or longevity – gets obfuscated at times.[61] To avoid confusion and appreciate the argumentative dynamics at play here, it is important to distinguish between laws of constituent units and trends in those laws as distinct bases of consensus, and to understand that each of them can be viewed from the perspective of temporality. Both consensus established on the basis of a majority of domestic legislation laws *and* consensus established on the basis of trends may be either recent or long-standing.

A hypothetical might shine better light on this difference. When courts seek consensus on the basis of domestic legislation of constituent units, they will look for a certain minimum number of states that follow a particular solution. In the case of the CoE with (now) 46 member states, let us presume 30 states. Whenever 30 states are in favour of a solution, the court will find that consensus on the basis of laws of constituent units exists. When courts examine if this consensus is recent or long-established, they will examine how long those 30 states have been following that solution; for instance, 30 states need to be in favour of the same solution for 10 years in order for the court to find consensus to exist. However, if courts look for the existence of a trend in domestic laws as a basis of consensus, they will examine the direction of change in the states' attitudes towards the issue at hand. It will not matter whether 30 states subscribe to a particular solution; it will only matter that the number of states subscribing to that solution is increasing with time. Finally, if a court examined trends from the viewpoint of temporality, the direction of change in the states' attitudes would have to be observable for a certain period of time; to borrow the words of SCOTUS, what would matter is 'the consistency of the direction of change'.[62] In our hypothetical, what would then matter is that the total number of states that subscribe to a solution would be on an upward trajectory for, say, a period of 10 years.

Therefore, any typological exercise on consensus analysis must reflect the distinction between trends as a basis of consensus and laws of constituent units from the perspective of temporality as a basis of consensus. Moreover, from the perspective of consensus as a legal mechanism of divergence or convergence, temporality may determine consensus' attitude towards diversity and its accommodation by diminishing the impact that consensus might have on the outcome of a case, as the discussion between the dissenters and the majority in *Atkins* demonstrates.

61 See, for instance, John Murray, 'Consensus: Concordance, or Hegemony of the Majority', *Dialogue between judges, European Court of Human Rights, Council of Europe, 2008* (2008) 12; Paul Mahoney and Rachael Kondak, 'Common Ground: A Starting Point or Destination for Comparative-Law Analysis by the European Court of Human Rights?' in Mads Andenas and Duncan Fairgrieve (eds), *Courts and Comparative Law* (Oxford University Press 2015) 132; *S.H. and Others v Austria* App no 57813/00 (ECtHR, 3 November 2011), para 96–7.

62 *Atkins v Virginia*, 536 U.S. 304 (2002) at 315.

5 Automaticity of Consensus

Finally, the fourth typological dimension of consensus analysis refers to how consensus influences the outcome of a case. Does the outcome of consensus analysis, i.e. the (non)existence of consensus, fully determine the outcome of a case, or do courts also decide cases against consensus, or perhaps look for additional arguments to justify their conclusions? In other words, do courts regard the outcome of consensus analysis as binding or not? This question has been discussed many times by authors discussing different courts and across institutional contexts. There is an agreement amongst them that consensus analysis is generally not considered as binding by courts; it is just one of the many factors and argumentative practices that constitute the decision-making process.[63]

This is certainly true in many cases. For instance, in *Graham* v. *Florida*, SCOTUS ruled that capital punishment imposed on a minor for a non-homicidal offence is in violation of the Cruel and Unusual Punishment Clause of the Eighth Amendment. After assessing whether there was a national consensus in favour or against the impugned punishment, the Court held that guided by '"the Court's own understanding and interpretation of the Eighth Amendment's text, history, meaning, and purpose," [...], the Court must determine in the exercise of its own independent judgment whether the punishment in question violates the Constitution.'[64] Put differently, the state of national consensus did not automatically determine the outcome of the case and the Court did not feel bound by the (non) existence of consensus; it was the Court's own assessment that, in the end, determines the outcome of the case.

In other cases, however, courts have been more deferential to consensus, even to the extent that the (non)existence of consensus could be considered as automatically determining the outcome of the dispute. In *Oliari and Others* v. *Italy*, the ECtHR ruled that Article 12 of the ECHR does not grant the right to marry to same-sex couples solely because there is no consensus amongst states parties to the ECHR on the issue. This is the entirety of the Court's reasoning regarding the Article 12 claim:

63 Francisco Javier Mena Parras, 'Democracy, Diversity and the Margin of Appreciation: A Theoretical Analysis from the Perspective of the International and Constitutional Functions of the European Court of Human Rights' [2015] Revista Electrónica de Estudios Internacionales 11; O'Mahony and Dzehtsiarou (n 4) 336; Youngjae Lee, 'Federalism and the Eighth Amendment' (2013) 98 Iowa Law Review 69, 73; Wildhaber, Hjartarson and Donnelly (n 7) 248–50, 256; John Murray, 'The Influence of the European Convention on Fundamental Rights on Community Law' (2009) 33 Fordham International Law Journal 1388, 1414; Murray (n 61); Michael S Moore, 'Morality in Eighth Amendment Jurisprudence' (2008) 31 Harvard Journal of Law & Public Policy 47, 52; Wayne Myers, 'Roper v. Simmons: The Collision of National Consensus and Proportionality Review' (2006) 96 Journal of Criminal Law and Criminology 947, 951; Eyal Benvenisti, 'Margin of Appreciation, Consensus, and Universal Standards' (1999) 31 New York University Journal of International Law and Politics 843, 851.

64 *Graham v Florida*, 560 U.S. 48 (2010) at 2022.

> The Court notes that in Schalk and Kopf the Court found under Article 12 that [...], as matters stood (at the time only six out of forty-seven CoE member States allowed same-sex marriage), the question whether or not to allow same-sex marriage was left to regulation by the national law of the Contracting State. The Court felt it must not rush to substitute its own judgment in place of that of the national authorities [...] The same conclusion was reiterated in the more recent Hämäläinen (cited above, § 96), where the Court held that while it is true that some Contracting States have extended marriage to same-sex partners, Article 12 cannot be construed as imposing an obligation on the Contracting States to grant access to marriage to same-sex couples.
>
> The Court notes that despite the gradual evolution of States on the matter (today there are eleven CoE states that have recognised same-sex marriage) the findings reached in the cases mentioned above remain pertinent. In consequence the Court reiterates that Article 12 of the Convention does not impose an obligation on the respondent Government to grant a same-sex couple like the applicants access to marriage.[65]

It would be difficult to describe the effect of consensus analysis on the outcome of this case as anything but automatic. Without offering any other arguments to justify the outcome, the Court rejected the applicants' Article 12 claim solely on the account of it not being able to find a consensus amongst CoE member states in favour of same-sex marriage, be it on the basis of a trend in domestic legislation, or on the basis of a majority of laws of constituent states. It rejected the notion that the legislative trend in favour of the recognition of same-sex marriage that had emerged since *Schalk and Kopf*[66] via *Hämäläinen*[67] and through *Oliari* was sufficient to find the existence of an (emerging) consensus. Nor was there a majority of states in favour of same-sex marriage to justify the finding of consensus on the basis of laws of constituent units. As the outcome of consensus analysis that the Court had conduced pointed against the protection of same-sex marriage, the Court automatically concluded that Article 12 did not protect the right of same-sex couples to marry; the Court did not examine any other arguments other than the absence of a consensus in reaching that conclusion.

Admittedly, however, much like the categories that were discussed in relation to generality and temporality of consensus, 'automatic' and 'non-automatic' consensus analysis are also simply analytical categories of a phenomenon that is not inherently discrete. Here as well, automaticity of consensus is a category that lies on a continuum and should be accounted for in this way: in individual cases, courts can consider consensus analysis as completely binding, completely non-binding, or anything in between. In the context of the ECHR, Dzehtsiarou has proposed a helpful

65 *Oliari and Others v Italy* App nos 18766/11 and 36030/11 (ECtHR, 21 July 2015), paras 191–2.

66 *Schalk and Kopf v Austria* App no 30141/04 (ECtHR, 24 June 2010), paras 61–3.

67 *Hämäläinen v Finland* App no 37359/09 (ECtHR, 16 July 2014), para 96.

framework that transcends the 'automatic' versus 'non-automatic' distinction and better reflects the continuous nature of automaticity of consensus. According to this framework, consensus creates a 'presumption that favours the solution to a human rights issue which is adopted by the majority of the Contracting Parties. This presumption can be rebutted if the Contracting Party in question offers a compelling justification.'[68] In other words, the stronger the consensus on an issue, the stronger the presumption in favour of that solution. And on the flipside, the stronger the presumption in favour of a solution, the stronger the justification needed to rebut it. On the extreme polar ends of this continuum lie the 'automatic' and 'non-automatic' consensus analysis. In the former case, consensus is so overwhelming that is establishes such a strong presumptions in favour of it that no justification could rebut it; while in the latter, the absence or fragility of consensus establishes such a weak presumption that any potential justification would be sufficient to rebut it. *Oliari*, then, could be read as establishing such a strong presumption against same-sex marriage due to an overwhelming lack of consensus that no justification that would be strong enough to rebut it, explaining why the Court did not even bother to include any reasons other consensus analysis in its justification.

Automaticity is also crucially important from the perspective of the diversity accommodating nature of consensus as it determines the role that consensus analysis has in the decision-making processes of courts. In *Oliari*, for instance, consensus seems to have automatically determined the issue, thereby further entrenching the existing divergences between states in their approach to same-sex marriage. In an alternate universe, the ECtHR could have used consensus in a non-automatic way, deciding that there are cogent reasons, despite the lack of consensus, to read Article 12 of the ECHR as granting the right to same-sex marriage and thus diminish the role of consensus as entrenching divergences. Therefore, by manipulating the role consensus has on an individual case, courts can also manipulate the wider role it has in how divergences amongst states are accommodated.

6 Conclusion

At the end of the day, the picture of consensus analysis that emerges across all four typological variables is a complex one. The method is far from being a monolith; courts have an extremely wide discretion in how they employ consensus in each individual case. This decision can have important repercussions not only for the outcome of that case and for the parties involved in it, but also the structural relationships between constituent units in multilevel polities. Table 9.3 collates all the typological considerations and variables discussed in this chapter and gives the complexity of the generalised view of consensus analysis a visual representation.

68 Dzehtsiarou (n 5) 9. He also identified three justifications that can override consensus in the ECHR context: (i) the text of the ECHR; (ii) historical and political justifications; and (iii) moral sensitivity of the matter in question. See ibid 30–6.

Table 9.3 A general typology of consensus analysis

Consensus analysis			
Bases of consensus	*Core meaning*	Laws of constituent units	
		Practices of constituent units	
	Peripheral meanings	International treaties	
		Decisions of international tribunals	
		Regional law	
		International soft law	
		Regional soft law	
		Internal soft law	
		Foreign legal orders	
		Trends in laws of constituent units	
		International trends	
		Margin by which legislation of constituent units is passed	
		Judges' perception of social consensus	
		Scientific developments and the views of experts	
		Statements of religious authorities	
		Polling data	
Level of generality		Legal principles (spectrum)	Legal rules (spectrum)
Temporality of consensus		Long-standing (spectrum)	Recent (spectrum)
Automaticity of consensus		Automatic (spectrum)	Non-automatic (spectrum)

But it may well be that even a graphic representation in the form of a table does not do justice to the complexity of the method and the many options courts have when employing it. Perhaps some numbers might help: even under the most benevolent assumption that the generality, temporality, and automaticity of consensus are discrete dichotomous variables and are not on a continuum, courts can use consensus in its core meaning in at least 6,264 different ways.[69] If we add the peripheral meanings of consensus to the calculation, the number is over $8.2\text{x}10^{15}$ different ways of justifying judicial decisions through consensus.[70] It is only by deconstructing the method, as we have done in this chapter by creating a general typology of consensus analysis, that such complexity can be grasped and

69 This calculation conservatively assumes that there are three different types of required majorities when counting laws and practices of constituent units (simple, qualified, unanimity) and that levels of generality, temporality and automaticity of consensus are discrete dichotomous variables. With these assumptions in mind, the number of combinations of consensus analysis in its core meaning is obtained through the expression: $n = 8(54+27^2) = 6{,}264$.

70 This calculation makes the same assumptions as above. The number of combinations of consensus analysis in its core and peripheral meanings is obtained using the expression: $n = 8(2(27\text{x}15!)+27^2\text{x}15!)$.

meaningfully analysed. Indeed, only in this way can we begin to fully understand all the ways in which courts in multilevel systems can manipulate consensus as a diversity accommodating mechanism; one through which courts can either impose uniform standards and constitute convergences, or one through which courts can give the constituent units a *carte blanche* to regulate an issue as they will, thereby legally entrenching the existent divergences.

10 Convergence, Divergence, and Strategic Interactions of International Courts

Lessons From the Protection of Business Premises for Legal Persons in Europe

*Audrey M. Plan**

1 European Courts and the Elusive 'Judicial Dialogue'

How do the European Court of Justice (ECJ) and the European Court of Human Rights (ECtHR) co-exist in a common legal space? How does this coexistence affect the fragmentation, or coherence, of European human rights law? Despite some attempts to formalise their relationship by having the EU become party to the ECtHR, they are still to this day two entirely separate and non-hierarchical courts. This has led to multiple jurisprudential sagas whereby the two courts have converged and diverged with each other when presented with similar questions.[1] There is no rule organising this overlap and no unified trend across issue-areas regarding which court leads and which court follows. They have been engaged in both formal and informal forms of 'judicial dialogue'.[2] But the concept of judicial

* Previous versions of this paper have been presented at the Department of Political Science of Trinity College Dublin (June 2021), the Conference (Playing) Constitutional Twister: The Mechanisms of Convergence and Divergence within Multilevel Legal Orders (Ljubljana, October 2021), the Annual Political Science Association of Ireland Conference (October 2021), I am most grateful for the feedback provided by Jacqueline Hayden, Chief Justice Frank Clarke, Samuel A. T. Johnston, Jesper Lindqvist, Benjamin Swift, and William Phelan for their useful comments. My sincere gratitude also goes to the reviewers and editors of this volume, for their availability, patience, and guidance during the revision process, as well as Sophie A. Cooper (University of St Andrews) for her proof-reading. This research has been funded by the TCD Provost PhD Award and the Irish Research Council Postgraduate Research Award (Grant GOIPG/2021/354).

1 Sébastien Platon, 'CJUE et Cour EDH: la dialectique du maître et de l'esclave?' [2020] Revue québécoise de droit international 533.

2 Monica Claes and Maartje de Visser, 'Are You Networked Yet? On Dialogues in European Judicial Networks' (2012) 8 Utrecht Law Review 100. See also, beyond European courts: Anne-Marie Slaughter, 'A Typology of Transjudicial Communication' (1994) 29 University of Richmond Law Review 99; Anne-Marie Slaughter, 'Court to Court' (1998) 92 American Journal of International Law 708; Anne-Marie Slaughter, *A New World Order* (Princeton University Press 2005).

DOI: 10.4324/9781003355762-10

dialogue only takes act of a sociological reality; it remains elusive, difficult to explore empirically[3] and crucially does not offer an explanation as to the various patterns of convergence and divergence that have been observed between the two European courts over the years.

This chapter will explore the interactions and judicial dialogue between ECJ and ECHR. It presents a theory explaining why strategic decision-making by either court can result in either coherence or fragmentation of this legal space, providing empirical examples of a series of cases brought before these courts regarding the right of moral persons to privacy. It shows that these courts respond to threats to their authority by using convergence with another international court as a costly, but an effective, self-legitimisation tool. Its contribution is therefore two-fold: first, it will offer a new methodology to systematically and empirically assess the extent to which these courts converge or diverge from each other over time, beyond the mere presence or absence of cross-citations. Second, it will provide correlation for these patterns of convergence and divergence between both courts which have so far not been explained.

2 A New Theory: Judicial Dialogue as a Strategic Legitimising Tool

Courts, including international courts, such as the ECJ and the ECtHR, can be approached as strategic actors. They attempt to maximise their goals in the face of various constraints[4] and strike a careful balance between different goals. This can lead them to make compromises when these goals are contradictory.[5] Such can be the case with the ***authority, legitimacy***, and ***specific goals related to the function*** of an international court.

Indeed, international courts have various goals or preferred outcomes, related broadly to their functional role. Beyond the heterogeneity of approaches among the two courts,[6] each court is steered toward specific goals based on its function. For example, a human rights court such as the ECtHR prioritises safeguarding a European level of protection of human rights, whereas the court of a supranational organisation such as the ECJ would rather seek the effective implementation of that organisation's supranational policies through judicial activism.[7] Not prioritising these goals when

3 Amrei Müller and Hege Elisabeth Kjos (eds), *Judicial Dialogue and Human Rights* (Cambridge University Press 2017) 4–9.

4 Alec Stone-Sweet, *Governing with Judges: Constitutional Politics in Europe* (Oxford University Press 2000) 140.

5 Yuval Shany, 'Assessing the Effectiveness of International Courts: A Goal-Based Approach' (2012) 106 The American Journal of International Law 225, 262.

6 Erik Voeten, 'The Impartiality of International Judges: Evidence from the European Court of Human Rights' (2008) 102 American Political Science Review 417; Michael Malecki, 'Do ECJ Judges All Speak with the Same Voice? Evidence of Divergent Preferences from the Judgments of Chambers' (2012) 19 Journal of European Public Policy 59.

7 Bruno de Witte, Elise Muir and Mark Dawson, *Judicial Activism at the European Court of Justice* (Edward Elgar Publishing 2013).

presented with a case where they are relevant would be contrary to each Court's mission and the teleologies of their respective legal orders. Nonetheless, their ability to reach these goals through judicial decision-making requires them to have sufficient authority.

This chapter will approach the concept of supranational judicial authority narrowly,[8] understood as an ability to have the rulings implemented at the domestic level. This is a deliberately restrictive understanding of authority, very similar to a goal-based approach to a court's effectiveness[9] or sociological authority and different from normative authority. Such a limited and empirically grounded understanding of authority was chosen for two reasons. First, non-implementation – or threat of non-implementation – is the clearest and most serious challenge with which an international court can be presented.[10] Therefore, if a threat to the authority of either court is to impact their behaviour, then surely this should be verified when this authority is the *most* challenged – that is, by the (threat of) non-implementation of its rulings. Second, this allows for a transparent assessment of what is, and is not, an attack on European courts' authority; a broader understanding of 'authority' would be more difficult to empirically assess in a single contribution. Compliance requires implementation by the actors, who then have to undertake a positive step to enforce the ruling, or could otherwise effectively prevent the implementation.

Closely related to the concept of authority is that of legitimacy. Of particular interest to this contribution will be the *perceived* or *sociological* legitimacy of the court.[11] It can be defined as the 'belief [...] within a given constituency [...] that a political institution's exercise of authority is appropriate'.[12] Distinct from (although related to) trust or public support,[13]

8 Other conceptions of authority can be broader, to encompass all the indirect and diffuse influence an (international) court may have on the actors in (and out) of its jurisdiction see for example: Karen J Alter, Laurence R Helfer and Mikael Rask Madsen (eds), *International Court Authority* (Oxford University Press 2018).

9 Yuval Shany, *Assessing the Effectiveness of International Courts* (Oxford University Press 2016).

10 Fiona de Londras and Kanstantsin Dzehtsiarou, 'Mission Impossible? Addressing Non-Execution through Infringement Proceedings in the European Court of Human Rights' (2017) 66 International & Comparative Law Quarterly 467; Yuval Shany, 'Compliance with Decisions of International Courts as Indicative of Their Effectiveness: A Goal-Based Analysis' (2010) 04–10 Hebrew University of Jerusalem Faculty of Law Research Paper.

11 Gregory A Caldeira and James L Gibson, 'The Legitimacy of the Court of Justice in the European Union: Models of Institutional Support' (1995) 89 American Political Science Review 356.

12 Jonas Tallberg and Michael Zürn, 'The Legitimacy and Legitimation of International Organizations: Introduction and Framework' (2019) 14 The Review of International Organizations 581, 585.

13 Patricia Popelier and others, 'A Research Agenda for Trust and Distrust in a Multilevel Judicial System' (2022) 29 Maastricht Journal of European and Comparative Law 351.

legitimacy ensures acceptance of the decision by the constituency of its rulings, rendering force unnecessary for compliance, regardless of the actual content of the decision.[14] But while many institutions' legitimacy hinges on their democratic nature, a court's legitimacy stems from being a 'neutral servant [...] of the law'.[15] In the words of Dothan, 'courts are supposed to apply norms and not their own discretion, therefore an appearance of constraint can usually help international courts gain support for their judgments'.[16] Consequently, factors that support this appearance of neutrality enhance the legitimacy of either European court.

Legitimacy precedes authority: 'before the court can make authoritative policy that other institutions, the states, and the public will view as binding on them, it must have some level of respect'.[17] Therefore, one way for the ECJ or the ECtHR to enhance their authority and achieve their respective goals is to enhance their legitimacy.[18] Convergence among courts can be seen as such a legitimacy-enhancing strategy, relying on both the inherent legitimacy of legal reasoning itself, as well as the persuasive authority that another Court's case law can have when employed to bolster one's own reasoning.[19] When one European Court converges with the other, it strengthens its own legal reasoning, gives it external validity, and co-opts the legitimacy of the other court in turn. Of course, this means that this second court must have a sufficiently high legitimacy itself. This convergence can take different forms: often, it consists in citing the other court's rulings (also called 'borrowing' or 'cross citation')[20] but convergence can also be achieved by using the same legal standards, and/or adopting the same outcomes.

However, this strategy is costly: relying on the precedent of another court while keeping the coherence of legal reasoning intact means reaching an outcome at least partly closer to the preferred outcome of this second court. European Courts must

14 Archibald Cox, *The Role of the Supreme Court in American Government* (Oxford University Press 1977); Shai Dothan, 'How International Courts Enhance Their Legitimacy' (2013) 14 Theoretical Inquiries in Law 455.

15 Martin Shapiro and Alec Stone-Sweet, *On Law, Politics, and Judicialization* (Oxford University Press 2002); Stone-Sweet (n 4) ch 1.

16 Dothan (n 14) 468.

17 Lee J Epstein and Jack Knight, *The Choices Justices Make* (1st edition, CQ Press 1997) 12–13.

18 Dothan (n 14) 459.

19 Erik Voeten, 'Why Cite External Legal Sources? Theory and Evidence from the European Court of Human Rights' in Clara Giorgetti and Mark A Pollack (eds), *Beyond Fragmentation: Cross-Fertilization, Cooperation, and Competition among International Courts* (Cambridge University Press 2022).

20 Erik Voeten, 'Borrowing and Nonborrowing among International Courts' (2010) 39 The Journal of Legal Studies 547; Wayne Sandholtz, 'Human Rights Courts and Global Constitutionalism: Coordination through Judicial Dialogue' (2020) 10 Global Constitutionalism 1; Sabrina D'Andrea and others, 'Asymmetric Cross-Citations in Private Law: An Empirical Study of 28 Supreme Courts in the EU' (2021) 28 Maastricht Journal of European and Comparative Law 498.

preserve the appearance of coherent legal reasoning to maintain the mask of law and neutrality,[21] as '[c]ourts cannot escape the logic of legal arguments'.[22] This is important since the ECJ and the ECtHR have different mandates and goals. When one converges with the other, it will have to accept a trade-off between its enhanced legitimacy and its ability to fully pursue its goals in any given subject area.

Therefore, convergence with another international court is a strategy a court will engage in only when the threat to its authority is perceived as sufficiently credible and serious. Formally, the theory poses the threat to the authority of the international court as the independent variable (IV), and the reaction of an international court, in the form of convergence or divergence with another international court, as the dependent variable (DV) (Figure 10.1).

International courts, therefore, react to 'threats to authority', but threats *from whom?* The constituency of an international court would include its member states, national judiciaries, but also the legal 'field', in a sociological sense.[23] Although the European Commission could also have an impact on the implementation of ECJ's rulings, it is not considered here to be a relevant actor for this study.[24]

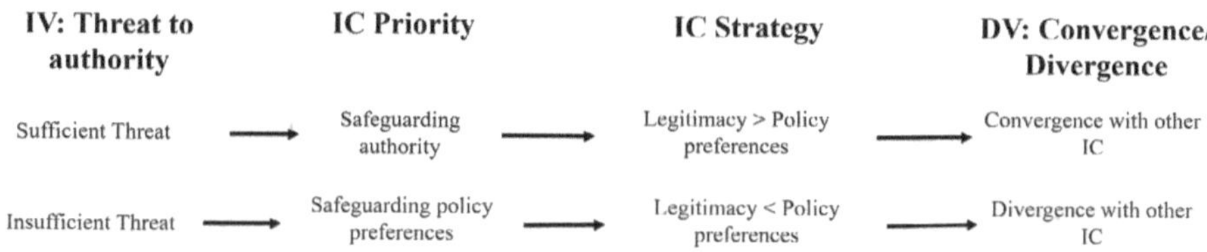

Figure 10.1 Causal chain hypothesised

21 Stone-Sweet (n 4); Anne-Marie Burley and Walter Mattli, 'Europe before the Court: A Political Theory of Legal Integration' (1993) 47 International Organization 41.

22 Frank Schimmelfennig, 'Competition and Community: Constitutional Courts, Rhetorical Action, and the Institutionalization of Human Rights in the European Union' (2006) 13 Journal of European Public Policy 1247, 1250.

23 R Daniel Kelemen, 'The Court of Justice of the European Union in the Twenty-First Century' (2016) 79 Law and Contemporary Problems 117.

24 There are two key reasons that support this decision. First, only a minority of cases could see their implementation impeded by the Commission itself: if the issue lies with domestic law's conformity with EU law (or the fundamental rights litigants would like to see included in EU law), the ball is in the hands of member states; if it lies within the EU regulation/directive the Commission relies on, then Member States are the one who need to reform it. Second, even when the Commission is in a position to impede the implementation of an ECJ ruling, to my knowledge, there is no case where the Commission's decision was annulled, and the Commission stubbornly did not change; whereas these situations have been repeatedly found from governments and domestic courts. Therefore, the Commission could be included in the theoretical framework as a potential threat, yet one which empirically is not found to be substantial enough to be effective.

As a result, Figure 10.1 indicates that for European courts, actors in charge of implementing rulings are domestic courts; governments of their Member States (understood broadly as all state authorities); and the other European court. Other European institutions, in this framework, are either too distantly related to matters of implementation (European Parliament) and/or are representatives of the majority of State interests and preferences rather than actors independent from their member States (Council of the EU, European Council, EU Commission).[25]

The theoretical expectations are therefore as follows: the more threats an international court will be under, the more likely it will be to converge with another international court, preferably one with overlapping competences, to rhetorically defend itself against these threats.

3. Research Design

The validity of this theory will be tested through an empirical case study, where the progressive convergence and divergence between two international courts on a given topic can be systematically assessed, along with the mechanism causing it to unfold. To preface, it must be acknowledged that a single longitudinal case study will not make the theory fully generalisable. The goal is not to explain, in an

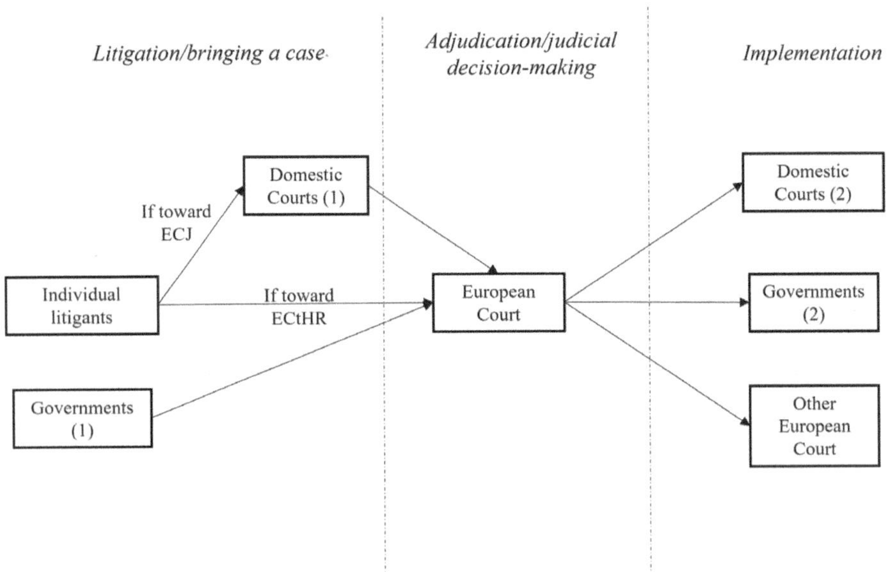

Figure 10.2 Procedure of adjudication before European courts

25 For the EU Commission in particular, we refer to Mark A Pollack, 'Delegation, Agency, and Agenda Setting in the European Community' (1997) 51 International Organization 99.

absolute manner, every single reference or absence of reference to the ECJ in the ECtHR's ruling, and vice-versa. Rather, this is a single case study – albeit covering multiple decades of cases – on a topic with the particularity of having a very low degree of salience in the legal and political debate. A trade-off of this in-depth qualitative and mechanism-oriented case study is the question of the external validity of the findings: in other words, their generalisability.[26] This contribution recognises this limit, as the goal is primarily to establish a credible, empirically documented and therefore stable mechanism for a theoretical framework which has not been explored so far. While the entire theory might not be generalisable with one case study; it will still give evidence that the mechanism envisioned is credible and warrants further research.

In this chapter, the focus will be on a jurisprudential saga which unfolded between 1989 and 2016, involving the ECJ and the ECtHR, where the main question at hand was: *Do legal persons benefit from the protection of their business premises under their right to privacy, and if so, to what extent?* All the cases relevant to this question from both courts were collected through a rigorous search of the two Courts' respective databases. This yielded 12 different cases across both courts which make up this jurisprudential saga.

An index (Table 10.1) was developed specifically for this project to measure the degree of similitude and dissimilitude between two courts on a specific matter at a given time. This measure can then be repeated, in order to track the evolution of this similitude/dissimilitude over time. This new index accounts for the multiple ways international courts can converge and diverge with each other, beyond mere cross-citations. Indeed, while borrowing and non-borrowing are one of the main practices international courts can engage in to converge or diverge from each other;[27] it is also a very restrictive approach. One could envision a convergence of the ECJ with the ECtHR without explicitly mentioning the ECtHR, for example, or alternatively, a reference to the case law of the ECtHR without substantive alignment in the end. Therefore, the index accounts for different ways in which these courts can end up having a similar or dissimilar case law on a given question.

- Substantive outcome on specific sub-questions: Are business premises of companies protected under article 8 ECHR, and then if they are, is it with a similar standard as individuals?
- Test/legal standards used: Do both courts use the same test to examine the potential breach of fundamental rights? Indeed, to examine whether there has been a breach of fundamental rights, each court developed its own test. The coding of this section is understood narrowly: it relies on which test the court claims to apply, rather than its substantive use. This cannot capture all the nuances of legal reasoning but ensures that coding is systematic. Moreover, it accounts for a court partially referring to the test used by the other or

26 Gary Goertz and James Mahoney, *A Tale of Two Cultures – Qualitative and Quantitative Research in the Social Sciences* (2014) 237–8.

27 Voeten, 'Borrowing and Nonborrowing among International Courts' (n 20); Sandholtz (n 20).

mentioning it without using it (for example: the ECtHR mentioning arbitrariness within its assessment of necessity).[28]

- Existence of cross-references: with a distinction in the score attributed, depending on whether the reference is coherently included in the reasoning, cherry-picked and/or just name-dropped.[29]

How these different aspects were assessed and turned into an index is presented in Table 10.1.

Table 10.1 Index of Convergence/Divergence

		Answer (Score associated)		*Maximum/ Minimum score*	
Category		*Dissimilarity*	*Similarity*		
Test/legal standard used by the Court	An identical test is...		Used (0) >Mentioned but not used /partly used (0.5) >None (1)	Max: 1 >Min: 0	Max: 3 >Min: 1
	A different test is...	Used (2) >Mentioned but not used /partly used (1.5) >None (1)		Max: 2 >Min: 1	
Outcome of the case	On protection of business premises for legal person:	Dissimilar (1.5) >Uncertain (1)	Identical (0), >On a different legal basis (0.5), >Uncertain (1)	Max: 1.5 >Min: 0	Max: 3 >Min: 0
	On the possible difference between the protection of legal and natural persons	Dissimilar (1.5) >Uncertain (1)	Similar (0) >Uncertain (1)	Max: 1.5 >Min: 0	
References to the other Court's case-law	Some pertinent case-law of the other Court is mentioned	No (2)	Yes (0) >Mentions the other Court without specific case law (+0.5)	Max: 2 >Min: 0	Max: 3 >Min 0
	If YES, the case law is cherry-picked/ irrelevant	YES (0.5)	No (0)	Max: 0.5 >Min: 0	
	If NOT cherry-picked, the Court	Explicitly does not follow (1)	Explicitly follows (0) >Implicitly does not follow (0.5)	Max: 1 >Min: 0	
Similarity/Dissimilarity Score				Maximum: 9 >Minimum: 1	

28 Wieser and Bicos Beteiligungen v Austria (2008) 46 EHRR 5, para 56.

29 Similar to Krommendijk's 'by-the-way' references, or Gelter and Siems' 'ornamental references'; see Jasper Krommendijk, 'The Use of ECtHR Case Law by the Court of

Taking the most recent ruling of the other European court as a reference, a European ruling is compared on all of these items, and points are attributed depending on the content of this ruling. A higher score means more dissimilarity; a lower score means more similarity. This score on its own does not capture the entirety of a court's legal reasoning, and the score attributed can be used to identify trends rather than being considered an exact 'quantification' of judicial dialogue. It merely purports to help identify trends over time, based on a systematic assessment of each ruling, as has been done for this research in the analysis section. For the same reason, any potential outlier case should not be dismissed, but instead carefully analysed to understand how it fits within the overall trend of the flow of cases.

By repeating this for each successive ruling, always comparing it with the most recent one from the opposite court, we can see what the general evolution of the jurisprudence of both courts was overall (Figure 10.3).

The score associated with the various rulings on moral persons' rights to privacy of the two European courts started high, but with a trend of getting lower and lower as time went on. This means that initially, there was a strong dissimilarity on this topic between both courts; but as time went on, their rulings got more and more aligned with each other.

However, this does not say much regarding which court was the one *causing* the divergence, or which one was the one *resolving* it and converging with the other. Was

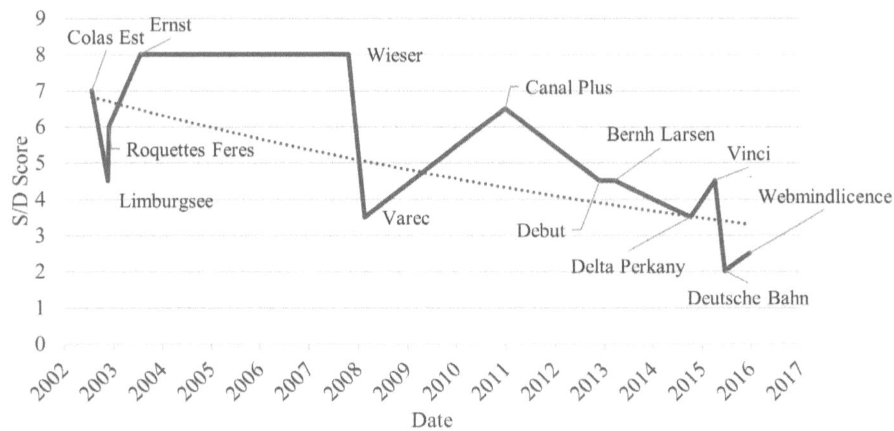

Figure 10.3 Evolution of the Similarity/Dissimilarity Score of European rulings for the case-study[30]

Justice after Lisbon' (2015) 22 Maastricht Journal of European and Comparative Law 812; Martin Gelter and Mathias Siems, 'Citations to Foreign Courts – Illegitimate and Superfluous, or Unavoidable? Evidence from Europe' (2014) 62 American Journal of Comparative Law 35.

30 The first ruling of the ECJ, Joined cases 46/87 and 227/88 *Hoechst AG v Commission* [1989] ECR 2859, is missing, as there is no previous ruling of the ECtHR to compare it to.

this a trend for both courts? Or is it that only one of them bridged the gap, as the other stood its ground? To answer this, each ruling is assigned a second score, a Convergence/Divergence Score ('C/D Score'). It is obtained by subtracting the S/D score of a ruling from the S/D score of the previous ruling. A positive Convergence/Divergence Score will mean that the international court *moved toward* the other international court ('Convergence'); whereas a negative score will mean that the international court *moved away*, with *less similarity* than before ('Divergence').[31] In other words, while the S/D score captures the state of relation between the two courts at a given time, the C/D score captures the action of a court in a given ruling: converging or diverging with the other (Figure 10.4).

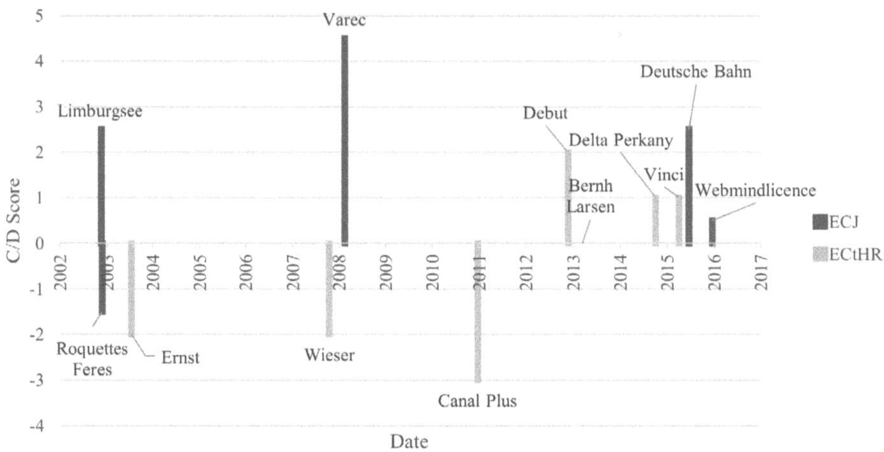

Figure 10.4 Evolution of the C/D Score of European rulings for the case-study[32]

An overview of all the relevant cases and their associated scores is presented in Table 10.2.

Table 10.2 List of all relevant cases and associated scores

Case	*Date*	*Court*	*S/D Score*	*C/D Score*
Hoechst	21/09/1989	ECJ	N/A	N/A
Colas Est	16/07/2002	ECtHR	7	N/A
Limburgse	15/11/2002	ECJ	4.5	2.5

31 This is because for two successive rulings A and B, regardless of the European Court delivering them: if $SD_A > SD_B$ meaning B presented more similarities with rulings of the opposite Court than A, then $CDB = SD_A - SD_B > 0$. On the other hand, if $SD_A < SD_B$ meaning A presented more similarities with rulings of the opposite Court than B, then $CDB = SD_A - SD_B < 0$.

32 The ECtHR's first ruling *Colas Est and others v France* (2002) 39 EHRR 17 is absent as there is no previous case to which its SD score could be subtracted.

Case	*Date*	*Court*	*S/D Score*	*C/D Score*
Roquettes Feres	22/11/2002	ECJ	6	-1.5
Ernst	15/07/2003	ECtHR	8	-2
Wieser	16/10/2007	ECtHR	8	-2
Varec	14/02/2008	ECJ	3.5	4.5
Canal Plus	21/12/2010	ECtHR	6.5	-3
Debut	20/11/2012	ECtHR	4.5	2
Bernh Larsen	14/03/2013	ECtHR	4.5	0
Delta Perkany	02/10/2014	ECtHR	3.5	1
Vinci	02/04/2015	ECtHR	4.5	1
Deutsche Bahn	18/06/2015	ECJ	2	2.5
Webmindlicence	17/12/2015	ECJ	2.5	0.5

Lastly, the operationalisation of the potential threats from different actors as presented in Figure 110. was based on a list of observable implications from each of these actors, such as states' positions, domestic courts' positions, and other European courts' positions (Table 10.3).

Table 10.3 Indicators of the Dependant Variables

	NON-THREAT	*THREAT*
STATES' POSITIONS	• Expresses support for the case law of a specific ruling in an issue-area • Has supported a legal reasoning, test, standard or outcome similar to the one adopted by the court • Does not submit amicus curiae or publicly comment on a case it is not party to	• Expresses criticism for the case law of a specific ruling in an issue-area • Has supported a legal reasoning, test, standard or outcome different from the one adopted by the court • Submit amicus curiae, observations or publicly comment even on a case it is not party to
DOMESTIC COURTS' POSITIONS	• Enforces / complies with the European court's ruling • Possibly with explicit confirmation / reference to the European court in question	• Refusal to implement jurisprudence (issue-specific or systematic) of the European court. • Threat of non-implementation (issue-specific or systematic) if the given European court does not change its position • Raises the question directly to the court
OTHER EUROPEAN COURT'S POSITION	• Reference to the autonomy/ independence of the other court or its legal order • Reliance on concepts of 'equivalent protection', left unquestioned or with a very lax control only.	• Jurisprudential divergence in the previous rulings AND • Explicit control and possibly full rebuttal of the presumption of equivalent protection

With this methodological roadmap set, it is now possible to move on to the empirical analysis of the case study.

4 Business Premises of Companies and the Asymmetrical Road(s) Toward a Coherent European Solution

Following the scores indicated in Figure 10.4, two periods can be distinguished for the purpose of this analysis. The first one goes up to and including the *Canal Plus* case in 2010: it is characterised by the ECtHR consistently diverging from the ECJ, and the ECJ on the other hand was slowly converging with the ECtHR. The second period saw a change in this trend for the ECtHR, which started, in turn, to converge with the ECJ. The ECJ, for its part, kept its slow convergence going as well. For each period, the constellation of challenges toward both courts will be laid out, to then move on to the impact they had on each of them individually.

4.1 2002–2010: The One-Sided Convergence of the ECJ

This first period includes cases *Colas Est* (2002), *Ernst* (2003), *Wieser* (2007) and *Canal Plus* (2010) for the ECtHR,[33] and *Limburgse* (2002), *Roquettes Freres* (2002), and *Varec* (2008) for the ECJ.[34] The ECJ found itself under sufficient threat to its authority, and therefore converged with the ECtHR, albeit keeping a certain degree of dissimilitude. On the other hand, an analysis of the challenges to the authority of the ECtHR shows that the Strasbourg court did not have to make such a trade-off, and could maintain a diverging position vis-à-vis the ECJ, prioritising its own preferred outcome: more extensive protection of fundamental rights, including for legal persons.

4.1.1 Overview of the Constellation of Challenges to the Authority of the Courts

This first period saw different actors granting varying levels of attention to the matter of fundamental rights for companies.

First, domestic legislation of the EU Member States leaned toward more protection of business premises at the domestic level, although not necessarily through the achievement of *fundamental rights* status for legal persons' protection of business premises.[35] Before the ECtHR, France did not argue against the

33 Respectively: *Colas Est* (n 32), *Ernst and others v Belgium* App. no. 33400/96 (ECtHR 15 July 2003); *Wieser* (n 28); *Canal Plus v France* App. No. 29408/08 (ECtHR 21 December 2010).

34 Respectively: Joined cases C-238/99 P, C-244/99 P, C-245/99 P, C-247/99 P, C-250/99 P to C-252/99 P and C-254/99 P *Limburgse Vinyl Maatschappij NV and others v Commission of the European Communities* [2002] ECR I-8375; C-94/00 *Roquettes Freres SA v DGCCRF and Commission of the European Communities* [2001] ECR I-9011; C-450/06 *Varec SA v Belgian State* [2008] ECR I-581.

35 *Hoechst* (n 30), Opinion of Advocate General Mischo.

protection of legal persons' business premises under Article 8 altogether, only that the standard of protection for moral persons was to be lower than for natural persons.[36] That is not to say that this was a full consensus across Europe, especially in the whole of the ECtHR's constituency. For example, Turkey and Russia, both then under the jurisdiction of the ECtHR, did not even require a warrant or judicial authorisation for an inspection of business premises belonging to a company to be conducted, let alone grant them any fundamental right to privacy.[37]

However, it is telling that no State submitted any *amicus curiae* briefs for any relevant ECtHR case during this period; and only a handful of observations were submitted to the ECJ during the same time.[38] The lack of salience inferred by the lack of *amicus curiae* briefs or observations submitted can only lead to a conclusion of a lack of threat to the authority of any court at this point.

On the other hand, multiple higher courts in the EU at least had made their preference on that specific question known in the previous years: the Spanish Constitutional Court[39] and the French Conseil Constitutionnel[40] had both decided in the 1980s that business premises for companies were protected by a right to privacy. But two more specific rulings deserve our attention. First, in its 2002 ruling sending the preliminary question to the ECJ in the *Roquette Freres* case, the French Cour de Cassation is fairly critical of the ECJ's lack of protection of fundamental rights for companies in these situations, and reminds the ECJ that the French court needs 'to carry out the review required by its *national constitutional law*'.[41]

The second interesting ruling comes from the Belgian Cour d'Arbitrage. In the *Varec* case, the lower court sent two questions within the same ruling: one to the ECJ, and one to its Constitutional Court. When the latter gave its decision before the ECJ's Advocate General had even written her conclusions, it was to state that Article 8 of the ECHR was fully applicable to moral persons.[42] This ruling may not have been mentioned by the ECJ, but it was explicitly covered by the AG,[43] ensuring the Luxembourg judges knew a ruling on the very case on which they were about to deliberate had already been partially provided with an answer, from a court which knew very well that the ECJ's turn would come after them.

36 *Colas Est* (n 32).
37 *Law of the RSFSR No. 948-I of March 22 of 1991 on Competition and Restriction of Monopolistic Activity in Commodity Markets* (March 22, 1991), Art. 13; *Act 4054, on the Protection of Competition* (December 7, 1994) Art. 14–15.
38 Excluding the States which were directly involved in the case before the ECJ, only Germany, Greece, Italy, the United Kingdom and Norway submitted observations during the *Roquettes Freres* case; only Austria submitted observations in *Varec* case; no observations were submitted in *Hoechst, Dow Chemicals, Dow Iberica* and *Limburgse* cases.
39 STC 137/1985, of Oct.17.
40 Cons. Const., 29 Dec 1983, n° 83–164 DC (emphasis added).
41 Cass. Com. 7 March 2000, n° 98–30.389 Bull. IV N° 47 p. 41.
42 C.C., 19 Sept 2007, n° 118/2007, A 2.2 (Cour Constitutionnelle, Belgium).
43 *Varec* (n 34) Opinion of Advocate General Sharpston.

Lastly, the more general politico-legal context of the relationship between the ECJ and domestic court matters. In 2005, the German Constitutional Court expressed serious doubts about the fundamental rights standards set by EU law in its Third Pillar, (as well as a ruling of the ECJ on this issue), and confirmed that it was willing to review EU Acts in light of its own standards when necessary.[44] Authors such as Wind and Bobek have also identified broader trends during the 2000s whereby national courts in Denmark, Sweden, and Central and East European Members of the EU were very reluctant to engage with the ECJ's *de facto* power of judicial review.[45] The ECJ had to worry about maintaining its authority over courts disagreeing with its positions both on the specific issue of privacy for companies, and for fundamental rights in general, without an equivalent threat facing the ECtHR.

As for the relationship between both European courts, the ECtHR officialised what would become the *Bosphorus* doctrine in 2004, whereby it would presume that EU law offered a protection 'equivalent' to the ECtHR's for fundamental rights.[46] There is a consensus in the literature to consider that this was an approach very deferential for the ECJ, and respectful of its autonomy, for example, observed by Lock: '[a]s a rebuttal of the presumption is unlikely to occur in practice, the key implication is that it results in immunity from review for the CJEU [...]'.[47]

On its side, the ECJ had so far shown a lot of goodwill toward the ECtHR: it had consistently recognised and given increasing importance to the ECHR, mentioning it as a source, then naming individual articles in its own rulings from 1975[48] and onward, giving it 'particular significance' for the first time in 1989's *Hoechst*, and in 1996 started citing ECtHR rulings specifically.[49] While it put some conditions on the possible accession of the EU to the ECHR, they were mainly formal ones and not a threat to the Strasbourg court.[50] Between 2002 and 2009, the ECJ continued to rely on the ECtHR's case law. The Charter of Fundamental Rights was still largely in limbo, and Luxembourg judges referred to it for the first time only in 2006,[51] addressing its exact legal value even later, in 2010.[52]

44 BVerG, Order of 18 July 200, 2 BvR 2236/04; Kelemen (n 23) 135.

45 Marlene Wind, 'The Nordics, the EU and the Reluctance Towards Supranational Judicial Review' (2010) 48 Journal of Common Market Studies 1039; Michal Bobek, 'Learning to Talk; Preliminary Rulings; the Courts of the New Member States and the Court of Justice' (2008) 45 Common Market Law Review 1611.

46 *Bosphorus v Ireland* (2006) 42 EHRR 1; *Avotinš v Latvia* (2017) 64 EHRR 2.

47 Tobias Lock, *The European Court of Justice and International Courts* (OUP 2015) 196; Lize R Glas and Jasper Krommendijk, 'From Opinion 2/13 to Avotinš: Recent Developments in the Relationship between the Luxembourg and Strasbourg Courts' (2017) 17 Human Rights Law Review 567, 5.

48 C-36/75 *Roland Rutili v Ministre de l'intérieur* [1975] ECR 1219.

49 Starting with C-13/94 *P v. S and Cornwall County Council* (1996) ECR I-2143.

50 *Opinion 2/94 Accession to the ECHR* [1996] ECR I-01759 mainly requiring that the accession to the ECHR be inscribed in EU Treaties first.

51 C-540/03 *European Parliament v Council* [2006] ECR I-05769.

52 C-555/07 *Seda Kücükdeveci v Swedex GmbH & Co. KG* [2010] ECR I-365.

Discussions between judges of the two courts regarding the accession of the EU to the ECHR were underway, with Presidents Wildhaber and Iglesias meeting regularly and publicly to this end.[53]

4.1.2 Convincing Domestic Courts: The Forced Partial Convergence of the ECJ

The ECJ was therefore faced with threats to its authority from domestic courts and, more moderately, from the ECtHR. This led to a partial convergence, as shown by the score in Figure 10.4. Luxembourg judges gave up a lot of ground while not actually aligning the ECJ with the ECtHR. In this period, the ECJ recognised the protection of business companies as a fundamental right protected by the ECHR, which was therefore also protected as 'a general principle of Community law'.[54]

However, while the ECJ acknowledged the jurisprudence of the ECtHR in this ruling,[55] it ignored it when litigants tried to rely on this same jurisprudence in *Limburgse*.[56] Lastly, it converged even more in *Varec*, when it acknowledged that there was indeed a 'fundamental right' to respect for private life,[57] and applied this to one of the litigants, a company. But the convergence is still only partial, as the ECJ continues using the same 'non-arbitrary or disproportionate' test,[58] while the ECtHR applies a more stringent one.

Can this clear but limited convergence be attributed to a self-legitimisation strategy from Luxembourg judges? Different elements support this claim.

The implementation and effectiveness of the EU competition policy and the Commission's decisions was one of the ECJ's concerns throughout its decisions on this matter.[59] Granting the protection of Article 8 to businesses adds a risk of discrepancies between different legal orders, where domestic courts would have different appreciations of that right, of the possible exceptions, of the requirement to still

53 Gil Carlos Rodríguez Iglesias, Speech delivered at the formal sitting held as part of the celebrations to mark the 50th anniversary of the Court (Luxembourg, 4 December 2002) < https://www.cvce.eu/obj/speech_by_gil_carlos_rodriguez_iglesias_luxembourg_4_december_2002-en-88c6d43e-e3cb-4b3d-b54d-a11451adbf46.html> accessed 01 October 2022; Gil Carlos Rodríguez Iglesias speech delivered on the occasion of the opening of the judicial year (Strasbourg, 31 January 2002) <. https://www.echr.coe.int/Documents/Annual_report_2001_ENG.pdf > accessed 01 October 2022; Laurent Scheeck, 'Solving Europe's Binary Human Rights Puzzle. The Interaction between Supranational Courts as a Parameter of European Governance' [2005] Questions de Recherche, Sciences Po 40.

54 *Hoechst* (n 30) para 19; *Limburgse* (n 34) paras 240, 252, keeping the notion of 'General Principle' used by the Court of First Instance; *Roquettes Frères* (n 34) paras 27, 28.

55 *Ibid.* paras 48, 52.

56 It can be noted that the opinion of the AG for *Roquettes Freres* actually was given before *Colas Est* ruling, but the ECJ can always depart from the AG's opinion, and had already done so in *Hoechst* (n 30) for example.

57 *Varec* (n 34).

58 *Roquettes Frères* (n 34), para 52; *Limburgse* (n 34), para 240.

59 Case 31/59 *Acciaieria e Tubificio di Brescia v High Authority of the European Coal and Steel Community* [1960] ECR 71.

conduct investigations, etc.[60] The best way to avoid such risks and discrepancies, which would have affected the effectiveness of EU law, would therefore have been either no application of Article 8 to business premises or application with limited safeguards, to avoid running into the aforementioned problems.

This is where it must be highlighted that the ECJ did not lean into the divergence at any point. Nonetheless, it converged quickly but covertly, pretending that the discrepancy never existed in the first place. The ECJ never fully acknowledged any potential divergence with the ECtHR, and instead downplayed it whenever it could. The *Colas Est* ruling from the ECtHR is universally interpreted by the legal scholarship as a departure from the ECJ's approach, a frank recognition of the right of business premises to be protected as a home when the ECJ had not done so in *Hoechst AG* previously.[61] Yet, the AG for the *Limburgse* case considered that this new ruling by the ECtHR did not contradict the ECJ's previously standing *Hoechst AG* case: the ECJ had provided some form of protection,[62] and the two tests used by the courts were similar[63] – which was not the way most legal scholars had interpreted *Colas Est*![64]

The ECJ judges went out of their way to constantly frame the ECtHR as agreeing with them, co-opting its authority and legitimacy on that particular issue. The ECJ had to give some ground, and self-legitimise during this period, both in the eyes of the ECtHR and of domestic courts.

4.1.3 Wait and See: The Status Quo of the ECtHR

The ECtHR's authority was not threatened by any actor and therefore the court was able to pursue its own goals, as a human rights court. Different elements prove that this was a deliberate choice of the Strasbourg judges, rather than simply an oversight of the divergence with the ECJ it caused.

First, the same domestic courts that were exerting pressure on the ECJ for higher standards were de facto aligning themselves with the ECtHR's approach – as the Belgian Conseil Constitutionnel did in 2007, explicitly citing the 2002 *Colas Est* ruling.[65]

But what about the signs from the ECJ? One possibility is that the ECtHR did not diverge willingly from the ECJ, did not make a strategic choice, and indeed simply was not aware of, or did not account for, this jurisprudence. But

60 *Hoechst* (n 30) para 17. See also *Roquettes Freres* (n 34), Opinion of AG Mischo, para 91.

61 Marius Emberland, 'Protection against Unwarranted Searches and Seizures of Corporate Premises under Article 8 of the European Convention on Human Rights: The COLAS Est Sa v. France Approach' (2003) 25 Michigan Journal of International Law 77, 95–96; Rick A Lawson, 'Confusion and Conflict? Diverging Interpretations of the European Conuvenution on Human Rights in Strasbourg and Luxembourg' in Rick A Lawson (ed), *The Dynamics of the Protection of Human Rights in Europe*, vol III (Kluwer Academic Publications 1994) 241.

62 *Roquettes Freres* (n 34), Opinion of Advocate General Mischo para 256.

63 *Ibid.* para 260.

64 For example: Lawson (n 61) 245.

65 CC, 19 September 2007 n° 118/2007.

there is much evidence proving that the ECtHR simply decided to stand its ground: in *Colas Est*, the ECtHR proved particularly knowledgeable about the state of the ECJ's current case law: it makes explicit reference to the relevant standing precedent, by extensively citing cases *Hoechst*, *Dow Benelux*, *Dow Iberica*, and the subsequent case *AKZO* which confirmed them. Impressively, it goes as far as citing a case from the Court of First Instance of the European Communities (which had not yet become the General Court), a case which had been decided barely months before the ECtHR's decision itself: proof that Strasbourg was attentively keeping up with the activities of the ECJ on that matter.[66] If the ECtHR does not cite the ECJ in its later cases (*Ernst* and *Wieser*[67]), it also cannot be assumed to be because the judges were somehow not aware of the more recent cases, for the ECJ's 2002 *Roquette Freres* case had been very widely commented on by the scholarship – the ECtHR simply decided to ignore it.

The *way* the ECtHR used the previous Luxembourg case law in its 2002 case also deserves much attention. It could be assumed that, by cross-referencing the ECJ thoroughly, Strasbourg judges were showing deference and respect to these rulings, taking them into account; this is typically how cross-referencing is interpreted. This is particularly true when we consider that in the *Colas Est* case, reference to EU law was not necessary. *Colas Est* was not a case of implementation of an EU decision or EU policies – it was a purely domestic French case. Could such reference, therefore, be a way for the ECtHR to seek support for its own reasoning? Quite the opposite. The ECtHR explicitly stated the ECJ's case law under the heading 'Case-law of the Court of Justice of the European Communities and of the Court of First Instance'. The ECJ explicitly showed that it was aware of the ECJ's refusal to grant the right to privacy to business premises for companies when it did not have to do so. Then in the very same ruling, it put forward its own preferred outcome very explicitly, stating that 'the Convention is a living instrument which must be interpreted in the light of present-day conditions' with a 'dynamic interpretation',[68] to conclude in a way that openly opposes the ECJ's. That *Colas Est* would be a departure from the ECJ's case law was not missed by Strasbourg judges; it was the goal.

Therefore, there was an absence of threat to the authority of the ECtHR from domestic constituencies, and the ECJ was also acknowledging the authority of the Strasbourg court more and more.

4.2 2010–2016: Confrontation, and the Push and Pull of European Courts

The relevant cases for this second period are *Debut* (2012), *Bernh Larssen* (2013), *Delate Perkany* (2014) and *Vinci* (2015) for the ECtHR;[69] *Deutsche Bahn* (2015)

66 *Colas Est* (n 32), para 27; the cases in question were Joined Cases T-305/94, T-307/94, T-313/94, T-316/94, T-318/94, T-325/94, T-328/94, T-329/94 and T-335/94 *LVM v. Commission* [1999] ECR II-931.
67 *Ernst* (n 33); *Wieser* (n 28).
68 *Colas Est* (n 32).
69 *DEBÚT Zrt. and Others v Hungary* App No 24851/10 (ECtHR 20 November 2012); *Bernh Larsen Holding AS and Others v Norway* App No 24117/08 (ECtHR 4

and *WebmindLicences* (2015) for the ECJ.[70] The index used for coding the cases shows that the ECJ was always slowly converging with the ECtHR, in particular by constantly referring to it in its rulings. Interestingly, the ECtHR switched to very slow, minor convergence (positive C/D Score), with some very limited references to the ECJ's case law.

4.2.1 Overview of the Constellation of Challenges to the Authority of the Courts

As could be expected, the very narrow question of the right to privacy of companies was still not at the forefront of European States' preoccupations after 2007. Once again, no State presented *amicus curiae* briefs to the ECtHR. As for the ECJ, only two EU Member States not involved in a case submitted observations: Spain and Portugal.[71]

Looking at submissions to the ECtHR by States who were involved in proceedings, however, yields a different insight, through the *Bernh Larsen* case, where the Norwegian government did its utmost to lower the standard of protection afforded to companies.[72] The Czech Republic also expressed a preference for a lower standard of protection, this time not by excluding part of the investigation from the protection of the home, but by leaning into a 'more far-reaching' right of interference of the State when it comes to companies, compared to individuals,[73] trying to defend the lacking requirement of a judicial authorisation to conduct this sort of search. This argument must be placed in perspective: it is the one the ECJ was still pushing at this point.

Overall, while the issue is still fairly non-salient, States were more in favour of a right to privacy for companies, albeit one with a lower standard than for individuals. While this may not have reached the level of a 'threat' to the authority of the ECtHR in particular, the fact that two States in a row argued this way before Strasbourg judges must be kept in mind.

At this point, domestic courts also present an interesting picture. Where the previous period was characterised by a real push in favour of the protection of these companies against government interferences, national courts were now more reluctant to engage with the question: in all four cases covered, domestic courts either found no violation where the European court did (*Delta Perkány, Debut*[74]), or avoided the question of Article 8 (*Bernh Larsen*[75] *and Vinci*[76]). Moreover, in *Delta Perkány* the lower Czech judges attempted to rely on the ECJ's 1989 *Hoechst* ruling to argumentatively support

March 2013); *Affaire DELTA PEKÁRNY a.s. c République Tchèque* (2014) ECHR 279; *Affaire Vinci Construction et GTM Génie Civil et Services c France* App Nos 63629/10 and 60567/10 (ECtHR 2 April 2015).

70 C-583/13 P *Deutsche Bahn AG and others v Commission* EU:C:2015:404; C-419/14 *WebMindLicenses* EU:C:2015:832.

71 Spain in *Deutsche Bahn*; Portugal in *WebMindLicences*. Even then, the latter actually had an interest in the case, as one of the parties before the domestic proceedings was a Portuguese company.

72 *Bernh Larsen* (n 69), paras 98–102.

73 *DELTA PEKÁRNY* (n 69), para 77.

74 *Debút* (n 69).

75 *Bernh Larsen* (n 69).

76 Crim. 8 Apr 2010, N°08–87.415.

their position, which was the older precedent by which the ECJ had fully refused to grant protection to company business premises.

Therefore, from the perspective of the ECtHR in particular, domestic courts seemed to either avoid the matter (a downgrade in terms of support for the ECtHR compared to the previous period) or for the first time sided with the ECJ rather than the ECtHR. It is possible to conclude that there existed a light challenge to the authority of the ECtHR, specifically fuelled by the divergences between the ECJ and the ECtHR on that issue.

The third – and most pronounced – change compared to the previous period was in the relationship between the ECJ and the ECtHR themselves. If the previous years had seen a cooperative, positive, commentary relationship, this period saw their relationship become colder and move toward a point of rupture.

On the particular question of the companies' rights to privacy, in *Delta Perkány* the ECtHR reviewed recent developments in the ECJ's case law, most notably *Roquettes Freres.*[77] However, this reference is very ambivalent: while the case had an element of EU law to it, the ECtHR did not *need* to review EU law and practices, nor the ECJ's case law, to solve the dispute. Indeed, it does not need to refer to either of them in its own argumentation. This is reminiscent of the first time the ECtHR did this sort of *aparte* in its ruling, back in 2002's *Roquettes Freres.*

The tensions were also on much more sensitive matters. Indeed, during this period, after the full entry into force of the EU Charter of Fundamental Rights, the ECJ started to reference the ECHR and the ECtHR's case-law[78] less and less frequently, diverging from the Strasbourg Court's position on various high-profile questions.[79] In turn, the ECtHR was engaged in a tense judicial exchange with the ECJ regarding the EU's asylum instruments and their implementation during the 'migration crisis',[80] as well as on the matter of the European Arrest Warrant.[81]

77 *Delta Perkany* (n 69), paras 44–5.
78 Gráinne de Búrca, 'After the EU Charter of Fundamental Rights: The Court of Justice as a Human Rights Adjudicator?' (2013) 20 Maastricht Journal of European and Comparative Law 168, 74–6.
79 Platon (n 1).
80 Giulia Vicini, 'The Dublin Regulation between Strasbourg and Luxembourg: Reshaping Non-Refoulement in the Name of Mutual Trust' (2015) 8 European Journal of Legal Studies 50; Vassilis Pergantis, 'The "Sovereignty Clause" of the Dublin Regulations in the Case-Law of the ECtHR and the CJEU: The Mirage of a Jurisprudential Convergence?' in Giovanni Carlo Bruno, Fulvio Maria Palumbino and Adriana Di Stefano (eds), *Migration Issues before International Courts and Tribunals* (CNR Edizioni 2019); Samantha Velluti and Francesca Ippolito, 'The Relationship between the ECJ and the ECtHR: The Case of Asylum' in Kanstantsin Dzehtsiarou and others (eds), *Human Rights Law in Europe: The Influence, Overlaps and Contradictions of the EU and ECHR* (Routledge 2014).
81 Michal Dorociak, 'A Check Move for the Principle of Mutual Trust from Dublin: The Celmer Case' (2018) 3 European Papers 857; Asif Efrat, 'Assessing Mutual Trust among EU Members: Evidence from the European Arrest Warrant' (2019) 26 Journal of European Public Policy 656; Szilárd Gáspár-Szilágyi, 'Joined Cases Aranyosi and Căldăraru. Converging Human Rights Standards, Mutual Trust and a New Ground for Postponing a European Arrest Warrant' (2016) 24 European Journal of Crime, Criminal Law and Criminal Justice 197.

The last straw would come in 2014. The ECJ had been asked to provide a legal opinion regarding the draft Accession Agreement to evaluate its compatibility with the EU Treaties.[82] The Opinion, against all expectations, turned out to be a negative one. Legal commentary on this decision called it a sign of 'autarky',[83] expecting the caveat raised by the ECJ to turn into 'locks'.[84] This is especially true considering the arguments used by the ECJ to justify this negative opinion. The ECJ refused to grant any authority to the ECtHR over the EU legal order as long as it would not respect the autonomy and specificity of EU law[85]: a much taller order than 1994's Opinion 2/94 on the same question.[86] This decision had a notoriously chilling effect on the relationship between the two courts.[87]

Overall, the ECJ found itself threatened by the ECtHR, but with less threat to its authority from domestic courts and the governments at this point. On the other hand, the ECtHR not only had to worry about the ECJ clearly challenging its authority but also had much less support from domestic courts and governments for its preferred outcome regarding the standards of protection for companies. While it is difficult to talk of a threat from States at this point, domestic courts, for their part, were expressing a preference for the ECJ's standards, and a willingness to follow these rather than the ECtHR's.

4.2.2 The ECJ's Continued Convergence

The ECJ was therefore challenged on two fronts: by the ECtHR and by domestic courts. It used the last two cases to fully converge with the ECtHR. Both *Deutsche Bahn* and *WebMindLicences* contain explicit references to relevant ECtHR cases and are explicitly aligned with them.[88] If the ECJ did not fully adopt the three-step test of the ECtHR, it still ended up referring to the requirement of a legal basis and proportionality in *WebMindLicences*.[89]

Once again, several clues indicate that this convinced the ECJ to compromise on its goals as a Court of the EU ensuring the effectiveness of EU competition law to instead bolster the legitimacy of its ruling and secure authority over its constituency – 'keeping it safe' from the ECtHR.

First, litigants were still willing to bring up any potential divergence between the ECJ and the ECtHR, as in *the Deutsche Bahn* cases. The plaintiff argued that

82 *Opinion 2/13 Accession to the ECHR* [2014] ECR I-4635.
83 Piet Eeckhout, 'Opinion 2/13 on EU Accession to the ECHR and Judicial Dialogue: Autonomy or Autarky' (2015) 38 Fordham International Law Journal 955.
84 Adam Łazowski and Ramses A Wessel, 'When Caveats Turn into Locks: Opinion 2/13 on Accession of the European Union to the ECHR' (2015) 16 German Law Journal 179.
85 *Opinion 2/13* (n 82).
86 *Opinion 2/94* (n 50).
87 Eeckhout (n 83); Daniel Halberstam, '"It's the Autonomy, Stupid!" A Modest Defense of Opinion 2/13 on EU Accession to the ECHR, and the Way Forward' (2015) 16 German Law Journal 105.
88 *Deutsche Bahn* (n 70), paras 10–22; *WebMindLicence* (n 70), para 72.
89 *WebMindLicence* (n 70), para 73.

the ECJ had disregarded the *Colas Est* and *Canal Plus* rulings[90], and plaintiffs in *Delta Perkany* also argued that, had the ECtHR's case law been properly followed, rather than the ECJ's, they would have had a more favourable outcome.[91] This means that, as before, the ECtHR could be given more opportunities to disagree with the ECJ. Moreover, so far, no case involving the actual direct implementation of EU law (or even a Commission decision) had made it to the ECtHR. Since litigants had seen that the ECtHR's case law tended to be more favourable to them than the ECJ's on this question, this could create an interesting opportunity for strategic litigants. In this situation, the ECtHR would use the *Bosphorus* rule, creating uncertainty about whether it would disavow the ECJ explicitly or not – even though at this point, it had never actually rebuked the presumption of equivalent protection.

Krommendijk's interviews with ECJ Judges and Advocate Generals conducted very appropriately in December 2014, provide more insight into the reason why the ECJ was pushed to refer the ECtHR's case law. By adding references to the ECtHR's case law, the Court was 'reassur[ing] national (constitutional) courts and secur[ing] compliance with a Court of Justice judgment, because it makes it more difficult for national courts to object', despite knowing that citing this court too frequently would be tantamount to acknowledging that the ECJ on its own did not have sufficient authority.[92] It also appears from the interviews that since the ECtHR is not part of its constituency, ECJ judges do not cite it purely to convince Luxembourg judges. But still, the AG in *Deutsche Bahn* does not dismiss the plaintiff's grounds of appeal based on the TEU potentially disregarding the ECtHR's jurisprudence. Instead, AG Wahl carefully evaluated the compatibility between the TEU's ruling and the ECtHR's case law, in particular *Colas Est, Canal Plus* and *Liotard Freres*,[93] and even went further than what the plaintiffs argued, since he also accounted for *Bernh Larssen* and *Delta Perkany*.[94]

4.2.3 The ECtHR: New Threats and Forced Slow Convergence

It appears that there was a threat to the authority of the ECtHR from the ECJ. Although systemic rather than specific to the issue of Article 8 and business premises, it could still become a stepping stone for further threats coming from other EU governments dissatisfied with the court's case law on this issue.

Overall, the Strasbourg judges managed to keep a certain dissimilarity with the ECJ by maintaining that the protection of business premises under Article 8 for companies was indeed a fundamental right. The only slight adjustment is that the ECtHR seems to have acknowledged that the margin of appreciation for States in the case of actions infringing on the right to the protection of the home is indeed

90 *Deutsche Bahn* (n 70), para 14.
91 *Delta Perkany* (n 69), para 20.
92 Krommendijk (n 29) 832.
93 *Deutsche Bahn* (n 70), Opinion of Advocate General Wahl.
94 *Ibid.* paras 37–8.

more far-reaching for legal persons than for natural ones.[95] Why would the ECtHR, which had so far managed to maintain its original position, start to partially converge with the ECJ? Different elements support the theory that threats from the ECJ and some domestic courts correlate with this convergence, but that these challenges were at the same time mild enough to only lead to a partial convergence with Luxembourg.

2012's *Debut* was decided against a background of already rising and then sustained tensions between the courts regarding criminal law,[96] asylum,[97] and social rights.[98] Before *Debut*, the ECtHR had always maintained that the protection of moral and natural persons' business premises was identical, or had sidestepped the question,[99] or had left open the 'possibility' that the power of the state may be 'more far-reaching' for corporate business premises, but had never actually made use of this possibility; it did so for the first time in *Debut.* However, the threat the ECtHR felt at this point might have been too low for this solution to be sustained: in 2013's *Bernh Larsen,* a different section of the ECtHR went back to stating that 'entitlement might well be more far-reaching where professional or business activities or premises were involved than would otherwise be the case'.[100] But when faced with the *third* case in a row where domestic courts had either dismissed the applicability of Article 8 and/or expressed an explicit ideal outcome for (the ECJ's) lower level of protection, the ECtHR relented and confirmed that for companies 'the right of interference of state can be more far-reaching'.[101]

It was following this move that the ECJ delivered Opinion 2/13 with its declaration of independence and autonomy from the ECtHR. Reactions from the ECtHR itself came quickly[102] with President Spielmann calling it a 'great disappointment'.[103] According to Stargaard:

95 *DEBÚT* (n 69), para 3; *Bernh Larsen* (n 69), para 104; *Delta Perkany* (n 69), para 77.

96 Alexandros-Ioannis Kargopoulos, 'The Presumption of Equivalent Protection Rebutted: The Right to a Fair Trial in Criminal Proceedings in the ECHR and EU Law' in Kanstantsin Dzehtsiarou and others (eds), *Human Rights Law in Europe: The influence, overlaps and contradictions of the EU and the ECHR* (Routledge 2014).

97 Vicini (n 80); Cathryn Costello, 'Dublin-Case NS/ME: Finally, an End to Blind Trust across the EU?' (2012) 2 Asiel en Migrantenrecht 83; Pergantis (n 80).

98 Amy Ludlow, 'The Right to Strike: A Jurisprudential Gulf Between the CJEU and ECtHR' in Theodore Konstadinides and others (eds), *Human Rights Law in Europe - The Influence, Overlaps and Contradictions of the EU and the ECHR* (Routledge 2014).

99 Marius Emberland, *The Human Rights of Companies: Exploring the Structure of ECHR Protection* (Oxford University Press 2006) 174.

100 *Bernh Larsen* (n 69).

101 *DELTA PEKÁRNY* (n 69), para 77.

102 See for example Dean Spielmann, President of the ECJ, 'Opinion 2/13 and Other Matters' (Lecture at University of Cambridge, Cambridge, 14 March 2015) < https://podcasts.apple.com/gb/podcast/opinion-2-13-and-other-matters-echr-president-dean/id469010611?i=1000411345668 > accessed 26 September 2022.

103 European Court of Human Rights, Annual Report 2014 (Strasbourg, 2015), p. 6, but also in Dean Spielmann, 'Human Rights Case Law in the Strasbourg and Luxembourg Courts: Conflicts, Inconsistencies, and Complementarities' in Philip Alston (ed), *The EU and human rights* (Oxford University Press 1999). Spielmann (n 102).

> [A] failure of the ECtHR to object [...] to the CJEU's depiction of itself as the supreme European fundamental rights court comes with the risk that the Strasbourg Court's authority in the eyes of national judiciaries and many Member States is (further) weakened.[104]

What could the ECtHR do in response? It had to give more ground, although this was done in a very limited way. It never went back on its decision to indeed give a lower level of protection to companies compared to individuals, but when the French government (mistakenly?) did not try to use this line of argument in the 2015 case *Vinci*, the ECtHR was careful to not raise it either at all and found a violation of Article 8.

The ECtHR may have converged with the ECJ due to a rising challenge to its authority by the ECJ, coupled with a new lack of support from domestic courts and Governments. But it is interesting to note that, the ECtHR has a different way to converge with the ECJ than the other way around. Except for *Delta Perkány* – explained previously –, there is not a single reference to the Luxembourg case law from the ECtHR in the second period of this study (Table 10.4).

This means that, where the ECJ refers to ECtHR cases, but then does not fully follow them or frame them argumentatively to make them appear as if supporting its own jurisprudence, the ECtHR converges differently: it gives some ground substantially but avoids explicit reference to the ECJ.

Table 10.4 Evolution of the references of the ECtHR to the ECJ's test

Case	*Reference to Abuse/Arbitrariness?*	*Period*
Colas Est	None (except when citing verbatim the ECJ)	Period 1 *(2002-2013)*
Ernst	None	
Wieser	None	
Canal Plus	None	
Debut	Mentions the *'lack of arbitrariness'* (para 3)	*Period 2 (2013-2016)*
Bernh Larsen	Mentions *'The risk of abuse and arbitrariness'(* para 144)	
Delta Perkany	Mentions that the decision could *be 'arbitrary'* (paras 82, 84, 93)	
Vinci	Mentions that the decision could be *'abusive and arbitrary'* (para 64)	

104 Louise Halleskov Storgaard, 'EU Law Autonomy versus European Fundamental Rights Protection—On Opinion 2/13 on EU Accession to the ECHR' (2015) 15 Human Rights Law Review 485, 521.

5 Conclusion: A Research Agenda for the Strategic Judicial Dialogue of International Courts

The ECJ and the ECtHR's dialogue is multi-faceted and ever-changing. The goal of this exploratory case study has been to explore some of the drivers of this dialogue, which affect how each court relates to the other, through a strategic engagement where one court can refer to another in hope of legitimising its own position. Yet this is a double-edged sword: in doing so, the said court is forced to give up at least some of its preferred outcomes for the sake of the coherence of its legal argumentation. In the case study presented here, it is the ECJ that had to give up more ground than the ECtHR, as it was faced with more challenges by multiple relevant actors.

This theory offers multiple ways forward for further research. First, the complexity and wealth of case law of the ECJ and the ECtHR calls for further testing of this theory. This would include more salient or politically sensitive issues which have been at stake in other jurisprudential sagas of the two European courts, such as the right to strike,[105] the protection of transgender persons,[106] women's rights,[107] the European Arrest Warrant,[108] data protection,[109] or asylum cases.[110] Such testing would improve the generalisability of the theoretical framework.

Moreover, one factor has been mentioned throughout but not included as a variable per se: the litigants themselves. Whether international law is fragmented or remains coherent can only be known if the potential for a conflict between two legal orders is activated.[111] Understanding how (strategic) litigants approach the situation of overlapping international courts, in particular in the case of courts as influential as the ECJ and the ECtHR, could yield much-needed insight for scholars researching European human rights law and international adjudication.

105 Ludlow (n 99); Albertine Veldman, 'Protection of the Fundamental Right to Strike within the Context of the European Internal Market: Implications of the Forthcoming Accession of the EU to the ECHR' (2013) 9 Utrecht Law Review 104.

106 Angus Campbell and Heather Lardy, 'Transsexuals – The ECHR in Transition' (2003) 54 Northern Ireland Legal Quarterly 209.

107 Samantha Besson, 'Gender Discrimination under EU and ECHR Law: Never Shall the Twain Meet?' (2008) 8 Human Rights Law Review 647; Janneke Gerards, 'Non-Discrimination, the European Court of Justice and the European Court of Human Rights: Who Takes the Lead?' in Thomas Giegerich (ed), *The European Union as Protector and Promoter of Equality* (Springer International Publishing 2020).

108 Gáspár-Szilágyi (n 81).

109 Síofra O'Leary, 'Balancing Rights in a Digital Age' (2018) 59 Irish Jurist 59.

110 Velluti and Ippolito (n 80).

111 Christian Kreuder-Sonnen and Michael Zürn, 'After Fragmentation: Norm Collisions, Interface Conflicts, and Conflict Management' (2020) 9 Global Constitutionalism 241.

11 Converging on Structures – The Influence of Court Structure on Convergence and Divergence among Judges

*Alexander Lazović**

Every legal system requires a level of stability that is surprisingly hard to achieve. Law is a notoriously contested practice. Divergent understandings of even the simplest of norms run rampant. This is even more so the case in multilevel legal orders in which judges from diverse national backgrounds bring to bear their divergent traditions and understandings. This paper focuses on one of these multilevel legal orders, namely the European Union's Court of Justice (subsequently 'the Court').[1] Here, the principle of representation of Member States leads to a relatively large court with a relatively diverse makeup. Certain other aspects such as the length of service and the appointment process exacerbate the risk of divergence further. And yet, the Court's case-law is relatively stable and has provided relatively effective guidance for the national legal systems. After discussing why convergence and divergence matter not just on the normative level but also for the functionality of a multilevel legal order (Section 1), I will turn to why the law itself is not necessarily much help in creating the necessary convergence. To determine, what we may turn to instead, we should understand convergence and divergence through the Bourdieusian concept of habitus which leads us to study the conditions under which judges practice law (Section 2). I will then turn to the Court and analyse the situation there: what are the external factors that exacerbate the problem of divergence in the EU context (Section 3)? And what are the internal structures that facilitate convergence and which ones allow for continued divergence among the judges (Section 4)? In the final section, in lieu of a conclusion, I will reflect on the problems of balancing the convergence and divergence in the setting of the Court by briefly addressing three recurring issues, namely the 'federalist' stacking of the Court Presidencies, the working language of the Court, and the single-voice approach, concluding that in the debates about a reform of the Court, functional aspects should not be overlooked (Section 5).

* The author would like to thank the anonymous reviewer for the helpful comments and all participants of the Ljubljana Multilevel Conference for the intriguing discussions.

1 The term is slightly vague but a consequence of the unfortunate naming conventions regarding the EU courts. I am referring to the 'Court of Justice' as the court within the institution 'Court of Justice of the European Union.'

DOI: 10.4324/9781003355762-11

1 Why Do We Care about Divergence?

In his work on legal argumentation, Luhmann identifies two conflicting requirements that need to be fulfilled by a legal system to function *as a system*.[2] On the one hand, legal argumentation must facilitate redundancy, that is, select information by filtering out that which is not system relevant, creating connexions between what is newly created (new legal decisions) and what is already recognised as part of the system (laws, case-law, and so on). This reduces the amount of new information (i.e., legally recognised arguments) that needs to be processed by the system. On the other hand, the system requires variety. It must remain responsive to an undetermined (and undeterminable) number of different situations. Redundancy prevents decisions from becoming isolated, disconnected instances, while variety makes sure that new information can still be processed. Luhmann refers to this as *dynamic stability*, the continued existence of the legal system *as a system* despite its continued evolution.[3] Even where new legal decisions are produced, these are recognisable as relating to that which has come before them.[4] When I talk about the necessary stability of a legal system, it is this (created) coherence, the connectability of new decisions to the system by use of legal categories and concepts (whether by repetition, analogy or distinction) to which I am referring.

If we leave system theory and move to the practical dilemmas faced by a multilevel legal order such as that of the European Union, we find a conflict of remarkable similarity. On the one hand, as with any legal order, EU legal practice requires shared concepts of meaning around which judges converge and through which they understand, discuss, and solve legal problems. That is to say, there needs to be some guarantee that a diverse set of judges from different judicial, professional, and national backgrounds will (by and large) decide cases consistently and coherently. This relates to normative requirements of legal certainty, but also functionally to the need to construct EU law as a meaningful source of information to which national decision-makers can connect their own decisions. A legal praxis that is constantly changing would be meaningless, remain isolated, and appear as instances of judicial *fiat*.[5] Likewise, these concepts must not be too broad or vague, too accommodating to the differences of national systems, as this would devoid them of any effective impact. In this sense, convergence around common concepts, that supersede nationally distinct modes of understanding, serves a similar role to redundancy in the Luhmannian sense.

At the same time, this rift between the national and the supranational level must not become too deep. For one, national legal systems themselves function based on redundancy and must be able to recognise decisions by the Court as relevant

2 On the following see in particular, Niklas Luhmann, *Das Recht Der Gesellschaft* (6th edn, Suhrkamp 2013) 352–61.
3 ibid 241–2.
4 ibid 349–51.
5 Cf ibid 274 fn 53.

information. Besides, in a multilevel system, the upper level must remain responsive to the lower levels, too. Only thus can it retain the ability to understand national legal problems in a way that allows it to give an answer that is meaningful for the national court,[6] and conform to the normative requirement to be representative of its constituting lower legal systems.[7] To do so, judges must retain the ability to diverge from the common concepts. The latter must not be so rigid as to become calcified lest it loses any usefulness to respond to new problems.

Hence, the multilevel system requires both: convergence around common understandings that allow to reduce the input of national sensitivities and sustain a truly autonomous system; and the ability to diverge from such concepts when necessary to preserve its function as guiding national courts in concrete instances of legal application. Or negatively put, a multi-level system in which judges diverge from common concepts persistently is no system at all, but an accumulation of incoherent case-law; whereas a system in which convergence is calcified will not be able to adapt to changing social requirements or take into account of differences in the legal systems of which it is comprised. This problem is specifically exacerbated in a supra-national context due to the larger variety of legal systems (or: legal thinking) with which connectability must be sustained. This is not to say that aspects of the problem do not also occur in federal systems, particularly those where the lower-level systems have distinct legal traditions (such as the relationship between the French-influenced legal system of Louisiana and the Common law tradition of the United States). These legal systems, however, commonly have other ways to create convergence, for example by greater standardisation in legal education. In the following, I will exclusively deal with the relationship of the European Union legal system to those of the Member States.

2 How to Think about Law

2.1 The Problem with Law

In an idealised (or: caricatured) legal system, whether multileveled or centralised, a convergent understanding of law would be a non-issue. After all, judges are bound by the law, they merely have to apply it to the case at hand. Should that not be enough to create coherence and unity among their decisions? However, lawyers are notoriously bickering in their profession, judges overrule each other, and academics fill libraries with arguments and counterarguments. The causes are commonly seen in the indeterminacy of

6 Michal Bobek, 'Of Feasibility and Silent Elephants. The Legitimacy of the Court of Justice through the Eyes of National Courts' in Maurice Adams, Henri de Waele and Johan Meeusen (eds), *Judging Europe's Judges. The Legitimacy of the Case Law of the European Court of Justice* (Bloomsbury Publishing 2013) 199–202; David Edward, 'How the Court of Justice Works' (1995) 20 European Law Review 539, 548.

7 Edward (n 6) 548, 553.

language more generally, the fact that all understanding requires interpretation and remains, thus, ambiguous[8] and subjective.[9] Even presumably clear rules can at times be called into question.[10] Any interpretation once found can be challenged, requiring the interpreter to give reasons.[11] These reasons can again be challenged and must be defended by further reasons, and so on.[12] With regard to EU law, the fact that all language versions, by now 24, are equally authoritative and valid does not help to mollify the ambiguity.[13] How, one may wonder, is it even possible in such a situation that case-law remains relatively stable? In other words: how come, that, by and large, lawyers converge around certain interpretations?

2.2 Pre-judice and Habitus

If the answer is not to be found in the law, then it must be found instead in the interpreters, that is, (usually) the lawyers and judges. Interpretation by and large functions because the interpreters already have some idea of what they think the law will require (in the abstract). They commonly turn to what they already know: ideas of legal concepts or categories,[14] grounded in their experience and background knowledge.[15] This pre-understanding has variously been called

8 Joxerramon Bengoetxea, *The Legal Reasoning of the European Court of Justice: Towards a European Jurisprudence* (Clarendon Press; Oxford University Press 1993) 123–33, 221–3; Luhmann (n 2) 364.

9 Regina Ogorek, 'Der Wortlaut des Gesetzes - Auslegungsgrenze oder Freibrief?' in Elena Barnert (ed), Regina Ogorek, *Aufklärung über Justiz*, vol 1 (2., unveränd. Aufl, Klostermann 2008) 129.

10 Brian Bix, *Law, Language, and Legal Determinacy* (Clarendon Press; Oxford University Press 1995) ch 3; Luhmann (n 2) 255–6; for a common example, see Anthony D'Amato, 'Aspects of Deconstruction: The 'Easy Case' of the Under-Aged President' (1989) 84 Northwestern University Law Review 250.

11 Neil MacCormick, *Rhetoric and the Rule of Law. A Theory of Legal Reasoning* (Oxford University Press 2005) 14–15.

12 Luhmann (n 2) 347–8; with regard to 'clear' laws, see Neil MacCormick and Robert S Summers, 'Interpretation and Justification' in Neil MacCormick and Robert S Summers (eds), *Interpreting Statutes. A Comparative Study* (Routledge 1991) 516–17; likewise, Ogorek (n 9) 125–6.

13 Francis G Jacobs, 'Approaches to the Interpretation in a Plurilingual Legal System' in Mark Hoskin and William Robinson (eds), *A True European: Essays for Judge David Edward* (Hart Publishing 2004) 302; Suvi Sankari, *European Court of Justice Legal Reasoning in Context* (Europa Law Publishing 2013) 101.

14 Karl N Llewellyn, *The Bramble Bush. Our Law and Its Study* (Oceana Publications 1930) 36, 47–8.

15 Walter Lance Bennett and Martha S Feldman, *Reconstructing Reality in the Courtroom. Justice and Judgment in American Culture* (Rutgers University Press 1981) 49–65, especially 54–5; Drosdeck, Thomas, 'Der Rechtsfall als Konstrukt' in Jeanette Schmid, Thomas Drosdeck and Detlef Koch (eds), *Der Rechtsfall – ein richterliches Konstrukt* (Nomos 1997) 18–19.

horse-sense,[16] or prejudice.[17] From where do these concepts gain their, at least partially, shared character?

For this, I turn to Pierre Bourdieu, the concept of the judges' habitus, the 'subjective but not individual system of internalised structures, schemes of perception, conception, and action common to all members of the same group or class.'[18] Habitus informs practice by providing what Bourdieu calls 'structuring structures' which give meaning to social action.[19] These structures are internalised through a continuous inculcation process in the family, school, professional life, and so on, in which the early experiences determine the perception (and thus reception) of the latter.[20] This creates a distinct trajectory that makes each habitus 'subjective but not individual.'[21]

For our purposes, habitus can be thought of as the legal concepts or understandings that judges share when they practice law.[22] These concepts serve a double purpose. They are applied implicitly by judges when practicing law (by forming or informing the repertoire of legal categories, through which judges understand their practice).[23] And they structure legal practice in that they sanction a specific set of legal categories as intersubjectively acceptable, thus stabilising themselves.[24]

This way, the concept of habitus can account for both convergence and divergence in law. The inculcation of a legal habitus provides judges with shared categories through which to understand a problem as a legal problem and to formulate legal solutions. They converge around such categories insofar as they acquire their habitus in similar circumstances. Yet, because each person arrives at their habitus through a different trajectory, their habitus differs, each being a 'certain specification of the collective history.'[25] Hence, while they share similar understandings, to varying degrees, they retain the ability to

16 Karl N Llewellyn, *The Common Law Tradition: Deciding Appeals* (Little, Brown and Company 1960) 4–5, 121.

17 Josef Esser, *Vorverständnis und Methodenwahl in der Rechtsfindung: Rationalitätsgrundlagen richterlicher Entscheidungspraxis* (Durchges und erg Ausg, Athenäum-Fischer-Taschenbuch-Verl 1972) 136–9.

18 Pierre Bourdieu, *Outline of a Theory of Practice* (Richard Nice tr, Cambridge University Press 1977) 31.

19 ibid 72, 78–9; Yves Dezalay and Mikael Rask Madsen, 'The Force of Law and Lawyers: Pierre Bourdieu and the Reflexive Sociology of Law' (2012) 8 Annual Review of Law and Social Science 433, 442.

20 Bourdieu, *Outline of a Theory of Practice* (n 18) 87.

21 ibid 86.

22 Pierre Bourdieu, 'The Force of Law: Toward a Sociology of the Judicial Field' (1987) 38 Hastings L.J. 814, 818–9; see similarly, Stanley Eugene Fish, 'Why No One's Afraid of Wolfgang Iser' (Clarendon Press 1989) 83–4.

23 Pierre Bourdieu, *The Logic of Practice* (Richard Nice tr, Polity Press 1992) 94; similarly, Geoffrey Samuel, *A Short Introduction to Judging and to Legal Reasoning* (Edward Elgar Publishing 2016) 92–3.

24 Bourdieu, *Outline of a Theory of Practice* (n 18) 169–71; Bourdieu, 'The Force of Law' (n 22) 837–9, 847–8.

25 Bourdieu, *Outline of a Theory of Practice* (n 18) 86.

act strategically[26] in their struggle for the right to consecrate their understanding of a problem as (legally) correct.[27] Yet in this strategic action, they remain guided by their habitus, as 'pious hypocrites' fully subscribing to what they understand to be the 'rules of the game.'[28] This explains the genuine sincerity with which lawyers practice law.

The remainder of this paper will now turn to the structures of practice that determine the level of convergence and the possibility of divergence among the judges at the Court. In doing so, I will first address why the problem of convergence is exacerbated in the EU context due to a lack of external convergence factors, before turning to internal factors that may help to facilitate convergence.

3 The Problem with (EU) Judges

The primary mode of inculcating judges' habitus with a common idea of law is a shared legal education.[29] Throughout the various education systems, future judges 'learn their trade,' acquire techniques and methods, and most importantly, a base grasp of 'the law' as understood in their country and legal system.[30] The problem is, of course, that these traditions are local. Certainly, the European legal system shares certain traits and modes of thought. But a judge educated in one of the systems will hold idiosyncrasies distinct from those of others.[31] Differences in the ways of 'doing law' have in the past caused some misgivings and misunderstandings between lawyers of different Member States.[32] This was exacerbated by the fact that knowledge of EU law was not a requirement for nomination to the Court.[33] Consequently, one of the

26 ibid 88.
27 Bourdieu, 'The Force of Law' (n 22) 837–8.
28 Pierre Bourdieu, 'Die Juristen. Torhüter der kollektiven Heuchelei' in Andrea Kretschmann (ed), Sergej Seitz and Anna Wieder (trs), *Das Rechtsdenken Pierre Bourdieus* (Velbrück Wissenschaft 2019) 30–1; Pierre Bourdieu, 'Is a Disinterested Act Possible?' in Randal Johnson (tr), *Practical Reason* (Polity Press 1998) 78.
29 Joxerramon Bengoetxea, Neil MacCormick and Leonor Moral Soriano, 'Integration and Integrity in the Legal Reasoning of the European Court of Justice' in Grainne de Burca and Joseph HH Weiler (eds), *The European Court of Justice* (Oxford University Press 2001) 48–49; Bourdieu, 'The Force of Law' (n 22) 833; Llewellyn (n 16) 19–20.
30 Llewellyn (n 16) 201–202.
31 Dezalay and Madsen (n 19) 442.
32 E.g., the reception of the teleological approach in the UK Eleanor Sharpston, 'The Shock Troops Arrive in Force. Horizontal Direct Effect of a Treaty Provision and Temporal Limitation of Judgments Join the Armoury of EC Law' in Miguel Maduro and Loïc Azoulai, *The Past and Future of EU Law: The Classics of EU Law Revisited on the 50th Anniversary of the Rome Treaty* (Bloomsbury Publishing 2010) 256–258; generally, Giuseppe Federico Mancini and David T Keeling, 'Language, Culture and Politics in the Life of the European Court of Justice' (1995) 1 Columbia Journal of European Law 397, 399–402.
33 To this day, Article 255 TFEU requires merely that judges does not explicitly require knowledge in EU law. However, the so called 255-panel, evaluates a candidate's capability 'of rising to the challenges involved in the application of European Union law', see Council of the European Union and Panel provided for by Article 255 of the

most relevant factors in the trajectory that would inculcate a shared habitus is missing at the Court of Justice.

This is also the case for the judges' professional experience. While there are differences between the Member States, there is usually in each one of them a 'typical' path to the judicial office. The opportunity to rise inside the judicial hierarchy can provide a considerable incentive for judges to conform to role expectations and internal (informal) values and institutions.[34] Yet, this 'typical career path' is missing from the Court.[35]

Finally, the appointment in practice follows a tradition of one judge per Member State, which fulfills the normative requirement of equal Member States representation.[36] But it also bears the risk of considerable divergence by facilitating the appointment of judges on political grounds.[37] The Members are selected by the Member States, they have various backgrounds as judges, academics, bureaucrats, or even politicians.[38] Each of these brings different attitudes towards law and judgment, and other institutional values to the bench in Luxembourg.[39] Vauchez and Cohen point out, that despite these differences, some quite considerable levels of convergence among the social background of the judges existed in the early years of the Court.[40] Yet, the professional homogeneity of the Court did not last long.[41] Already some of its early members had been politically active, and the dominant professional background of the Court shifted over time.[42] An additional problem with relying on professional background for a shared habitus among the Court's members remains that the Court itself has little agency over who joins its ranks. The establishment of the 255-panel has brought some change here, as the President

Treaty on the Functioning of the European Union, *Sixth Activity Report.* (Publications Office 2019) 18.

34 Raymund Werle, *Justizorganisation und Selbstverständnis der Richter. Eine empirische Untersuchung* (Athenäum Verlag 1977) 92.

35 Sally J Kenney, 'The Members of the Court of Justice of the European Communities' (1998) 5 Columbia Journal of European Law 101, 101; Damian Chalmers, 'Judicial Performance, Membership, and Design at the Court of Justice' in Michal Bobek (ed), *Selecting Europe's Judges. A Critical Review of the Appointment Procedures to the European Courts* (Oxford University Press 2015).

36 Michal Bobek, 'The Court of Justice of the European Union' in Anthony Arnull and Damian Chalmers (eds), *The Handbook of European Union Law* (Oxford University Press 2015) 162–163.

37 Jens Frankenreiter, 'Judges, Politics, and the Law. Empirical Studies on Judge Behavior, with a Focus on the European Court of Justice' (Doctoral Thesis, ETH Zürich 2016) 42.

38 For an overview, see Chalmers (n 35).

39 Antonin Cohen and Antoine Vauchez, 'The Social Construction of Law: The European Court of Justice and Its Legal Revolution Revisited' (2011) 7 Annual Review of Law and Social Science 417, 419–20; Chalmers (n 35) 51.

40 Cohen and Vauchez (n 39) 422–3.

41 Sabine Saurugger and Fabien Terpan, *The Court of Justice of the European Union and the Politics of Law* (Palgrave Macmillan Education 2017) 55–61.

42 Chalmers (n 35) 56–7.

of the Court proposes its members and can thus influence its standards at least indirectly.[43]

In light of this lack of external convergence-creating factors, the need for convergence needs to be addressed at the level of the Court. The next section seeks to highlight some mechanisms which exist at the Court to ensure that judges, after all, still practice law, and converge around common understanding and concepts that inform this legal practice. These are the factors through which the Court's judges' habitus is inculcated, under the assumption that this organisation at least partially aims at socialising judges to a common approach to EU law.[44] I will also point out which structural features ensure that the possibility of divergence among the judges (the openness of the legal system for adaptation to the Member States' systems) persists.[45]

Convergence is created by factors that incentivise judges to adapt to the objective structures of the Court. On the other hand, where the structures simplify the possibility to adapt concepts to the judges' pre-Court perception, they facilitate divergence. The more rigid these structures prove, the more they will create uniformity between the habitus. If they are weaker, the judges will assimilate less, and there will be greater divergence.

4 Subject and Scope of Control

4.1 Individual Advancement and Reinforcement

So far, I have presented the external influence factors that would hamper strong convergence of judges around common approaches to EU law; factors like the legal education and selection of its future members, over which the Court has no direct control. It is for the Court itself, or rather the working mechanisms within the Court, to absorb this lack of socialisation, to instill in the judges a sense of professional identity, and create convergence around common legal categories.

4.1.1 Professional Identity

The first element is to invite new members to think of themselves as judges, not political decision-makers, or representatives of their government. Creating among them an identification with their judicial office already carries with it a number of legal values that they must implicitly subscribe to, such as impartiality.[46] While Llewellyn dismisses the influence of such an identification on the national level as a

43 TFEU, article 255 subpara 2 clause 3; Christoph Krenn, 'Self-Government at the Court of Justice of the European Union: A Bedrock for Institutional Success' (2018) 19 German Law Journal 2007, 2016–2017.

44 Werle (n 34) 80.

45 The list of these factors is not meant to be exhaustive. For reasons of space, it is a selection of factors that are discussed in more detail as part of my PhD thesis.

46 Llewellyn (n 16) 47–8; Werle (n 34) 87; similarly, Bourdieu, 'The Force of Law' (n 22) 830.

'form without content'[47] that does nothing to address differences in the judges' background,[48] such a professional identity can serve as a gateway for other norms or values associated with the organisation. For the Court, Chalmers found that its members develop a strong group identity around their belonging not only to a court but precisely a European Union Court, which makes them prone to take an EU perspective, as well as one based on the traditional liberal rights-based values typically associated with the EU's founding document.[49]

4.1.2 Career Advancement

Werle has pointed to promotion and advancement within the judicial organisation as one of the central traditional means by which to create such an identification.[50] While the Court does not offer the possibility for career advancement in the traditional sense – all judges are theoretically equals, with the President first among them – it does offer elected positions as President, Vice-President, and President of a chamber, that come with both higher compensation and, likely, more importantly, higher prestige. Indeed, in a sense, the Court has made a virtue out of necessity. Since neither the Court nor the judges can influence directly whether they are reappointed, their career lies in the hands of the nominating Member State. Yet, there is a mechanism by which this connection is modeled in such a way that career advancement and convergence around the Court's legal practice are intertwined. The Court takes the secrecy of its deliberations incredibly seriously, more so than would perhaps legally be required. There is almost no way to divine which decision can be attributed to which judge or judges beyond speculations about the influence of Judge-Rapporteurs. This makes it difficult for judges to promote themselves for re-appointment or other career advancements with the nominating government.[51] As Hermansen and Naurin argue, the only way that their performance can be assessed is by reference to their standing within the Court, that is, by the types of cases they are assigned as Judge-Rapporteur or their election to one of the presidencies.[52] This incentivises them to conform to the Court's majority position to enable their rise within this (unofficial) hierarchy.[53] If we take seriously the idea that practising law successfully requires

47 Llewellyn (n 16) 203.
48 ibid 49.
49 Damian Chalmers, 'Judicial Preferences and the Community Legal Order' (1997) 60 The Modern Law Review 164, 168–9.
50 Werle (n 34) 92–7.
51 Krenn (n 43) 2023–4.
52 Silje Synnøve Lyder Hermansen and Daniel Naurin, 'Will Do? Selecting Judges on the Basis of Policy Preferences or Performance Indicators' (2019) 30–35, available at https://siljehermansen.github.io/project/court-of-justice-of-the-european-union/WillDo_HermansenNaurin.pdf, last accessed 20 September 2021.
53 ibid 13, 39–40; Christoph Krenn, 'A Sense of Common Purpose. On the Role of Case Assignment and the Judge-Rapporteur at the European Court of Justice' [2020] SSRN Electronic Journal 11–12 available at https://www.ssrn.com/abstract=3680454, last accessed 29 April2021; Frankenreiter (n 37) 143.

recognition of the underlying logic of that very practice,[54] then this cannot remain without effect on the judges rising through the ranks. The judges who are in a position to influence newcomers' success are likely to have themselves gone through this process and already subscribed to the prevalent legal understandings that the new judges now have to adopt.

Central in this regard is the President of the Court and the allocation of cases to Judge-Rapporteurs, in which the President has complete discretion. The President of the Court is elected by the judges every three years,[55] yet re-elections are common. Indeed, there has been only one President in the history of the Court that was not re-elected while continuing to serve at the Court.[56] Furthermore, the electees tend to be judges who have already served some time at the Court. With the exception of the Courts first two Presidents, President Skouris was the youngest electee in terms of service, being elected after four years at the Court. This indicates that the Presidential office, despite being elected, is commonly held by judges who have already had time to adapt their habitus to the Court.

4.1.3 The Judge-Rapporteur

Besides a variety of administrative and representative functions, a central task of the President is to select a Judge-Rapporteur for each case. The Judge-Rapporteur prepares and administers the case from the moment they are assigned until the decision is made. They first prepare a report for the general meeting, in which they summarise the case and may even indicate preferences of how it should be solved. They suggest central steps in the case progression, such as requesting further information from the national court, or the size of the chamber in which the case should be decided.[57] Granted, in central matters such as chamber size, their suggestion is voted upon by all judges of the Court in the General Meeting,[58] but the Judge-Rapporteur, having the best knowledge of the case files at this point is well positioned to have their suggestions adopted. They are also the ones who will write the first draft of the judgment which will then be discussed with the other judges sitting in the chamber.[59]

This allocation of cases serves a socialising function at the Court.[60] As Krenn found in a recent study, newer judges tend to be assigned to cases that end up being decided in smaller chambers, and rise over time first to cases for five-judge

54 Bourdieu, 'Is a Disinterested Act Possible?' (n 28) 78; Bourdieu, 'Die Juristen' (n 28) 30–1.
55 TFEU, article 252 paragraph 2 clause 1.
56 Kenney (n 35) 108 fn 29.
57 Bengoetxea, MacCormick and Moral Soriano (n 29) 51–2; Gil Carlos Rodríguez Iglesias and Fernando Castillo de la Torre, 'The Procedure Before the Court of Justice of the European Communities' in Carlos Jiménez Piernas (ed), *The Legal Practice in International Law and European Community Law. A Spanish Perspective* (Martinus Nijhoff Publishers 2006) 357–9.
58 Rules of Procedure, article 25.
59 Edward (n 6) 555–556.
60 Krenn (n 53) 10–12.

chambers and finally to Grand Chamber cases, although not all judges end up in this 'higher echelon.'[61] This suggests that early on, judges can prove themselves by showing their mastery of the concepts and traditions that define the Court. As the President will likely already have been inculcated by this practice, it is thereby 'passed down' to the next generation of judges who may define the Court and elect a future President who will conform to the ideas of the Court that have been instilled in them, and so forth.

4.2 The Form of the Decision

In contrast to the more subtle influence of the socialisation incentives discussed above, this subsection focuses on those elements of the decision-making progress, that are most closely connected to the sanctioned legal categories through which judges decide cases, namely the style and language of the judgment.

The style of the Court is commonly considered to be deductive and terse, with little discussion of arguments presented by the parties, or even itself.[62] This clarity may appear to act as a 'stylistic corset,' requiring the adoption of fairly restricted forms of argumentation.[63] However, on closer inspection, this is not quite how it works. In fact, the terse style may be a gateway for divergence to persist, as it obscures them behind a façade of formulaic argumentation.[64] Indeed, it may lead to the use of more abstract principles on which the judges can agree, but which remain undecisive in their actual application in individual decisions.[65] Hence, while creating some convergence on the abstract level, this style allows for considerable divergence in the immediate practical application. Pierdominici further points out, that the style is less strictly observed than often assumed and that indeed the Judge-Rapporteurs can bring aspects of their national legal system's style into the decision.[66]

In contrast, the multilingualism of the Court may at first glance appear to further divergence. After all, 24 different authentic language versions, each carrying with it different connotations, assumptions, and allusions,[67] would allow each

61 ibid 4–6.

62 Anthony Arnull, 'The Working Language of the CJEU: Time for a Change?' (2018) 43 European Law Review 904, 908; Bengoetxea (n 8) 221; Jan Komárek, 'Legal Reasoning in EU Law' in Damian Chalmers and Anthony Arnull (eds), *The Oxford Handbook of European Union Law* (Oxford University Press 2015) 50.

63 Fernanda G Nicola, 'National Legal Traditions at Work in the Jurisprudence of the Court of Justice of the European Union' (2016) 64 American Journal of Comparative Law 865, 873.

64 Mitchel de S-O-l'E Lasser, *Judicial Deliberations: A Comparative Analysis of Judicial Transparency and Legitimacy* (Oxford University Press 2004) 356–7.

65 Michal Bobek, 'Legal Reasoning of the Court of Justice of the EU' (2014) 39 European Law Review 418, 233–4.

66 Leonardo Pierdominici, *The Mimetic Evolution of the Court of Justice of the EU: A Comparative Law Perspective* (Palgrave Macmillan 2020) 223–7.

67 Pierre Bourdieu, 'Authorized Language. The Social Conditions for the Effectiveness of Ritual Discourse' in John B Thompson (ed), Gino Raymond and Mathew

member of the Court to think and work in their own language version which may carry implicit connexions to their national legal system. However, research by McAuliffe has shown that the language regime may actually be a unifying factor in the work at the Court. From the very beginning, the Court has used French as a working language. It developed over time its own idioms and connotations and is today referred to by some as 'Court French,' distinctly 'European' in its style.[68] Former members have remarked on the importance of the use of Court French to establish among the judges an esprit de corps.[69] Considering the proximity between legal language and legal culture,[70] this marks Court French as a major convergence factor.[71] It is the language in which European legal concepts are born and filled with meaning in subsequent decisions. Adopting it as a working language inculcates its distinctions and history in the practitioners' habitus.

In addition to this, while each case at the Court is authoritative in the language of the case (in preliminary reference procedures usually the language of the referring Court), the judgments are translated into the official languages of all Member States.[72] To make the translation even more feasible, decisions must be written with translatability in mind. This means that there is a pressure that formulations and concepts that have been used in the past to express certain ideas should be used again, rather than new concepts introduced.[73] As a result, judges must adapt to a relatively formulaic and redundant language that is risen out of past decisions of the Court.[74] They must 'think inside the box' – a strong convergent factor that makes it difficult for judges to introduce new, divergent, nationally determined concepts.

4.2.1 The Decision-Making

While the previous subsection dealt with the *form* of the decision taken, the following subsection will consider the effect of the decision-making process itself.

Adamson (trs), *Language and Symbolic Power* (Polity Press 1991) 109; Edward Clay and Karen McAuliffe, 'Reconceptualising the Third Space of Legal Translation: A Study of the Court of Justice of the European Union' (2021) 45 Comparative Legilinguistics 93, 99–100.

68 Joxerramon Bengoetxea, 'Multilingual and Multicultural Legal Reasoning: The European Court of Justice' in Anne Lise Kjær and Silvia Adamo (eds), *Linguistic Diversity and European Democracy* (Ashgate Pub 2011) 108–110; Clay and McAuliffe (n 67) 108–10.

69 Mancini and Keeling (n 32) 398.

70 Elina Paunio, *Legal Certainty in Multilingual EU Law: Language, Discourse, and Reasoning at the European Court of Justice* (Ashgate 2013) 9–10; Karen McAuliffe, 'Translating Ambiguity' (2014) 9 Journal of Comparative Law 65, 70, 76.

71 Similarly, Pierdominici (n 66) 329–30.

72 Leo Mulders, 'Translation at the Court of Justice of the European Communities' in Sacha Prechal and Bert van Roermund (eds), *The Coherence of EU Law: The Search for Unity in Divergent Concepts* (Oxford University Press 2008) 49–50.

73 McAuliffe (n 70) 77; Mulders (n 72) 50; Pierdominici (n 66) 334–6.

74 Karen McAuliffe, 'Precedent at the Court of Justice of the European Union: The Linguistic Aspect' in Michael Freeman and Fiona Smith (eds), *Law and Language*, vol 15 (Oxford University Press 2013) 90; Mulders (n 72) 47.

Decisions are taken by the Court in chambers and issued with a single voice, both of which have influence on the degree of convergence among the judges.

4.2.2 The Chamber System

The chamber system has seen some considerable rework over the Court's existence, the current system being primarily a response to the enlargement.[75] The Court found it unfeasible to decide in full plenum after growing first to 25 and finally to 28 judges. Hence, with the Treaty of Nice, the five-judge chamber was made the regular composition for decision-making with routine cases going to three-judge chambers. Additionally, the Grand Chamber was introduced to decide cases where 'the difficulty or importance of the case or particular circumstances' require it. The Grand Chamber originally consisted of nine judges but has grown by now to fifteen. Its composition today includes the President and Vice-President of the Court, three of the five Presidents of the five-judge chambers in rotation and the Judge-Rapporteur. The remaining places are filled with the reaming judges based on alternating seniority.[76]

The introduction of the new chamber system has caused some concerns about fragmentation of case-law and the emergence of chamber traditions.[77] Taking decisions in chambers bears the risk of lessening the convergent pull on newcomers, creating a habitus informed by the chamber rather than the Court. There are, however, mechanisms to prevent this effect. The Grand Chamber is meant to provide a guarantee for the coherence of the case-law. When chambers start to diverge from one another in their decision-making, future cases dealing with similar topics can be allocated to the Grand Chamber where they can be discussed by a larger plenum, which will decide which of these divergent approaches will be sanctioned and become (or be confirmed as) official.[78] The structure of the Grand Chamber favours an approach that makes divergence from once-established concepts difficult. Most judges sit on the Grand Chamber seldomly, given that they rotate among a larger number of judges. In contrast, the President and Vice-President sit on every single case and the Presidents of the five-judge chambers sit

75 Sacha Prechal, 'The Many Formations of the Court of Justice: 15 Years after Nice' (2016) 39 Fordham International Law Journal 1273, 1274–5.

76 For an overview, see ibid 1275–7.

77 Court of Justice, 'Report of the Court of Justice on Certain Aspects of the Application of the Treaty on European Union' (1995) 6 available at http://www.cvce.eu/obj/report_of_the_court_of_justice_of_the_european_communities_luxembourg_may_1995-en-3644862f-2e8f-4170-9616-e573a41b61c5.html, last accessed 16 May 2021; R Daniel Kelemen, 'The Political Foundations of Judicial Independence in the European Union' (2012) 19 Journal of European Public Policy 43, 51; Leif Sevón, 'Experiencing the Court of Justice of the European Communities' in Fernand Schockweiler and Gil Carlos Rodríguez Iglesias (eds), *Mélanges en hommage à Fernand Schockweiler* (1. Aufl, Nomos 1999) 584.

78 Kelemen (n 77) 52; Prechal (n 75) 1280–1281; Lorna Woods, 'Consistency in the Chambers of the ECJ. A Case Study on the Free Movement of Goods' (2012) 31 Civil Justice Quarterly 339, 349.

relatively often (rotating three seats among five Presidents). They form a relatively stable core,[79] and, considering the internal advancement of judges in the Court,[80] they are more likely to be at least somewhat senior, with their habitus relatively convergent. Hence, they are likely to take more seriously the concepts established at the Court. This structure further allows the Presidents of the five-judge chambers to carry the logic that informed a Grand Chamber decision into their own chambers, where they sit on every case.[81] In the other direction, the close working relationship between the President of the Court and those of the five-judge chambers allows the former to gain information on the performance of newcomers in the chambers,[82] which the President can then take into account when allocating new cases, perpetuating the socialisation pressure that the case-allocation system brings with it.

4.2.3 The Single-Voice Approach

However, discussing cases in the Grand Chamber does not only create convergence pressure but also allows for divergence to sustain. This is because the Court gives its judgments with a single voice, there are no dissenting opinions. One may think that this would further convergence, as it consecrates only one perception of the case, suppressing alternative accounts.[83] However, these single-voice judgments are not the result of a win-all, loose-all struggle, but rather, by all accounts, the product of a mediated, collegiate process.[84] In order to compensate for the lack of dissenting opinions, as many of the outvoted judges as possible are brought on board with the judgment. They participate in writing the decision, which often leads to compromise solutions: where no consensus can be reached, a passage may be stricken, or alternative arguments may be included.[85] This is exacerbated in Grand Chamber cases: not only are there more judges that need to consent, making it more difficult to find compromises. Since the cases tend to be legally complicated, the categories through which they are understood are also more likely to be contested. There is more room for strategic action, for divergent interpretations of the situation to take hold. Insofar as this leads to more compromise, it is also likely to increase the use of abstract principles in decisions passed by the Grand Chamber,[86] leaving it ultimately to the smaller chambers in subsequent cases to fill the decision with

79 Woods (n 78) 343.
80 See above, Secrtion 4.1.2.
81 Woods (n 78) 350.
82 From the German context, Werle (n 34) 124–5.
83 Angela Huyue Zhang, 'The Faceless Court' (2016) 38 University of Pennsylvania Journal of International Law 71, 112–13, 128.
84 Edward (n 6) 556; Rodríguez Iglesias and Castillo de la Torre (n 57) 365; generally, Llewellyn (n 16) 31–2.
85 McAuliffe (n 74) 491; Christoph Schönberger, 'Mi attendu, mi dissertation.Le style des décisions de la Cour de justice de l'Union européenne' (2015) 91 Droit et Société 505, 518.
86 Bobek, 'The Court of Justice' (n 36) 170–1.

meaning.[87] Hence, the chamber system in combination with the single-voice approach strikes a balance between convergence and divergence. It provides incentives to converge around existing modes of understanding by reinforcing the internal hierarchy of the Court and provides the possibility to rectify divergences in judgments by smaller chambers in subsequent cases. Yet, in particular, when deciding new cases, the consensus approach allows judges to bring divergent understandings to bear by using abstract principles without committing to concrete interpretations.

5 Balance Struck?

To recapitulate briefly the main points I have made: courts in a multilevel legal order must fulfill two functional requirements: they must ensure the effectiveness of their own jurisprudence by establishing a case-law that determines its own selection criteria for what does and what does not count as legally relevant information (valid arguments, legally expressed problems, and so on). Therefore, it must not be subject to permanent shifts in its practice due to a changing membership struggling to advocate national or political interests in the guise of legal decisions. At the same time, it must remain responsive to lower-level legal systems, so that it can provide meaningful guidance for national judges, preventing its own case-law from becoming calcified and isolated. In order to do so, it must ensure that its judges converge around shared legal concepts and understandings while allowing divergence to persist. Bourdieu's concept of habitus helps to explain how this balancing act is fulfilled: objective structures inculcate in the judges' habitus a common understanding of how the law is practiced, while the distinct trajectory of the judges means that subjective understandings still persist.

At the Court, the appointment process is stacked in favour of creating a diverse set of judges with different political backgrounds, legal educations, and professional experience. While this satisfies the normative requirement of representation of all Member States, it also bears the danger of turning a legal into political practice. However, this is counterbalanced by the prevailing practice within the Court. New-comers find themselves in an unofficial hierarchy in which they are incentivised to express any political positions or national peculiarities they may have in the form and language of legal concepts established in the Court. Especially the emergence of a core composed of the President, the Vice-President, and the Presidents of the five-judge chambers in Grand Chamber decisions, well positioned to also influence the advancement of newcomers, creates pressure to think inside the box. This requires them to adopt, and adapt to, the existing practice, inculcating in their habitus the structures of the Court's legal practice. This does not, however, rule out divergence completely. Judges still struggle to impose their own visions and understanding which will also (partially) be informed by political beliefs, national traditions, and so on. The terseness of style and the collegiate approach illustrates well that a balance is stricken here. These allow judges to

87 McAuliffe (n 74) 491; Woods (n 78) 347–8.

adopt legal concepts on a relatively high abstract level which are when they first emerge, unlikely to be strongly determinate for future decisions. Hence, where no long-standing case-law exists, they need to converge only on broad principles and can continue to struggle for their own interpretation of these principles in subsequent decisions.

In this paper, I advocated the use of this 'functional' lens as an additional concern when considering changes to the Court. Changing elements of the practice can end up shifting the balance currently struck. For example, the introduction of the Grand Chamber system due to the EU enlargement in the early 2000s caused critique of a 'federalist coup' in the Court.[88] Yet, while this approach may have favoured a 'federalist' outlook, functionally, it created the conditions for a continued stability in the practice under drastically changed conditions. The later changes to the Grand Chamber system, that introduced the rotation system also for Presidents of the five-judge chambers, reduced the consistency with which the 'core' sits together, and may have lessened convergence: it is now possible that a follow-up case to a Grand Chamber decision may be heard by a chamber whose President did not partake in the original case. But it also came at a time when the 'socialisation' of the new Member State's judges and the reciprocal adaptation of the EU legal system and the new Member State legal systems had already progressed.

The danger of ruptures in the stability of the EU legal system is even more prominent when it comes to calls for changing the working language to English.[89] If we take seriously the connexion between law and language, changing the working language of the Court will facilitate, if not necessitate, the introduction of new (more Common law-oriented) concepts and lessen the connexion to concepts associated with or stemming from the French tradition of the Court. This should not be overstated: existing EU legal concepts have been part of the Common law legal culture (and via translation: its legal language) for a considerable time now so a change of the working language would not sever the connexion completely. But it should also not be easily dismissed, as a change in the approach towards law could lessen the stringency of the Court's decisions.[90]

Finally, another constant point of contention with the Court is the single-voice approach. Many scholars argue for the introduction of dissenting opinions.[91]

88 Hjalte Rasmussen, 'Present and Future European Judicial Problems after the Enlargement and the Post-2005 Ideological Revolt' (2007) 44 Common Market Law Review 1661, 1674.

89 Arnull (n 62); Ninon Colneric, 'Multilingual and Supranational Law in the EU: "United in Diversity" or "Tower of Babel"?' in Friedemann Vogel (ed), *Legal Linguistics Beyond Borders: Language and Law in a World of Media, Globalisation and Social Conflicts: Relaunching the International Language and Law Association (ILLA)* (1st edn, Duncker & Humblot 2019) 181–3; Huyue Zhang (n 83) 129.

90 Pierdominici (n 66) 332–4.

91 Prominently, Joseph HH Weiler, 'Epilogue: Judging the Judges – Apology and Critique' in Maurice Adams and others (eds), *Judging Europe's Judges. The Legitimacy of the Case Law of the European Court of Justice* (Hart Publishing Limited 2013) 252;

Without going into detail, the claim is common that this may improve the reasoning of the Court since it will have to address possible critique from its own members.[92] However, as I have argued, the single-voice approach allows the Court not only to 'hide' its motives, as often supposed but also to create convergence among its judges around more abstract concepts and values, that are still adaptable by national legal systems. Judges who do not find their position (or: their legal system) represented in the decision can push for more abstract reasoning to keep the decision adaptable. A more discursive decision, flanked by dissenting opinions, may in this sense not only lower convergence among the judges– judges do not have to subscribe to the reasoning, and adapt it as their own for future decisions – but may also lower the adaptability of the system if the binding decision itself is less open.

All of this may be normatively desirable. There is a normative case to be made that, for example, the dominance of French (and French legal thinking) lowers the access to the Court to lawyers from Member States where French is not widely spoken.[93] This, in turn, means that the EU legal system is less adaptable and responsive to these systems. The convergence around stabilised EU legal systems may become calcified and less useful for judges in these Member States. However, these normative desires should be clearly articulated. And in any such discourse, the functional aspects that I have highlighted should not be forgotten. Stability, in the sense of a convergence around shared concepts, is itself normatively desirable for the proper and continued functioning of the system.

Huyue Zhang (n 83) 112–13; Hjalte Rasmussen and Louise Nan Rasmussen, 'Comment on Katalin Kelemen – Activist EU Court 'Feeds' on the Existing Ban on Dissenting Opinions. Lifting the Ban Is Likely to Improve the Quality of EU Judgments' (2013) 14 German Law Journal 1373.

92 Huyue Zhang (n 83) 128–9; Rasmussen and Rasmussen (n 91) 1384–5.

93 Colneric (n 89) 183; Huyue Zhang (n 83) 93.

12 Multilevel Governance in the EU Through Deliberative Democracy

Zooming into the Mechanism of the European Citizens' Initiative

Agata Magdalena Poznańska

1 Introduction

This chapter argues for the mechanism of the European Citizens' Initiative (ECI) deployed as a model of deliberative democracy, to be a practical tool for facing the challenge stemming from the tension between a visible recourse to preserving diversity/national identity and an ongoing further integration in the European Union (EU). The given phrases, diversity accompanied by national identity and integration, are often juxtaposed. Unquestionably, the EU has recently been facing disintegrative trends, which happen to be backed by arguments ascribing the utmost value to national identity. At the same time, EU governance is steering towards more complex levels of political, legal and economic integration. Arguably, moving ahead in the direction of tighter unity can cause reluctance, especially if those who are embraced by it, i.e. the European citizens, are not a part of the process. In effect, the people of the EU and its governing centre diverge. I argue that this can be rectified by mechanisms of convergence such as the ECI, specifically in the framework of deliberative democracy.

The chapter is structured in the following way: the first part reflects on the theoretical account of the EU. It argues for the Habermasian model of *pouvoir constituant mixte* as a reflection of the EU's shared sovereignty. It is an important starting point for further discussions, as building on this understanding of European demos, the argument is that the EU should strive for a democracy in a post-national form. This in turn leads to the consideration of said tension between integration and diversity inherent in post-national polities. It is argued that deliberative democracy can accommodate this dichotomy through deliberative instruments such as the ECI. The second part of the chapter zooms into the practical role that the ECI can play as a mechanism of convergence in the EU when its deliberative potential is fully deployed.

2 The EU as Multilevel Polity – The Theoretical Account

2.1 Who is The Sovereign?

Looking pragmatically, 'Who is the sovereign?' is the first question which needs to be answered when theorising about multilevel polities such as the EU. Since the

DOI: 10.4324/9781003355762-12

milestone works of Hobbes, Locke and Rousseau we associate the sovereign with the people of a given polity – its citizens. The world's first constitutions were revolutionary, presenting themselves as reflections of the sovereign;[1] a text which comes about through their assent. Thus, sovereignty and constituent power are inextricably linked: sovereignty as a legal concept traces back to the constitution as its tangible representation, with the latter being a product of the constituent power.

How can constituent power in the EU be normatively characterised? The term can be used in a narrow meaning: as the power of the people to shape the constitution. However, I take the definition to be wider: the constituent power as a kind of power connected to the democratic process in general; as the power of the people to shape the law that binds them. As Rubinelli explains '[a]t least since the French Revolution, the idea of constituent power has been used to indicate the power the people have to create legal-political orders. [...] the history of constituent power is deeply tied to the principle of popular power and, through it, to the history of democracy'.[2] Patberg argues that constituent power is indeed the right term to be used in the context of the EU governance – he understands it 'as the freedom of citizens to decide on the structure and competence of their political system in a democratic process'.[3] In looking at the EU I, therefore, understand the constituent power as essentially democratic power; its *demos*. Different theories aim at explaining the constituent power of the EU, with a wide spectrum of meanings ascribed to demos. I will focus here on the conceptualisation of Jürgen Habermas.[4]

Habermas started out with a thought experiment of a 'double sovereign' of the EU,[5] which later developed into the idea of *pouvoir constituant*

1 See the references to 'people' or 'nation' in the first American (1787), Polish (1789) and French (1789) constitutions – the first three in the world. From a sociological perspective the concept of national consciousness started appearing around that time, deployed by thinkers such as Johann Gottfried Herder.

2 Joel I Colón-Ríos and others, 'Constituent Power and Its Institutions' (2021) Contemporary Political Theory 1. My emphasis.

3 Markus Patberg, *Constituent Power in the European Union* (Oxford University Press 2020) 23. To be precise, there is a conceptual difference between 'democratic process' and 'democracy', as the former does not necessarily presuppose the latter, but in this context the 'process' has to be understood as a part of the whole democratic system.

4 To be sure, a plethora of other academic accounts explaining the EU's constituent power exists. A remarkable work in this regard has been conducted e.g. by Markus Patberg, who in his book (n 3) explores four academic theories of the EU's constituent power, corresponding to four 'public narratives': regional cosmopolitanism, democracy, dual constituent power (which can be understood as what I refer to as Habermas' mixed constituent power) and destituent power.

5 Jürgen Habermas, 'The Crisis of the European Union in the Light of a Constitutionalization of International Law' (2012) 23 European Journal of International Law 335; Habermas 'Democracy in Europe: Why the Development of the EU into a Transnational Democracy Is Necessary and How It Is Possible' (2015) European Law Journal 546.

mixte.[6] The theory rests on the concept that the EU is constituted of two sovereigns existing on an equal footing: the Member States and the citizens (understood collectively as the citizens of the EU). The relationship between the two sovereigns is heterarchical: both sovereigns are on an equal footing in the process of opinion and will formation. They are co-original in their capacity of being a constituent power.[7] For Habermas, the key question which underlies the theory is whether such a normative understanding of the legitimising powers of the EU can allow for its further, post-national democratic development: 'can the process of European unification lead to a form of democracy that is at once supranational and situated above the organisational level of a state?'.[8] According to him, such an aim is plausible and the *pouvoir constituant mixte* understanding of the EU polity allows for this conceptualisation of European democracy. Habermas uses the method of rational reconstruction to picture how the EU was from the outset legitimised by an amalgam of constituent power: he proposes to imagine that from the very conception of the EU, the citizens in their dual roles (as citizens of the Member States and citizens of the Union) have taken part in building its constitution.[9] Establishing the mixed constituent power of the EU leads to the conclusion that sovereignty can, and in fact, *should* be shared in the EU.[10] When a polity, like the EU, affects the life of its citizens in a way of imposing a directly applicable legal order, it needs to be directly accountable,[11] which hence leads to the conclusion that there must a be sovereign, to which it is accountable. It is the mixed sovereign acting in its dual capacity.

6 Habermas 'Citizen and State Equality in a Supranational Political Community: Degressive Proportionality and the Pouvoir Constituant Mixte'. (As Patberg explains the term itself was coined earlier by Anne Peters and Vlad Constantinesco – see Markus Patberg, 'Introduction: The EU's *Pouvoir Constituant Mixte* - Exploring the Systematic Potential of an Innovative Category: The EU's *Pouvoir Constituant Mixte*' (2017) 55 JCMS: Journal of Common Market Studies 165).
7 Neil Walker, 'Habermas's European Constitution: Catalyst, Reconstruction, Refounding' (2019) 25 European Law Journal 508, 512.
8 Habermas (n 5) 'Democracy in Europe' 546.
9 ibid 556.
10 The question if sovereignty in the EU is (or *can* at all) be shared is a topic of debate in and of itself. Richard Bellamy has famously argued that in a supranational structure like the EU only state sovereignty can guarantee the lack of mutual domination by the states (see Richard Bellamy, 'A European Republic of Sovereign States: Sovereignty, Republicanism and the European Union' (2017) 16 European Journal of Political Theory 188). Dieter Grimm claimed that sovereignty cannot be divided, hence all members of the EU are individually sovereign but the EU as a construct does not have shared sovereignty (see Dieter Grimm 'Does Europe Need a Constitution' European Law Journal (1995) 282 or *idem* 'Sovereignty in Europe' in *The Constitution of European Democracy* (Oxford University Press 2017)). In response to this Habermas argued that it has to be shared (see Jürgen Habermas 'Remarks on Dieter Grimm's: Does Europe Need a Constitution' European Law Journal (1995) 303). The latter is a normative standpoint of this chapter and it will be explored in the following sections.
11 Patberg (n 3) 19.

Arguably, the *pouvoir constituant mixte* seems to be both the most descriptively accurate and normatively plausible account of constituent power in the EU: it embraces the EU's complexity and uniqueness while allowing for its further democratic development and giving voice to the people in their capacity as European citizens. The link to the democratic community of one's own country is not denied; nonetheless, room is left for creating a new community of democratic will formation on the international level. It can be said that the account of the mixed constituent power offers a 'constrained' normative theory: on the one hand, it sets a clear normative aim for the EU's constitutional development, while on the other it accepts the Union as a dynamic legal order, being in the process of constant formation. A democratic Union is then the underlying normative principle, but a development towards that goal can only take place within certain institutional and practical constraints; like acting within the powers of the Treaties or acknowledging conflicting interests between the Member States. The *pouvoir constituant mixte* thus corresponds to the dynamic development paradigm, as flexible and responsive to practical constraints.

Habermas argues that forms of loyalty or attachment to the state as a political unit are not set in stone but historically have been fluid. Thus, nothing precludes the development of such loyalty on a post-national level. Habermas emphasises that it is political rather than social integration, which plays a role: 'No nation, if we understand the word in its modern sense, arose without political mobilisation of the masses. Nations are composed of citizens and form political communities that did not develop spontaneously, but were instead legally constructed'.[12] This is important because it shows that the EU with its legal capacity can aim at such post-national community building. Arguably, this position best clarifies what should be the normative understanding of the EU's quest for democracy as a multilevel polity and what is the theoretical foundation of multilevel governance in the EU. Hence, to list the building blocks of the argument in order: mixed constituent power implies shared sovereignty, which leads to the post-national form of democracy.

2.2 Post-national democracy – the role for deliberative democracy?

Post-national democracy rests on the idea that a democratic system can be built outside of the confines of the nation state. This implies integration between the people of the EU through common democratic procedures. Knowingly, however, the EU is far from such integration in many respects, while there is a visible resentment towards that goal. 'United in diversity' – the motto of the Constitutional Treaty, has become the flag EU slogan; a phrase to describe the identity of the EU – in essence, its DNA. Incorporating diverse structures of the Member States into one system, while preserving their uniqueness, is arguably inscribed in the EU's *telos* and is something that the Union wants to proudly emphasise.[13]

12 Habermas (n 5) 'Democracy in Europe' 552.
13 Johan Fornäs, *Signifying Europe* (Intellect Books 2012) 105.

This is important in the context of deliberative democracy, which embraces the same goal of accommodating diversity under the aegis of unity in finding common ground through the rules of rational argumentation.

The tension between diversity and integration should not on its own be seen as problematic. The two do not stand in opposition; in fact, diversity should be accommodated by unity. However, when the balance between diversity and unity is upset, diversity can become a factor leading to disintegration. The challenge, therefore, does not lie in the presence of diversity but in its radical polarisation, which leads to understanding 'integration' as forced homogeneity and 'identity' as the last bastion of autonomy. The fact that diversity or identity claims are often evoked as an argument against various EU policies is arguably symptomatic of a bigger problem. Namely, the EU's quest for unity on the political level does not meet with the expression of diversity on the citizens' level. The most important challenge here is the disconnection of the citizens' opinion and will formation from the decision-taking and law-making core of European power and politics. Joerges argues that the principal democratic deficit of the EU is that in its decision-making process it cannot take into account the opinion of those who are affected by these decisions.[14] This in effect causes distrust, frustration and in the end further polarisation; often through the prism of integration vs diversity, with the emphasis on the EU misunderstanding and trumping the latter by the 'forced unity'. This is a gap, which can arguably be filled by instruments of convergence such as the ECI. Giving the citizens an opportunity to put their ideas to the fore and articulate their proposals is a way of soothing the tension. Deliberation plays a special role in that process, as the key step in opinion and will formation. The ECI can be a mechanism of convergence precisely through its deliberative potential.

Deliberative democracy offers a paradigm shift, whereby unity is built bottom-up through a common effort of engaging citizens in diagnosing the existing problems and finding solutions for them. Crucially, diversity is an inherent part of rational deliberation understood in Rawlsian or Habermasian terms. For example, for Habermas, the underlying distinction lies between values and norms. The former guide questions of 'the good life' and are private to a given individual, while it is impossible that they could ever be shared by the whole society. The latter pertain to fairness and refer to the question of how procedures regulating the civic life should be organised.[15] These, on the contrary, can and should,

14 Christian Joerges, 'How Is a Closer Union Conceivable under Conditions of Ever More Socio-Economic and Political Diversity? Constitutionalising Europe's *Unitas in Pluralitate*' (2018) 24 European Law Journal 257, 265.

15 For a detailed explanation of Habermas' distinction between morality (norms) and ethics (values) see: Matthew King, 'Clarifying the Foucault-Habermas Debate: Morality, Ethics, and 'Normative Foundations' (2009) 35 Philosophy & Social Criticism 287, 290. See also, the conceptual differentiation between norms and values thoroughly explained in Martijn W. Hesselink, 'Private Law and the European Constitutionalisation of Values' Amsterdam Law School Research Paper No. 2016-26, Centre for the Study of European Contract Law Working Paper Series No. 2016-07, Available at http://dx.doi.org/10.2139/ssrn.2785536 (last accessed 5 October 2022).

through deliberation, be agreed to by society. Only then it can be said that the laws are truly valid.[16] Unity, therefore, does not trump inherent diversity but is built through building consensus over the laws and rules that shall be binding. Importantly, convergence in this sense shall be understood as the said process of accommodating the inherent differences within a common whole. That is why arguably the mechanism of citizens' initiative can work as an instrument of convergence.

In light of this understanding of deliberative democracy, as a normative framework which facilitates the accommodation of diversity within the unity paradigm of a post-national democratic system, the second part of the chapter will focus on how the ECI can work as a mechanism of convergence in the EU when deployed in the framework of deliberative democracy theory.

3 The European Citizens' Initiative as a Mechanism of Convergence

3.1 The Functioning of the ECI

The mechanism of the European Citizens' Initiative was introduced into EU law in 2009 in the Lisbon Treaty and it is operational since 2012[17]; however, its history traces back to the Constitutional Treaty. During the drafting of the Treaty in 2003, it was proposed by the German social-democrat MP, and member of the Convention, Jürgen Mayer. He argued that the initiative 'represents a large step in the democratisation of the Union' and that it 'will bring Europe closer to the people'.[18] Upon its introduction, it was praised as a mechanism for bridging the gap between the EU citizenry and the regulatory power.[19]

The basic framework of the mechanism is specified in Article 11(4) TEU (included in the set of the so-called 'democratic' provisions introduced by the Lisbon Treaty).[20] It sets out that at least one million citizens can take an initiative to invite the European Commission to submit a proposal for a legal act when they consider that such an act should be adopted 'to implement the Treaties'. The specific operation of the mechanism is governed by the Regulation,[21] which sets out that seven citizens from seven different Member States need to form an organising committee, which first prepares the project of the initiative and then is

16 The famous Habermasian 'discourse principle' which is discussed further below.
17 Which is when the first Regulation governing the ECI entered into force.
18 Luis Bouza García, Víctor Cuesta López, and Elitsa Mincheva, Dorota Szeligowska, 'The European Citizens' Initiative – A First Assessment', *Bruges Political Research Papers* (2012) 8.
19 Maximilian Conrad, Annette Knaut and Katrin Böttger (eds), *Bridging the Gap? Opportunities and Constraints of the European Citizens' Initiative* (1st edn, Nomos 2016).
20 Chapter II of the Lisbon Treaty; A von Bogdandy, 'The European Lesson for International Democracy: The Significance of Articles 9 to 12 EU Treaty for International Organizations' (2012) 23 European Journal of International Law 315, 322.
21 First Regulation 211/2011/EU, now repealed by the new Regulation (EU) 2019/788, which entered into force on 1 January 2020. Hereinafter referred to as 'the Regulation'.

tasked with gathering the – at least – one million signatures across the EU, with the minimum number of signatories being specified for each country. After formulating the text of an initiative, the organisers need to submit it to the Commission, which triggers the first step of the project: registration. Following Article 6(3) of the Regulation, the Commission can decide to either register the initiative or decline it. The said provision specifies the requirements that the project has to satisfy: the initiative cannot 'manifestly fall outside the framework of the Commission's powers to submit a proposal for a legal act of the Union for the purpose of implementing the Treaties'; it cannot be 'manifestly abusive, frivolous or vexatious'; and cannot be 'manifestly contrary to the values of the Union as set out in Article 2 TEU'. When the required amount of signatures is collected, the project is again submitted to the Commission, which triggers the second step of the procedure: the Commission's assessment. Within one month of the submission, the Commission must invite the organisers to Brussels to present the initiative and explain it in detail.[22] The organisers also have the right to a public hearing in the European Parliament.[23] The Commission, which has the final word, has six months to decide on the fate of the initiative.

So far, there have been 94 registered initiatives;[24] of which six have gathered at least one million signatures;[25] two have been approved by the Commission as a basis for proposals; and only one has been effectively turned into law. For ten years of operation, the numbers of successful initiatives are strikingly low, which has been triggering questions on the deficiencies of the mechanism and its effectiveness as an instrument enhancing the democratic credentials of the EU, just as it was initially praised. In the specific context of this chapter the low success rate can raise one fundamental question: can the ECI at all function as a mechanism of convergence? In the end, if the initiatives do not make a tangible legal impact, the potential force of the instrument remains symbolic.

Nonetheless, I maintain that it can work as a mechanism of convergence within the multilevel governance of the EU, specifically when taken as stemming from the roots of deliberative democratic theory. Taking into consideration the challenge caused by the integration vs diversity tension discussed above, I claim that the ECI could be one of the solutions if it is taken seriously as an instrument of deliberative democracy. With this guiding framework, I will bring in two important aspects in which the ECI should be guided by the core of the idea of deliberative democracy, namely: its operation as an emanation of the public sphere and its institutional embedding.

3.2 ECI in the Paradigm of Deliberative Democracy

The theory of deliberative democracy is a broad name for certain modes of democratic engagement. On the most basic level, it encompasses the idea that

22 Article 15(1) of the Regulation.
23 Article 14(2) of the Regulation.
24 Data for 5 October 22
25 Verification of the signatures is ongoing for four others.

deliberation between citizens provides the best and most legitimate way for their opinion and will formation in the democratic process. It is not a rival model to the classic representative (or aggregative)[26] conception of democracy, but should be treated as a supplement to it that extends the understanding of democratic engagement into something more than simply casting a ballot in elections.[27] The theory emphasises the process of deliberation as leading to legal and regulatory solutions, which thus gain utmost legitimacy by being an outcome of citizens' opinions. In essence: 'deliberative democracy puts meaningful communication at the heart of democracy'.[28]

I propose to take the deliberative democracy theory as a normative basis for further discussing the ECI as a mechanism of multilevel governance. Deliberative democracy understood as an account of democracy based on opinion and will-formation between the citizens rather than simple votes aggregation, is an especially apt model for multilevel governance in the context of the EU. It is arguably the most plausible solution for the challenge stemming from the tensions discussed above: to attach importance to citizen-made solutions, brought up as an outcome of their mutual communication. Anchoring democracy in citizens' deliberation is thus even more urgently needed on the EU level than on the national ones, as it provides a tangible remedy for the issues inherent to multilevel polities.

3.3 Emanation of the Public Sphere

The ECI should be understood as enhancing the operation of the public sphere on the European level.[29] Arguably, the public sphere is a concept inseparable from the theory of deliberative democracy. Understood as a space for the citizens to freely exchange their views and form opinions on matters of public and political life, it performs a crucial role as the platform for deliberation. That theme is especially important in the Habermasian strand of thought, which emphasises the public sphere as one of the prerequisites of a well-functioning democracy. In Habermas' conceptualisation, the public sphere is very distinct from the official state institutions and does not merge with the state authorities. It acts as a form of 'criticism and control' of those in power.[30] In Habermas' model of the 'circulation

26 Chantal Mouffe, 'Deliberative Democracy or Agonistic Pluralism' [2000] Reihe Politikwissenschaft Political Science Series 1.

27 André Bächtiger and others (eds), *The Oxford Handbook of Deliberative Democracy* (First edition, Oxford University Press 2018) 2; Michael A Neblo, *Deliberative Democracy between Theory and Practice* (2015).

28 Bächtiger (n 27) 2.

29 Whether there is an EU-wide public sphere is quite another question. This has been an element of the long lasting debate on the EU's democratic deficit, where one of the arguments for the existence of the deficit has been that the EU public sphere does not exist. I argue that it does exist, even if in an elementary form, which is an important assumption for the present discussion, however delving into this debate it is beyond the scope of this piece.

30 Habermas 'The Public Sphere: an encyclopedia article' (1974) New German Critique 49.

of power', the political system consists of the periphery and the core, where the former denotes the general public – people in their capacity as citizens, far from the decision-making power, and the latter refers to those who have an actual influence on decision making in a given polity.[31] In Habermas' account, for the public sphere to function well, ideas need to flow freely from the periphery to the core. In his terms 'communicative power' of the citizens exercised within the public sphere must influence the 'administrative power' of the state.[32] Moreover, the public sphere necessarily involves freedom of access, freedom of assembly and association.[33] Therefore only unimpeded access to the public sphere makes the periphery attuned to its conceptual traces. If the periphery becomes secluded by money or other barriers, then it cannot be called a genuine periphery anymore. Thus arguably, if the ECI is to be an instrument bridging the periphery and the core, it has to be inclusive in its deliberative potential.

When it comes to multilevel governance model understood as a *democratic* model, such public space allowing for opinion and will formation beyond the state. Taking that Habermasian understanding, the argument is, therefore, that the ECI should be a tool for facilitating the public sphere on the European level, essentially a convergence mechanism. This fits with the mixed constituent power account of the EU argued for above, namely, the mechanism engages the citizens in their dual capacity: both as citizens of particular Member States (since there always need to be at least seven different states involved) and as citizens of the EU as a collective (one underlying aim of the initiative, common for the whole EU). Whether the mechanism indeed fosters the phenomenon of a European public sphere, is a question to be pondered on. On the one hand, indeed availing of the mechanism itself demands exercising communication on matters of public concern beyond the state level; it also necessitates creating and conducting a campaign promoting the given initiative, as well as the whole process of effectively convincing at least one-million citizens across the whole EU to support the project. On the other hand, the potential organisers are faced with a handful of practical issues, such as organising a campaign with a wide outreach of audience and thus also getting sponsors and gaining know-how on promoting their ideas to the lay public. This poses questions as to freedom of access to the public sphere and the possible colonisation of the process of opinion and will formation for example by the money from sponsoring entities.

3.4 Institutional Embedding

This leads to the second issue linked with the role of the Commission, as the 'administrative power' in the mechanism of the ECI. As specified in the ECI Regulation, the Commission retains a significant role in the whole process. It is

31 Hugh Baxter, *Habermas: The Discourse Theory of Law and Democracy* (Stanford Law Books 2011) 155.
32 ibid.
33 Habermas (n 30) 49.

the gatekeeper for all initiatives and, importantly, has the last word over either accepting or rejecting an initiative. This issue plays out interestingly with the constitutional question of the Commission's sole right of legislative initiative in the EU. The Commission retains considerable discretion over assessing whether the criteria from the Regulation are met, which raises questions relating to the systemic balance of power within the operation of the mechanism. While the Commission technically enjoys credibility as an unbiased assessor of the initiatives,[34] arguably the issue lies in the fact that the deliberative democratic potential of the ECI is not fully realised in the life-cycle of an initiative, which is also connected to the argument about the access to the public sphere referred to above. As a result, the Commission's dominant role in the ECI process hampers the latter's potential as an instrument of deliberative democracy. Its gatekeeping role stands in the way of true access to the public sphere. As explained above, at the initial stage, the organisers meet with the Commission officials to explain the initiative in detail, and they have a right to a public hearing in the European Parliament. However, that closes the list of opportunities to deliberate on the ideas contained in an initiative, in the framework of the institutional setting of the mechanism. If the Commission decides that a given ECI cannot be transformed into a proposal despite the required number of signatories, it states its reasons behind the decision in an official communication. That is where the issue with the Commission's role lies: it reduces the exercises of reason-giving, crucial for the paradigm of deliberative democracy. This does not mean that the reasons presented by the Commission in its communications should be discounted. Clearly, one million signatures, which is circa 0.2% of the total EU population, should not override the assessment of the Commission. It is hence not *per se* problematic that it retains the last word over the proposals and in this sense its power to decline initiatives should remain unchanged. What proves a problem, however, is that the dialogue with the citizens willing to make an impact is dominated by the Commission's technical communications and it is not sufficiently deliberative. As the communications sent out by the Commission do not leave room for the exchange of reasons but rather stifle any potential for further discussions, the organisers are left with a final decision, without the possibility to express their mind on its content. This is the biggest issue from the perspective of deliberative democracy.

34 Whether the Commission is always unbiased in its assessments of the ECIs is a matter of debate. Some academic commentary, especially at the initial period of the functioning of the ECI pointed to the fact that the reasoning of the Commission is not always clear and objective. In this regard see: James Organ, 'Decommissioning Direct Democracy? A Critical Analysis of Commission Decision-Making on the Legal Admissibility of European Citizens Initiative Proposals' (2014) 10 European Constitutional Law Review 422; Anastasia Karatzia, 'Revisiting the Registration of European Citizens' Initiatives: The Evolution of the Legal Admissibility Test' (2018) 20 Cambridge Yearbook of European Legal Studies 147 or Erik Longo, 'The European Citizens' Initiative: Too Much Democracy for EU Polity?' (2019) 20 German Law Journal 181.

3.5 The Way Forward Towards More Deliberation

If the ECI is to be treated as an instrument of post-national deliberative democracy, as discussed above, the power of the outcomes of citizens' deliberations cannot be dependent on one institution only. This is a valid point, especially taking into account that currently citizens' say in the EU is mostly reduced to a vote in second-order elections,[35] in turn, reduced to national political allegiances. It is therefore especially important that the normative deliberative democratic aim of an authentic gathering of citizens' voices is realised through the mechanism. Otherwise, the question is how far the endeavour of preparing a successful initiative can be understood as falling outside of the sphere of administrative power of the EU and to what extent it becomes an effort that in the end aims to please the Commission and its own legislative agenda. If we look into the six initiatives, which can so far be considered successful, only two of them gained the Commission's acceptance as projects suitable for EU legal acts.[36] The Commission's sole responsibility for transposing the initiatives into legal proposals leads to an imbalance of power from the constitutional perspective. A solution for this problem could be assigning a stronger role to the European Parliament in the process.

In July 2021, the Committee of Petitions of the European Parliament convened with Věra Jourová, the Commissioner for Values and Transparency, to discuss the currently ongoing ECIs and express its stance on the actions of the Commission. It is striking that the approach of the MEPs towards the steps taken by the Commissions and in fact, its role in the ECI mechanism was very sceptical. Yana Toom, a member of the Renew Europe Group and the Vice-Chair of the Committee said very openly: 'we [the MEPs] are elected, while the Commission is appointed. We are the mediator between the Commission and the European citizens but in today's situation we cannot fulfil this duty'.[37] Whereas the Commission is a body, which, as Jourová argued in her response, has the credit of an unpolitical assessment of the initiatives, it is also a body which evidently has less democratic credentials than the EP.

The Commission has always enjoyed a special place within the institutional architecture of the EU. Its right of legislative initiative is rooted in the beginnings of the EU; specifically, the European Coal and Steel Community (ECSC). The High Authority of the ECSC, which was the predecessor of the current Commission[38] was

35 On the argument about second order elections see e.g. Andreas Follesdal and Simon Hix, 'Why There Is a Democratic Deficit in the EU: A Response to Majone and Moravcsik' (2006) 44 JCMS: Journal of Common Market Studies 533.

36 As for 5 October 2022 these are: 'Water and sanitation are a human right! Water is a public good, not a commodity!' ECI(2012)000003 and 'End the Cage Age' ECI (2018)000004.

37 My own transcript from the meeting of the Committee on 16 July 2021 https://multimedia.europarl.europa.eu/en/committee-on-petitions_20210715-1130-COMMITTEE-PETI_vd (accessed 8 September 2021).

38 The exact genealogy is more complex: in 1957 the European Economic Community (EEC) and the European Atomic Energy Community (Euratom) were created by respectively the Treaty of Rome and the Euratom Treaty. Two new Communities had

initially envisaged by Monnet to be a purely technocratic and non-partisan body. This was supposed to be a guarantee for it to be acting in the general interest of the Community and not in the interests of any particular Member State. Interestingly, at that time the democratic dimension of the High Authority was not discussed and the legitimacy of its executive mandate was simply presupposed through pooling the national interests.[39] The Commission's role in the EU power-share has, however, significantly evolved over time with the gradually increasing democratisation of the EU legislative process. This ties in with a broader paradigm shift of the EU's legislative landscape, whereby since the entry into force of the Single European Act in 1987, the position of the European Parliament started gaining more prominence.[40] Especially the ordinary legislative procedure introduced by the Maastricht Treaty (then referred to as the co-decision procedure) proved to be a milestone in that development, as the Parliament was accorded equal status to the Council in the legislative process. Initially only applicable to a few areas, with the next Treaties the ordinary legislative procedure started becoming much more relevant and today it is the most used procedure. Gradually, the EP gained more say in the legislative process, also marking the incremental lessening of the Commission's unique position within the EU's power share. Historically entrusted with the prerogative of legislative initiative, to this day mainly the Commission wields that power, however, data shows that its role in coming up with 'innovative proposals' (i.e. those not being merely reactive to other institutions) has decreased.[41]

This visible shift should be mirrored in the regulation of the ECI, allowing for a stronger presence of the EP. One possibility of engaging the Parliament within the deliberative democratic framework would be for it to become a platform for the missing reason-giving exercise. Concretely, I propose that the role of the EP could embrace organising and hosting ***deliberative meetings*** with the ECI organisers and the Commission officials, where the MEPs would also be present themselves and take an active part. As mentioned earlier, as per Article 14 of the Regulation, the organisers have an opportunity to present their successful initiative at a public hearing organised by the EP, where the Commission is represented, whereas the Council and other institutions also have a chance to take part. As per Article 15, the organisers of a successful initiative also meet with the Commission's representative within a month of submission. The deliberative meeting I propose, however, would take a different format from the public hearing envisaged by the Regulation. Furthermore, it would take place at a different moment of the ECI

their own counterparts of the ECSC's High Authority called 'Commissions'. In 1965 the institutions of the three Communities merged through the Merger Treaty, which resulted also in joining the two Commissions and the ECSC's High Authority into one body, called 'The Commission'.

39 Neill Nugent and Mark Rhinard, *The European Commission* (Second edition, Palgrave Macmillan 2015) 24.

40 Marck A. Pollack 'The Commission as an agent' in Neil Nugent (ed.) *At the Heart of the Union* (Palgrave Macmillan 2000) 121; Nugent and Rhinard (n 39) 229.

41 Daniela Corona, Costanza Hermanin and Paolo Ponzano, 'The Power of Initiative of the European Commission: A Progressive Erosion?' (Notre Europe 2012).

lifecycle and with a different purpose. The two meetings put forward by the Regulation happen after a given ECI is officially signed by the required number of supporters and submitted to the Commission but before the Commission has conducted its formal assessment and taken decisions on further actions towards the initiative. The deliberative meeting, on the other hand, would first and foremost be focused on *reason-giving*, therefore it would have to happen at a later stage when the Commission has already conducted its formal assessment and the Parliament has also taken its own stance on the proposal. Where, for the other two meetings envisaged by the Regulation, the organisers are placed in the centre, their role being to respectively 'present the initiative at a public hearing' in the Parliament and 'explain in detail the objectives of the initiative' to the Commission,[42] the centre of gravity of the deliberative meeting would be the exchange of reasons behind the stances of all parties. Importantly, an equal weight would have to be accorded to the voice and arguments of all sides, in accordance with the guiding principles of deliberative democracy. One possibility is that these meetings could take a similar form to trilogues, which became a part and parcel of the legislative process in the EU. Arguably, giving the citizens the possibility to hear the Commission explicating its conclusions on the initiative and actively engaging with them in presence of the Members of the Parliament would offer a new avenue of deploying the deliberative potential of the ECI instrument, which is not fully realised at present. In practice, this means that, even if not directly influencing the decisions of the Commission, it would foremost enhance its accountability vis-à-vis democratic initiatives and it would oblige it to enter into a conversation with the organisers. As discussed above, currently the responsibility of the Commission to provide motivations for its decisions is left at the stage of the final letter and it cuts the possibility of an exchange of reasons with the citizens who prepare and support the initiative. Thus the potential of deliberation is prematurely cut, while the citizens who stand behind the initiatives are not given an equal voice in the debate.

3.6 Joining the Threads: How can the ECI be a Tool for Enhancing Balanced Multilevel Governance?

To wrap up the argument, the ECI mechanism can act as a tool that helps in balancing multilevel governance in the EU. Adopting the normative basis of deliberative democracy, which emphasises the importance of the epistemic dimension of democracy as its moral value, puts citizens' engagement in dialogue at the central place. As discussed in the first part, the main challenge stemming from the tension between diversity and further integration in the EU is the disconnection of the citizens from the law-making centre. To use Habermas' terminology of circulation of power, it means that the periphery is disconnected from the core and the ideas cannot flow freely from the former to the latter. In such a case, following the argument deployed in the first part of the chapter that sovereignty in the EU is shared, the EU sovereign is not able to be adequately

42 Articles 14 and 15 of the Regulation.

represented in its mixed constituent power capacity. *Pouvoir constituant mixte* envisages that the citizens of the EU engage in democratic governance both within their own national fields, as well as on the post-national level. Taking into account the ongoing and deepening European integration in many areas of policy and law-making, if the citizens are not involved in that post-national governance, they become further disconnected from their role as an EU sovereign, while entrenched in their national political boundaries. As a result, there appears a recourse to preserving national identity in the EU, which in fact often serves as a label for a sheer nationalistic discourse. National diversity as an utmost value is simplistically put in opposition to further integration or, more generally, the EU unity paradigm, whereas the narrative of disintegration as an alternative gains prominence. Because of this the EU and its people diverge. The ECI was brought into existence as a tool meant to alleviate that problem, and it has the potential to do so if deployed in line with the ideals of deliberative democracy. Taking into account how the ECI is operationalised in practice, specifically two aspects are important here: the ECI's potential to foster a deliberative public sphere and its institutional character, which should arguably give more way to the European Parliament to intervene in the process. Another intermediate step in the ECI life-cycle, which would be a meeting of the initiative organisers with the representatives of the Commission and the Parliament, organised and hosted by the latter – could alleviate this. Already the ECI offers EU citizens a tangible form of democratic engagement. Anchoring it more concretely in the deliberative democratic framework could increase its power as a mechanism of convergence of a European 'public'.

4 Conclusions

To be sure, the EU is an intriguing case of a multilevel polity. It is a *sui generis* creation under a constant ongoing development, which is importantly underpinned by democratic ideals. It has a plural constituent power, best understood by the account of the *pouvoir constituant mixte*, as I claim. The shared sovereignty paradigm presupposes the development of a post-national form of democracy, where integration takes place through democratic procedures. These factors unquestionably lead to tensions in governance. The tension between integration and diversity is and surely will remain an inherent feature of the EU as a multilevel polity. Its existence is, however, not a problem in itself, as arguably recognition and appreciation of diversity are desirable in the EU's context. It becomes problematic when diversity takes priority over unity (which can also be induced by the EU's own actions). I have argued that the way to deal with this shall be sought in applying more democratic solutions to EU law-making, specifically within the framework of deliberative democracy. I have proposed making use of the mechanism of the European Citizens' Initiative in this context, given that through its operation it fulfils its aim of enhancing the European public sphere and that it better responds to the institutional balance of the Union, as seen from the perspective of the EU's constitutional law. Concretely, I have proposed the introduction of a new step in the ECI procedural framework, whereby the European Parliament would gain a special role in organising a deliberative meeting with the citizens in charge of a given initiative and the representatives of the Commission, which would differ from the already existing possibility of a public hearing in the Parliament or a meeting with the Commission. Arguably, this would allow to make use of the ECI more in a deliberative democratic framework. It would also ultimately enhance its potential as a mechanism of convergence, which clearly exists.

13 EU law's Contribution in Streamlining Member State Enforcement Structures

A Promising Mechanism for Convergence?

Pieter Van Cleynenbreugel

1 Introduction

The implementation and enforcement of EU law still take place predominantly at the level of the Member States.[1] In that context, each Member State retains a degree of autonomy to designate the appropriate bodies and to allocate enforcement capacities in accordance with their national institutional framework and preferences. Although respecting the constitutional and administrative identities of the Member States,[2] this setup poses a significant risk of divergence in the enforcement of otherwise uniform, harmonised or at least converging supranational substantive law norms.

To address those risks, the European Union legislator increasingly determines how national enforcement authorities have to be organised and in accordance with which enforcement activities at Member State level need to take place.[3] To that extent, instruments of secondary legislation – i.e. Regulations or Directives[4] – in an increasing amount of EU policy fields contain obligations to set up independent national authorities and/or to confer a number of minimum EU-imposed enforcement powers and capacities on Member States' enforcement bodies. In doing so, the EU imposes a series of additional obligations on Member States seeking to bring more convergence in their administrative organisation. Those obligations essentially constitute second-order convergence mechanisms that

1 As confirmed by Article 291 of the Treaty on the Functioning of the European Union (TFEU). It has been note, however, that this traditional understanding of indirect enforcement is increasingly challenged across various EU policy fields. See in more detail Miroslava Scholten, 'Mind the trend! Enforcement of EU law has been moving to Brussels' (2017) 24 *Journal of European Public Policy* 1348–66.

2 As required by Article 4(2) of the Treaty on European Union (TEU); see also Elke Cloots, *National identity in EU law* (Oxford University Press 2015).

3 See for a more general conceptualisation Lincey Bastings, Ellen Mastenbroek and Esther Versluis, 'The other face of Eurolegalism: the multifaceted convergence of national enforcement styles' (2017) 11 *Regulation & Governance* 299–314.

4 Per Article 288 TFEU. On the legal acts and legislative procedures of the European Union, see in detail, Kieran St. Bradley, 'Legislating in the European Union' in Catherine Barnard and Steve Peers (eds.), *European Union law* (2nd edn, Oxford University Press 2021), 93–135.

DOI: 10.4324/9781003355762-13

complement the first-order legal framework of uniform or harmonised substantive law rules.

This chapter undertakes to conceptualise and illustrate the extent of those convergence mechanisms prior to framing them within the constitutional framework of EU integration. The chapter will outline first how EU law has contributed to converging the institutional organisation and enforcement capabilities of national administrative authorities. To that extent, it identifies the building blocks of that template and its contribution to the convergence among different Member States' enforcement structures. Although not fully identical, the EU clearly imposes similar legislative techniques as a means to enhance convergence in the implementation and enforcement of harmonised EU law (Section 2). The chapter subsequently argues that the use of secondary legislation takes place in an attempt to increase and maintain the effective enforcement of EU law. It questions whether that effectiveness policy rationale could be considered compatible with the overall constitutional setup of EU multi-level governance. Although the EU constitutional framework a priori would not seem to resist the use of secondary legislation in the interest of effective EU law enforcement, important practical questions can be raised as to the legitimacy and coherence of the envisaged convergence mechanisms. This part of the chapter, therefore, calls for a broader debate on what kind of administrative convergence the EU legal order wants to achieve (Section 3).

2 Enforcement Convergence Through EU Secondary Legislation

Despite the increasing importance and extending competences of European Union (EU) agencies,[5] the enforcement of European Union law has been left traditionally to its Member States.[6] In accordance with the principle of national institutional autonomy, Member States remain free to designate, organise and structure the actors responsible for such enforcement.[7] As a result, enforcement structures and capacities have diverged significantly among different Member States. Apart from general obligations flowing from the principle of sincere cooperation,[8] European Union law for a long time paid little attention to any kind of streamlining of Member States' enforcement structures.

With the increase in EU legislative interventions across different policy domains, divergent enforcement structures became increasingly less desirable. As a result,

5 See for an overview of the stakes of the EU agencification debate, Merijn Chamon, *EU Agencies: legal and political limits to the transformation of the EU administration* (Oxford University Press 2016).

6 See Robert Schütze, 'From Rome to Lisbon: "Executive federalism" in the (New) European Union', (201) 47 *Common Market Law Review* 1413.

7 Sébastien Platon, 'L'autonomie institutionelle des États membres de l'Union européenne – parent pauvre ou branche forte du príncipe d'autonomie institutionnelle et procédurale?' in Laurence Potvin-Solis (ed.), *Le statut d'Etat membre de l'Union européenne* (Bruylant 2018), 461–90.

8 As manifested in Article 4(3) of the Treaty on European Union (TEU), see also Markus Klamert, *The principle of loyalty in EU law* (Oxford University Press 2014).

over the past three decades, however, the European Union gradually began to streamline the organisation and enforcement capacities of different enforcement actors across its Member States. In EU policy fields ranging from data protection law and telecom/energy regulation to competition law and digital services, the EU increasingly required Member States' enforcement bodies to be streamlined. Somewhat remarkably, across those different fields, similar convergence tools have been relied on by the EU legislator. In practice, Member States are required to set up independent administrative authorities with a series of harmonised enforcement and sanctioning powers. In addition, those authorities increasingly have to cooperate within EU-structured networks, adding to the need for converging Member State structures. This part of the chapter illustrates how those similar requirements have played out in different policy fields (Section 2.1). The overall picture that follows is an increasingly converging administrative space as a result of increasingly detailed EU secondary legislation obligations on national authorities. Although the intensity with which EU law intervenes in this context still differs across policy fields, a clear tendency towards similar convergence techniques can be highlighted (Section 2.2).

2.1 Legal Obligations Imposed on Member States' Enforcement Structures

In an attempt to streamline how substantive EU law obligations were enforced, EU secondary legislation began to impose requirements on national enforcement authorities or divisions. Those requirements are essentially threefold. First, EU law required, in a number of fields, the establishment of independent administrative authorities at Member State level (Section 2.1.1). Second, in addition to or independently from independence requirements, EU secondary legislation also harmonised minimum enforcement powers and capacities of Member States' administrative enforcement bodies (Section 2.1.2). Third, EU secondary legislation frequently provides for the establishment of an EU-structured enforcement coordination network, seeking to streamline and coordinate enforcement between and across the Member States (Section 2.1.3).

2.1.1 Independent Administrative Authorities or Bodies Required by EU Law

The EU legislator increasingly requires national administrations tasked with the implementation and enforcement of harmonised law to be independent. Independence means that national administrations or authorities need to function separately from private interests or general public administration structures. As a result, different independent administrative authorities have seen the light of day as a direct result of EU secondary legislation. The EU legislator imposes more or less detailed requirements as to how independence is to be rendered operational. This may include conditions and procedures regarding the appointment of members of the authority and their accountability. In general, the obligations imposed leave little room for manoeuvre at the Member State level. Starting in the 1990s in the fields of data protection, telecommunications and energy regulation, independence requirements can now be found in fields as disparate as competition law, budgetary law, digital services law, asylum law and human rights law. Although not all fields covered by EU law have been subject to independent authority requirements, it is clear that a tendency increasingly to impose such requirements is taking place. The following seven illustrations show the variety of independence obligations put in place by EU secondary legislation.

First, in the field of data protection, the 1995 Data Protection Directive required independent data protection supervisors to be set up at Member State level. The reason for this was to ensure transparency of processing in the Member States and to guarantee that the rules of protection are properly respected throughout the European Union.[9] At the end of the 1990s, Article 8(2) of the Charter of Fundamental Rights of the European Union directly confirmed that data protection guarantees need to be enforced by independent authorities. In doing so, EU primary law directly requires data protection authorities to be independent. The EU legislator can only implement that constitutional obligation and make it operational in practice. The 2016 General Data Protection Regulation (GDPR) further developed those requirements.[10] For its part, the Court of Justice confirmed that authorities have to be independent bodies from every public or private actor, although they may depend on their budget on Parliaments.[11]

Second, in the framework of energy regulation, similar independence requirements arrived in the early 2000s. As part of a more general program to liberalise those sectors, EU law required operators and network owners to be separated, in order for competition to emerge between those operators. The obligation to establish national regulatory authorities (NRAs) was directly mandated by 2003 and 2009 Directives.[12] Each Member State is obliged to designate a single

9 Recitals 62–64 and Article 28 of Directive 95/46/EC of the European Parliament and of the Council of 24 October 1995 on the protection of individuals with regard to the processing of personal data and on the free movement of such data, [1995] OJ L281/31.

10 See Articles 51–52 of Regulation 2016/679 of the European Parliament and of the Council of 27 April 2016 on the protection of natural persons with regard to the processing of personal data and on the free movement of such data, and repealing Directive 95/46/EC (General Data Protection Regulation), [2016] OJ L119/1 (hereafter GDPR).

11 CJEU, Case C-518/07, *Commission v Germany*, EU:C:2010:125 and Case C-614/10, *Commission v Austria*, EU:C:2012:631.

12 See Article 23 Directive 2003/54/EC of the European Parliament and of the Council of 26 June 2003 concerning common rules for the internal market in electricity and repealing Directive 96/92/EC, [2003] OJ L176/37 and Article 25 of Directive 2003/55/EC of the European Parliament and of the Council of 26 June 2003 concerning common rules for the internal market in gas and repealing Directive 98/30/EC, [2003] OJ L176/57 and Directive 2009/72/EC of the European Parliament and of the Council of 13 July 2009 concerning common rules for the internal market in electricity and repealing Directive 2003/54/EC, [2009] OJ L211/53 (and Directive 2009/73/EC of the European Parliament and of the Council of 13 July 2009 concerning common rules for the internal market in natural gas and repealing Directive 2003/55/EC, [2009] OJ L211/94) (hereinafter referred to as 2009 Natural Gas

regulatory authority at the national level, with the option of creating additional regional authorities and the establishment of specific regulatory authorities for small systems on a geographically separate region.[13] Energy NRAs have to be legally distinct and functionally independent from any other public or private entity and should act independently from any market interest.[14] Authorities cannot seek or take direct instructions from any government or other public or private entity when carrying out regulatory tasks. NRAs should equally exercise their powers impartially and transparently.[15]

Third, matched to the framework of energy regulation, EU electronic communications law also required independent authorities, also referred to as national regulatory authorities or NRAs, to oversee the liberalisation process. In the same way, those authorities have to be legally distinct and functionally independent from any other public or private entity and should act independently from any market interest.[16] Authorities cannot seek or take direct instructions from any government or other public or private entity when carrying out regulatory tasks. NRAs should equally exercise their powers impartially and transparently.[17]

Fourth, in the framework of the budgetary surveillance program set up in the wake of the sovereign debt crisis in the early 2010s, the EU legislator imposed detailed rules on budgetary predictions and controls. Regulation 473/2013 granted an important role to independent bodies in that regard. According to that Regulation, such bodies need to be structurally independent or endowed with functional autonomy vis-à-vis the budgetary authorities of the Member State.[18] Their role is to monitor compliance with EU budgetary rules put in place.

Directive). The 2009 Electricity Directive has in the meantime been replaced by Directive 2019/944 of the European Parliament and of the Council of 5 June 2019 on common rules for the internal market for electricity and amending Directive 2012/27/EU, [2019] OJ L158/125 (hereafter 2019 Electricity Directive).

13 Article 39(1) 2009 Natural Gas Directive and Article 57(1) 2019 Electricity Directive. See also Article 57(2), stating that the designation of a single authority shall be without prejudice to the designation of other regulatory authorities at regional level within Member States. For general objectives, see Article 40 2009 Natural Gas Directive and Article 58 2019 Electricity Directive.

14 Article 39(4)(a) 2009 Natural Gas Directive; Article 57(4)(a) 2019 Electricity Directive.

15 Article 39(4), first sentence 2009 Natural Gas Directive; Article 57(4), first sentence 2019 Electricity Directive; See also Article 39(4)(b)(ii) and 57(4)(b)(ii), which oblige Member States to make sure that management and staff of the NRA do not seek or take direct instructions from any government or other public or private entity when carrying out the regulatory tasks.

16 See originally Article 3 of Directive 2002/21/EC of the European Parliament and of the Council of 7 March 2002 on a common regulatory framework for electronic communications networks and services (Framework Directive), [2002] OJ L108/33, currently featuring in Articles 5 to 7 of Directive 2018/1972 of the European Parliament and of the Council of 11 December 2018 establishing the European Electronic Communications Code (Recast), [2018] OJ L321/36.

17 Article 6(1) of Directive 2018/1972.

18 Article 5 of Regulation 473/2013 of the European Parliament and of the Council of 21 May 2013 on common provisions for monitoring and assessing draft budgetary

Fifth, in the field of competition law, Directive 2019/1 also imposed independence requirements on national authorities charged with the application of Articles 101 and 102 TFEU. The latter provisions prohibit anticompetitive agreements and abuses of a dominant economic position and are enforced largely by the European Commission. However, since the entry into force of Regulation 1/2003, national authorities are also obliged to apply those provisions in certain circumstances. The latter regulation did not impose requirements on those national competition authorities.[19] Directive 2019/1 imposed more detailed institutional design obligations on national authorities for the sake of effectiveness.[20] It is now required that 'Member States shall ensure that such authorities perform their duties and exercise their powers impartially and in the interests of the effective and uniform application of [Articles 101 and 102 TFEU], subject to proportionate accountability requirements.'[21]

Sixth, a similar institutional design setup can be detected in the so-called Digital Services Act (DSA), which is still being finalised by the EU legislator. The aim of that Act is above all to regulate digital services providers and to impose important transparency and content moderation obligations on (some of) them.[22] Against that particular background, the DSA requires Member States to designate one or more competent authorities as responsible for its application and enforcement. One of those authorities has to be designated as Digital Services Coordinator.[23] Digital Services Coordinators need to perform their tasks under this Regulation in an impartial, transparent and timely manner. To achieve this, they need to act with complete independence and are required to remain free from any external influence, whether direct or indirect or from instructions from any other public authority or any private party.[24]

Seventh, the field of EU equality law requires Member States to provide for bodies ensuring assistance to victims of discriminatory treatment.[25] The assistance

plans and ensuring the correction of excessive deficit of the Member States in the euro area, [2013] OJ L140/11.

19 See Article 35 of Council Regulation 1/2003 of 16 December 2002 on the implementation of the rules on competition laid down in Articles 81 and 82 of the Treaty, [2003] OJ L1/1.

20 Directive 2019/1 of the European Parliament and of the Council of 11 December 2018 to empower the competition authorities of the Member States to be more effective enforcers and to ensure the proper functioning of the internal market, [2019] OJ L11/3.

21 Article 4(1) of Directive 2019/1.

22 By way of example, Article 26 of the Proposal for a Regulation of the European Parliament and of the Council on a Single Market For Digital Services (Digital Services Act) and amending Directive 2000/31/EC, COM 2020/825/FINAL (hereafter DSA proposal).

23 Article 38(2) and 40 DSA proposal.

24 Article 39 DSA proposal.

25 Article 13(1) of Council Directive 2000/43/EC of 29 June 2000 implementing the principle of equal treatment between persons irrespective of racial or ethnic origin, [2000] OJ L180/22; Article 12(1) of Council Directive 2004/113/EC of 13 December 2004 implementing the principle of equal treatment between men and

offered must be independent and effective.[26] Although the Directives do not explicitly impose the creation of independent bodies, the European Commission recommends the Member States to set up such bodies.[27] In order to make this happen, modifications to the legal framework are contemplated at present.[28] If implemented, EU secondary legislation would mandate much more explicitly the establishment of independent bodies, directly in line with the Commission's recommendations.

The previous illustrations highlight that the obligation to set up independent administrative authorities has been implemented or is appearing across a wide variety of policy fields. Although independence is not required from national administrations across all fields covered by European Union law, the EU legislator incrementally imposes independence obligations on national authorities in an increasing number of EU policy fields.

2.1.2 Streamlined Enforcement Powers and Capacities

Another means EU secondary legislation relies on to streamline Member States' enforcement practices is by harmonising enforcement powers and procedures at Member State level. In that context, EU legislation imposes minimum enforcement powers and procedures on Member State authorities.

Six of the seven fields illustrated in the previous section are characterised by EU secondary legislation outlining in detail the enforcement powers authorities must have. First, in the field of data protection, the GDPR contains a detailed list of minimum enforcement powers each data protection supervisor must have in place.[29] Those powers include imposing administrative fines on those disrespecting GDPR provisions.[30] Second, as far as energy regulation goes, national regulatory authorities have to be able to issue binding decisions on electricity and natural gas undertakings, carry out investigations into the functioning of electricity and gas markets and impose effective, proportionate and dissuasive penalties on

women in the access to and supply of goods and services, [2004] OJ L373/37; Article 20(1) of Directive 2006/54/EC of the European Parliament and of the Council of 5 July 2006 on the implementation of the principle of equal opportunities and equal treatment of men and women in matters of employment and occupation, [2006] OJ L204/23; Article 11(1) of Directive 2010/41/EU of the European Parliament and of the Council of 7 July 2010 on the application of the principle of equal treatment between men and women engaged in an activity in a self-employed capacity and repealing Council Directive 86/613/EEC, [2010] OJ L180/1.

26 Article 13(2) of Directive 2000/43/EC; Article 12(2) of Directive 2004/113/EC; Article 20(2) of Directive 2006/54/EC; Article 11(2) of Directive 2010/41/EU.

27 Commission Recommendation C(2018) 3850 final of 22 June 2018 on standards for national equality bodies. See for the text of this 2018 Commission Recommendation, https://ec.europa.eu/info/files/commission-recommendation-standards-equality-bodies-0_en.

28 See more particularly, https://ec.europa.eu/info/law/better-regulation/have-your-say/initiatives/13098-Equality-bodies-binding-standards_en.

29 Article 58 GDPR.

30 Article 83 GDPR.

undertakings.[31] Third, electronic communications regulators need to have powers similar to the ones applying to energy regulators.[32] Fourth, in competition law, Directive 2019/1 outlines inspection, decision-making and sanctioning powers national competition authorities have to put in place.[33] Fifth, EU digital services regulation also outlines in detail the powers and enforcement procedures digital services coordinators would have to respect.[34] Sixth, in the field of equality protection, the EU legislator imposes rather specific requirements on how Member State administrations should handle complaints. Although not formally requiring independent bodies to be in place, EU secondary legislation does not hesitate to streamline enforcement and complaint-handling procedures.[35] It is only in the context of budgetary control that no such streamlining has been provided for. This is since it is the European Commission that ultimately controls, validates and enforces budgetary rules against the Member States.[36]

A similar tendency to harmonise Member States' enforcement powers can also be detected in fields where no direct or indirect independence requirements have been imposed by EU secondary legislation. A good illustration of this is EU consumer law. In that context, no specific independence requirements have been imposed on national enforcement authorities. EU secondary legislation nevertheless outlines the enforcement powers public authorities responsible for the enforcement of this branch of EU law must have.[37]

It follows from the illustrations given here that, although the level of detail varies among sectors, the EU legislator clearly prefers to ensure the enforcement powers of national authorities are uniform or at least converge towards a singular structure. In addition, in fields where EU law does not mandate the establishment of independent Member State administrative authorities, secondary legislation also imposes detailed enforcement powers and sanctioning practices administrations must maintain. It follows from this that harmonising or streamlining enforcement practices also constitutes a means by which EU secondary legislation seeks to bring convergence in the implementation and enforcement of harmonised substantive rules at Member State level.

2.1.3 Participation in EU-Structured Enforcement Networks

The putting in place of streamlined enforcement authorities and capacities by means of EU secondary legislation generally does not operate in isolation. In the

31 Article 41(4) 2009 Natural Gas Directive; Article 59(3) 2019 Electricity Directive.
32 Article 5(1) Directive 2018/1972.
33 Articles 6 to 16 Directive 2019/1.
34 Article 41 DSA Proposal.
35 Article 13(2) of Directive 2000/43/EC; Article 12(2) of Directive 2004/113/EC; Article 20(2) of Directive 2006/54/EC; Article 11(2) of Directive 2010/41/EU.
36 Article 6 of Regulation 473/2013.
37 See Article 9 of Regulation (EU) 2017/2394 of the European Parliament and of the Council of 12 December 2017 on cooperation between national authorities responsible for the enforcement of consumer protection laws and repealing Regulation (EC) No 2006/2004, [2017] OJ L345/1.

different examples highlighted in the previous section, the newly established or modified enforcement authorities also participate in the framework of an institutionalised EU enforcement network. Although the features and powers of those networks differ across different policy fields, they all seem to serve as an additional tool to enable convergence of enforcement procedures and practices to develop.

First, in the field of data protection law, independent national authorities have to operate within the confines of the European Data Protection Board.[38] The GDPR enforcement framework relies on a one-stop-shop enforcement mechanism, in which one national supervisory authority is the lead supervisor. That supervisor is in principle responsible for the oversight of data processors falling within its jurisdiction. A mutual assistance and cooperation mechanism has nevertheless been set up and coordinated within the Board.[39] The presence of similarly structured national authorities with similar enforcement powers and responsibilities seems to have been considered a precondition To ensure the smooth operations of this mechanism. In cases of conflict, the Board can take binding decisions on case allocation or enforcement action.[40]

Second, within the framework of EU energy law, an institutionalised network, a European Regulators Group for Electricity and Gas (ERGEG) had been set up. In 2009, however, this network was replaced by a full-fledged European agency,[41] the Agency for the Cooperation of Energy Regulators (ACER).[42] That Agency is nevertheless still structured as an institutionalised network of national regulatory authorities and functions in that manner as well.[43]

Third, in EU electronic communications law, a Board of European Regulators of Electronic Communications (BEREC) allows the different authorities to meet and exchange information and best practices. The European Commission coordinates BEREC's activities, which seek to ensure that authorities of different Member States keep talking to and learning from each other.[44]

38 Article 68 GDPR.
39 Articles 60–61 GDPR.
40 Article 65 GDPR.
41 See Commission Decision 2011/280/EU of 16 May 2011 on repealing Decision 2003/796/EC on establishing the European Regulators Group for Electricity and Gas, [2011] OJ L129/14.
42 See for background, https://www.acer.europa.eu/the-agency/about-acer.
43 Article 2(1) Regulation 713/2009 of the European Parliament and of the Council of 13 July 2009 establishing an Agency for the Cooperation of Energy Regulators, [2009] OJ L211/1; this Regulation has been recast into Regulation 2019/942 of the European Parliament and of the Council of 5 June 2019 establishing a European Union Agency for the Cooperation of Energy Regulators, [2019] OJ L158/22 (hereinafter referred to as ACER Regulation). See Marco Zinzani, *Market integration through 'Network Governance'* (Intersentia 2012), 133–34 for an overview of alternative institutional options considered.
44 See Regulation (EU) 2018/1971 of the European Parliament and of the Council of 11 December 2018 establishing the Body of European Regulators for Electronic Communications (BEREC) and the Agency for Support for BEREC (BEREC Office), amending Regulation (EU) 2015/2120 and repealing Regulation (EC) No 1211/2009, [2018] OJ L321/1.

Fourth, within the context of EU competition law, a European Competition Network (ECN) has been set up. That network is composed of the representatives of different competition authorities and is chaired by the European Commission.[45] The main ambitions of the ECN members are to inform each other of new cases and envisaged enforcement decisions; coordinate and help each other with investigations; exchange evidence and other information; and discuss various issues of common interest.[46] One of the major tasks that can take place within the network concerns the allocation of cases to the best-placed national competition authority or authorities. The operations of the network have been influential in requiring an increasingly streamlined institutional and enforcement organisation of different national competition authorities by means of Directive 2019/1.[47]

Fifth, the framework set up by the Digital Services Act also seeks to embed freshly established independent digital services coordinators within a networked structure. In an attempt to streamline and coordinate enforcement between different authorities, an EU-structured network of national enforcement agencies will be set up: a European Board for Digital Services.[48] The Board's role will be to exchange information, to ensure coordinated enforcement and to recommend a Digital Services Coordinator to take action, Should a recommendation by the Board to a Digital Services Coordinator to act be ignored, the Commission and not the Board can request the Coordinator concerned to take action.[49] It would seem that such a request constitutes a binding Commission decision that is binding upon the Coordinator concerned.[50]

Sixth, a European Network of Equality bodies (Equinet) has been set up.[51] The role of the network is to coordinate and exchange information on how discrimination cases are addressed and tackled in different Member States. The network encompasses representatives of other (non-EU Member) States as well, enhancing the scope for potential implementation and enforcement convergence.

Seventh, in the framework of competition law, a Consumer Protection Coordination (CPC) network has been set up. The network regroups the different authorities or bodies at Member State level responsible for the implementation and enforcement of EU consumer law.[52] CPC's role again consists in exchanging information and enhancing best practices among different Member States' authorities.

45 Recital 15 of Council Regulation 1/2003.
46 See https://ec.europa.eu/competition-policy/european-competition-network_en.
47 Wouter Wils, 'The European Commission's "ECN+' Proposal for a Directive to empower the competition authorities of the Member States to be more effective enforcers"', 2017 *Concurrences* 60–80.
48 Article 48 DSA proposal.
49 Article 45(5) DSA proposal.
50 Article 45(7) DSA proposal.
51 See for more information and background on the specifics of this network, https://equineteurope.org/.
52 See for background on the consumer enforcement network, https://ec.europa.eu/info/live-work-travel-eu/consumer-rights-and-complaints/enforcement-consumer-protection/consumer-protection-cooperation-network_en.

It follows from the foregoing that across the different policy domains illustrated here, a network of national enforcement bodies of some sort has seen the light of day. EU secondary legislation not only formally establishes those networks but also determines their composition, operations and powers. In doing so, the EU legislator clearly wants to ensure that convergence between national enforcement structures does not only take place on paper. By including the latter in an EU-structured enforcement network coordinated by the European Commission directly or indirectly, Member States are invited to behave in accordance with the network logic that underpins such structures.[53] In practice, that constitutes a clear invitation to streamline and further converge their implementation and enforcement operations.

2.2 EU Secondary Legislation as an Enforcement Convergence Instrument

Despite the existence of different policy rationales or reasons to envisage more streamlined enforcement structures, the emergence of comparable enforcement structures can be identified. In all the examples highlighted above, EU secondary legislation serves as a tool to bring convergence among previously diverging enforcement practices. Whether it is by mandating the establishment of independent authorities and/or by streamlining enforcement and sanctioning powers, the European Union effectively asks – albeit at times somewhat implicitly – its Member States to converge their administrative enforcement capacities around a comparable template. In doing so, it can hardly be denied that EU law put in place a mechanism aimed at converging enforcement practices.

In the same way, the emergence of coordinating networks is a phenomenon re-appearing in different sectors. Despite the differences in powers and operations of the different networks as illustrated above, it is clear that the streamlining in the organisation and enforcement powers of national authorities are essentially meant to contribute to the effective functioning of those networks or enforcement coordination boards. The use of secondary legislation as a tool to ensure that different authorities can more effectively talk to one another and coordinate their operations is accommodated by the setting up of such networks.

It follows from the illustrations given here that EU secondary legislation itself serves as a means to address divergences in Member States' enforcement practices. As such, EU legal norms and obligations constitute a tool to enable convergence in enforcement practices across different Member States. Although the obligation to set up independent bodies or the establishment of enforcement networks do not feature with the same intensity in all policy fields covered by EU law, it is submitted that the EU legislator's reliance on legal norms to make administrative enforcement capacities converge is no longer a taboo. On the contrary, even, the use of EU secondary legislation as an enforcement convergence instrument does

53 See for that argument already, Pieter Van Cleynenbreugel, *Market supervision in the European Union. Integrated administration in constitutional context* (Brill 2014) 9–86.

not seem to be questioned at all when doing so. It only seems to make sense to impose, by means of legislation, institutional design and enforcement capacity obligations on the Member States.

At first sight, the use of secondary legislation to bring convergence in enforcement structures allows making enforcement convergence choices that are the result of a democratically legitimated process. In that constellation, Member States themselves play a legislative role as members of the Council. As such, they vote on the administrative or procedural reorganisations they will have to implement themselves. That also means that, in most cases, at least a qualified majority of them agreed to the harmonisation of streamlining proposed in EU harmonisation instruments.[54] Inserting enforcement convergence mechanisms directly into legislation additionally also gives the Commission or other Member States the tools to act should a Member State fail to comply with the rules adopted. Infringement proceedings in accordance with Articles 258 and 259 TFEU could further force Member States to upgrade their institutional design. The Court of Justice has been given the opportunity to rule on such upgrades in the context of data protection. In those cases, Member States have been forced to adapt their authorities in order fully to comply with EU independence requirements.[55] Having those rules inserted in a binding legal instrument facilitates their monitoring to some extent.

3 Enforcement Convergence Mechanisms: *a priori* Constitutional But Not Free From Challenges

The previous section offered an overview of the use of secondary legislation as an instrument to streamline and enhance convergence in the enforcement of EU law. It is submitted that reliance on secondary legislation directly contributes to a more general objective of enhancing the effective implementation and enforcement of EU rules across different Member States. From that point of view, streamlining national authorities' design and enforcement capacities is not an end in itself, but above all a means to enhance the effective enforcement of EU law. The fact that harmonised national authorities almost always form part of a more general effort at coordinating enforcement between national authorities constitutes the best illustration of that claim. Mostly, coordinated enforcement predominantly takes place within networks of national authorities, with more or less coordinating or binding decision-making powers. At times, however, the European Union has gone farther by transforming some of those networks in EU agencies. The best example of that approach can be found in energy regulation. In that context, a previously existing network of national supervisory authorities had been upgraded to an agency with coordinating and – subsidiary – binding individual decision-making powers.

54 See on the legislative process, Kieran St. Bradley, n. 4, for background on the voting procedures used in EU legislative acts.

55 As highlighted by Saskia Lavrijssen and Annetje Ottow, 'Independent Supervisory Authorities: A Fragile Concept' (2012) b39 Legal Issues of Economic Integration 419–46.

Although the format of such coordination may be different, the agencies thus created essentially also constitute formalised networks of national supervisory authorities. In that template, those authorities also have to be streamlined in order for them to be embedded effectively in the operations of coordinated enforcement taking place within those agencies.

The overall picture that emerges from those developments is that the European Union uses harmonised rules to streamline its enforcement processes. Although it may be one step too far to say that the EU requires the Member States to set up European union agents at the Member State level, the rules it imposes most directly serve as a mechanism to impose and further promote convergence in the functioning and operation of national supervisory or enforcement authorities. EU law is in any case relied upon as a mechanism to speed up or stimulate a more converging approach to law enforcement in those fields.

As the EU increases its reliance on convergence through secondary legislation, questions nevertheless deserve to be raised as to whether the EU constitutional framework[56] allows for such mechanisms to be created (Section 3.1). At present, the Court of Justice of the European Union has not been able to address that question directly. Absent such assessments, it would seem that, *a priori,* no major EU constitutional issues would arise. Despite streamlined or coordinated enforcement mechanisms not being considered problematic from an EU constitutional law point of view, their increased use warrants attention as they raise coherence and legitimacy challenges within the Member States in which they are implemented. To acknowledge and address those challenges, a more open debate on the scope and format of enforcement convergence appears necessary (Section 3.2).

3.1 Enforcement Convergence and the Constitutional Foundations of EU Law

From an EU constitutional law perspective, few if any limits appear to be imposed at first sight on the establishment of streamlined authorities and enforcement coordination networks. Despite the European Union enjoying no formal legal powers in this realm,[57] streamlining enforcement structures could be understood as a complement of substantive harmonisation powers.

Although several Treaty provisions would make such enforcement convergence possible, no single provision of EU primary law governs the setup of Member States' enforcement authorities. In the field of data protection, Article 16 TFEU requires the Member States to have in place independent supervisory authorities responsible for overseeing the processing of personal data. That provision does not as such impose minimum powers on those authorities. However, that provision does grant a broad mandate to those authorities to ensure compliance with data

56 By constitutional, I refer above all to the provisions of EU primary law, as well as the general principles of law accompanying it. Constitutional law in that understanding is used as an umbrella term to cover those provisions and principles.

57 Article 197 TFEU only allows for supporting measures in Member States' initiatives to improve their administrative enforcement capacities.

protection law, making it not impossible to envisage harmonised enforcement powers. In other fields, the harmonisation of enforcement structures and powers is understood to be a corollary of existing provisions allowing for the harmonisation of substantive law rules. In competition law, Article 103 TFEU plays a key role and for other domains touching upon the EU internal market, Article 114 TFEU is considered the go-to provision. That provision has been held to allow for enforcement coordination to take place within the confines of an EU agency as well.[58]

In addition, the principle of sincere cooperation featured in Article 4(3) TEU serves as a constitutional catch-all provision governing mutual duties and obligations between the national and supranational levels.[59] In accordance with that principle, both supranational and national authorities are called upon to assist each other in fulfilling the tasks which flow from the Treaties. Member States shall in particular assist the Union and refrain from any action or inaction that could jeopardise the Union's actions. Thus formulated, the provision reflects a particular set of obligations predominantly imposed on Member States.

The Court of Justice has held that the principle of sincere cooperation also applies to Union institutions.[60] In that understanding, sincere cooperation incorporates a set of mutual cooperation obligations that frame and structure the interactions between different administrations and institutions. That understanding continues to guide the institutional organisation of enforcement structures, albeit to a different extent. In the present regulatory framework, cooperative obligations are matched by the image of cooperative rights. From a sincere cooperation point of view, the ability of EU law to remove national institutional obstacles and the resulting diminution of national institutional autonomy is deemed essential for the functioning of a supranationally integrated enforcement and coordination system. The translation of mutual loyalty obligations into mutual cooperation duties paves the way for more intensified enforcement convergence initiatives. Obligations to cooperate with national authorities imply that EU institutions should be able to effectively intervene in national supervisory operations and the organisation of national authorities. The principle of sincere cooperation appears to justify an increasing intervention in Member States' enforcement designs.

A combined reading of relevant EU primary law provisions would therefore seem to conclude that EU law is not opposed to the setting up of streamlined enforcement and coordination mechanisms. Although such mechanisms have not been mandated directly by the Treaties, the latter are not against it either. As a result, the EU constitutional law framework allows for significant leeway to set up such enforcement convergence structures. As long as the principle of sincere

58 See on that provision, Pieter Van Cleynenbreugel, 'Meroni circumvented? Article 114 TFEU and EU regulatory agencies', 21 Maastricht Journal of European and Comparative Law (2014), 64–88.

59 Geert De Baere and Timothy Roes, 'EU loyalty as good faith' (2015) 64 International and Comparative Law Quarterly 829–74.

60 CJEU, Case C-2/88 IMM, *Zwartveld*, EU:C:1990:440, para 17–18.

cooperation and the limits of what can be harmonised are considered, it would be perfectly constitutional under EU law to proceed with the extension of independence requirements, harmonised enforcement procedures and enforcement coordination networks.

An important nuance nevertheless needs to be added to the previous analysis. At this stage, the Court of Justice has not had the opportunity to pronounce itself explicitly on the scope of sincere cooperation duties in the framework of harmonised enforcement designs. As a result, it remains unclear for now what the exact limits are as to what the EU legislator can do in this context. It cannot be excluded therefore that the contours of how much integration the EU constitutional framework would allow will only become clear in the near future. As long as the Court of Justice has not definitively carved out the limits of sincere cooperation in this context, the constitutionality of the measures taken by the EU legislator to some extent remains in limbo. Although CJEU precedents seem to indicate that no constitutional problems would arise, the question still remains open to some extent.

3.2 Towards a More Transparent Administrative Convergence Discussion in the EU Legal Order?

The fact that the expansion enforcement convergence through secondary legislation may at first sight not seem unconstitutional as a matter of EU law, does not mean it is free from other policy challenges. Those challenges essentially are twofold and concern the internal coherence within Member States and the legitimacy of streamlined authorities' decision-making.

First, the establishment of streamlined authorities with similar powers enables the European Union to have in place similar enforcement bodies in the different Member States. At the same time, however, those bodies at times become increasingly detached from Member States' own administrative enforcement traditions.[61] This phenomenon, which relates to the 'legal transplants' literature, could manifest itself in the EU context as well. To take one example, in some Member States such as Belgium, the concept of independent administrative authorities is not known in national administrative law.[62] As a consequence, the imposition of such requirements by EU law generates tensions and creates unforeseen legal issues in the day-to-day operations of those authorities embedded in the Member States concerned. It cannot be excluded therefore that despite the overall contribution to EU law's effective enforcement, the convergence initiatives paradoxically create more divergence within Member States' administrative organisation. The risk thus emerges that two separate administrative tracks – one directly conditioned by EU law and one more grounded in national administrative

61 See for background, Edoardo Chiti, 'Is EU administrative law failing in some of its crucial tasks?', (2019) 22 *European Law Journal* 476–96.

62 For those difficulties, see Emmanuel Slautsky, *L'organisation administrative nationale face au droit européen du marché intérieur* (Larcier 2018).

law traditions – will be consolidated and create coherence challenges at Member State level. In any case, Member states would be called upon to accommodate, within their national laws, the EU-structured authorities in one way or another.

Second, the EU-structured authorities have significant powers of enforcement and can intervene very directly in the life of businesses and individuals. Such interventions require that authorities' decisions are perceived as legitimate. To the extent that those authorities emanate from the Member States, the latter must be able to justify and defend the authorities' actions. However, their powers emanate principally from EU legislation and are justified by concerns to increase the effective enforcement of EU law. To that extent, cases may be transferred and information exchanged within the context of EU coordination mechanisms. It is true that Member States' governments have adopted and accepted those rules in the EU legislative process, but that fact alone is not necessarily sufficient to justify the nature of intrusion made across those decisional processes. The establishment of newfound EU enforcement coordination structures is therefore likely to raise the same legitimacy problems that confront the European Union as a whole.[63] Member States taking part in those mechanisms are at risk of exacerbating those legitimacy challenges, ultimately risking to undermine the very coordinated system they have set up.

It follows from the foregoing that the convergence mechanisms proposed by means of legal norms streamlining administrative authorities suffer from the same coherence and legitimacy defects that characterise the EU legal order as a whole. The additional risk in this particular context is that, by intervening directly in the organisation of national administrative law systems, those defects are brought closer to individuals and businesses confronted with national administrations. That in itself warrants careful attention, as the effective enforcement of EU law must be accompanied by sufficient attention to rules and enforcement practices being deemed legitimate.

This is not the place to offer a fully developed way forward out of those challenges. It is submitted, however, that one constructive way to address them could be at least to acknowledge their evolution and the challenges brought. So far, the streamlining of national administrative authorities' enforcement powers has taken place as a complement to sector-specific legislation harmonising EU substantive rules. As a result, streamlining efforts have taken place somewhat in the shadow of such harmonisation. A consequence of this is that attention to streamlining developments as convergence tools have received limited general attention beyond the confines of sector-specific regulation. Despite the emergence of a governance template across sectors, limited discussions on the desired scope and consequences of administrative streamlining have taken place. It may therefore be warranted to

63 On those issues, see Max Haller, 'Is the European Union Legitimate? To what extent?' (2009) 60 International Social Science Journal (2009), 223. See also Fritz Scharpf, *Governing in Europe. Effective and Democratic?* (Oxford University Press 1999); see also, Giadomenico Majone, 'Europe's Democratic Deficit' (1998) 4 European Law Journal 5–28.

conduct a more open debate within the confines of the EU institutions – including within the Council, which would be directly between the different Member States – on what kind of administrative law convergence EU law seeks to bring about and how its challenges can be addressed. Doing so would not only recognise the potential for convergence administrative streamlining offers, but also enable the EU better to accommodate the challenges it brings about.

4 Conclusion

This chapter sketched secondary legislation's contribution to streamlining Member States' enforcement designs in the interest of increasing the effective enforcement of EU law. Despite Member States remaining primarily responsible for the enforcement of EU substantive rules, European Union law has made significant attempts to streamline existing enforcement authorities and powers. The instrument relied on to do so has been EU secondary legislation. In different fields of EU law, secondary legislation imposes more or less rigorous independence, impartiality and procedural fairness requirements on national authorities, in addition to requiring them to hold minimum enforcement powers and to participate in EU enforcement coordination structures. In so doing, EU law essentially seeks to create a converging enforcement framework across different Member States, accommodating Member States diversity to a relatively limited extent only. Although this evolution so far did not raise problems from an EU constitutional law perspective, its increase in use across regulatory fields is likely to raise coherence and legitimacy challenges at Member State level. The chapter submitted that a wider and cross-sector debate on the need for and challenges of this type of convergence may be useful to at least acknowledge and potentially address those challenges in the future.

14 Conclusion

Oscillating Between Unity and Diversity

Jakob Gašperin Wischhoff and Julian Scholtes

1 Normative Considerations – Effectivity, Stability, and Supranational Democratic Legitimacy

The book addresses an old question in a unique context: How do we resolve the tensions in multilevel constitutional orders between the demands of effective unity on the one hand, and the appropriate scope of autonomy and respect for the diversity of its constituent elements, on the other hand?

By mapping some of the ways in which movements of convergence and divergence in multilevel settings are managed, balanced, fostered, and configured, we shed more light on the interplay of diversity and unity in multilevel settings. Rather than 'side' with either convergence or divergence, this volume takes the contradictions inherent in multilevel settings as something to be accepted and reckoned with – not as something to overcome. Multilevel orders are not unfinished products, waiting to be finally consolidated into something more coherent. Instead, they are often a legitimate and even preferable constitutional setting because, rather than despite, of their fractured, or open-textured, appearance.[1] In other words, and in the example of the European Union, 'an ever closer union' does not necessarily entail the goal that diversity is eventually subsumed in a more compelling unity. Rather, the system aims to establish a dynamic balance between national diversities and European unity.[2]

This book explores the various legal mechanisms of divergence and convergence that can help establish (and upset) this dynamic balance. This balance is contested, adjusted, discussed, and settled in various ways, many of which are discussed in this book: Proportionality, distribution of competencies, interlegal balancing, constitutional asymmetry, margins of appreciation, judicial dialogue, identity claims, consensus analysis, deliberative democracy, harmonisation, derogation clauses, and international cooperation. These mechanisms, however, cannot solve the underlying question of *appropriate* accommodation of diversities in multilevel constitutional orders by the mere virtue of their existence and application.

1 Signe Rehling Larsen, *The Constitutional Theory of the Federation and the European Union* (Oxford University Press 2021).

2 Matej Avbelj and Jan Komárek, *Constitutional Pluralism in the European Union and Beyond* (UK edn, Hart Publishing 2012).

DOI: 10.4324/9781003355762-14

Whereas the book demonstrates that legal mechanisms serve to address diversities, it cannot provide a definitive answer as to *how* they ought to be used. Oftentimes they can be used to both ends, to either strengthen unity or protect diversity. Rather than the mechanisms themselves, the various underlying normative considerations of appropriate balance determine their application in practice and thus the nature of multilevel legal order accordingly.

This is what renders these mechanisms worth studying: The ends to which they are used and the balance they establish is inherently contestable. Neither convergence nor divergence are in and of themselves the preferable course. More than that, the normative factors that are supposed to help determine such a balance – stability, democracy, the rule of law, etc. – can often point in different directions, or not be helpful altogether. In some contexts, it may be that the stability and effectiveness of a multilevel polity requires greater unity of its component parts.[3] In other contexts, stability might require greater divergence and diversity among its component parts to accommodate underlying socio-political divergences in identity and allegiance.[4] In some cases, the principle of democracy might seem to demand that the cross-border effects of national decision-making be 'mediated' through supranational or federal legal principles and political processes, in order to internalise some of its 'external effects'. But such 'mediation' itself can threaten to substitute, virtualise, and render intangible, democracy as a process of the self-determination of a political community.[5] Furthermore, the rule of law might demand that the laws of the supranational unit or the federal level override countervailing local laws – elsewhere, the rule of law might require more deference to local solutions, depending on where the relative authority on a relevant issue is the strongest.[6]

The diverse instruments, tools and mechanisms of divergence and convergence in multilevel constitutional orders discussed in this book have shown how context-sensitive the balance between diversity and unity in multilevel settings is, and that there is no 'one' answer to the question of how to strike that balance. In fact, the normative *unsettlement* of justifications for either convergence or divergence play among the factors that render the study of these developments so interesting.

2 Theoretical Accounts of Convergence and Divergence

The first part of this book devoted itself to a more theoretically grounded discussion of convergence and divergence in multilevel systems. How do we facilitate mutual accommodation and harmonic interaction between different legal systems? After all, each legal system establishes its own coordinate system of authority and is not *per se* conducive to inter-systemic dialogue.

3 See chapters by Verellen and van Cleynenbreugel.
4 See chapters by Sahadžić and Kos.
5 See Alexander Somek, 'The Argument from Transnational Effects I: Representing Outsiders through Freedom of Movement' (2010) 16 European Law Journal 315.
6 See chapters by Encinas and Gasperin Wischhoff.

Interlegality, explored in Chapter 2, offers a constitutional vision providing a common language that can serve the communication *between* legal systems, rather than surrendering to the idea that different legal orders are bound to talk past each other. Pluralist accounts of boundary conflicts often convey the sense that there is little in the way of law that can be used to settle such conflicts. Gabriel Encinas counters this rather fatalistic account by focusing on exploring the *interlegal* mechanisms that can help finding a final common answer where different legalities overlap. For Encinas, interlegality 'approaches the question of diverse applicable standards sourced in different legalities from a different perspective; namely, from cases at hand and their applicable norms as invoked by the affected parties.'[7] In analysing the patterns of conflict resolution through interlegal balancing, Encinas highlights how four major tools, already employed in legal practice, mirror the idea of interlegal balancing. The margin of appreciation doctrine, equivalent protection doctrines, arguments of national constitutional identity, and *ultra vires* arguments. This makes his account a realistic practice rather than a 'utopian abstraction'.[8] At the same time, Encinas is not oblivious to the limits and obstacles facing the broader idea of 'interlegality': Given the lack of any common objective standards to provide an authoritative inter-legal 'yardstick', interlegality might amount to something much more modest that cannot, of itself, eliminate the risks of fragmentation and judicial perspectivism.

Asymmetry and *dynamic stability* are presented as keys to accommodate diversity within federal and other multilevel systems in Maja Sahadžić's Chapter 3. Constitutional asymmetry appears to matter particularly where socio-cultural factors influencing political allegiance and loyalty are so significantly divergent in one or more parts of the federal unit, as opposed to the other parts, that they require accommodation. Sahadžić thus highlights Belgium, Iraq, Indonesia, and Bosnia and Herzegovina as examples of constitutional asymmetry. Such asymmetric solutions can help manage plurality and constitutional differences by introducing 'variations in status, powers, and/or fiscal matters for specific levels and actors within a particular multilevel system.'[9] However, it is also fraught with the danger that constitutional imbalances eventually can lead to more severe fragmentation. In order to manage this tension, Sahadžić argues that adaptiveness, trust, and interaction within the system can enhance the system's cohesion and eventually create the desired stability. Stability, she argues, should be understood as *dynamic* concept.[10] Not every system needs to achieve the same balance between convergence and divergence, and the balance in the respective system does not need to be frozen in time either. Rather, dynamic stability is based on dense coordination across levels and actors, which in turn requires cohesive relationships and trust.

7 Encinas 4.
8 Encinas 16.
9 Sahadžić 4.
10 Sahadžić 11.

Differentiation, a final theoretical account of diversity accommodation with more specific reference to the EU context, considers respect for national constitutional differences as a prerequisite for a functioning multilevel constitutional order. As argued by Marjan Kos in Chapter 4, acceptance of constitutional idiosyncrasies, as long as they respect the common values laid down in the EU Treaties, may strengthen the multilevel order and even increase its legitimacy.[11] Kos argues that constitutional *differentiation* in that way protects national sovereignty,[12] and can concurrently 'serve as an efficient instrument of preventive neutralisation of conflicts between EU law and national constitutional demands.'[13] According to Kos, an 'ever closer union' does not require complete unity. To the contrary, insisting on such may even produce backlash and yield the opposite effect from the desired progressive integration and effective EU law. Kos argues constitutional differentiation does not necessarily undermine integration, and demands for differentiation due to national constitutional specificities should not be *a priori* rejected as illegitimate, but seen as a way of overcoming constitutional tensions. According to Kos, a mature legal order such as the EU no longer needs to categorically insist on uniformity for the sake of its preservation, but rather embrace constitutional diversities and allow for constitutional differentiation.

What all three of these accounts suggest is that diversities in multilevel constitutional orders cannot and should not be simply dismissed. Rather, a common language must be found through which divergences can be negotiated, reconciled or accommodated. Moreover, accommodation of diversities proves to be a highly complex, contingent, and context-sensitive task. It requires the good faith of all agents involved and the openness of legal orders to amicably search for constructive solutions. What is more, it needs to be based on dialogue where one side does not categorically rule over the other. Furthermore, any framework of diversity accommodation rarely provides a clear-cut answer or solution. Asymmetrical constitutional frameworks are tailored to divergences found on the ground; constitutional differentiation has to take into account the constitutional particularities to which it is tailored; and interlegal balancing itself cannot tell us in which cases one or the other side has to yield in favour of greater divergence or convergence.

Accordingly, to effectively tackle these multilevel constitutional differences, one should take a closer look into several legal mechanisms of divergence and convergence, as more closely addressed in the book. As we have seen, while some mechanisms pull multilevel constitutional order together, and others secure the diversities within, many legal mechanisms can undertake both tasks, of convergence and/or divergence. It might depend on the intentions of those engaged, or on the specificities of the context, whether a legal mechanism in a particular circumstance leads to convergence or divergence.

11 Kos 21.
12 Kos 10.
13 Kos 22.

3 Legal Mechanisms of Divergence and Convergence

The second part of this book moves from broader concepts to more precise tools, instruments, and mechanisms of convergence and divergence. Each of these tools plays a different role and pursues different aims. Some, such as harmonisation, can be clearly conducive to convergence – by design, they pull a multilevel constitutional order together, making it more coherent and centralised. Others, such as the invocation of constitutional identity, serve to legitimate divergence, protecting constitutional specificities of various constituent parts to maintain a certain level of pluralism and differentiation. However, the majority of legal mechanisms described in the book do not have an underlying normative goal by design. Rather one can use them for either goal – managing divergence or inducing convergence. Depending on the context, particular case law, and the underlying motivation of the respective agent, different instruments, tools, and mechanisms will yield different outcomes. Finally, some mechanisms have the ability to bring closer multilevel constitutional order and its constituent parts – not in the sense of convergence and centralisation as in the first example, but rather as a constructive dispute mechanism which eases and reduces the constitutional tensions and even constitutional disputes without necessarily changing the constitutional balance of multilevel order and its parts towards more diversity or more unity.

As seen in Chapter 7, Thomas Verellen shows how the distribution of competences in the foreign policy sphere, an area in which both the EU and the Member States are empowered to act, led the CJEU to apply different strategies to avoid and, if necessary, resolve the conflicts between unity and diversity. However, always into the direction of protecting the external autonomy of the Union. At first, the CJEU applied the strategy of conflict avoidance through exclusivity. Later on, it moved away from this approach and developed an alternative technique, constraining the external autonomy of the Member States even in areas of shared competence. Based on the principle of sincere cooperation, the 'EU's foreign affairs constitution privileges unity over diversity in an effort to construct the EU as a foreign policy actor in its own right.'[14] While the diversity of the Member States is protected through representation in the Council, this protection mainly takes place 'within the confines of the EU legal order'.[15] The mechanisms applied by the Court were specifically directed towards the protection of the unity of the Union while taking into consideration the Member States and their interests.

Similarly, the diverse structure of the CJEU with 27 judges from all the Member States with various jurisdictions, different legal cultures and five decades of judicial practice could imply diversity and continuous changes in the said institution. Yet, as shown by Alexander Lazović in Chapter 11, a special mechanism of intra-institutional dialogue enables the Court to maintain a considerable degree of consistency in its case law. By using the 'federalist' stacking of the Court

14 Verellen 25.
15 ibid.

Presidencies, the working language of the Court, and the single-voice approach, the Court maintains a high level of convergence, cohesiveness, and stability.[16]

In Chapter 13, Pieter van Cleynenbreugel demonstrates how the EU managed to considerably harmonise the enforcement of EU law by giving the Member States concrete instructions as to the nature, organisation, and capacities of their independent national enforcement authorities.[17] Accordingly, with the creation of national independent authorities with autonomous capacities construed according to the converging enforcement template created by the EU, the field of implementation and enforcement became increasingly harmonised across the Member States despite the lack of explicit competencies of the EU thereof.

Other tools discussed in this book have not yet been used thoroughly enough to unleash their full potential of bringing about convergence. As Agata Poznańska's discussion of the European Citizens' Initiative in Chapter 12 shows, the potential of the ECI as a tool of deliberative democracy has not yet been fully seized. Taking it seriously could aid convergence in a much different – and, arguably, considerably more significant – way than judicial, legal, or regulatory convergence: the convergence of a true European public sphere.

Contrary to the converging mechanisms above, the invocation of national constitutional identity as discussed by Jakob Gašperin Wischhoff in Chapter 6 specifically protects constitutional diversities and thus functions as instrument of divergence. Gašperin Wischhoff demonstrates how a multilevel fundamental rights landscape with various coexisting standards of protection is a normatively desired outcome, whereas the national constitutional identity argument often undertakes the role of a constitutional dispute resolution mechanism to mitigate the tensions resulting thereof. Despite the critical observations about the existence of identity claims in constitutional law in general, the protection of constitutional identity is one of the most straightforward legal tools that directly safeguard national constitutional essentials and idiosyncracies in relation to EU law.[18]

Similar things can be stated regarding the idea of consensus, as Jaka Kukavica explicates in Chapter 9. Kukavica shows that 'consensus can be used by courts either as a divergence entrenching or convergence constituting mechanism.'[19] In these circumstances the mechanisms only serve as the means to achieve the goal one aims to follow. Moreover, several legal mechanisms mainly serve to ease the constitutional tensions and constructively overcome constitutional conflicts. In Chapter 5 Pieter Aertgeerts presents a normatively attractive model of what he calls 'constitutional trilogue'. He argues that multilevel fundamental rights landscape can best function should one connect the CJEU and the national apex courts together with the EU legislation, functioning as a catalyst.[20] Creating this

16 Lazović 2.
17 van Cleynenbreugel 16.
18 Gašperin Wischhoff 1.
19 Kukavica 17.
20 Aertgeerts 27.

type of intense dialogue among all respective sides can accommodate both requirements of diversity and unity.

In addition, one can observe a similar conclusion in relation to the legal mechanism of inter-institutional dialogue, concretely in strategic interactions of international courts as shown in Chapter 10 by Audrey Plan. While several international courts, most notably the CJEU and the ECtHR, strategically 'refer to another in hope of legitimizing its own position',[21] the courts thereby give up some of their policy preferences to increase the level of coherence of legal argumentation among the respective courts. According to Plan, these soft dynamic interactions, motivated by strategic legitimacy building, occasionally converging and elsewhere diverging, can slowly bring legal systems together and elegantly resolve some of the potential constitutional conflicts.

Finally, Pedro Coutinho argues that national and European economic constitutions impact one another in a reciprocal relationship. In Chapter 8 on the example of the Portuguese economic constitution, he shows how EU institutions increasingly tend to mimic the responses to crises typical at the national level, thus bridging the gap between the 'economic constitutional identities' of both the Member States and the Union.[22] Conversely, the Member States also had to amend their constitutions to reflect the common and shared economic identities as reflected in the Treaties. This two-way relationship not only leads to a convergence among the economic identities of the Member States and the Union but, according to Coutinho, also maintains tension among them. That results in a continuous search for a balance between excessive protectionism and excessive state intervention at the national level, and potentially excessive liberal tendencies at the EU level.[23]

4 Concluding Remarks: Looking beyond Europe

Most of the chapters in this book have approached the topic of convergence and divergence in multilevel legal orders through a European – and, more specifically, EU-centric – lens. As one of the world's most complex multilevel polities, the EU lends itself well to discussing issues regarding convergence and divergence. However, that should not induce the reader to think that these issues should, let alone could, only be approached through a European perspective. Questions about the accommodation of diversity in complex polities, federations, and international organisations arise globally – be it with a view to the management of diversity in multi-ethnic and multinational polities[24], the relationship between state law and indigenous legal systems[25] or human rights courts such as the Inter-American

21 M. Plan 23.
22 Coutinho 18.
23 Coutinho 19.
24 See Sahadžić, ch 3.
25 Nicole Roughan's book on 'relative authority' provides an incredible insight on the theory of authority where authorities overlap, discussing both the EU and Crown-Maōri relationships in New Zealand through this lense. See Nicole Roughan, ***Authorities: Conflicts, Cooperation, and Transnational Legal Theory*** (Oxford University Press 2018).

Court of Human Rights.[26] In this sense, the seemingly neat concept of multilevel legal order (itself not immune to suspicions of Eurocentrism[27]) that this book relied on should not be separated from but placed into a wider context of *legal pluralism*.[28]

Despite its predominantly European focus, this book has drawn on global examples wherever this was adequate. For instance, Kukavica's chapter presents 'consensus analysis' not as something exclusive to the European Court of Human Rights but as a global tool of use to federations and other supranational courts alike. Sahadžić's chapter uses the concept of 'asymmetry' as something cutting across both supranational polities, such as the EU, and ethnically, culturally, or linguistically diverse or divided States such as Indonesia, Bosnia and Herzegovina, and Iraq. Encinas' chapter on interlegality discusses not merely the example of constitutional conflict in the EU, but similarly engages with the Inter-American Court of Human Rights.

Other contributions, focused more specifically on the EU context, may well lend themselves as comparative insight for other, similarly shaped, contexts elsewhere. For instance, Lazovic's chapter on how a supranational court with a bench as diverse as the European Court of Justice manages to consistently speak with one voice, bolstering its authority vis-à-vis the Member States, may be insightful for other international courts. In addition, Audrey Plan's methodological approach to convergence and divergence in the light of judicial authority may similarly lend itself to studying broader judicial interactions in other contexts. While the book most notably explored and highlighted the mechanisms of convergence and divergence in multilevel constitutional systems in the European context, hopefully its findings will be able to also contribute to broader global debates on constitutional convergence and divergence, and the accommodation of diversity, that focus on different contexts.

26 Armin von Bogdandy's newest book illustrates what the European Court of Justice can learn from the Inter-American Court of Human Rights in building a mandate of transformative constitutionalism for itself. See Armin von Bogdandy, *Strukturwandel des öffentlichen Rechts: Entstehung und Demokratisierung der europäischen Gesellschaft* (Suhrkamp Verlag AG 2022).

27 The terms 'multilevel legal order' and 'multilevel constitutionalism' are most frequently used with reference to the European Union. We have attempted to give the term a broader meaning in this book, by applying it to federal states and international human rights systems alike.

28 Gunther Teubner, 'Global Bukowina: Legal Pluralism in the World-Society' (1996) <https://papers.ssrn.com/abstract=896478> accessed 27 October 2022; Boaventura de Sousa Santos, 'Law: A Map of Misreading. Toward a Postmodern Conception of Law' (1987) 14 Journal of Law and Society 279.

Index

Kolibri 360 GmbH
Ferdinand-Jühlke-Straße 7
99095 Erfurt, Deutschland
produktsicherheit@kolibri360.de